Famous Wisconsin Film Stars

Lights, Camera- Enjoy!

Kristin Gilpatrick

Badger Books Inc.
Oregon, WI

© Copyright 2002 by Kristin Gilpatrick Halverson
All Rights Reserved.
Published by Badger Books Inc.
Edited by Patrick Reardon and Julie Shirley
Cover design by Ann Christianson
Printed by McNaughton & Gunn of Saline, Michigan

ISBN 1-878569-86-4

No part of this book may be reproduced, stored in a retrieval system, or transmitted in any form or by any means, electronic, mechanical, photocopying, recording or otherwise, without prior permission from the publisher. Contact:

Badger Books Inc.
P.O. Box 192
Oregon, WI 53575
Toll-free phone: (800) 928-2372
Fax: (608) 835-3638
Email: books@badgerbooks.com
Web site: www.badgerbooks.com

To my forever friend, my sister Shelly, who was always the first to rush out and see the premiere of the latest Hollywood epic, to buy the newest book on her favorite star, and to laugh the hardest at the antics upon the movie screen.

To all the Wisconsin movie fans like her.

And, especially to all the Badger State's movie star dreamers.

May we one day be as proud to see your name in lights as we are of the dozens of Wisconsinites, who went as far as they dared to dream and touched the Silver Screen.

CONTENTS

INTRODUCTION	7
FOREWORD	9
SPENCER TRACY	12
AGNES MOOREHEAD	26
ORSON WELLES	35
CAROLE LANDIS	55
JEFFREY HUNTER	60
GREGG SHERWOOD DODGE	76
FRED MACMURRAY	87
DON AMECHE	98
PAT O'BRIEN	106
FREDRIC MARCH	117
COLLEEN DEWHURST	129
JAMES & TYNE DALY	140
STANLEY & JOHN BLYSTONE	149
GENA ROWLANDS	158
NICHOLAS RAY	166
DENNIS MORGAN	173
JACK CARSON	186
EDUARD FRANZ	193
BRIAN DONLEVY	196
RAY "CRASH" CORRIGAN	201
CHARLES WINNINGER	207
JOSEPH LOSEY	210
CHARLOTTE RAE	214
TOM HULCE	219
ELLEN CORBY	223
GENE WILDER	228
WILLEM DAFOE	238
BILL REBANE	247
CHRIS FARLEY	254
TONY SHALHOUB	268
DAVID & JERRY ZUCKER	271
JERRY ZIESMER	283
COLLEGIATE CLOUT	295
THEY ALSO STARRED	310
LIGHTS, CAMERA, ACTION!	322
ACKNOWLEDGMENTS	327
ABOUT THE AUTHOR	331
INDEX	333

INTRODUCTION

There are Wisconsin folk in every area of the movie business. And, after more than 30 years in Hollywood, we've found that what makes the Wisconsin actors and crew members we meet most unique is their warm, excited greeting at having found a fellow Wisconsinite.

We've also found that these actors and filmmakers are just like most Wisconsinites; they come from a sound upbringing of strong family and personal values coupled with a wonderful work ethic.

Oh, dog-eat-dog might help you if you do a movie at a time. But, if you're planning to have a long career in Hollywood, you'll go a lot further and faster — and last a lot longer — remembering your Wisconsin roots and the human qualities that got you to Hollywood in the first place.

Nothing could have prepared us better for years in Hollywood than the warm respect for those around us and strong work ethic that our Wisconsin roots have given us. We are certain that other Wisconsin actors and producers would say the same.

— Jerry & Suzanne Ziesmer
First Assistant Director & Production Crew Assistant
Los Angeles, California

FOREWORD

"The whole cheese thing is very organic to all of us Wisconsinites. I've definitely tapped into my Cheddar power."
— *Brad Rowe, rising movie star and Milwaukee native*

When Badger Books first asked me to write about all of Wisconsin's famous film stars, I thought, "Well, that will be a short book."

After all, I was quite certain that there were only about five Wisconsinites who had "tapped into their cheddar power," as Rowe has, to reach the Silver Screen: Orson Welles, Spencer Tracy, Don Ameche, Chris Farley and ... I thought I'd heard something about Gene Wilder and Milwaukee once.

After a couple of quick calls to the Wisconsin Film Office in Madison and the Wisconsin Performing Artists Hall of Fame in Milwaukee, however, I realized that I had a lot of nibbling to do.

As a Badger, I was proud to learn that almost 100 one-time Wisconsinites have seen their name in Hollywood lights, and that list of cinema Cheeseheads included some of the greatest and most famous actors and actresses of all time!

 • **Harrison Ford** and **Arnold Schwarzenegger** went to college here.
 • Celebrated director and movie star **Orson Welles** was born in Kenosha and attended grade school in Madison.
 • Versatile actor **Willem Dafoe** found the stage as a boy in Appleton.
 • Endearing TV father and Walt Disney star **Fred MacMurray** grew up in Beaver Dam.
 • Two of seven actors in Hollywood history to win a pair of Best Actor Oscars — **Spencer Tracy** and **Fredric March** — grew up in Milwaukee and Racine, respectively.
 • Oscar winning director **Nicholas Ray** was born in La Crosse.
 • Top 1930s and '40s movie stars **Dennis Morgan** and **Jack Carson** made a film featuring the town that gave them their start, *Two Guys From Milwaukee*, in 1946.
 • Beautiful but tragic pinup girl **Carole Landis** was born in

Fairchild.
- Radio and movie legend **Don Ameche** was born in Kenosha.
- One of the actresses with the most Oscar nominations ever, **Agnes Moorehead** (who was nominated four times), taught school in Soldier's Grove.
- Father and daughter Wisconsinites actor **James** and **Tyne Daly** were born in Wisconsin Rapids and Madison, respectively.
- Oscar nominated actress **Gena Rowlands** hails from Cambria.
- 1950s and 60s Hollywood heartthrob **Jeffrey Hunter** graduated from Whitefish Bay High School.

The list of the famous and infamous Wisconsin screen stars was so long that I knew right away I'd have at least one sequel to write.

To keep this first book under 400 pages, I decided to set some criteria.

In order to be featured, a movie star had to be a true Cheesehead, not merely one who was educated in the state. They had to have been born and/or raised in Wisconsin and have at least five movies to their credit, including one well-known movie and/or have been nominated for an Oscar. To provide a cutoff point, they also had to achieve stardom prior to 2000. Today's up and coming stars like Milwaukee's **Brad Rowe** — who so eloquently summarizes above how Wisconsin influenced his Hollywood success — will be featured in a future *Famous Wisconsin* book.

Finally, I did not completely eliminate those who didn't make these arbitrary criteria, however. In the back of *Famous Wisconsin Film Stars* you'll find several chapters. *They Also Starred* features Wisconsinites who appear in films but are better known for stage, television, or movie production roles, such as **Uta Hagen**, **Salome Jens**, **Jane Kaczmarek, Bradley Whitford** and **Tom Wopat**. *Collegiate Clout* features some of the one-time Wisconsin college students who made it big in Hollywood, like Ford and Schwarzenegger, **Ralph Bellamy** and **Campbell Scott**. And, *Lights, Camera, Action! ... In the Badger State* provides a list of many movies filmed in Wisconsin, such as *Deep End of the Ocean* (1999), *Rudy* (1993), *Back to School* (1986), *The Blues Brothers* (1980), and *The Giant Spider Invasion* (1975).

In most cases, the actors, actresses, and directors profiled in this book are those who are best known for their movie roles. However, as is an author's prerogative, I've made some excep-

tions to my own rules and included such stars as:
- Racine's **Ellen Corby**, who despite her fame as Grandma Walton, is profiled based on the hundred-plus movies she's featured in.
- Madison's **Chris Farley,** who is certainly better known as a *Saturday Night Live* comedian than a movie star but who was on the verge of movie stardom when he died.
- Beloit's **Gregg Sherwood Dodge,** who only appeared in five movies, but led such a star-studded and infamous life that I had to tell her story.

Even with such exceptions, astute readers will surely note that some big names are missing from this book such as legendary stage actors **Alfred Lunt** and his wife **Lynn Fontanne,** who lived in Genesee Depot, Wisconsin. Like Milwaukee's **Liberace** and Appleton's **Houdini** — who were far more famous for their stage performances than their movie work — their stories will be told in future *Famous Wisconsin* books.

If you were hoping to get more dirt on a favorite Hollywood star, or to find out what color underwear they prefer, you'd be best served by the *National Enquirer.*

If, instead, you want to know where your favorite stars grew up and hung out in high school and how they used their "Cheddar power" to reach the Hollywood spotlight, turn the page.

— **Kristin Gilpatrick
September 2002**

SPENCER TRACY

He is one of the few stars in the history of motion pictures to win the theatrical Triple Crown as the audience favorite, the critic's choice and the actor's actor.

Besides winning two Best Actor Oscars and being nominated for nine Academy Awards, Milwaukee native Spencer Tracy's best movie performances span three decades and every movie genre: comedies, dramas, action films and romances.

Tracy's ability to make a role seem so natural and believable is what earned him enduring and endearing praise from his acting peers. When asked in 1950 to choose the best movie actor from among their own, 200 moviemakers who'd been creating films for 25 years or more told *Daily Variety* that Spencer Tracy was their overwhelming choice.

"It's inspiring to play opposite Spencer Tracy," noted actress Joan Crawford, who costarred with him in 1937's *Mannequin*. "He walks through a scene just as he walks through life." And he "makes us believe he is what he is playing," added costar and lifelong friend Humphrey Bogart.

Tracy's believability on screen was so strong that directors like Stanley Kramer cast him whenever they could get him because, "A silent close-up reaction of Spencer Tracy said it all."

Though he became one of the most respected and well known movie actors of all time, Spencer Bonaventure Tracy seemed more destined for church confessionals, on either side of the curtain, when he was a truant school boy dreaming of priesthood in Milwaukee.

Tracy was born the younger of two brothers to Sterling Motor Truck Company general sales manager John Edward Tracy and his wife Caroline (Brown) on April 5, 1900, in a Prospect Avenue apartment in Milwaukee.

The St. Rosa Parochial School boy spent most of his impressionable youth playing baseball, fighting, and skipping school. When he would sit still long enough, Tracy was a Boy Scout, served as an altar boy at St. Rosa's Catholic Church, and worked as a lamplighter, lighting fifty gas street lights a night and polishing their globes with old newspapers for $3.50 per week.

Tracy also enjoyed entertaining neighborhood friends with backyard tent productions for the admission price of one or two safety pins.

And, his brother Carroll recalled in an Associated Press biography from March 1, 1951, Tracy enjoyed watching films whenever he could get to a local theater.

He watched Bronco Billy Anderson's Westerns so many times that his brother found him asleep in the theater one day. When Carroll woke him, "Spencer told me, 'that's what I'm going to be: an actor,'" explained the brother who later became the star's business manager.

For reasons even the actor later admitted were unclear, Tracy also spent some of his boyhood days running away from home in search of greater adventures, he recalled in Donald Deschner's 1968 book, *The Films of Spencer Tracy*.

"We lived in a pleasant environment in Milwaukee, yet they tell me that when I was 7, I ran away. ... They found me a little after dark. I was down on the South Side playing in an alley with two youngsters known as Mousie and Rattle. They were sons of a bartender, tough eggs, but we became good friends," the actor said. "I remember my mother grabbed me and wept when I got back home. That should have cured me of running away, but it didn't."

Though he stayed at St. Rosa's for his grade school classes, Tracy bounced between a half dozen high schools before finally getting a diploma.

The future star first studied at Wauwatosa High School and then St. John's Cathedral School in Milwaukee before the family moved for six months to Kansas City, Missouri, where Tracy attended St. Mary's high school and the Rockhurst Academy in Topeka. After the family returned to Milwaukee, Tracy enrolled at Marquette Academy, where he played baseball and the tuba.

It was at Marquette, in 1917, that Tracy met a boy who shared his dream — at first of becoming a priest and later of becoming a movie star — William "Pat" O'Brien.

Spence and Bill (as the pair were known to friends) decided they should be serving their country, not their teachers, during World War I. Tracy gladly left the textbooks that always bored him in search of greater lessons in the military. At first, the then 17-year-old hoped to join the U.S. Marines but was turned away as underage at the recruiting office near the Schlitz Hotel in Milwaukee. So, Tracy followed pal O'Brien's boot steps into the Navy, and the Marquette duo was soon training at Great Lakes Naval

Training Station near Chicago.

Neither made it past the U.S. border during World War I, however, with Tracy serving his Navy tour as a Norfolk Navy Yard seaman in Virginia. After the war, Tracy enrolled at the Northwestern Military and Naval Academy in Lake Geneva, Wisconsin, in 1919, where he earned his high school diploma. The seaman soon tired of further military classes and opted to be discharged from the service and academy Sept. 30, 1921.

That same year, Tracy enrolled at Ripon College in Ripon, Wisconsin, to study pre-med with the idea of becoming a plastic surgeon. The gregarious freshman quickly became popular on campus and served on the All-College Prom Committee. In 1921, his classmates voted him their "most popular" as well as "cleverest and most talented" classmate.

It was college teacher H. P. Boody who encouraged the talent he saw in the outgoing student, urging Tracy to try out for the college's debate team.

"To my vast surprise, I liked it," Tracy noted in Deschner's book. "It helped me develop memory of lines. ... It gave me something of a stage presence, and it helped get rid of my awkwardness.

Debate also helped Tracy develop "the ability to speak extemporaneously, which has stood me in good stead many a time when a cue has been missed" — a skill he became quite respected for as an actor. In Hollywood, it was well known that Tracy could keep working through any misspoken line with such finesse that costars were left wondering if it was *they* who were mistaken.

Tracy was a talented enough college debater to be elected to the debate honor society, Phi Kappa Delta. He also joined the Theta Alpha Phi theater fraternity after Professor J. Clark Graham convinced the Milwaukee native to give speaking on the theatrical stage a try.

The professor later told Deschner that, from the beginning, he saw "a certain decisiveness" in Tracy's speech, "a clipped firmness of expression indicating poise, self-control, and confidence."

Whatever he saw, Graham knew he wanted it on his college stage and cast Tracy as the warden in the spring commencement play *The Truth*. That fall, he cast his new star as a heroic prisoner in *The Valiant* and followed with lead roles for Tracy in *Dregs*, *The Great Divide*, and *Sintram of Skaserack*.

According to Ripon's *College Days* paper, Tracy proved himself on the stage from the beginning. "His steadiness, reserve strength and suppressed emotion were a surprise to all who heard him," the paper noted in 1921.

"Before the end of the semester, he was talking about a career as an actor," Graham recalled of Tracy's enthusiasm for acting Ripon had stirred in him. "His parents came on a visit and we had a family conference" where Tracy's father agreed to pay one semester's tuition at the American Academy of Dramatic Arts in New York if Tracy could live on a $30 per month education allowance from the Navy.

Just whose idea it was to attend the academy and pursue fame in New York on a Navy stipend remains a mystery. Somehow, before the parental meeting at Ripon, Tracy and his old Navy buddy O'Brien (who had already been performing in New York but had to return to work briefly during a family emergency) had hatched just such a plan.

O'Brien, who insisted the plan was his idea, reports in his autobiography, *The Wind at My Back*, that when he asked Tracy if he would join him in New York, his Marquette Academy friend responded, "Can a shamrock be anything but green?"

The two rented a small 98th street apartment where they practiced their lines — even moving the furniture to act out scenes — dreamed of the future and tried to make ends meet. Money was tight, and they sustained themselves on rice, pretzels, and water and shared one good suit between them.

A publicity shot of Spencer Tracy. Photo courtesy of the Wisconsin Center for Film and Theater Research. Image No. WCFTR-3757.

"I was broke several days before the end of each month," Tracy recalled in Deschner's book. "Sometimes I'd borrow a couple dollars from Pat, and sometimes he was broke ahead of me."

The friends took their first stage step toward stardom together as well. Tracy and O'Brien both landed $15 a week roles as nonspeaking robots in R.U.R., though it didn't take Tracy long to get a speaking part in that play and several others on and off Broadway.

By 1923, Tracy was established in New York and was working regularly in stock company productions in White Plains, N.Y., for $20 a week. Tracy soon became a $42.50 a week featured stock company player.

Through stock company productions, Tracy and O'Brien were introduced to other future stars and longtime friends Frank McHugh, Edna Hibbard and William Boyd. They later became good friends with Will Rogers and James Cagney.

Tracy, however, was most interested in one particular actress, Louise Treadwell, whom he married Sept. 12, 1923, in Cincinnati. For a short time between stock company work in Cincinnati, Tracy sold pianos there to help make ends meet for his growing family.

By 1924, the new Mrs. Tracy had moved in with Tracy's parents in Milwaukee and gave birth to a son, John, on June 26. The joy of the baby's birth was dampened, but only temporarily, when the Tracys learned their son had been born deaf. Using their later experiences in raising a deaf child, the Tracys founded the John Tracy Clinic for the Deaf in 1942 to teach families how to break the barriers of silence and help deaf children excel in a hearing world, as John Tracy later did, graduating from college, marrying in 1952 and presenting the Tracys with a grandson in 1953.

The same year that Tracy was struggling with the news of his son's deafness, the actor was struggling to get past one of his first and only bad reviews. On his performance in *A Royal Fandango*, "one caustic critic commented I looked as if I had been picked up by the property man. I can laugh about that now but it did burn me up at the time," Tracy admitted in Deschner's book.

The review was a small shadow on an otherwise bright stage horizon for the Milwaukee native and his wife, who had rejoined Tracy on the road and on stage by 1927.

By the late 1920s, Tracy was earning the respect of stage producers and actors and gaining even greater roles.

It was stage producer George M. Cohan who first told Tracy he was destined to be a great star himself when Tracy was playing a small role in Cohan's production of *Yellow* in 1926.

In the 1981 book *Together Again: Stories of the Great Hollywood Teams* by Garson Kanin, Tracy recalled seeing his idol Cohan coming toward him after rehearsal and then passing him by. Since Cohan had not been talking with Tracy as he had the other young actors during the play, the Wisconsinite was afraid he was going to be fired. Instead, when Cohan reached the theater's apron, Cohan turned to Tracy and said, 'Young man. You're the best damn actor I ever saw.'"

Movie director John Ford thought so too when he saw Tracy portray a death row killer in the early 1930 play *The Last Mile*. Tracy himself was unsure of his stage performance, telling O'Brien not to see the show because it was "one hell of a flop. ... (and) I've got no confidence in it."

The so-called flop, which earned rave reviews, catapulted Tracy into movie stardom.

Based on his *Last Mile* performance, Ford asked Tracy to appear in a 1930 prison movie he was making with Humphrey Bogart called *Up the River*. Tracy — who had acted in a few New York produced short subject films such as *Hard Guy* (1930) and told friends he saw no future for himself in movies — signed a 20th Century Fox Studios movie contract within a year.

Up the River also proved the start of a beautiful friendship between its famous star and soon-to-be famous costars, Bogart and Tracy. The two were so close that, according to Deschner, Tracy, and Katharine Hepburn were some of the few daily visitors Bogart received when he was dying of cancer in 1956-1957.

"They would sit together at Bogie's bedside for half an hour or so every evening in the months and weeks leading up to his death," the author wrote. "After Bogie's death, (wife Lauren) Bacall requested that Spencer deliver the eulogy at the funeral. Spence apologetically declined saying it would simply be ... too emotional. ... John Huston delivered the eulogy instead."

The Milwaukee native rushed his family out to meet his newfound Hollywood friends and fame so fast in 1931 that the Tracys reportedly had to enjoy Thanksgiving dinner on the train. The Tracys settled into a San Fernando Valley ranch and welcomed a daughter Louise "Susie" July 1, 1932.

While Tracy was building a family, he was also laying the foundation of a movie career. From 1931 to 1932, Tracy was featured in supporting roles in such films as *Six-Cylinder Love*, *Goldie*, *Sky Devils*, *Disorderly Conduct*, *Young America*, *Society Girl*, *My Gal*, and *She Wanted a Millionaire*.

Then, in 1933, Fox lent its new supporting actor out first to Warner Bros. to play a prisoner in *20,000 Years in Sing Sing* and then to Columbia where he starred in *Man's Castle* with Loretta Young, one of several actresses Tracy was reported to have had affairs with over the next thirty years.

By all accounts, Tracy did not feel challenged by what Hollywood was offering him and made some of his displeasure well known, drowning some of that frustration in alcohol — a liquid nemesis that would haunt the star for all his Hollywood days.

Tracy had a wild reputation, especially in the 1930s, reported his frequent director and friend Stanley Kramer in Deschner's book. "Nobody could drink, fight and cause more trouble than Tracy in his early Hollywood days."

Though Fox began to offer the red-haired, hot-headed actor some bigger roles in such films as *Face in the Sky* (1933), *The Power and the Glory* (1933), *Looking for Trouble* (1934), and *Dante's Inferno* (1935), Tracy's skills still weren't really tested as an actor and his fame as a movie star not really realized until after his Fox contract expired in 1935.

Tracy signed with Metro-Goldwyn-Mayer that same year and was cast in his first movie pairing with Clark Gable in *San Francisco* (1936). He received his first of nine Oscar nominations for his work in the film. The two eventually costarred in other movies, such as 1940s *Boom Town,* and became fast friends. Gable, a major star, often commented that his friend Tracy was the most polished and talented actor he had ever worked with, saying, "Whenever I'm asked what my definition of a professional is in our business, I tell 'em to talk to Spence."

By the late 1930s, the Milwaukee native was already the stuff of acting legend when he became the first man to win back-to-back Oscars, an honor he held until modern-day star Tom Hanks tied him.

Tracy won his first Oscar for his portrayal of a Portuguese fisherman, Manuel, in the 1937 hit *Captains Courageous*, though the Academy of Motion Pictures web site at *www.oscars.com* notes that his original gold statue was actually inscribed "Dick Tracy."

Though it eventually became one of his personal favorites, Tracy admitted that he was leery about taking the sailor role at first. "I thought I was doing the worst job of my life," Deschner quoted. "I felt sure I wouldn't survive the singing, the dialect, the curled hair (of the character)."

Tracy "survived" that and more, winning his second Oscar for his 1938 portrayal of Father Flanagan in *Boys Town*. This time, though, the actor didn't even keep his (correctly inscribed) statue. Instead, Tracy handed it to the real Father Edward Flanagan, founder of the charitable youth community in Nebraska, upon whose work the movie was based. "You earned it, not I," he reportedly told the priest.

Tracy followed his mesmerizing Oscar performances with roles of differing depth and character. He gave voice to the famous line "Dr. Livingstone, I presume," as Henry Stanley in the 1939 20th Century Fox movie *Stanley and Livingstone*, teamed up with Gable again as Gunner Morris in *Test Pilot* (1938), played Major Robert Rogers in the 1940 hit *Northwest Passage* (1940), and portrayed U.S. inventor Thomas Edison in *Edison The Man* (1940). The Milwaukee native pulled off a split personality with double the believability as the lead in the 1941 version of *Dr. Jekyll and Mr. Hyde* and returned to his Oscar-winning role of Father Flanagan for a 1941 sequel, *Men of Boys Town*.

In 1942, Tracy found perhaps his best fit on screen and off when he was paired with Katharine Hepburn for the comedy *The Philadelphia Story: Woman of the Year*. It was the first of nine now legendary battle-of-the-sexes styled, intelligent love stories that the couple heated up the screen with in the 1940s, 1950s, and the 1960s.

"Tracy and Hepburn are the best two screen partners I've ever seen. Their interplay and action and reaction, talking and listening, sense of spontaneity, invention, are all of the highest order," stressed Garson Kanin in his 1981 book, *Together Again: Stories of the Great Hollywood Teams*.

Considered by most to be one of the greatest screen pairs in Hollywood history, Tracy starred with Hepburn in:

• *Keeper of the Flame* (1942), as journalist Steve O'Malley interviewing a war hero widow (Katharine Hepburn);

• *Sea of Grass* (1942), as ruthless rancher James Brewton and his unfaithful wife Lutie.

• *Without Love* (1945), as scientist Pat Jamieson and his assistant Jamie Rowan who find love through a marriage of convenience.

• *State of the Union* (1948), as industrialist presidential candidate Grant Matthews, who with his wife, Mary, lose their integrity to the political machine.

• *Adam's Rib*, as lawyer-prosecutor Adam married to defense attorney Amanda Bonner. They face each other in a heated shooting trial.

• *Pat & Mike*, as sports promoter Mike Conovan with Hepburn as golf champ Pat Pemberton.

• *Desk Set* as computer installer Richard Summer with Hepburn as determined office department head Bunny Watson.

• *Guess Who's Coming to Dinner?* As Matt Drayton who with his wife, Christina, faces challenges to their beliefs when their daugh-

A young Spencer Tracy fishes on the Muskegon River. Photo courtesy of Wisconsin Center for Film and Theater Research. Image No. WCFTR-3757.

ter brings her black fiance (Sidney Poitier) home for dinner.

Tracy always got top billing in his films with Hepburn despite their costar status. When he was once asked why a gentleman didn't let the lady's name appear first, the actor reportedly retorted, "Because this is a movie, not a lifeboat!" The Associated Press biography piece noted.

Though they publicly, and quite effectively, denied rumors for years, Hepburn and Tracy enjoyed an even more passionate romance and friendship off camera, the actress admitted in her autobiography, *Me*.

Tracy's wife was reportedly well aware of the affair, one of several Tracy had during their marriage. However, as a devout Catholic, Tracy refused to ever divorce Louise and thus entered into a cordial agreement whereby he would appear married in public and still discreetly spend his nights with Hepburn.

According to Robert Osborne in a Turner Classic Movie biography about Tracy, the star and Hepburn were "devoted to each other" and often traveled together. They also "shared nearby cottages (but never the same living quarters) on the grounds of George Cukor's estate in Hollywood."

When he wasn't enjoying Hepburn's company, Tracy was starring in such MGM productions as Pilon in *Tortilla Flat* (1942), real-life war hero Lt. Col. Jimmy Doolittle in *Thirty Seconds Over Tokyo* (1944), and Arnold Boult in *Edward, My Son* (1949).

Famous Wisconsin Film Stars

During World War II, the Navy veteran also worked in the Hollywood Canteen, visited hospitals, and narrated films for the U.S. Office of War Information. In 1944, the actor returned to the Badger State on a tour of Midwest Navy bases and became the mascot of Wisconsin-built submarine Icefish (SS-367), which reportedly sank two Japanese ships that year, according to the 1997 U.S. Naval Institute Press book *Stars in Blue*.

In 1945, Tracy took a brief hiatus from Hollywood to return to the Broadway stage for the first time in fifteen years, starring in *The Rugged Path*.

He wasn't far from Hollywood, and Hepburn, for long however. The two reunited on film in the 1948 hit *State of the Union*.

In 1951, Tracy teamed with another favorite partner when he asked producers to cast Pat O'Brien as his costar in *The People Against O'Hara* in 1951. Though that movie received a lukewarm reception, Tracy continued to turn in solid performances in such 1950 films as *The Actress* (1953), *Broken Lance* (1954), and *The Mountain* (1956).

By this time, Tracy's drinking was excessive. The star would reportedly vanish from sets for days or even weeks on drinking binges. And, when he wasn't drinking, Tracy remained a moody and often impatient person.

Even Katharine Hepburn remarked in Deschner's book that Tracy was usually "much too impatient for the time and place in which he found himself."

The actor was especially impatient where reporters and unprepared actors were concerned.

According to a 1967 Associated Press obituary, when a reporter asked him what makes a woman attractive, Tracy gave him thirty seconds to come up with a better question. When the writer couldn't, Tracy left.

To the young actors constantly seeking the star's advice, Tracy had little better to offer about, say, what motivation to use to enter a scene. Deschner noted that Tracy's frustrated advice was simply, "You come in the goddamn door because there's no other way to come into the goddamn room!"

Another gem of advice he borrowed a bit from Wisconsin stage actor Alfred Lunt (who used to advise, "learn your lines and don't bump into the furniture"). Tracy is often quoted suggesting actors "come to work on time, know their lines and don't bump into other actors."

Deschner also noted that Tracy once said he'd tell aspiring

actors to "throw the gum away and keep cigarettes out of their mugs," adding that he didn't believe he had much more advice to offer. "I couldn't teach them a thing because I don't know anything about acting."

"I've never known what acting is," Tracy said in Deschner's book. ... (But) I wonder what actors are supposed to be, if not themselves? ... When I begin a part, I say to myself, 'this is Spencer Tracy as a judge, as a president, or as a lawyer and let it go at that.'"

For the little he claimed he knew about acting, "Tracy as anything" was better than nearly anybody as anyone else.

Despite the constant battle with booze and his own personality, Tracy turned in some of the best performances of his career. Tracy also remained a private person who insisted on leaving the set by 5 p.m. regardless of the shooting schedule. The actor was a consummate professional with a concentrated mind who knew his lines, had the stage presence to cover a flub with near seamless dialogue, respected the opinions of others, believed steadfastly in the rights and abilities of each individual, had a good sense of humor — and especially enjoyed a funny anecdote — and liked to relax by sailing, deep sea fishing, reading and, in his early years, playing polo.

Tracy used all his quirks and talents to set the performance bar high in his portrayal of Elizabeth Taylor's father Stanley Banks in the hit 1950 movie *Father of the Bride* — a performance for which he was again nominated for an Oscar. It was a role he repeated in the nearly-as-well received sequel, *Father's Little Dividend* in 1951 and a performance that actor and comedian Steve Martin would try to emulate in a 1991 version of the film.

Tracy was nominated for two more Oscars in the 1950s, one for his 1955 performance as a one-armed war veteran John MacCreedy in *Bad Day at Black Rock* and the next for his second fisherman role, that of the "old man" in 1958's *The Old Man and the Sea*, which is said to be one Tracy's personal favorites.

Though he had begun to suffer the effects of the heart ailment that would eventually take his life, the now gray-haired, seasoned actor teamed up again with the director who gave him his start. John Ford cast Tracy as aging Boston political boss mayor Frank Skeffington in his 1958 movie *The Last Hurrah*, which costarred fellow Wisconsinites Jeffrey Hunter as the mayor's nephew and Pat O'Brien as the mayor's friend.

Tracy didn't let up on the quality of his performances in the

1960s, though he did slow down the number of movies he made in his final decade of stardom-a decade that would see Tracy nominated for three more Oscars.

In 1960, Tracy was nominated for his portrayal of the Clarence Darrow character, Henry Drummond, in Stanley Kramer's classic movie *Inherit the Wind*, which pitted him in the Scopes monkey trial against veteran Wisconsin actor Fredric March, as the opposing attorney, the William Jenning Bryan character.

During filming, the two Wisconsinites would reportedly bring the set house down by feigning boredom when the other actor was giving his long, passionate summation. According to Deschner, March fanned himself "endlessly each time Tracy rose to deliver his courtroom lines." Tracy repeated the snub by picking his nose behind March during March's four-minute summation.

Tracy earned his second nomination of the decade — another back-to-back honor — for presiding over Nazi war trials as Judge Hayward in 1961's *Judgment at Nuremberg*.

Besides his top performances, Tracy played a priest in 1961's *The Devil at 4 O'Clock*, narrated *How the West Was Won* in 1962 and played the underpaid and overstressed police captain T.G. Culpeper chasing of some of the top comedians of the day in 1963's comedy classic *It's a Mad Mad Mad Mad World* before fading from the screen for four years, in part to recover from a respiratory infection.

After some prodding by his friend and director Stanley Kramer, some coaxing from his favorite costar Hepburn, and the promise of a $300,000 salary, Tracy agreed to return to movies in 1967.

In what proved to be — and by all accounts Tracy guessed would be — his last performance, he played Matt Drayton in the racial commentary movie *Guess Who's Coming to Dinner?*

Spence had been "frightened for all of us that he might not get through the picture," Kramer noted in Deschner's book. Four days before shooting ended, "he put an arm around me and said, 'you know I read the script again last night and if I were to die on the way home tonight you can still release the picture with what you've got.'"

Tracy received his ninth and final Oscar nomination posthumously for his *Guess Who's Coming to Dinner?* performance. He died of a heart attack June 10, 1967, just weeks after filming his scenes for the film. He was posthumously inducted into the Wisconsin Performing Artists Hall of Fame.

Though at the time of his death Hollywood press agents said it was the star's brother Carroll who found him, Katharine Hepburn said she was with Tracy when he died. In her book *Me*, Hepburn relates that Tracy had left her side in the middle of the night to get some tea. The actress ran to the kitchen when she heard a cup crash and found Tracy dead.

The fact that Tracy's last movie performance was in a film that dealt with individual rights and freedoms was as fine a screen eulogy as any, said his good friend U.S. Supreme Court Justice William O. Douglas in the introduction to Deschner's 1968 book *The Films of Spencer Tracy*.

"I never knew anyone more American," the judge stressed. "(Tracy) was Thoreau, Emerson, Frost. ... He was no respecter of prejudice; his society was classless except for men and women of talent. To that aristocracy all were welcome."

As Tracy passed into Hollywood history, the star left a mark of excellence that few future actors have been able to match.

Perhaps it was the man who first discovered that legendary and nearly unmatchable talent, Ripon College Professor Graham, who best summed up the actor and his talent while presenting Tracy with an honorary Ripon College degree in 1940 (as recorded in Deschner's book).

The teacher said of the student that day, "The world knows you as many people but Ripon College knows you in another role-that of the eager youth who spoke his lines impromptu to the cues of life. ... The task of the actor, as Shakespeare remarked, is and ever has been to hold the mirror up to nature to interpret the deepest passions of the human soul and thereby to cleanse it. To that distinguished company, Spencer Tracy, you belong."

Famous Wisconsin Film Stars

ON SCREEN

To catch a legend on the Silver Screen, movie watchers need only see any one of Tracy's many films, including:

Guess Who's Coming to Dinner (1967)
MGM's Big Parade of Comedy (1964)
It's a Mad Mad Mad Mad World (1963)
How the West Was Won (1962) (voice)
Judgment at Nuremberg (1961)
The Devil at 4 O'Clock (1961)
Inherit the Wind (1960)
The Last Hurrah (1958)
The Old Man and the Sea (1958)
Desk Set (1957)
The Mountain (1956) .
Bad Day at Black Rock (1955)
Broken Lance (1954)
The Actress (1953)
Plymouth Adventure (1952)
Pat and Mike (1952)
For Defense for Freedom for Humanity (1951) (uncredited)
The People Against O'Hara (1951)
Father's Little Dividend (1951)
Father of the Bride (1950)
Edward, My Son (1949)
Malaya (1949)
Adam's Rib (1949)
State of the Union (1948)
Cass Timberlane (1947)
The Sea of Grass (1947)
Without Love (1945)
Thirty Seconds Over Tokyo (1944)
The Seventh Cross (1944)
His New World (1943) (voice)
A Guy Named Joe (1943)
Keeper of the Flame (1942)
Tortilla Flat (1942)
Ring of Steel (1942)
Woman of the Year (1942)
Dr. Jekyll and Mr. Hyde (1941)
Men of Boys Town (1941)
Boom Town (1940)
Edison, the Man (1940)
Northwest Passage (1940)
Northward, Ho! (1940)
Young Tom Edison (1940)
I Take This Woman (1939)
Stanley and Livingstone (1939)
Hollywood Hobbies (1939)
Hollywood Goes to Town (1938)
Boys Town (1938)
Test Pilot (1938)
Mannequin (1937)
Big City (1937)
Captains Courageous (1937)
They Gave Him a Gun (1937)
Libeled Lady (1936)
San Francisco (1936)
Fury (1936)
Riffraff (1936)
Whipsaw (1935)
Dante's Inferno (1935)
The Murder Man (1935)
It's a Small World (1935)
Marie Galante (1934)
Shoot the Works (1934)
Now I'll Tell (1934)
Bottoms Up (1934)
Looking for Trouble (1934)
The Show-Off (1934)
The Mad Game (1933)
Man's Castle (1933)
The Power and the Glory (1933)
Shanghai Madness (1933)
The Face in the Sky (1933)
20,000 Years in Sing Sing (1932)
Me and My Gal (1932)
The Painted Woman (1932)
Society Girl (1932)
Young America (1932)
Disorderly Conduct (1932)
Sky Devils (1932)
She Wanted a Millionaire (1932)
Goldie (1931)
Six Cylinder Love (1931)
Quick Millions (1931)
The Strong Arm (1930)
Up the River (1930)
The Hard Guy (1930)
Taxi Talks (1930)

AGNES MOOREHEAD

She was born a minister's daughter December 6, 1900, in Clinton, Massachusetts. She grew up to be a witch — on television anyway, as Endora, the meddling mother-in-law on the hit 1960s series *Bewitched*.

Endora may have been a mean-spirited woman, but those who knew Agnes Robertson Moorehead when she lived in Reedsburg and Soldier's Grove, Wisconsin, say the actress was just playing a part.

"She was remembered very fondly by those who knew her in the area. In all my research for the *2000 Agnes Moorehead Film Festival* in Viroqua, I could never find anyone who had anything bad to say about her," noted Viroqua funeral home director John Sime, who was one of the coordinators of a festival designed to honor the actress who had once lived in the area and to raise money to restore the Temple Theater, where she likely took in shows.

Moorehead came to the Viroqua area — specifically to Soldier's Grove — to teach English, declamation, and other classes shortly after she got a bachelor's degree and took a few masters-level English courses at Muskingum College in New Concord, Ohio (a university her uncle founded).

The actress took the Soldier's Grove job to be near her parents, the Reverend Dr. John H. and Mary Moorehead, who had accepted the ministry of Reedsburg's Presbyterian Church several years before. It is reported that Moorehead actually moved with them her senior year of high school and graduated from Reedsburg High School (though St. Louis, Missouri, where Moorehead grew up, disputes this, saying she graduated from high school there in 1919).

Regardless, it is clear that Moorehead lived and taught in the Reedsburg, Viroqua, and Soldier's Grove area at least from 1923 to 1927.

Her primary teaching job was at Soldier's Grove High School, where, according to the *Kickapoo Scout,* she coached the oratory teams to numerous speech contest championships and produced high school plays. She had one junior class recite the *Hamlet* soliloquy and also reportedly directed some plays at Reedsburg High

School.

One of the students from her first year of teaching, Orland Helgeson, who is now in his 90s and living in the Viroqua area, remembers Moorehead as a good teacher.

"I was interested in geometry and physics at that time, and since she didn't teach subjects I was interested in, I didn't pay as close attention as I should. She taught ancient history and coached our school plays. We all thought she was a good teacher. She was nice and nice looking, but I didn't fully appreciate her because I was interested in other subjects at that time," Helgeson recalls.

Agnes Moorehead as a child. Photo courtesy of Wisconsin Center for Film and Theater Research. Image No. WCFTR-3769.

Moorehead threw herself into her drama club work, adds Sime, who uncovered reports of an especially elaborate production of *Peter Pan*. "It was supposed to be the senior class play but by the time she was done, nearly everyone in the school was involved. The production got out of control size wise; the cast just got bigger and bigger, but it was very well done and received."

The teacher also tried hard to instill the wholesome values she was raised with, asking her students to maintain the standards she set and rigidly upheld for herself such as self-improvement, neatness, and good study habits. "I feel so strong about them that to compromise any one of them would be, for me an act of hypocrisy. And a teacher who is not true to his or her own values, is not a teacher at all," she told *TV Picture Life* interviewer Daisy Charles in 1971.

In what spare time she had, the teacher completed her master's degree in English and public speaking at the University of Wisconsin in Madison (and later received a doctorate in literature from Bradley University in Illinois). She also sang in her father's church choir as well as in local singing groups she organized.

Meanwhile, the drama coach was saving her money to pursue a dream of performing on her own in New York City.

By 1926, Moorehead had saved enough to try out for the American Academy of Dramatic Arts. When she was accepted, Soldier's Grove threw her a fine *bon voyage* party in 1927.

Somehow between Soldier's Grove and New York City, the 27-year-old teacher became a 21-year-old actress. Many records still incorrectly list her as having been born in 1906.

Though her age got fuzzy, Moorehead's acting talents only sharpened in New York. Her parents reportedly recognized their daughter's gift for characterizations early on and let her perform on stage when she was only 3. They also often played along when their daughter acted like someone else, usually a neighbor or parishioner, for whole days at a time as a child. As a pre-teen she began dancing and singing with the St. Louis Municipal Opera Company and performed in St. Louis summer stock theater for four or five years. She fine-tuned her skills in college, where she sang in the glee club and acted in summer stock.

Moorehead's time in Soldier's Grove added an appreciation of the director's perspective to her raw talent, a combination that helped the actress graduate the American Academy of Dramatic Arts with honors in 1929 and quickly propelled her into the New York spotlight. The teacher found small roles in such Broadway productions as *Courage*, *Soldiers and Women*, and *All the King's Horses*.

Just as she was getting her dramatic feet wet, however, The Great Depression hit. As theater work grew hard to come by, Moorehead turned her talents to radio acting.

In the early 1930s, Moorehead was acting in as many as six radio shows a day, including as a regular on NBC's *Seth Parker Family Hour* and *The March of Time*, which aired from 1935 to 1951 and often featured Moorehead impersonating Eleanor Roosevelt.

It was in the 1930s that Moorehead began relationships with two of the most important men in her life. One was her first husband, an actor she met at the academy and married June 5, 1930, Jack G. Lee, with whom she later adopted a son, Sean. The second was a man who had Wisconsin ties — child prodigy stage star and radio actor, Orson Welles.

Welles was so impressed with Moorehead's acting talents on the radio shows they did together, such as *The March of Time*, that he brought her in on the ground floor of the renegade Mercury Theater he cofounded in 1937 with John Houseman. Welles cast Moorehead in such stage productions as *Jane Eyre*, *Treasure Island* and *Julius Caesar*. He also made Moorehead a fixture in *The Mercury Theatre of the Air* (later the Campbell [Soup] Playhouse) and then cast her with him in one of his most famous — and infamous — radio productions, the 1938 overly realistic presentation of H.G. Wells' *The War of the Worlds*.

Moorehead built herself into a national radio celebrity. Welles made her a movie star.

The actor/director who often said, "Give the role to Agnes, she can play anything," continually pushed her acting talents. He cast Moorehead as Kane's mother in his masterpiece *Citizen Kane* in 1941 and then cast her as Aunt Fanny in 1942's *Magnificent Ambersons,* a part for which she got an Academy Award nomination. She later appeared in such Welles films as *Journey Into Fear* (1943) and *Jane Eyre* (1944).

Meanwhile, mainstream Hollywood was seeing what Welles had noticed long ago. Agnes could play anything, from a neurotic woman to the Queen of England, and the teacher became one of Hollywood's great character actors.

Scripts poured Moorehead's way for the next 25 years. Her movie performances earned her three more Academy Award nominations for playing the title role in *Mrs. Parkington* (1944), Aggie McDonald in *Johnny Belinda* (1948), and the maid in *Hush ... Hush, Sweet Charlotte* (1964). In all, Moorehead starred in more than 70 Hollywood and television movies, from playing a murderess in *The Dark Passage* (1947) to a captain's wife in *Show Boat* (1951) and from a nurse in *Magnificent Obsession* to a queen in *The Swan*.

For Wisconsin movie fans, Moorehead's more significant roles may have been as Bruna Johnson in the 1945 film, *Our Vines Have Tender Grapes,* about a struggling Wisconsin farm family and her 1948 supporting role in *Station West*, which had its world premiere in Milwaukee in the fall of 1948. According to a November 3, 1995, *Milwaukee Journal Sentinel* article by Jackie Loohauis, star Jane Greer and costar Moorehead came to Milwaukee for the Riverside Theater premiere. Comic Jack Paar was the master of ceremonies for the extravaganza that "spilled over (from the theater) to the Schlitz Brown Bottle pub," Loohauis reported.

While she built her Hollywood career, Moorehead never left her radio success. She continued to act on *The March of Time* and other programs. In 1943, she starred as the invalid who overhears someone planning her murder in one of the most famous radio broadcasts of all time: CBS's *Sorry, Wrong Number*. She repeated the performance for which she won a Golden Mike Award time and again for eager audiences and recorded it for Decca in 1947. Ironically, when the movie *Sorry, Wrong Number* debuted in 1947 it was Barbara Stanwyck, not Moorehead, in the starring role.

"Of course I wanted the Stanwyck part," Moorehead later told Ronald Bowers for his 1960s article "Agnes Moorehead Thinks Acting Is More a Matter of Magic Than of Craft." "It had been written for me (for radio) by Lucille Fletcher and I must have done it on radio about eighteen times. I went to Hal Wallis at Paramount when they were casting it to put my hat in the ring, but he said he owed Barbara a picture. ... I'm not bitter about it," though she added, laughing, "they played my recording constantly on the set."

By the late 1950s, Moorehead was moving away from movies and radio and into other venues. She appeared in the first episode of *The Twilight Zone* TV series and several TV movies such as *Alice Through the Looking Glass* (1966), *What's the Matter with Helen* (1971), *Night of Terror* (1972) and *Frankenstein: The True Story* (1972).

She also quietly worked as a dialogue coach and drama teacher for many Hollywood stars and was the uncredited dialogue coach for fellow Wisconsinite Jeffrey Hunter in *King of Kings* (1961), with whom she starred in his first movie, *Fourteen Hours* in 1951.

In the meantime, Moorehead divorced Lee and married actor, and later TV director, Robert Gist in 1953. They divorced in 1958.

Some rumored that her marriages failed because Moorehead was one of Hollywood's closet lesbians (as alleged in the 2000 *The Theater History Studies* section "The Witching of Agnes Moorehead," on p. 105 of Volume 20).

But, in an October 1966 *Photoplay Magazine* story, Moorehead said it was her success that led to the divorces.

The actress explained that she preferred to keep her son Sean out of acting because of its many "sorrows and disappointments" and because "I think (acting) is even harder for a man, who has to be the breadwinner. To marry someone in the business is even worse. ... No two careers blossom at the same rate. It's terrible for a man to see his wife famous if he is a performer too and not so well known. It's much easier the other way around."

In the middle of her marriage to Gist, Moorehead was busy touring the country performing *Don Juan in Hell* with Charles Boyer, Charles Laughton and Sir Cedric Hardwicke, a talented troupe calling itself the First Drama Quartette. She also developed a popular one-woman stage show for herself called *The Fabulous Redhead*.

The actress had to put such performances aside, however, when she was cast in 1964 as Elizabeth Montgomery's overbearing mother, the witch Endora, on TV's *Bewitched*. Endora remains the character she is probably best known for today.

Endora's flamboyant nature wasn't all too separate from the actress who played her, at least where colors are concerned. Moorehead was known for years as "The Lavender Lady" because of her intense love of purple. She drove a purple Ford Thunderbird and had her dressing trailer on the *Bewitched* set redone entirely in purple, often telling the curious that, "I wear as much purple as I can *safely* put on."

The Lavender Lady agreed to do *Bewitched* only if she could perform in just eight of every twelve shows to allow her time to continue with stage and movie roles. It was a promise the producers kept throughout the series' eight-year run.

The flexible schedule allowed Moorehead to perform her one-woman show from time to time, make TV movies and, most significantly, earn her fourth Academy Award nomination for her *Hush... Hush, Sweet Charlotte* performance in 1964 and win an Emmy for her role as Emma Valentine in the "Night of the Vicious Valentine" episode of the TV series *The Wild, Wild West*.

When the actress returned to her childhood hometown of St. Louis in August of 1973 for what proved to be the last time to play Aunt Alicia in *Gigi*, she talked with *St. Louis Post Dispatch* reporter John M. McGuire about how ethereal even her best and award-winning work really was. "Theater is a thankless art," she told him. "When the curtain goes down, that is all. It doesn't really mean anything. Memories are very short, and fame is extremely fleeting."

Moorehead made that final 1973 stage tour stricken with cancer. That same year, she struggled through her illness to perform as Delilah in *Dear Dead Delilah* and to provide the voice of the stuttering goose in *Charlotte's Web*, which featured Debbie Reynolds' voice as Charlotte.

The animated film proved to be Moorehead's final movie performance. She died of cancer April 30, 1974, at Mayo Clinic in Rochester, Minnesota. The actress chose to be buried near her family farm in Ohio and is interred at Dayton Memorial Park in Dayton, Ohio.

According to movie critic Leonard Maltin's biography, she may have fallen victim to cancer because of work she did in the 1954's *The Conquerer*, which was filmed near a government nuclear testing site in Utah. For visual matching purposes, the production crew also hauled red dirt from the location into the studio set in California where John Wayne, Dick Powell, Susan Hayward, Pedro Armendarez and Lee Van Cleef all worked. Like Moorehead, all those cast members later died of cancer.

Though Moorehead had lived primarily between her two homes — a Beverly Hills mansion she called "Villa Agnese" and a 320-acre family farm in Ohio — the actress did reportedly visit her parents in Reedsburg over the years. Her ties to Wisconsin were close enough that Moorehead donated many of her scripts and other papers to the Wisconsin State Historical Society. Moorehead's mother, Mary, outlived her and sold some of the actress's things in a Reedsburg auction. A Richland Center woman reportedly bought some of Moorehead's dresses; a former Soldier's Grove student bought her cello.

The Wisconsin teacher was remembered by Viroqua residents at the 2000 Agnes Moorehead Film Festival, which featured the showing of her films *Our Vines Have Tender Grapes* and *Johnny Belinda*, and by all of Wisconsin in the state's Performing Artists Hall of Fame into which she was inducted posthumously.

Hollywood remembers her well, and fans can view her star on the Hollywood Walk of Fame. If they look closely, fans might also note an odder tribute nearby, Sime adds.

A publicity photo of Agnes Moorehead. Photo courtesy of Wisconsin Center for Film and Theater Research. Image WCFTR-3768.

Famous Wisconsin Film Stars

"There is a white wall near her star that a dedicated bunch of local weirdos constantly paints 'Agnes Moorehead is God' on. The town keeps painting over it, but the saying keeps coming back."

That a popular witch like Endora would be thought of in the same sentence as God would probably please the actress.

Above all else in her life, Moorehead was religious, keeping a Bible by her bedside and in her dressing rooms.

"If we give our lives over to God and dedicate ourselves to Him, we are then living life as it should be lived," the minister's daughter told interviewer Daisy Charles from *TV Picture Life* for a September 1971 article, "Agnes Moorehead Reveals Beauty Secrets From the Bible."

"I have never worked for an honor or prize. ... I work primarily to please Him, since it is His commandment that we are honest in all things we do," she added. "We are told by Scriptures that it is good to work and good to take pride in your work. The Bible tells us that it's not what you do but *how* you do your work that is important."

With 75 movies and TV shows, four Oscar nominations, a Golden Mike and an Emmy to her credit, Wisconsin can be proud of the teacher who did her work so well.

ON SCREEN

Fans can spot the award winning stage and screen star-and former high school teacher- Agnes Moorehead in the following:

Rex Harrison Presents Stories of Love (1974) (TV)
Charlotte's Web (1973) (voice)
Dear Dead Delilah (1972
Frankenstein: The True Story (1972) (TV)
Night of Terror (1972) (TV)
Rolling Man (1972) (TV)
The Strange Monster of Strawberry Cove (1971) (TV)
What's the Matter with Helen? (1971)
Suddenly Single (1971) (TV)
Marriage: Year One (1971) (TV)
The Ballad of Andy Crocker (1969) (TV)
Mr. Blackwell Presents (1968) (TV guest)
Alice Through the Looking Glass (1966) (TV)
The Singing Nun (1965)
Hush... Hush, Sweet Charlotte (1964)
Bewitched (1964) TV Series
Who's Minding the Store? (1963)
How the West Was Won (1962)
Jessica (1962)
Bachelor in Paradise (1961)
Twenty Plus Two (1961)
The Land of Oz (1960) (TV)
Pollyanna (1960)
Night of the Quarter Moon (1959)
The Bat (1959)
La Tempesta (1958)
A Tale of Two Cities (1958) (TV)
Operation Raintree (1957) (uncredited)
The True Story of Jesse James (1957)
Raintree County (1957)
The Story of Mankind (1957)
Jeanne Eagels (1957)

Meet Me in Las Vegas (1956)
The Opposite Sex (1956)
Pardners (1956)
The Revolt of Mamie Stover (1956)
The Swan (1956)
The Conqueror (1956)
All That Heaven Allows (1955)
The Left Hand of God (1955)
Untamed (1955)
Magnificent Obsession (1954)
The Story of Three Loves (1953)
Those Redheads from Seattle (1953)
Main Street to Broadway (1953)
Scandal at Scourie (1953)
The Blazing Forest (1952)
The Blue Veil (1951)
Fourteen Hours (1951)
Show Boat (1951)
Adventures of Captain Fabian (1951)
Black Jack (1950)
Caged (1950)
Without Honor (1950)
The Great Sinner (1949)
The Stratton Story (1949)
Station West (1948)
Johnny Belinda (1948)
The Woman in White (1948)
Summer Holiday (1948)
The Lost Moment (1947)
Dark Passage (1947)
The Beginning or the End (1947)
(scenes deleted)
Keep Your Powder Dry (1945)
Our Vines Have Tender Grapes (1945)
Her Highness and the Bellboy (1945)
Dragon Seed (1944)
Tomorrow the World! (1944)
Mrs. Parkington (1944)
The Seventh Cross (1944)
Since You Went Away (1944)
Jane Eyre (1944)
Government Girl (1943)
The Youngest Profession (1943)
Journey Into Fear (1942)
The Big Street (1942)
The Magnificent Ambersons (1942)
Citizen Kane (1941)

ORSON WELLES

"The public," Oscar Wilde once said, "... forgives every thing except genius." It's a fitting way for director and author Peter Bogdanovich to start the semi-autobiographical book, *This is Orson Welles*, which he cowrote with the genius moviemaker and published after Welles' death. After all, Welles's vision was not only forever ahead of his time, but ahead of the people running the clocks as well.

Hollywood insiders and stars alike publicly praised Welles for his creative genius, naming him their most talented director and calling him divinely inspired. Humorist Dorothy Parker said that meeting Orson Welles was "like meeting God without dying."

Despite all the public admiration, few opened their pocketbooks or their minds to support the Kenosha, Wisconsin, native's cutting-edge efforts.

George Orson Welles was born May 6, 1915, on Park Street (now Seventh Avenue) in Kenosha, Wisconsin. Richard and Beatrice (Ives) Welles, named their ten-pound infant either after uncles Orson and George or after two bachelors (comic author George Ade and rich investor Orson Collins Wells) his parents met on a cruise while Beatrice was pregnant.

Welles had been born into a formidable and somewhat eccentric family. His father was a respected inventor from a prominent Kenosha family who had patented, among other things, headlamps for the first automobiles as well as a "steam-driven plane that crashed on its first flight and a regulation Army mess kit," Joseph McBride reported in a September 14, 1970, *Wisconsin State Journal* article.

Welles's mother was a strikingly beautiful musician from Chicago who reportedly became one of the first women in Wisconsin to be elected to office when she gained a seat on the Kenosha School Board. She was also puritanical and ran the town's censorship board, which banned anyone younger than 21 from seeing movies that showed bare shouldered women, men without shirts, and other immoral images, noted Charles Higham in his book, *Orson Welles: The Rise and Fall of an American Genius*.

Nearly from the start, Orson was showered with family praise

Agnes Moorehead and Orson Welles. Photo courtesy of Wisconsin Center for Film and Theater Research. Image No. WCFTR-3768.

as the near perfect talent combination of his creative inventor father and artistic mother, an impatient mechanical thinker and visionary poet all in one.

Meanwhile, the intelligent, achievement-focused upper middle class family all but ignored Orson's older brother Richard Ives Welles, ten years his senior, who stuttered and seemed slower witted.

Welles's older brother had enjoyed a prosperous upbringing, thanks to the Welles family's past wealth and the patent money his father earned at Badger Brass and Bain. However, by the time Orson was born the family was facing leaner times, thanks to his alcoholic father's addiction to liquor and bad investments.

By 1913, Higham notes, the family was renting the lower rooms of its Park Street home to traveling salesmen.

All was not bliss in other areas either. Tortured death and suffering — a theme depicted in many of his movies — haunted Welles' childhood. His first such experiences came as a toddler as he watched and heard his grandmother Lucy Ives' agonizing

> "I'm not ashamed of being from Wisconsin, just being from Kenosha. It's a terrible place."
> — Orson Welles

death from stomach cancer while she was living with the family in Kenosha.

At the same time, he watched his father drink himself further into ruin and despair and his mother begin an affair with the doctor who'd treated Lucy Ives, Dr. Bernstein, Higham notes.

Beatrice Welles divorced Richard when Orson was 6 and moved with her young son to an apartment on East Superior Street in Chicago where she began giving piano lessons and asked her son to recite Shakespeare, an author he'd begun reading as early as age 2. It was the doctor who bought the precocious, hot-tempered, arrogant, and creative boy a puppet theater and a box of magic tricks to keep him occupied. Welles reportedly wrote plays for his puppets to perform and developed a lifelong passion for magic.

When he wasn't creating shows, young Orson was eating, especially sweets, and was often teased by other kids about his chubby appearance. Eating was an obsession that would add a great many pounds to accent those chubby cheeks over the years; Welles weighed three hundred pounds when he died.

Most weekends, the family (including Richards Jr. and Sr.) would travel to Grand Detour, Illinois. Beatrice and Dr. Bernstein lived in a home on Route 3, complete with a live-in nanny for Orson, while the two Richards took a room at the Sheffield House hotel.

Despite all the attention and activities, Orson complained constantly about being bored in Grand Detour, Higham relays. "In despair as to how to please him, (his father) went to Chicago and bought him a houseful of toys — including a train Orson loved to play with for hours — (and) then created a large-sized toy house to put them in."

When Orson was 9, he endured a second more tortuous death of his mother. Beatrice contracted hepatitis in Chicago and died within a week. Orson's father proved little comfort to his sons as he increasingly sought his own comfort in the bottle.

Meanwhile, Orson's paternal grandmother Mary Welles — a Christian Scientist and domineering family matriarch who hated the theater — terrified young Orson on his visits to see her at the family's Kenosha mansion. Later in life, Welles insisted that Mary Welles practiced black magic and even sacrificed birds in her home. Though no lasting signs of any witchcraft have ever been found, Higham reports that a former resident of Mary Welles's home, Mary Page, did find a wooden altar with a painted multicolored window above it in one of the home's closets.

Without a mother or a reliable father, Orson remained in the care of Dr. Bernstein either in Grand Detour or in Highland Park, Illinois, near Chicago, where Welles was able to attend many symphony and theater performances.

Welles continued to perform for friends, family, and household help, especially in Grand Detour where the future star once chased acting dreams with a young girl staying at the Sheffield House hotel.

The acting team "went door to door, raising money that they could use to embark on their careers as child actors," Higham recounts. With money in hand they ran away, slept in the woods, and were eventually found "performing on a street corner for a penny a show."

In 1926, Orson Welles returned to Wisconsin for more than just a family visit. His father and Dr. Bernstein enrolled Welles in Madison public schools and the 11-year-old lived with the doctor's friend Frederick Mueller (perhaps spelled Miller), a psychologist and lecturer. Before this, Welles had no formal education. Despite the lack of class time, he proved himself an exceptional student who excelled in writing, drawing, music, history, and geography.

His skills were so advanced that the school moved Welles up a grade from fourth to fifth, where teachers Lowell Frautschi and Dorothy Chapman encouraged artistic talents in the "quiet pupil," Chapman told the *Wisconsin State Journal*'s McBride in 1970.

"His interests were definitely directed toward art and dramatics," she told the *Wisconsin State Journal* March 15, 1938. "He disliked arithmetic and found the regular school curriculum much to his disliking. He was permitted to take special art courses, in which he showed marked adeptness."

In an Oct. 11, 1985, story in the newspaper, Chapman further relayed that Welles participated in school productions including *The First Thanksgiving*. He had a lead role in the class's 1924 production of *A Christmas Carol* as well and built the set's fireplace — a prop used for years by later classes, the teacher noted.

While in Madison, Welles also attended Camp Indianola where he edited and illustrated the *Indianola Trail* paper and gave hours-long performances. In the 1938 *Wisconsin State Journal* article, Lowell Frautschi, who was the camp's athletic director, relates that Welles staged "his own mono-actor version of *Dr. Jekyll and Mr. Hyde*" as the camp's summer program finale in 1925 — (a performance) that was "definitely the hit of the season."

Higham reported that the young prodigy also dictated a poem he wrote, "The Passing of a Lord," to Mueller. It read in part, "an aristocrat who sat upon a satin chair, 'his trousers ironed without a singe,' ... "The Lord sat still and was unaware. A moment before there had been a shot. The aim was true but the Lord knew not. The next day they found him in a pool of his blood."

After a year in Madison, Dr. Mueller and Richard Sr. decided that their child genius would be best served at the Todd School in Woodstock, Illinois. Welles would later insist that his change of venue was the result of a midnight dash away from the camp and to Chicago as a railroad runaway, the *Wisconsin State Journal* reported.

By this time, Welles's 21-year-old brother was a drifter working at fisheries in Montana. In 1927, Richard Sr. had his namesake son declared insane and institutionalized in Illinois. Though he remained at the Kankakee State Institution for ten years, Orson seldom, if ever, visited his brother and reportedly only saw Richard Jr. a few more times in his life, both when his brother sought Welles out in New York. Richard Jr. was later reported to have become a counselor.

Welles did not return to Wisconsin often and had few good things to say about the town or state of his birth, often telling reporters that he'd been born in Brazil or Paris instead. Welles did remember Madison more fondly, calling it "a wonderful city."

"I'm not ashamed of being from Wisconsin, just being from Kenosha. It's a terrible place," Welles said in McBride's *Wisconsin State Journal* article.

In Illinois, Welles' creativity blossomed at Todd School, under the tutelage of headmaster Roger Hill. The talented student performed magic, sang in shows, and appeared in numerous plays and musicals including *It Won't Be Long Now* and *Finesse the Queen*.

According to his October 15, 1985, obituary in the *Daily Variety*, Welles' Todd School portrayal of both Antony and Cassius in the Chicago Drama League competition was so impressive that "the judges disqualified the production because two ringers obviously had been employed for the occasion."

The now six-foot, one-inch teenager was also known to carry his performances beyond the stage and sometimes fancied wearing stage makeup throughout the day, Higham reports.

While at Todd School, Welles learned that one of his earlier childhood locations, the Sheffield House, burned to the ground on his father's watch, and Richard Sr. barely escaped the flames with his life.

A teenage Welles had adjustments to make in his life with his doctor guardian as well.

Dr. Bernstein married Edith Mason, a star of the Chicago Opera Company who, according to Higham, continued, as part of the marriage agreement, her sexual relationship with former husband and conductor Giorgio Polacco. The strange arrangement, which Welles bore witness to, ended two years later when Edith remarried Polacco.

Welles had worldly educations of another kind when Dr. Bernstein took him on a trip to Cuba and sent him on a student trip to Germany in 1929.

In 1930, Welles's father took him on a trip to the Orient, an event that Welles would later embellish as a journey filled with extravagant adventure and the exotic charms of his father's home in Shanghai. The home never existed and, in reality, father and son merely enjoyed an Oriental cruise for Welles's birthday. It was the last good time they spent together.

Just after Christmas that same year, Welles endured another tragic death when his father died alone in his hotel room. Though a death certificate with many names missing and signed by Dr. Bernstein said Richard Sr. died of "chronic myocarditis and nephritis followed by cardiac failure," some believed Welles's father took his own life, notes Higham.

Following a funeral in Kenosha, Dr. Bernstein was officially made Welles's guardian until his high school graduation that June.

Instead of college, Welles talked Bernstein into letting him take a sketching tour of Ireland. And, though he enjoyed drawing all of his life, the 16-year-old high school graduate was about to put his paintbrushes aside and paint passions on a bigger canvas — the professional stage.

When money ran low in Ireland, Welles struck on the idea that he could earn money by performing in Ireland's top theater, The Gate, in Dublin. Ignoring his own lack of experience as an actor and with dreamed up New York connections to impress producers Hilton Edwards and Michael MacLiammoir, Welles stepped boldly into The Gate and asked for an audience with Edwards.

The producer was impressed enough with the teenager's reading of part of a script — though he never bought into Welles's supposed American theater ties — that he summoned his partner and said, "something strange has arrived from America. Come and see what you think of it," Higham notes.

Welles also painted sets for the theater while rehearsing his first role, Duke, for *Jew Suss*. After a long ovation and a good review from J.J. Hayes of *The New York Times,* who commented on Welles's "naturalness and ease about acting," The Gate cast the 16-year-old "child prodigy" in further productions. He appeared in one of the theater's only flops, *Mogu of the Desert* and then played middle-age millionaire Ralph Bentley in *The Dead Ride Fast*, played both Marshall Francois Bazaine and a Mexican colonel in *The Archdupe*, the ghost of Hamlet's father in *Hamlet,* and Baron Lamberto in *Death Takes a Holiday.*

Shortly after, Welles left Ireland to pursue his acting dreams in New York, where the future star was rejected at every turn.

Welles returned to Woodstock, Illinois, and partnered with Roger Hill in creating Todd Trouper productions. The two also traveled to the Chippewa Indian reservation near Lac du Flambeau, Wisconsin, where they wrote a play of their own, *Marching Song*, about freeing slaves, a subject Welles knew much about from his family's history as slave liberators in the Underground Railroad. Though a New York producer liked the play enough to search for backers, none were found, and the play remained only on paper.

Frustrated in Illinois, Welles again headed for Europe and Africa where he earned money writing magazine articles and, the actor later insisted, tried his hand at bullfighting in Spain.

By 1933, the 18-year-old was back at a party in Woodstock where he had a chance meeting with Thornton Wilder. According to Higham, Wilder remembered Welles from the Irish theater and was impressed enough to write letters of recommendation on the young man's behalf to influential people in New York.

The letters paid off, and Wilder's friend Alexander Woolcott introduced Welles to actress and road company theater producer Katherine Cornell, who cast him as Mercucio in a nationally touring production of *Romeo and Juliet*. After the play wound down, Welles returned for a time to Woodstock, Illinois, and convinced his former Irish bosses to join him there for the summer 1934 theater season.

With the Irish backers, Welles played Claudius in *Hamlet*, Count Pahlem in *Tsar Paul* and Svengali in *Trilby* to rave reviews, including a July 14, 1934, assessment by Lloyd Lewis of the *Chicago Daily*

News that Welles "shows remarkable vigor of imagination and dramatic instinct … He will, I think, go far on the stage."

When he wasn't on stage, Welles was working on a play, *Bright Lucifer*, about two men who travel with their ward to Northern Wisconsin. Though Higham says the work, which included homosexual themes, was "clumsy and poorly constructed," Welles's story referred to many of his childhood memories including his grandmother's alleged black magic.

The summer of 1934 was an especially busy one for Welles. Not only was he entertaining Chicago elite on stage and the Irish producers at night, Welles was falling in love with his costar in *Tsar Paul*, Virginia Nicholson, a Woodstock native. He cast the beautiful girl in one of his early, Woodstock-made short films, *Hearts of Age* (in which he played Death) and married her later that year. They had a daughter, Christopher, in 1937 and divorced in 1939, in part because of Welles's workaholic ways and because of his many reported affairs.

In that short five-year span, the newlyweds went from a low-rent apartment with a living room bathtub that doubled as a bed to the height of New York theater circles.

In the fall of 1934, Cornell brought Welles back to New York to star as Tybalt in her production of *Romeo & Juliet*. After meeting budding stage director and star John Houseman, Welles left Cornell to star in Houseman's production of *Panic*.

In addition, Welles began acting in and narrating radio shows. By 1936, he was a star of NBC's *The March of Time* and was lending his resonant bass voice to the popular drama, *The Shadow*. By 1941, Welles had written for, acted in, and directed well over a hundred radio dramas.

It was during this flurry of the airwaves that Welles' passions were ignited by John Houseman's work with the U.S. Work Progress Administration's Negro Theater Project. "Everything Houseman told Welles about the project excited" the Wisconsinite whose family had championed the cause of abolishing slavery in the 1800s, noted Higham.

In early 1936, Welles asked Houseman to let him bring an all-black version of Shakespeare's *Macbeth* to the stage. Welles "hated the Uncle Remus and mammy (African American) images of screen and theater (and) was delighted to be giving these striking performers an opportunity to work," Higham adds.

Welles cast Jack Carter in the title role and Henri Christophe as the king (of Haiti). The production incorporated black cultural elements as well, featuring black music and voodoo priests instead of witches. The show opened to a sold out crowd in Harlem in April 1936 and was soon playing to sellout crowds on Broadway, reportedly the first time an all-black cast performed for the mostly white Broadway audiences.

Welles and Houseman continued to produce top-selling plays with members of their black cast, including *Doctor Faustus* with Jack Carter starring opposite Welles. Eventually, though, the federal government began alleging that the plays were too political. When the company cast the leftist production *The Cradle Will Rock* in 1937, federal agents appeared at the theater with a notice forbidding them to "perform on stage." Welles and Houseman refused to be beaten, however. They hurried the cast, crew and audience up the street to a different theater and performed the opera in the theater aisles, thereby avoiding the stage. For all the government's efforts, *The Cradle Will Rock* was a hit.

Welles and Houseman left the WPA project and founded their own production company, the Mercury Players, in 1937. Among their best productions was a modern version of *Julius Caesar* that played to sellout crowds. It was during this period that Welles also created a short film that was to be shown during Mercury's *Too Much Johnson* production. But, the public reportedly never saw the film and it was later lost in a 1970 fire.

Meanwhile, Welles continued his hectic stage and radio performances that were so tightly scheduled "he would often be spirited by special ambulance to the theater in order to make the curtain," *The Daily Variety* noted in its obituary of Welles.

On May 9, 1938, *Time* magazine featured Welles on its cover, dressed as Capt. Shotover from the Mercury's *Heartbreak House*.

By now, Welles, just 22 years old, was being heralded as one of the top stage talents of all time.

The young star and Houseman took their players onto national radio in 1938, performing the classics as *The Mercury Theater of the Air* on CBS, in which Welles often cast fellow Wisconsinite Agnes Moorehead, an actress and friend he called "Aggie."

The group's most infamous radio production, *War of the Worlds*, aired Halloween night of 1938 and featured Welles breaking into a radio drama (which was all part of the larger drama) to report an invasion of Earth by Martians. The broadcast included news bulletins and eyewitness accounts. The problem was that many listeners didn't hear the repeated notice that this was simply a fictional theater account. The result was nationwide panic, even in

Madison, where the *Wisconsin State Journal* headline read, "Hysteria Sweeps Country as Radio Hoax Describes 'Invasion' by Mars Giants ... Listeners Faint ... Pray ... Prepare to Flee."

The *State Journal* recalled in an October 26, 1958, article that one man called WIBA radio hysterically demanding that the station get news of the invasion out right away while "several Madisonians called the *State Journal* asking if the reported invasion was true."

Welles apologized on air the next day, saying Mercury had intended to create only a good drama, not real panic.

The international attention from *War of the Worlds* caught more than a few Hollywood ears.

RKO-Radio Pictures studio soon signed Welles to a very generous contract for a first-time movie director, even allowing him to make final cuts on the film. The novice filmmaker took on the daunting task of not only writing, producing, and directing the movie, but starring in it as well. In the meantime, he continued to work on radio and stage in New York and, in 1939, won "TWA's prize as the airline's most traveled passenger (traveling 300,000 miles between Los Angeles and New York)," Higham reported.

After toying with other movie ideas for the RKO picture, the stage star cast himself and Mercury stars like Agnes Moorehead and Joseph Cotton, in a film reportedly based on American millionaires William Randolph Hearst and Robert McCormick about powerful publishing and political magnate Charles Foster Kane.

In 1941, Welles enjoyed the release of his now much celebrated first feature movie, *Citizen Kane*.

Welles made the film using revolutionary camera, sound, and even makeup techniques. In addition, as he did with most of his films, Welles shot the picture using high contrast black and white film and deep focus photography in which those in the background are as clear as those in the foreground, creating a visual and auditory experience not known to American movie audiences before.

Though it was critically acclaimed enough for nine Oscar nominations and is regarded today as one of the best films ever created, Welles enjoyed little public or studio praise for his first Hollywood effort. The film lost $150,000 for RKO. The 25-year-old did, however, win an Academy Award for the film's screenplay, which he cowrote with Herman Mankiewicz, and was one of only a handful of actors ever nominated for Best Actor in a debut movie role.

Despite the critical praise, the legendary movie never enjoyed commercial success until it was re-released for its 50th anniversary in 1991, Bogdanovich reports, noting that 1991 moviegoers often commented on how modern the 50-year-old movie seemed. In 1998, *Citizen Kane* was again named the "greatest American film ever made" by the American Film Institute.

If commercial dollars were the final judge of greatness, then Welles was a failure as a movie producer and director. Few if any of the films Welles created ever enjoyed commercial success.

Surely part of that failure rests with the Hollywood elite who tried to undermine and refused to finance and/or distribute Welles' movies. Some efforts were likely led by Hearst, who remained upset with the filmmaker for his not-so-disguised portrayal of the publisher in *Citizen Kane,* though Welles denied any such connection to his character at the time.

The actor/director did not help his own cause when he dug at the Hollywood elite in newspaper interviews in 1940. For example, in a United Press International story from April 14, 1940, Welles said movie actors were "really the same class as those who wait on tables," adding, "Of the movies, I will speak only of contempt."

The so-called "actor-waiters" offered their own public "backlash" toward Welles.

"I know some very nice waiters and waitresses. I only hope they don't mind being put in the same class with those of us in Hollywood," Bette Davis responded.

Actor and fellow Wisconsinite Pat O'Brien defended Welles, saying "I know it sounds awful screwy (what Welles said), but I met Orson once and he's really a nice kid."

Welles continued to enjoy backing in New York and in 1941 produced a highly praised production of *Native Son,* starring black actor Canada Lee as the accused killer.

In some respects, Welles said (as quoted in his October 15, 1985, *Daily Variety* obituary), he should have stayed in New York where he received praises from both the public and the critics.

"I would have been much better off if, after I made my first picture, I had gone back to the theater from which I came," Welles lamented. "(Film) is the most expensive mistress that anyone could have, and I've been trying to support her ever since."

Even though studio backing was slim, acting and narrating offers for the richly voiced actor were always on the table, and he took RKO up on playing Colonel Haki in *Journey Into Fear* in 1942 and Edward Rochester in the 1944 hit *Jane Eyre.* In between, he reportedly dated married actress Lena Horne and actress Delores del Rio before marrying pinup girl and actress Rita Hayworth in

1943.

For a short time at least, RKO still believed in the young director's possibilities. The studio gave Welles the okay to make a movie based on the radio program he'd already created from Booth Tarkington's book, *The Magnificent Ambersons*. While the film would again star many of Welles' Mercury Theater actors, including Wisconsin's Moorehead, Welles's himself would leave starring roles up to others, though he did narrate the film.

Welles told Bogdanovich that he especially respected Moorehead as an actress. Higham reported that Welles's admiration might have begun years before since Welles claimed he first met Moorehead when he was 5. A meeting between the two would have been possible when Welles was a bit older child because Moorehead was taking classes at the University of Wisconsin and helping out in local productions (from 1923 to 1927). Meanwhile, Welles was starring in Madison grade school and camp performances from 1926 to 1927.

By the time Moorehead and Welles completed shooting in South America, RKO management had changed for the worse where the renegade director was concerned. When the movie didn't fare well in previews, the studio edited it and shot additional scenes without Welles' knowledge or approval before releasing the film in 1942 while Welles was reportedly still in South America.

According to a 1994 Welles biography by Leonard Maltin on the Internet Movie Database, RKO went so far as to throw Welles' Mercury Productions out of studio headquarters and cancel the Wisconsin native's next film already being shot in South America, *It's All True*. (Incidentally, Maltin reports, some of the footage from this never-made film was pulled together and released in 1993.)

When he returned to Hollywood, Welles narrated several movies in his trademark radio voice such as *Duel in the Sun* (1946) and *Battle for Survival* before he was given his next directing opportunity in a 1946 thriller called *The Stranger* in which he starred as Charles Rankin and Franz Kindler. During the war years, Welles, who had been released from military obligation because of a bad back and other ailments, campaigned for President Roosevelt's re-election and toured as a magician with the *Mercury Wonder Show*, where he "sawed" celebrities like his wife, Rita Hayworth, in half.

In 1948, Welles parlayed the success of *The Stranger* into a writing, acting, and directing opportunity for Columbia Pictures' *The Lady From Shanghai* (1948), in which Welles starred as Michael

O'Hara with Hayworth. Welles and Hayworth had a daughter, Rebecca, in 1944 before they divorced in 1948.

Welles was then hired to produce a low-budget version of *Macbeth* in which the director cast himself in the lead and many Mercury players in supporting roles. It was the last Hollywood directing job Welles had for ten years.

The actor/director gave up on Hollywood and moved to Europe, hoping to find a more welcoming audience for his films. Where acting was concerned, the move paid off. In 1949 the outcast director starred as Harry Lime in the well-received film *The Third Man* and then took roles in European-made movies to help finance the films he wanted to make, starring in *Black Magic* (1949), *Prince of Foxes* (1949), *Black Rose* (1950), *Trent's Last Case* (1952), *Man Beast and Virtue* (1953), *Royal Affairs in Versailles* (1953), *Napoleon* (1954), and *Moby Dick* (1956).

Meanwhile, Welles was trying desperately to earn and find enough backing to complete a movie based on *Othello*, which he'd begun shooting in Morocco in 1948. He succeeded and *Tragedy of Othello: The Moor of Venice* was finally released with Welles in the lead role.

Regardless of how tight funding was, there were some things Welles wouldn't do for money, he noted in a United Press International story Nov. 1, 1959. The producers of a popular Hollywood quiz show reportedly offered Welles $170,000 to play in a rigged game show that Welles was guaranteed to win. Welles said he turned the offer down because, "I would be competing against some college teacher or some poor widow who needed the money to pay the mortgage." He said the whole idea of quiz shows is "a gyp on the people."

Still, for all his charitable notions, Welles spent much of the money he earned not on movies, but on his lavish lifestyle, which reportedly included having steaks flown in and employing a full staff.

In addition, Welles's childhood guardian, Dr. Bernstein, and the actor's first wife, Virginia, were constantly after him for money. Virginia wanted more alimony and child support and originally got a settlement for Welles to pay half of her rent plus $500 a month toward their daughter. The doctor especially hounded Welles for many years implying that the star owed him money to repay the support he'd given him as a child.

In 1940, for example, Higham reports that Dr. Bernstein, who was living in Welles' home at the actor's expense, wrote Welles that he had only $700 left and needed money to live on for at least one year, for his own apartment, good clothes, etc. "You have helped so many stranded actors who meant nothing to you. I hope that I mean more than they did to you," he pleaded.

Despite the financial pressures, Welles was loyal to the father figure he had in Dr. Bernstein and was reportedly quite upset when the doctor died in 1964.

Thanks to the funding of some European backers, Welles was given the chance to film another of his screenplays. He produced, directed, and starred as Gregory Arkadin, in *Mr. Arkadin* in 1955. It was one of the last projects Welles would control from start to finish (though even his European hosts did some final editing to Welles's frustration).

That same year, Welles married Italian actress and countess Paoli Mori and had a daughter Beatrice. Though they remained married, Bogdanovich reports that Welles had a twenty-year intimate relationship with Yugoslavian sculptor Oja Kodar.

"Orson was different with Oja than with anyone else and different to others when she was there," Bogdanovich writes. "She had ways of sending him up, or taking the mickey out of him or just teasing him."

In 1958, the new father returned to the Hollywood movie set to direct *Touch of Evil* for Universal, playing the role of a corrupt police captain in the film that featured Charlton Heston. Heston later noted how impressed he'd been by Welles as a director saying, "He was the most talented man I've ever worked with —indeed, ever seen."

Again, Welles won critical acclaim and even a filmmaking prize at the 1958 World's Fair in Brussels, Belgium, but the American director remained a commercial failure in the United States.

When he wasn't pounding the pavement in search of backers, Welles took acting or narrating jobs in movies and television to help maintain his expensive tastes and fund future projects.

Most notably, Welles played the title role in a TV production of *King Lear* in 1953. He also hosted such television series as *Around the World with Orson Welles* (1955) and *Orson Welles and People* (1956).

On screen, Welles starred as Father Mapple in *Moby Dick* (1956), Will Varner in *The Long Hot Summer* (1958), and King Saul in *David and Goliath* (1961), and he narrated Wisconsin director Nicholas Ray's 1961 Biblical epic *King of Kings*.

In between the Wisconsin child prodigy tried to film his adaptation of the Don Quixote story. Though Welles never completed it, the movie was finished and released posthumously in 1992.

In 1963, Welles was asked to direct his adaptation of *The Trial* (1963), again earning critical praise but few American dollars.

He then wrote, directed, and starred as Falstaff in a European-made, Shakespeare-based film, *Chimes at Midnight*, which also received critical acclaim and even enjoyed some commercial success in the United States.

Though Welles later wrote and directed *The Immortal Story* (1968), most of the acclaimed director's projects never saw theater screens.

For example, from 1970 to 1976, Welles continually worked with John Huston to produce the movie, *The Other Side of the Wind*. Despite all his stage, TV and movie work to raise money, the film remains one of Welles's many unfinished projects, like *The Deep* (1970).

Though their project never came to fruition, the respect between Huston and Welles was mutual. In Welles' obituaries, Huston is often quoted as saying, "Orson once described me as a renaissance prince. Orson was a king."

The Hollywood praise of Welles's talents only grew larger as the financial pot with which he had to create grew smaller. The American Film Institute presented Welles with a lifetime achievement award in 1975, and the Directors Guild of America honored him with the D.W. Griffith Award in 1984. Even the Wisconsin Film Society got into the celebration of Welles's work and showed a retrospective of the renegade director's films at the Memorial Union in 1972.

Despite the accolades, Welles's last works as a director were unrealized efforts of frustration. His work as an actor, narrator, and spokesman never ended.

Most notably, Welles starred as Brig. General Dreedle in the hit *Catch 22* (1970), narrated *Start the Revolution Without Me* (1970), played Long John Silver in *Treasure Island* (1972), and narrated the television mini series *Shogun* (1980).

He also played a magician in the 1971 movie *A Safe Place*. Welles needed little preparation to portray a master magician because he was one. That little magic box that Dr. Bernstein had given Welles as a boy had never been discarded. The star kept up his magic talents enough to maintain his decades-long membership in the magicians union. Welles often performed as a magician on stage throughout his career and, later in life, appeared in magic

A classic Orson Welles publicity photo, courtesy of Wisconsin Center for Film and Theater Research. Image WCFTR-3760.

shows on television, including guest starring on *The Magic of David Copperfield* TV show in 1978 and hosting *The Orson Welles Magic Show* in 1985.

Welles also lent his voice to dozens of films, cartoons and commercials, most notably claiming for Paul Masson wine that, "We will sell no wine before it's time." The star appeared on many TV talk shows as well, including Johnny Carson's *Tonight Show*, which he hosted on occasion.

He narrated English versions of many foreign films and appeared on several TV shows. He played himself in an *I Love Lucy* episode as well as in a dream sequence in *Moonlighting* in 1985 and he appeared as Robin Masters's voice in episodes of *Magnum P.I.* in the 1980s.

Such performances may have seemed an odd choice for a classic stage actor and innovative movie director, but Welles admitted to Bogdanovich that he couldn't stop himself from performing, partly for money, partly for pleasure, regardless of the medium. "I hate television. I hate it as much as peanuts, but I can't stop eating peanuts," he told his protegee.

Welles, who once said of himself, "I started at the top and worked down," ended his critically acclaimed career in less than praiseworthy films, starring as Judge Rauch in 1981's *Butterfly*, Sheriff Paisley in 1983's *Hot Money*, and appearing in two movies released after his death, as Danny's Friend in 1987's *Someone to Love* and as the voice of Unicron in the 1986 cartoon movie *The Transformers*.

Still, Welles insisted he was less upset with how Hollywood treated him than how it had treated others. "I'm not bitter about Hollywood's treatment of me, but over its treatment of Griffith, Von Sternberg, Von Stroheim, Buster Keaton and a hundred others," the Wisconsin native once said, according to his Internet Movie Database biography.

On October 10, 1985, the movie maverick died of a heart attack while staying at a friend's home in Hollywood, reportedly collapsing across the typewriter on his bed sometime after 10 p.m. At Welles' request, the star's ashes were buried in Malaga, Spain, at the home of bullfighter Antonio Ordonez Ronda.

In the years since his death, appreciation and fame of Welles as a moviemaker have only grown, and a few of his uncompleted works have been released, including *Don Quixote* in 1992 and *The Big Brass Ring* in 1997/1999. He also was inducted into the Wisconsin Performing Artists Hall of Fame.

The visionary artist, it seems, had at last caught up with the time that his creative clocks had been keeping.

ON SCREEN

Catch the work of Orson Welles as a maverick director, a shining screen star and an actor taking any part for funding in the following films. *(Note: If a role such as (narrator) or (director) is not mentioned in the below list, Welles was likely the host of the show or played an uncredited role. Welles also often wrote and/or directed the TV shows he hosted. Movies made with foreign names are listed by the name that they were released under in the United States.)*

Magnificent Ambersons (2002) TV Mini Series (original screenplay writer)
The Big Brass Ring (1999) (original screenplay writer)
The Big Brass Ring (1997) (original screenplay writer)
Don Quixote (1992) (narrator, writer, director)
Someone to Love (1987) (actor)
The Transformers: The Movie (1986) (voice)
Orson Welles' Magic Show (1985) (TV) (writer, producer, director)
Scene of the Crime (1985) TV Series
Almonds and Raisins (1984) (narrator)
The Enchanted Journey (1984) (voice)
In Our Hands (1984)
The Spirit of Charles Lindbergh (1984) (writer, director)
The Road to Bresson (1984)
Hot Money (1983) (actor)
Orson Welles à la cinémathèque (1983)
A Salute to John Huston (1983) (TV)
Where Is Parsifal? (1983) (actor)
Slapstick (Of Another Kind) (1982) (voice)
Butterfly (1981) (actor)
Genocide (1981) (narrator)
Search for the Titanic (1981)
History of the World: Part I (1981) (narrator)
Tales of the Klondike (1981) TV Mini Series (narrator)
The Man Who Saw Tomorrow (1980) (narrator)
Shogun (1980) (mini) TV Series (narrator)
Shogun (1980) (TV) (narrator)
The Secret Life of Nikola Tesla (1980) (actor)
The Double McGuffin (1979) (narrator)
The Late Great Planet Earth (1979) (narrator)
The Muppet Movie (1979) (actor)
The Orson Welles Show (1979) TV Series (director)
Filming 'Othello' (1978) (writer, director)
The Magic of David Copperfield (1978) (TV)
Tut: The Boy King (1978) (TV) (actor)
A Woman Called Moses (1978) (TV) (narrator)
Il Grande attacco (1977) (narrator)
Hot Tomorrows (1977) (voice)
Rime of the Ancient Mariner (1977) (narrator)
Some Call It Greed (1977) (narrator)
It Happened One Christmas (1977) (TV) (actor)
Voyage of the Damned (1976) (actor)
Bugs Bunny Superstar (1975) (narrator)
A Salute to Orson Welles (1975) (TV)
Underwelles (1975) (archive footage)
F for Fake (1975) (actor, writer, director)
Who's Out There? (1975)
The Challenge... A Tribute to Modern Art (1974)
And Then There Were None (Ten Little Indians) (1974) (voice)
Great Mysteries (1973) TV Series
The Battle of Sutjeska (1973)

Famous Wisconsin Film Stars

Get to Know Your Rabbit (1972) (actor)
The Man Who Came to Dinner (1972) (TV) (actor)
Necromancy (1972) (actor)
Treasure Island (1972) (actor, writer)
Ten Days Wonder (1972) (actor)
The Other Side of the Wind (1972) (writer, director)
The Silent Years (1971) TV Series
Sentinels of Silence (1971) (narrator)
London (1971) (writer, director)
Malpertuis: The Legend of Doom House (1971) (actor)
Salvador Dalí (1971) (narrator)
Directed by John Ford (1971) (narrator)
A Safe Place (1971) (actor)
The Deep (1970) (actor, writer, producer, director)
Start the Revolution Without Me (1970) (narrator)
Upon This Rock (1970) (TV) (actor)
Waterloo (1970) (actor)
Catch-22 (1970) (actor)
12 + 1 (1970) (actor)
The Kremlin Letter (1970) (actor)
The Battle of Neretva (1969) (actor)
The Merchant of Venice (1969) (TV) (actor, director)
The Southern Star (1969) (actor, director)
Kampf um Rom II - Der Verrat (1969) (actor)
The Immortal Story (1968) (actor, director)
Long Live the Revolution (1968) (actor)
Vienna (1968) (director)
The Last Roman (1968) (actor)
Oedipus the King (1968) (actor)
House of Cards (1968) (actor)
Targets (1968) (writer) (uncredited)
Disorder Is 20 Years Old (1967)
I'll Never Forget What's'isname (1967) (actor)
The Sailor from Gibraltar (1967) (actor)
Casino Royale (1967) (actor)
A Man for All Seasons (1966) (actor)
Is Paris Burning? (1966) (actor)
A King's Story (1965) (narrator)
The Bible (1966) (writer) (uncredited)
Marco the Magnificent (1965) (actor)
Chimes at Midnight (1965) (actor, writer, director)
In the Land of Don Quixote (1964) TV Series (producer, director)
The Finest Hours (1964) (narrator)
Americans on Everest (1963) (TV) (narrator)
The V.I.P.s (1963) (actor)
The Trial (1963) (actor, writer, director)
Let's Have a Brainwash (1962)
No Exit (1962) (director)
Lafayette (1961) (actor)
The Tartars (1961) (actor)
King of Kings (1961) (narrator) (uncredited)
David and Goliath (1961) (actor, director of own scenes)
The Battle of Austerlitz (1960) (actor)
Crack in the Mirror (1960) (actor)
High Journey (1959) (narrator)
Masters of the Congo Jungle (1959) (narrator)
Ferry to Hong Kong (1959) (actor)
Compulsion (1959) (actor)
Portrait of Gina (1958) (TV) (writer, director)
The Roots of Heaven (1958) (actor)
The Vikings (1958) (narrator) (uncredited)
South Seas Adventure (1958) (narrator)
Touch of Evil (1958) (actor, director)
The Long, Hot Summer (1958) (actor)
Man in the Shadow (1957) (actor)
The Fountain of Youth (1956) (TV) (narrator, writer, director)
Orson Welles and People (1956) (TV) (narrator, writer, producer, director)
Moby Dick (1956) (actor)
Around the World with Orson Welles (1955) TV Series (director)
Mr. Arkadin (1955) (actor, writer, producer, director)

Three Cases of Murder (1955) (actor)
Napoléon (1955) (actor)
Royal Affairs in Versailles (1954) (actor, narrator)
King Lear (1953) (TV) (actor)
Trouble in the Glen (1953) (actor)
Man Beast and Virtue (1953) (actor)
The Tragedy of Othello: The Moor of Venice (1952) (actor, writer, producer, director)
Trent's Last Case (1952) (actor)
The Little World of Don Camillo (1951) (narrator) (uncredited)
Return to Glennascaul (1951)
The Black Rose (1950) (actor)
Black Magic (1949) (actor, director)
Prince of Foxes (1949) (actor)
The Third Man (1949) (actor)
Macbeth (1948) (writer, producer, director)
The Lady from Shanghai (1948) (actor, writer, producer, director)
Battle for Survival (1947) (narrator)
Monsieur Verdoux (1947) (writer/idea)
Duel in the Sun (1946) (narrator) (uncredited)
The Stranger (1946) (actor, director)
Tomorrow Is Forever (1946) (actor)
Follow the Boys (1944)
Jane Eyre (1944) (actor)
Show Business at War (1943)
Journey Into Fear (1942) (actor, re-writer, producer, director)
The Magnificent Ambersons (1942) (narrator, writer, producer, director)
Tanks (1942) (narrator)
Citizen Kane (1941) (actor, writer, producer, director)
Swiss Family Robinson (1940) (narrator) (uncredited)
Too Much Johnson (1938) (actor, writer, producer, director)
The Spanish Earth (1937) (original narrator)
Hearts of Age (1934) (actor, writer, director)
Around the World of Mike Todd (1934) (narrator)

CAROLE LANDIS

Long before America fell in love with Marilyn Monroe, it was infatuated with another tragic beauty, Wisconsin native turned Hollywood siren Carole Landis.

Landis was born Frances Lillian Mary Ridste in Fairchild, Wisconsin, on New Year's Day, 1919 (or '18 or '17 depending on the source). Her Norwegian father, Alfred, worked for a time as a railroad mechanic while her Polish mother, Clara, raised Landis, her brother Lawrence, and sister Dorothy.

Just exactly when her father skipped out on the family — while the kids were still small in Wisconsin or maybe after they'd moved as pre-teens to San Bernardino, California — is uncertain. What's clear is that the most significant man in the young girl's life had left. A natural beauty, Frances filled the gap by competing in beauty contests from the age of 12 and in sports, even reportedly trying out for the girls football team in high school.

Perhaps her father's absence explains why, at just 15, Frances married Irving Wheeler in January of 1934. Because she was underage, the marriage was annulled in February. However, the couple remarried on August 25, 1934, and moved to San Francisco where the young bride worked as a nightclub hula dancer and band singer under the stage name of Carole Landis. By 1937, she was under contract with Warner Bros., appearing in small, mostly nonspeaking parts in some fifteen films including *A Star is Born*.

The year 1939 was a critical one for the budding actress. Landis accepted an offer from Hal Roach to play the lead cavewoman Loana in *One Million B.C*, a part the 5-foot-5¾-inch actress earned because of her perfect (36 ¼"-by-24"-by-35") figure, stunning looks and impressive athletic abilities. As the movie work began, Landis divorced Wheeler, who tried to sue the movie studio executives for $250,000 for "stealing his wife away."

One Million B.C. was a success, and so was Landis. Audiences started calling her "The Ping Girl," a title first used by publicist Frank Seltzer as a shortened version of "purring." Landis, who was also known as "The Sweater Girl," was appalled by both monikers and protested such demeaning and chauvinistic names in a two-page article in *Life* magazine.

Landis made no secret of her feminist beliefs and also voiced her dislike of the term "starlet," among other "belittling names." She was often quoted as asking, "Why don't we have a diminutive, like 'starlet,' for the men?"

"We so much want to believe we are not just make-believe to men," she once said, according to her fan site at www.carolelandis.net, "not just mannequins, not just the equivalents of shiny, chromium-trimmed cars, sleek yachts, Charvet ties or other expensive accessories with which men advertise their importance to the world. Who wants to be an accessory?"

The feminist in Landis still wanted to be a wife, to have the husband/family package that she lost in her childhood. By many accounts Landis was a family-style girl at heart who loved mashed potatoes and ate most meals at home with her Great Dane, Sweetums, and her cat, Missy. On July 4, 1940, she married Willis Hunt Jr. with hopes of permanently sharing that home. The dream faded fast. They divorced November 13 that same year.

After three comedies for Warner Bros. — *Road Show*, *Topper Returns*, and *Turnabout*, where she starred as a wife who changed personalities with her husband — the studio sold her contract to 20th Century Fox in 1941. She earned solid reviews for her second-lead performances to Betty Grable in *Moon Over Miami* as the sister helping Grable land a rich husband and in *I Wake Up Screaming* as the beautiful blonde who gets murdered. Continuing her star streak, the Hollywood beauty played a gossipy spouse in *Orchestra Wives* and starred with Rita Hayworth in *My Gal Sal* in 1942 before taking part in a USO-sponsored Hollywood Victory Tour of the British Isles and North Africa to boost morale of American troops.

Landis spent much of 1943 on USO tours and was so dedicated that even after contracting malaria and later amoebic dysentery and a nearly fatal case of pneumonia, she refused to slow down the tour schedule. She returned home so physically weak that, years later, she was still plagued by related health problems.

Despite her bouts of illness, the blonde (and sometimes brunette) beauty also dedicated herself to helping others and to feminist causes. In fact, she was the top fundraising star for the American Cancer Society. She also never forgot about the soldiers she met on her tours and was known to send condolence letters when she learned of the death of any of the men she met, including a letter to the family of Lt. Joseph C. Reynolds of Frederick, Oklahoma, a B-17 pilot whom Landis met at the 91st Air Force Heavy Group base in England while on the USO tour.

Between her patriotic efforts, the girl friends called "honey" tried matrimony yet again, marrying Thomas C. Wallace January 5, 1943. She divorced him in July of 1945 and stacked his wedding ring upon the others she reportedly wore on the same finger.

The tireless tours she and other Hollywood stars gave toward the war effort inspired the actress to write about her experiences. Landis was confident she could write a book for Random House about the USO tours. Though she had little more than an eighth grade education, the well-read, quick-tongued, self-educated actress was, by all accounts, talented and intelligent as well as beautiful. Landis was an excellent amateur photographer who developed her own pictures and had a singing voice so fine that Hollywood rarely dubbed someone else's voice in her musicals. She also spoke French, played the piano, flew planes, and was a good target shooter.

A publicity photo of Carol Landis distributed by MCA Artists Ltd., courtesy of Wisconsin Center for Film and Theater Research. Image WCFTR-3749.

Her book, titled *Four Jills In a Jeep, The Rolliking Adventures of Four Hollywood Stars Who Entertained The Troops in Bermuda, England and Africa,* did well enough for Random House that 20th Century Fox turned it into a 1944 movie, *Four Jills In a Jeep,* starring Landis and other USO girls she had toured with, Martha Raye, Mitzi Mayfair and Kay Francis.

Reviewers called the movie "self serving," and thus wrote the beginning of the end for Landis's career ... and even her life.

Landis filmed just three more Fox movies, including a great comedy performance in *Having a Wonderful Crime,* before her contract was cancelled in 1945. That same year, still hoping to at last find happiness at home, Landis married W. Horace Schmidlapp December 8, 1945. Though she filed for divorce in early 1948, the troubled marriage actually ended with Landis's death on July 5 of that year.

Landis appeared for a short run on Broadway in 1945 and tried to return to Hollywood but could manage only B-movie roles, including *It Shouldn't Happen to a Dog* and *Out of the Blue.* Her last two films, *Noose* and *The Brass Monkey,* were filmed in England in 1948 because Hollywood had all but written her off. Despite her waning Hollywood fame, Americans and especially servicemen loved her so much so that American Generals Dwight D. Eisenhower and James Doolittle each sent personal letters of condolences after her death.

Hollywood snubbed the Wisconsin-born beauty not for any lack of talent but, in part, for her feminist attitude and sexual dalliances.

Landis reportedly had several affairs, even during her marriages, with Hollywood leading men including Charlie Chaplin and Rex Harrison as well as men she publicly dated such as Tyrone Power, Victor Mature and Gene Markey. It now seems apparent that Landis found love in the arms of some leading women as well, including *Valley of the Dolls* author Jacqueline Susann. Susann talked about their lesbian trysts, which were allegedly the basis for those she depicted in her best-selling autobiography *Scandalous Me.*

In *Hollywood Babylon II,* Kenneth Anger affirmed that Landis's sexual liaisons were plentiful. "She was the studio hooker ... the most constant visitor in attendance in the back room of (Fox studios' boss) Darryl F. Zanuck's office," he reported. Rumors also persisted that before making it to Hollywood, Landis made extra money in San Francisco as a call girl.

At the time of her death, Landis had been having an affair with married heartthrob Rex Harrison, while he was ironically filming the movie *Unfaithfully Yours.* On July 4, 1948, the two reportedly had dinner, and Harrison made it clear that he would not leave his wife, Lilli Palmer, for Landis. Landis, then 29, returned home and sometime in the night or early morning took a lethal overdose of Seconal. Harrison arrived at her home for a lunch date

July 5 and found his mistress dying in the bathroom. In his biography of Harrison, *Fatal Charm,* Alexander Walker reported that the actor summoned a doctor instead of calling an ambulance, opting "for damage-limitation and image-control. By the time a doctor saw her, she was way past reviving."

With her tragic death, Landis had avoided her long underlying fear of having to return to a life as a poor nobody. "I have no intention of ending my career in a rooming house, with full scrapbooks and an empty stomach," she once said.

Instead, Landis ended her life in her 13-room Spanish Bel Air home still a somebody, a beautiful star still burning, if not quite as brightly as she once had.

ON SCREEN

You can take in the beauty and charm that was Carole Landis in the following movies:

Varsity Show (1937)
The King and the Chorus Girl (1937)
Alcatraz Island (1937)
Adventurous Blonde (1937)
Over the Goal (1937)
Hollywood Hotel (1937)
A Star Is Born (1937)
A Day at the Races (1937)
Broadway Melody of 1938 (1937)
The Emperor's Candlesticks (1937)
Gold Diggers in Paris (1938)
Boy Meets Girl (1938)
He Couldn't Say No (1938)
Girls on Probation (1938)
Over the Wall (1938)
Love, Honor and Behave (1938)
A Slight Case of Murder (1938)
When Were You Born? (1938)
Blondes at Work (1938)
Men Are Such Fools (1938)
Four's a Crowd (1938)
Reno (1939)
Daredevils of the Red Circle (1939)
Three Texas Steers a.k.a. **Danger Rides the Range** (1939)
Cowboys from Texas (1939)
One Million B.C. (1940)
Turnabout (1940)
Mystery Sea Raider (1940)
Road Show (1941)
Topper Returns (1941)
Moon over Miami (1941)
Dance Hall (1941)
Cadet Girl (1941)
I Wake Up Screaming a.k.a. **Hot Spot** (1941)
A Gentleman at Heart (1942)
My Gal Sal (1942)
It Happened in Flatbush (1942)
Orchestra Wives (1942)
Manila Calling (1942)
The Powers Girl (1943)
Wintertime (1943)
Four Jills in a Jeep (1944)
Secret Command a.k.a. **Pilebuck** (1944)
Having Wonderful Crime (1945)
Behind Green Lights (1946)
Thieves' Holiday a.k.a. **A Scandal in Paris** (1946)
It Shouldn't Happen to a Dog (1946)
Out of the Blue (1947)
Noose a.k.a. **The Silk Noose** (1950)
The Brass Monkey a.k.a. **The Lucky Mascot** (1948)

JEFFREY HUNTER

"**A** symphony of sex appeal, talent and personality." That's how *Modern Screen* reporter Arthur Charles and most reporters of the 1950s and 60s described Milwaukee raised actor Jeffrey Hunter.

Hunter was a stunning combination of intelligence, versatility, compassion, athleticism, and humility — all wrapped into a set of perhaps the most penetrating blue eyes Hollywood has ever seen.

The only son of a manufacturing salesman, Henry Herman "Hank" McKinnies Jr., was born his father's namesake and his mother Edith's pride on Thanksgiving Day, November 25, 1926, on Panola Avenue in New Orleans, Louisiana, not long after his parents had moved there from Arkansas.

"Nobody at our house got any turkey that day. The turkey was me," their son would often quip.

Thanks to the Great Depression, the family didn't stay long in New Orleans and headed to Milwaukee when the future Hollywood heartthrob was 4 years old.

That first year in Milwaukee, the McKinnieses almost lost their only child. The 5-year-old lay near death in a Milwaukee hospital after suffering an appendicitis attack that caused both peritonitis and nephritis. After his recovery, the family returned to West Allis. They soon moved to Whitefish Bay and joined Christ Episcopal Church, where McKinnies often tended the altar as an acolyte.

As he grew, McKinnies and his father worked on electric trains in the basement, played ball and took many fishing trips to northern Wisconsin and Canada. "I remember one time Dad and I fished for fourteen hours straight without getting a single bite, but we still had a swell time together," he recalled in a July 1953 Dorothy O'Leary story for *Motion Picture and Television Magazine.*

The future actor also spent hours playing with the dogs he had over the years. "One of my favorites was a dachshund named Poochie. Another was a fox terrier named Buddy that we had for twelve years. I remember my father and I were both almost literally heartbroken when Buddy was run over by a neighbor's car," the actor recalled in 1953.

The movie star always remembered his childhood fondly, adding that he was blessed with "two very devoted people" for parents. "We had a big back yard and I was always putting on a carnival or circus, puppet show or magic show," and charging pennies for admission, he was quoted as saying in a 1974 *Filmograph* retrospective on his life (Vol. IV, No. 2).

When he wasn't playing in the back yard, Hank also went to see a lot of movies, recalled childhood friend Robert Head, who later visited the star twice in California, in a 2002 phone interview.

"Hank and I were especially close at and since my cousins lived on his street, we played a lot together after school. I remember we saw a lot of movies and especially remember Hank convincing his parents to let us see *Captains Courageous* (starring fellow Milwaukeean Spencer Tracy).

"We'd been playing outside and decided we wanted to see the movie again. But when we asked his mom, she wondered, 'didn't you see that already?' Hank admitted that we had but then, to convince her, he launched into reciting a whole scene from the movie. Well, his mom was so impressed that she let us go see it."

Jeffrey Hunter stands near an athletic field during his high school days. Photo courtesy of the Hunter family.

Hank loved movies, Head recalled. "In fact, whenever we'd be talking about what we were going to be when we grew up, I'd always say 'a major league baseball player,' and Hank would always say, 'a movie star.' Well, he sure succeeded in that dream," noted Head, who became a successful Realtor in the Milwaukee area.

His childhood friend always enjoyed performing, "being in front of or just with people," noted Head, who added that he was one of Hank's first costars. "We were in a school play together. I was dressed up as a girl and jumped into his lap, which caused quite a laugh from the audience!"

McKinnies recalled how excited he was as a boy to have the

opportunity to play a part or even entertain. As a child, he even saved up enough Ralston cereal box tops to get a Tom Mix makeup kit so he could dress up as different characters, he told Charles for a June 1952 *Modern Screen* article.

"I'd put on clown white and nose putty and make up stories and play all the characters," McKinnies, then named Jeffrey Hunter, recalled. "I'd act out the comic strips. I had a dream world in my room."

One time, when he was 12, such antics got him into hot water when he dressed as a monster, ran up the "dusk street and knocked on the front door of a neighbor's house. The woman who answered took one look, screamed, slammed the door and locked it," Charles reported. "Pushing his luck, Henry tore around to the back door and banged. This time the man of the house confronted him angrily, ripped away the fright wig, putty and false eyebrows and barked ... 'beat it right home this minute ... If you keep it up, some day you're going to get shot!'"

The young McKinnies was also acting in summer productions of the Wisconsin Children's Theater in Milwaukee and, when a New York summer stock company, the Port Players, moved from Port Washington, Wisconsin, to Whitefish Bay in 1942, McKinnies went on stage as a walk-on. He acted with the group for three summers in such productions as *Dinner at Eight* and *Boy Meets Girl*. He also reportedly shared the stage on occasion with a budding actress from Milwaukee named Charlotte Rae.

It was in these roles that McKinnies earned his first official review in July 18, 1943, *Milwaukee Journal* coverage of a Port Players production. "Important too in the cast is Henry McKinnies, a Whitefish Bay youth who this week has his first important role with the Port Players. He gives an excellent performance."

Besides the stage, McKinnies performed on Milwaukee radio as a pre-teen and teenager. According to his mother, it was Milwaukee radio personality and later *Milwaukee Journal* writer Larry Lawrence who unknowingly drew her son into radio.

In a July 2, 1951, *Milwaukee Journal* article, Lawrence relayed Edith McKinnies's story of her son's start in show business. She had taken Hank to watch Lawrence's show *Radio Rodeo* performed at the WTMJ studio. Lawrence had picked the boy from the audience to come say something into the microphone. McKinnies was too shy and froze at the thought of saying something over the air. When they returned home he told his mom, "If I ever get the chance to talk on radio again, I'm going to do it."

And he did. McKinnies's radio career started with roles in a fairy tale radio show narrated by Ann Ross and participating in WTMJ's *Children's Theater of the Air*. As a high school senior, McKinnies was also on radio in *Those Who Serve*, earning $12.50 a show and eventually a radio scholarship to Northwestern University.

When he wasn't performing in the community, McKinnies was on the school stage. In high school, he starred in many school plays and musicals including as the lead character, Henry Ingalls, in *The Goose Hangs High*. McKinnies also reportedly played the guitar, banjo, and piano.

In an eighth grade Whitefish Bay production of *The Birds' Christmas Carol*, McKinnies performed with a girl, Sally, whom he had a crush on at the time. The romantic scenes he was to play with her were reportedly spoiled by friends who hollered catcalls from the audience.

McKinnies, who was class president his sophomore year, student body president his senior year and an American Legion "outstanding boy" award recipient, was a popular student at Whitefish Bay High School.

"He was truly a nice person, sometimes almost too nice. He was handsome and very popular in school and popular with the girls. He dated a girl for quite a while who was a year ahead of him in school, Mary Mockley," Head notes.

McKinnies was also a good athlete and had dreams of pursuing a football career.

"I had only one ambition in life, college football," the actor told Charles in 1953.

At age 11, he won a statewide punt, pass and dropkick contest. From seventh grade on, he played fullback on Whitefish Bay school teams and was co-captain with Elmer Noonan of the championship high school football team.

While friend and high school teammate Paul Farley agreed McKinnies was a "strong athlete and good football player," he notes that his friend also had a "very protective mother. He was the only fellow at that time that would wear a mouth guard. His mom worried so much that, one time, when he broke his nose during a game, she went charging right into the locker room."

Despite his mother's best efforts, McKinnies did get hurt, breaking a nose, a rib and collarbone before eventually splintering an arch in his ankle late in his senior year.

"He didn't let injuries stop him from being in the game however," recalls Head, who also played on the team. "Hank just became a cheerleader, and a good one."

It was the splintered arch, essentially a football-career-ending injury then, that led Hunter to chase other ambitions. His idea was to take his love of performing to a career in radio. He'd won the scholarship to pursue that dream at Northwestern University but, when he graduated from high school in 1945, America was still fighting World War II.

McKinnies delayed his dreams and enlisted in the Navy, hoping to gain radar training. However, the Navy had enough radar men and sent McKinnies back for primary training with the idea that he'd be sent to fight in the Pacific if needed. The war ended in August 1945, and McKinnies' naval career didn't last long after that. He had worked as a radio technician and was working in teletype exchange at the Ninth Naval District Headquarters when the seaman contracted the measles. He had serious complications from the illness and received a medical discharge in 1946.

As soon as he was able, McKinnies enrolled at Northwestern, majoring in radio and speech and minoring in English and psychology. In between studies, he acted in university plays and on radio shows. During school breaks, he joined stock groups, acting one summer in Pennsylvania. And, he got his first taste of movie work when he was featured in a bit role in 1949's 16mm production of *Julius Caesar* starring Charlton Heston.

After college graduation in 1949, McKinnies headed for California in the car his father bought him. He went west not to pursue a Hollywood film career but to get his master's degree in radio at UCLA with hopes of being a radio actor and/or teacher some day. The radio actor found movie success so quickly that he could not find time to not return to the Badger State for nearly two years.

"I really worked to get practical experience along with educational training," he told O'Leary in 1953, adding he chose radio because it seemed a good field for beginning actors to break into. "I studied all phases of it, taking masters classes to teach radio 'if I didn't click behind the mike,'" he explained.

McKinnies was well on his way to completing that training when, in 1950, he was discovered by not one, but two, talent scouts on opening night of the UCLA production of *All My Sons*.

"I honestly thought it was some kind of gag at first. After all two talent scouts-one from Paramount and one from Fox studios-was a little too much to take. ... I figured some of my pals in the cast were trying to pull a fast one on me. Real honest-to-goodness talent scouts couldn't be interested in me!" he told Martha Buckley in a 1952 story for *Motion Picture & Television*.

Paramount brought him in for a screen test, setting him opposite established actor Ed Begley, who played the father in the original production of the play.

"I'd never been before a movie camera and I was scared," he told the *Milwaukee Journal* in a July 30, 1950 article. "I was so awestruck at first that I gawked wherever I went. Once on the Paramount lot, I saw Milwaukee's Nancy Olson, whom I've never met. Although I passed right by her, I got cold feet at the last minute and didn't even speak to her."

Jeffrey Hunter and son Todd. Photo courtesy of the Hunter family.

For all his nerves, McKinnies's screen test went so well that Paramount put him on option right away, to the reported disappointment of Fox Studios.

However, when Paramount inadvertently let its option lapse, Fox jumped in and had McKinnies on a plane for New York within forty-eight hours to shoot his first film, *Fourteen Hours*, where he plays a stock boy who meets Debra Paget in a crowd watching a man preparing to jump from a tall building.

After shooting, McKinnies's Fox agent called and said the actor could stay but the name had to go and, with publicity deadlines on the new film approaching fast, the studio needed that new name within the hour. So, the Midwest actor reportedly wrote down all the names he could think of on index cards. He pulled two from the pile — one said Jeffrey, the other Hunter — and Fox had its newest star. Jeffrey Hunter was soon playing a G.I. in *Call me Mister* and a university Casanova in *Take Care of My Little Girl*.

His parents had visited their star son on the set of *Take Care of My Little Girl* in 1951 and watched its Milwaukee premiere with *Milwaukee Journal* writer Lawrence in July, 1951. Though proud of her son's achievements, Edith McKinnies told Lawrence that the Casanova role was "a terrible role he's playing. It's absolutely against Hank's nature. He isn't like that at all."

And, the mother lamented, "I wish they'd give him a haircut."

The next three years, the McKinnieses watched their son often team up with Debra Paget and/or Robert Wagner in such movies as *Belles on Their Toes* (1952), *White Feather* (1955), and *Princess of the Nile* (1954) or star in such Western flicks as *Three Young Texans* (1954) and *Red Skies of Montana* (1952).

By the time Hunter returned home for Christmas in 1952, he was a genuine movie star, and autograph seekers descended on Whitefish Bay. Hunter was also a new father, so when 12-year-old Susan Randolph handed him a stuffed dog, he thought it was a gift for his infant son. Hunter did not realize the animal was her "autograph hound" and she merely wanted his signature until he returned to Hollywood, according to a May 24, 1953, *Milwaukee Journal* article.

The actor remedied the misunderstanding when he returned to Milwaukee in May of 1953 to accept the achiever of the year award from Junior Achievement Inc. in Milwaukee. Hunter had been a Junior Achievement member while working at WTMJ radio in high school.

After accepting the award and accolades from some two thousand fans, Hunter said he had something to give back to one fan. He personally delivered the autograph hound back to Susan, complete with his signature and more than a few extra autographs. "Signers included: Anthony Dexter, Joanne Dru, Arthur Kennedy, Rock Hudson, Audie Murphy, Wanda Hendrix, Joel McCrea, Marge and Gower Champion, John Ireland, Marilyn Maxwell, Ann Blyth, Phyllis Kirk, Steve Cochran, Peggy Lee, Tony Curtis, Janet Leigh, Peter Lawford, Polly Bergen, Dane Clark and Monica Lewis," the *Milwaukee Journal* reported.

Joining Hunter on this trip home were his son Christopher and wife Barbara Rush.

Hunter had noticed the beautiful actress at his first screen test, and the two met again thanks to mutual friends. They had their first date on the beach, though it was no "day at the beach," as Hunter reportedly took the actress out in a rubber raft where she waited while he speared fish.

In the 1952 interview with Charles, Rush said their next date was more traditional, with dinner at the Santa Ynez Inn and a walk along Pacific Palisades where Hank (as she also called him) said, "Nice Spot. Someday I'd like to build a house here. That is, if you'll marry me."

Rush didn't answer right away. But, a few months later, while Hunter was in the Virgin Islands shooting *The Frogmen* and she was in Arizona shooting *Devil's Canyon*, they called each other and decided to elope. They were married December 1, 1950, had a two-day honeymoon and went back to their sets.

In their first sixteen months of marriage, the newlyweds were reportedly together just eight months because of their hectic filming schedules. When they were together, they settled into and furnished a two-bedroom Westwood Village apartment and had Hollywood friends like Debbie Reynolds and Robert Wagner, John and Pati Derek, Nancy Gates and Bill Hayes, and Peter Hansen and Mitzi Gaynor over for dinner.

They both enjoyed singing, dancing, and playing the piano. Hunter took lessons on the organ, an instrument Rush already played well. Hunter, a skilled hobby carpenter, also set about fixing up the apartment, building cabinets and a milk can lamp for the living room, and pursued his other hobby — black and white photography.

"Jeff is the rare combination of scholar and athlete," noted Rush, who also called her husband "out-going, out-giving and even-tempered" in a July 1953 article for *Motion Picture and Television* magazine. "He's a fine pianist, talented artist and in contrast a great skier, swimmer, and skin diver."

He was also a fine father, she professed, after giving birth to their son, Christopher, on August 29, 1952, just days before Hunter had to leave for England to shoot *Sailor of the King*, one of the many roles Hunter chose for the "man against the odds" theme.

When he did finally get to hold his firstborn again, Hunter confessed to O'Leary that he was a bit nervous about the meeting.

"The first time I picked him up, I had the horrible feeling he might break but, by the third time, I had a good grip and I didn't worry any more. I understand all fathers go through that. The first time I lifted him I was also afraid he might cry because I was a stranger. He didn't."

Hunter worked hard at being a father, he told several reporters over the years, wanting to give his children a good foundation from which to follow their dreams.

"I believe the best that parents can give a child is a solid background, an unprejudiced look at things ... (and) the advantages that make for sound health and good education, with understanding," he told O'Leary in 1953.

While Hunter worked hard at fatherhood, he worked equally hard at his chosen craft, studying acting as he had radio and always working to improve.

"It's fun to work and improve," he told Charles. "I don't see why just because you're an actor, you have to be a screwball too."

Hunter had a strong work ethic and went beyond Hollywood protocol to ensure he was always acting somehow, somewhere. He was often quoted as stressing that a man has to be "well prepared when old man opportunity comes knocking," and often has to "make his own opportunities."

"The whole trouble in this profession here is complacency ... (actors) sit back and wait for a good part ... (or) hope for the best. That's no way to work for the future. In every other profession, a man has to go out and sell himself. Why not acting?" Hunter asked in a September 29, 1956, article for *Picturegoer* magazine.

Hunter often put his action where his talk was, working hard to get roles he wanted and to keep working in the profession he loved. Case in point was all that the budding actor went through to get the role he wanted in a John Wayne movie, *The Searchers*, being directed by John Ford in 1955.

Hunter first called Ford and was rebuffed by the director for being "nowhere near the type," the actor recalled in the *Picturegoer* article. "The next day I showed up at his office. I felt I should at least try to look something like a half Indian. I slicked back my black hair, wore a very open-necked sports shirt to display a healthy tan. When I was shown into his office, Ford said, 'take your shirt off.' I did just that and he grunted, 'I'll let you know,' and I thought this was just another of those Hollywood brushoffs. But then he said, 'don't cut your hair until you hear from me.' Somehow I felt I was in."

And in he was. "I was told I had arrived when they gave me almost as much ammunition as they gave John Wayne in *The Searchers*," Hunter often quipped.

Released in 1956, *The Searchers* was a great box office success, and Hunter was riding the wave of his hard work, appearing in five top pictures that year: *The Proud Ones*, *Gun for a Coward* with fellow Wisconsinite Fred MacMurray, Walt Disney's Civil War drama *The Great Locomotive Chase* and A *Kiss Before Dying*, a suspense thriller with Robert Wagner.

At the height of his career, Hunter had a brush with death beneath the waves of the Mediterranean Sea, he confessed in a May 1954 article, "Towards the Sun" that he wrote for *Modern Screen* magazine. Hunter explained that while snorkeling during a break from shooting, he had noticed a curious cave beneath the water and swam into it to investigate. When the actor turned around a few seconds later, he realized the cave ceiling was actually tilted downward and that he had been swimming further away from the surface than he realized.

"Don't let anyone tell you that a man can't sweat underwater," he wrote. "Around and behind me was murk and deep shadow. Ahead, through an opening, was sunlight streaming down ... like the light that used to fall on the altar of the church where I served as an acolyte. ... I knew again that for me there could never be any doubt. The difference between being in the church and out of it was like the difference between being in the sunshine which now warmed me and being in that cave."

While his faith was stronger than ever and his career was on solid footing, the Hunters' marriage was failing.

In divorce papers, Rush told Associated Press reporters in 1955 that it was all the time the two had spent apart chasing careers that finally separated them. They were divorced in March 1955.

Hunter echoed Rush's explanation to The Associated Press's Bob Thomas, saying, "We rarely fought; we just disagreed. Two careers and long separations never helped a marriage."

Still, Hunter didn't give up on the ideal and two years later married actress Joan Bartlett, whom he called "Dusty" and met on a movie set on July 7, 1957. The actress had a son, Steele, and Hunter soon adopted him. After a miscarriage in 1960, the Hunters added two boys of their own: Henry Herman "Todd Hunter" McKinnies III and Scott Hunter, to the family they brought to the marriage (Christopher and Steele).

The marriage got off to a somewhat rocky start as both became quite ill with hepatitis after unknowingly drinking rank water on a ship home from Europe.

Meanwhile, Hunter costarred with the Milwaukee actor he grew up watching, Spencer Tracy, in *The Last Hurrah* in 1958. In some respects, the title was foreshadowing Hunter's movie career. His Hollywood popularity began to wane in the 1960s.

The same year as his second wedding, Hunter made his first film for Wisconsin director Nicholas Ray, *The True Story of Jesse James*. That introduction led the way to the role for which Hunter is most famous, that of Jesus Christ in *The King of Kings* (1961).

Ray told *Modern Screen* magazine in 1961 that he specifically wanted Hunter to play Christ for his "robustness, masculine grace, peaceful visage — and his eyes."

"It is possible to do almost anything with makeup, but only Jeff Hunter has those eyes that have a penetrating depth, a mystical effect," he explained.

It was a part that several Hollywood friends warned him not to take. "They said that actors who play Jesus have a hard time getting other roles," Hunter explained in a January 30, 1965, interview with Joan Schmitt of the *Los Angeles Citizen News*. "But, I felt this was a myth. After all, how can you be typecast as Christ? There just aren't that many Jesus roles around."

Hunter was apprehensive about trying to capture the world's most well-known, studied, and revered religious figure. "You try to get the feel of any role, but it's much more difficult in the case of Christ because every one has their own personal image of Him. It's a role you take on knowing that no matter how you play it, you are going to disappoint many."

To help him better capture the holy man, Hunter enlisted the help of former Wisconsin teacher-turned-movie star Agnes Moorehead as his dialogue coach.

Nothing completely prepared the actor for what portraying such a significant figure would mean, he confessed in the Metro-Goldwyn-Mayer book, *Samuel Bronston's Production of King of Kings*.

"When I appeared in my robes, I saw to my astonishment that many dropped to their knees and made the sign of the cross ... They knew perfectly well, of course, that I was merely an actor. Still, I was the living representation of a figure they had regarded from childhood with most sacred awe. It was then that I realized what I had undertaken," he said.

While audiences found Hunter's resulting portrayal warm and sincere and even the Vatican reportedly approved of his reverent performance, some religious scholars were upset that some of Christ's most significant miracles were not depicted and felt it inappropriate for a divorced man and "Hollywood hunk" to play

Jesus.

Even the reviewers themselves were mixed. In November of 1961, *Films in Review* critic Edward Connor wrote, "The production as a whole is in good taste. Nicholas Ray's direction is effective and sometimes it is inventive ... and Jeffrey Hunter's face is made up and photographed to be, at least to my mind and heart, the kind of Christ image that stirs mankind."

Connor then added that Hunter was miscast as Christ. "It was painful for me to see him struggle amateurishly with the greatest of all roles."

After a bit of a film-making lag thereafter, Hunter's career picked up again when Warner Bros. signed him to a two year contract in 1963 and picked up a pilot of a Western TV show that Hunter's own production company, Hunter Enterprises, had produced. The result was an hour long show, *Temple Houston*, in which Hunter starred for thirty episodes until the show's cancellation in 1964.

Though Hunter hoped his production company would become his bread-winning enterprise, the actor continued filming movies. In 1962, Hunter played a lone man doing righteous battle in *No Man Is an Island* and played a soldier storming the beaches of Normandy in *The Longest Day*. He also played in *The Man From Galveston* in 1963 (a forerunner to the *Temple Houston* series) and *Gold for the Caesars* in 1965. But Hunter's career was leading toward television. He is said to have lobbied to portray Mike Brady in *The Brady Bunch* TV series and he was cast in an NBC series, *Journey Into Fear* (1966), that never aired.

In between, Hunter also did guest appearances on TV and radio programs, including: on NBC's *The George Gobel Show* in a live comedy sketch February 5, 1955, as well as on the network's radio program, *Bob Hope Presents The Chrysler Theater* in 1963 and 1964. Hunter also appeared in an episode of ABC's *Green Hornet* and two episodes each of *The F.B.I.* and *Insight*.

Hunter also was cast as the first captain of the U.S.S. Enterprise in a new, cutting-edge 1964 TV series pilot called *Star Trek*. He was intrigued with the concept of the series, he told *Los Angeles Citizen News* reporter Joan Schmitt January 30, 1965. "We run into prehistoric worlds, contemporary societies and civilizations far more developed than our own. It's a great format because writers have a free hand — they can have us land on a monster-infested planet or deal in human relations involving the large number of people who live together on this gigantic ship," he said.

Gene Roddenberry later told the Hunter family that he wanted

Hunter to play the lead role in the series because the Wisconsinite had the strength and sensitivity combination that Roddenberry wanted in his *Star Trek* captain.

After the pilot, Hunter opted out of playing the *Star Trek* captain in order to have more time to do movies, he told J.D. Spiro of *The Milwaukee Journal* July 4, 1965, when he was back visiting his parents' home, then on Skyline Lane in River Hills, a Milwaukee suburb. "Had I accepted it, I would have been tied up much longer than I care to be. I love doing motion pictures and expect to be as busy as I want to be in them," he explained. Others have said that his wife Dusty may have also contributed to the choice.

Had Hunter stayed in the TV series, the actor may finally have been able to carve out the home time he wanted with his family.

All the required traveling to exotic set locations is not as glamorous as it sounds, Hunter told Spiro. "I found you spend so much time on the job, working six days a week, that you don't do much else. Paris, Rome, Madrid — they're great for the tourist but as an actor in a picture, I might as well have been in Oshkosh."

Hunter added that traveling was definitely the downside of the business he loved. He hated being away for extended periods from his family.

"It was hard on our young sons. If we took them with us, (to locations, especially Europe the last five years), it made necessary, for one thing, changing schools. If we didn't, then we had to be parents by long distance, which is far from satisfactory," he explained.

From 1966 to 1969, Hunter's film career moved mostly to Europe, where he starred in such films as *Joe Navidad* (1967), *A Witch Without a Broom* (1968), and *Viva America!* (1969). He also had a starring role in the Bob Hope and Phyllis Diller movie *The Private Navy of Sergeant O'Farrell* in 1968.

In 1967 he and Dusty divorced, his wife charging that Hunter drank too much. In an *E! Mysteries and Scandals* TV program, Hunter's son Christopher, now a professional photographer, confirmed that by this point his father had a drinking problem that was "painful to see in someone you loved so much."

Hunter found fleeting happiness again in the arms of *General Hospital* soap opera actress Emily McLaughlin whom he met at a holiday party. After a whirlwind courtship, Hunter married his third wife Feb. 4, 1969 in Juarez, Mexico, with McLaughlin's son Bobby along for the ceremony. With fewer film roles and increasing alimony, money was tight and the newlyweds accepted the wedding gift of a car from Hunter's parents.

The two returned to a California home Hunter himself had partially rebuilt, adding rooms, a fireplace, and winding staircase.

The newlyweds were soon on their way to Spain, where Hunter was filming his latest movie. Hunter arrived with terrible burns on his legs suffered when juice from a pan of turkey they'd picked up at a restaurant the day before leaving the U.S., spilled and soaked his pants in hot grease, McLaughlin recalled for a *Movieland & Times* article in June 1970.

It was an ominous start to what would prove a tragic ending for Jeffrey Hunter.

While on set in Spain, "a car window blew up in his face instead of going the other way. He was badly hit on the head and received a bad concussion. ... (A few days later), a friend jokingly karate chopped him on the chin and his head hit a door and he was hurt pretty badly," McLaughlin recalled adding that through it all "Jeff kept insisting that he'd be okay."

Things went wrong with the filming itself, and the producers ran out of money to pay the Spanish crew. Hunter reportedly refused to be paid if the crew wasn't and returned to California.

"On the plane home, Jeff suddenly went into shock," McLaughlin recalled. "He couldn't speak. He could hardly move. We were met by an ambulance and put on an immediate flight to Los Angeles. ... Jeff was rushed to the Good Samaritan Hospital" but doctors could find nothing seriously wrong outside of his concussion and a displaced vertebra.

A month later, while he was taking it easy at home, Jeffrey Hunter suffered a massive inter-cranial hemorrhage, fell down a short flight of stairs, hit his head on the banister, and broke his skull. The 42-year-old died in surgery fourteen hours later on May 27, 1969, while doctors were trying to repair the fracture.

At the time of his death, the one-time Whitefish Bay altar boy and football star, had made fifty films and earned himself a reputation as a gracious, good-mannered, intelligent actor who was so much more than just a pretty face.

As movie critic Leonard Maltin said, Jeffrey Hunter was "almost absurdly handsome (and while) he probably couldn't have held his own with Olivier, his screen persona combined virility and sensitivity in a way atypical of most Hollywood leading men."

His impact on his fans, especially women who fell for the blue-eyed star, lasted for decades. His official fan club continued into the 1990s and, according to Whitefish Bay High School yearbook adviser Paul Fehlhaber, fans still occasionally call wanting a copy of Hunter's yearbook photo. He added that for a time the school got some especially "weird requests" from a small group of fans who "were like a cult." They thought there was "something significant about him because he played Jesus and then died young," the adviser noted.

Well beyond his charm and good looks, his friends and costars consistently remembered Hunter as the nice, hardworking Midwest boy who grew up to be the nice, hardworking actor who had earned the respect and friendship of those around him.

And he never lost the respect of his friends back home.

"Hank just enjoyed being with people. He had a great way about him that way. He was so nice that it would be very hard to say anything against him, and to this day, he was one of the nicest men I've ever known," said lifelong friend Robert Head on behalf of so many who knew the blue-eyed star.

"In fact, Jeffrey Hunter nearly always played a character that portrayed something positive because he was positive. And, I like that the image of my friend which carries into eternity is one of goodness."

Famous Wisconsin Film Stars

ON SCREEN

Look into Whitefish Bay actor Jeffrey Hunter's famous eyes on the big screen in the following movies:

Viva América! (1969)
Super Colt 38 (1969)
Frau Wirtin hat auch einen Grafen (1968)
Find a Place to Die (1968)
The Private Navy of Sgt. O'Farrell (1968)
A Witch Without a Broom (1967)
Joe Navidad (1967)
Custer of the West (1967)
A Guide for the Married Man (1967)
Dimension 5 (1966)
Strange Portrait (1966) never released
Murieta (1965)
Star Trek (1965) TV series pilot
Brainstorm (1965)
Gold for the Caesars (1963)
The Man From Galveston (1963)
The Longest Day (1962)
No Man Is an Island (1962)
King of Kings (1961)
Man-Trap (1961)
Hell to Eternity (1960)
Key Witness (1960)
Sergeant Rutledge (1960)
Count Five and Die (1958)
In Love and War (1958)
The Last Hurrah (1958)
Mardi Gras (1958)
No Down Payment (1957)
The True Story of Jesse James (1957)
The Way to the Gold (1957)
The Great Locomotive Chase (1956)
Gun for a Coward (1956)
A Kiss Before Dying (1956)
The Proud Ones (1956)
The Searchers (1956)
Seven Angry Men (1955)
Seven Cities of Gold (1955)
White Feather (1955)
Princess of the Nile (1954)
Three Young Texans (1954)
Single Handed (1953)
Belles on Their Toes (1952)
Dreamboat (1952)
Lure of the Wilderness (1952)
Red Skies of Montana (1952)
Fourteen Hours (1951)
The Frogmen (1951)
Take Care of My Little Girl (1951)
Call Me Mister (1951)
Julius Caesar (1950)

GREGG SHERWOOD DODGE

It's hard to choose between famous and infamous when it comes to Beloit model, showgirl, and aspiring actress Gregg Sherwood Dodge.

On one hand, the beautiful blonde had a reputation as a party girl and flirt. She married a serviceman, a salesman, a ticket taker, a police officer and one of the richest men in America. She was arrested for stealing cigarette lighters, hospitalized after a bar fight, considered a gold digger by a mother-in-law and convicted of embezzling from her son's bank account.

On the other hand, she was a determined small town girl with a charitable heart who chased her dreams to the heights of New York and Hollywood social circles and caught more than one star along the way. She danced on Broadway, dated Joe DiMaggio, appeared on screen with Rock Hudson and Abbott and Costello, and was the pinup girl of every boy's dreams.

Gregg Sherwood Dodge was born Dora Mae October 21, 1923, in New York City. When she was 3, Dora and her mother moved to Beloit where her mom soon married Mons Fjelstad, a janitor at Todd Elementary School who adopted the little girl as his own.

Dora grew up with brown, not blonde, hair and always had a flair for dramatics. At Beloit high school, where she graduated in 1941, the teenage beauty had a reputation as a flirtatious, outgoing girl who dreamed of being a star.

A former high school teacher, Joseph Rhodes, remembered her as "very outgoing, very popular, with many friends. I had classes on the first floor, and her locker was right outside my office door, and she was always very friendly, easy to talk to," he recalls in Beloit Historical Society notes.

Dora may have been a bit "too popular with the boys" for her own good. In high school, she had a reputation as a party girl who hung out with some of the fraternity boys at Beloit College, a reputation that earned her the nickname in town of "Dumb Dora."

The gregarious girl first chased her dreams to New York in the early 1940s where she enrolled at Powers Modeling School.

> "I spit fire. I always have, and I always will"
> — Gregg Sherwood Dodge

Though the brown-haired, natural beauty had some advertising gigs, her early career didn't pan out.

The brown-eyed girl returned to Beloit and worked in a department store, earning money to glamorize her looks.

Eventually, she had her teeth capped, her hair dyed blonde and renamed herself Gregg Sherwood, later explaining that she chose the unusual first name of Gregg after the Gregg-style of shorthand she once studied.

Around this same time, Sherwood married a U.S. serviceman, Willy Zebell, and moved to where he was stationed in North Carolina.

Cousin Jean Stowell said that while in the South, Sherwood competed in and won a 1943 Miss North Carolina pageant and took fifth place in the following national competition. Several later press releases indicated that Sherwood was a Miss Wisconsin who later competed in the Miss America pageant. But the official Miss America pageant archives could find no record of Gregg Sherwood or Dora Fjelstad. She may have competed in another national pageant such as the Miss USA pageant.

Regardless of where she won them, Sherwood's beauty pageant honors boosted her desires to return to New York for another shot at stardom.

Even after she moved with Zebell to a Beloit home in the 1300 block of West Grand, the small town girl with a wild side still longed for big-city life.

Sherwood's first marriage did not last long, and there were rumors that she was seeing a local liquor store owner both before and after her marriage ended.

By 1946, the divorcee was back in New York where she soon caught the theater district's eye, landing jobs as a model and cho-

The Wink magazine cover that featured Gregg Sherwood. Photo courtesy of the Beloit Historical Society.

rus girl.

Sherwood quickly became a recognizable model and pinup girl, appearing in traditional ads as well as in some girlie magazines of the day, like *WINK*, which was noted as a "fresh magazine" that featured girls in little more than stockings and high heels. In 1948, Sherwood posed in her bra, underwear and silk stockings for *WINK's* cover story on her, "A Whirl of a Girl."

The article noted that, at the time, Sherwood was "just about the most famous showgirl and model to ever invade the torrid atmosphere of New York nightlife."

The former Miss North Carolina gained national attention in 1947 when, for a publicity shoot, the chorus girl cut more revealing slits in her bathing suit and sewed satin letters on the suit to spell out the name of the Plymouth Theatre production she was appearing in, *WINK* reported. They quoted the model as saying that she knew to become famous she would have to put herself in the public eye.

The appropriate play name that was written across the pinup girl's voluptuous body? *A Young Man's Fancy*.

The stunt worked publicity wonders when the photo appeared in newspapers nationwide. Sherwood had caught the attention of Broadway talent scouts. Though her novice acting skill would never bring Sherwood true actress status, she had the talent to stay on the Broadway stage as a supporting player and chorus girl.

Sherwood's looks kept her busy as a model and showgirl. From the mid-1940s to late 1950s, she appeared in countless ads and promotions as "Salami Queen," "Miss Pucker Up," "Bubble-gum Baby," "Miss Plunging Neckline," the "National Donut Week Queen" and "Miss Bazooka of 1959."

She even graced the cover of the November 5, 1949, *TV Guide*, which reported that Sherwood was "the highest-paid showgirl in the country." She was also reportedly the model for Daisy Mae in the 'Lil Abner comic strip.

Blonde hair, some luck, and a lot of hard worked turned the beauty into an overnight sensation. "I moved back as a platinum blonde and was an instant success," the model said in a 1990 interview in *Fame* magazine.

Sherwood rode her chorus line and modeling talents to Broadway, playing a Secret Service woman and showgirl from November 1948 to January 1949 in the musical comedy *As the Girls Go*. She also had a small part in the 1949 Broadway production of

Gentlemen Prefer Blondes.

Just before appearing in *As the Girls Go*, Sherwood had her first movie role, landing an uncredited appearance as the dead body in the 1948 hit New York murder mystery movie *The Naked City*. Filmed almost entirely in New York, Sherwood shot her few scenes and continued working as an aspiring Broadway actress.

Her cousin Jean Stowell remembers going to see the movie with a friend and catching the opening scene of Sherwood playing dead and then a later scene where someone shows her picture. "My friend asked, 'Was that it?' And, I had to say it was," Stowell recalls.

By 1949, New York knew Sherwood as one of the "world's most beautiful showgirls," whose rare combination of "heavenly figure and an extremely facile brain" kept her in demand and in the eyes of most the men who saw her, *WINK* noted.

Sherwood certainly had plenty of pursuers, she acknowledged in a United Press International story January 16, 1947, saying she knew "how to contend with men who go 'wolfing' for pretty girls like her in New York City."

Though she turned many away, the aspiring actress did let a few wolfing admirers catch the fox.

For two years, the Beloit native dated baseball legend Joe DiMaggio and was seen on the arm of actor and performer Dean Martin.

Then, in the later 1940s, she married Walter Sherwin, a man she reportedly assumed to be an heir to the Sherwin paint dynasty or at least a big wig with the New York Yankees since he worked at Yankee Stadium. In fact, Sherwin was the ticket office manager for the Yankees, earning $90 a week.

Sherwood divorced Sherwin, telling the *Beloit Daily News* June 8, 1949, that she left her husband because he "wanted her to give up her career."

Two years later, in January 1951, her ex-husband pleaded guilty to grand larceny charges for stealing some $43,000 from the New York Yankees while he was the team's ticket office manager. Sherwin took the Yankees' money supposedly to help finance a home the couple built for Sherwood's parents in the 1100 block of Milwaukee Street in Beloit.

As divorce proceedings continued, Sherwood's career got a Hollywood boost. The chorus girl earned her second movie opportunity, this time with a credited 1949 role as Iris Anthony in *The Golden Gloves Story*, starring Dewey Martin and James Dunn.

Sherwood's scenes were filmed mostly in Chicago, close enough to Wisconsin that Standard Theater's district manager John S. Falco arranged to have forty members of the Beloit High School dramatics class travel to Chicago to watch the filming of the movie, reported the *Beloit Daily News* Dec. 6, 1949.

Sherwood's star was on a steady rise as she returned home in October of 1950 to appear on stage at Beloit's Majestic Theater for the local premier of the film, the *Beloit Daily News* said. The paper noted that Sherwood was next set to appear in the movie *Where the Sidewalk Ends*, though no listing of the Beloit actress appears in the credits.

Tom Conery, a friend who knew the model when he was a teenager and once presented Dodge with a portrait he'd painted of her, says the beauty was "always generous with advice" and with her and the Dodge's wealth during the many times he visited her and her parents in Beloit.

The retired Marshal Fields visual merchandiser especially remembers when Dodge ran into him at the Chicago store and offered to take him home to Beloit for the weekend since she was going that way, too. "I joined her and her son on their private rail car all the way to Beloit. It was beautiful and so was she. She was very generous."

Sherwood enjoyed visiting her hometown. On one occasion Sherwood modeled clothes for an Elks Charity Ball, sporting "one of John Heller's trophy-winning hairdos," the *Beloit Daily News* reported. Sherwood was photographed with "fire, police and city officials," appeared at the Optimist and Rotary clubs, and was named an honorary member of the Beloit Sigma Phi chapter.

In 1951, the aspiring actress earned another credited movie role, playing Gwendolyn in the boxing movie, *Iron Man*, featuring Rock Hudson. And, early in the 1950s, she made at least one guest appearance with Abbott and Costello on the television show, *The Colgate Comedy Hour*.

In 1952, the showgirl was typecast as a dancer from Paris's famous Maxim's in the Fernando Llamas and Lana Turner movie, *The Merry Widow*. The Wisconsin native made her last movie appearance as Franny in *The Girl Next Door*, a 1953 movie starring Dan Dailey as a comic strip writer who falls in love with his new next-door neighbor played by June Haver.

In between movie and stage roles, Sherwood was also playing the elite circles of Manhattan social life and started dating one of the town's wealthiest men, Horace Dodge, heir to the $57-million-plus Dodge family automobile fortune.

When Sherwood next returned home to visit her parents, in July of 1951, it was reportedly with Dodge in tow, the *Beloit Daily News* reported, noting: "There are reports that Miss Sherwood and Dodge plan to marry, but Dodge recently said stories that he's going to divorce his present wife and marry the actress-showgirl are unfounded."

They weren't unfounded for long, however, and Sherwood became Dodge's fifth wife in 1953. Dodge had officially proposed to Sherwood at a lavish party in a French Riviera resort home they'd rented for the occasion, reportedly presenting his bride to be with a $50,000 engagement ring. The couple even helped finance a home for Sherwood Dodge's parents in Beloit at 837 Sherwood Ave.

Married life with the rich and famous was not all bliss.

According to a 1954 story in the *Confidential* tabloid magazine, titled "Meet Horace Jr., The Only Dodge That Ever Ran on Bourbon," nurses had to hold Dodge's head off the table at the engagement party because he was so drunk.

Virtually everyone including his mother and new wife was well aware that drunk was Dodge's usual state. His mother was reportedly at first happy with her daughter-in-law because Sherwood had gotten her alcoholic son to drink only beer the first year of their marriage.

However, the mother-in-law's opinions soon changed when Horace returned to bourbon and Sherwood Dodge found other men more to her liking.

In 1952, the two had a fight about Dodge's drinking that culminated with Sherwood storming out of their New York home. According to *Confidential*, Dodge called police and had his wife arrested because she'd left with $60 worth of cigarette lighters.

"I can't compete with whiskey," Sherwood Dodge told police.

Dodge reportedly couldn't compete with his wife's many suitors. She was rumored to have had affairs with Dominican playboy Porfino Rubirosa, whom Sherwood always said was just "a family friend," and with Brooklyn actor Si Armus. *Confidential* reported in a November 1955 story that Armus would visit Sherwood's Hamsphire House hotel suite in New York as a grocery store boy making a delivery.

Despite the rumors and several public fights, the marriage held together and the couple bought a mansion on Ocean Drive in Palm Beach, Florida. In 1954, Dodge sponsored a speedboat named *My Sweetie Dora* for his wife in the President's Cup speedboat races on the Potomac River, in Washington, D.C. The boat came in second place overall.

Dodge's drinking continued to be problematic, even dangerous, and Sherwood Dodge reportedly left the millionaire because of it on more than one occasion.

In July 1954, *Confidential* reported about a particularly heated fight the two had after Sherwood Dodge discovered that her husband reportedly paid a Palm Beach society woman some $20,000 to ensure that his wife would be accepted in the community.

"Dodge got incredibly drunk and a fearful brawl ensued. ... The next day, Sherwood shoved up to New York and registered at Hampshire House with a different name. She phoned her press agent and said, 'If that — — wants to know where I am, lie "dead." I want to save the baby and another brawl like that and it's dead,'" the magazine reported.

Horace Dodge and Gregg Sherwood Dodge at a party in Cannes. Photo courtesy of Beloit Historical Society.

The baby Sherwood wanted to save was her only child, son Johnny Dodge, then about 1.

The year 1954 proved a big one for Sherwood Dodge as she continued to make news in heated marital arguments and even made national headlines when she returned to visit her parents in Beloit.

One of the *Beloit Daily News* photographers who followed Sherwood Dodge on some of her hometown visits was David Sandell, now a longtime photographer at the *Capital Times* newspaper in Madison.

"She was very blonde and very attractive. Whenever I photographed her, she was always nice in a movie star sort of way, saying 'Darling, how are you?'" Sandell said. "And, she had a charitable spot in her heart. She had a white Lincoln Continental Mark I, which was a very, very expensive car back then. When I was younger, my friends and I would see her parked downtown and hang out around the car, checking it over fender to fender. On more than one occasion she let us sit in it and pretend to drive. That was very nice."

Sandell says he also took pictures for the paper when Sherwood Dodge bought toys on charge at McNeeny's store to give to poor children in the area. However, he later heard, the Dodges never paid the charge for the toys.

The teenage staff photographer was just 15 years old when *Confidential* called the newspaper's photo department to see if someone could take a more controversial photo of Sherwood Dodge than he was used to.

Apparently Sherwood Dodge had been drinking at a hometown hangout, The Corral, and was pestering and hanging on dancer Jose Greco a little too hard. When he punched her in the nose to fend her off, Sherwood Dodge went outside and sat in the snow. An ambulance took her to the hospital.

"The *Confidential* wanted a picture of her in the hospital, and I answered the call when they phoned the newspaper looking for a photographer," Sandell recalls. "I ran home and, since I couldn't drive then, got my father to take me to the hospital."

The teenager offered his father little explanation of his assignment but told his puzzled dad to keep the car running since he didn't know what might happen inside.

"I gave the nurse $5 to tell me where Dora was, and she did that no problem. The nursing staff wasn't real crazy about her either. She and her mother were too demanding. When I got there, other patients were in the hallway so she could be accommodated," the photographer recalled in a 2002 phone interview.

"Dora's bed was against the wall and the nurse offered to carry a tray into the room and push the door aside so I could shoot the picture right past her," Sandell explained. "As soon as the flash went off, I heard yelling. It was Dora's mother, who was a constant presence with her. She came after me and I ran downstairs and kept running to the car and said, 'Come on, Dad, let's go!' Well of course, I had to explain to my father what that was all about on the way home."

Though *Confidential* paid Sandell for the photo, it never saw print.

The incident was only one of many over the years, before and during Sherwood Dodge's New York days, when the Beloit High School graduate caused a ruckus at more than one local hangout. Proprietors of the Wagon Wheel once asked her and her husband not to come back because of inappropriate behavior, and she reportedly got into a fight at the Key Club after another patron accused Sherwood Dodge of stealing her earrings.

Sherwood Dodge made headlines again, this time in California, when a Los Angeles police officer charged her with battery when she slapped him after he pulled a drunken Sherwood Dodge and gossip columnist Irv Kupcinet over on LaCienega Boulevard. According to a December 18, 2001, column by *Capital Times* newspaper columnist Doug Moe, Sherwood Dodge's reply at the time was that the two were "looking for Frank Sinatra, somewhere, but we missed him."

As wild as her nights occasionally were, Horace Dodge himself reported that his wife's spending habits were wilder. In 1961, he filed for divorce, saying, "I can't afford the woman" and alleging that Sherwood Dodge spent $300,000 in one year on jewelry, clothes, and luxuries that reportedly included two-carat diaper pins for their baby boy.

Dodge, already quite ill and often in a wheelchair from his years of heavy drinking, died before the divorce was final and the former pinup girl inherited $11 million.

In 1964, Gregg Sherwood Dodge sued her former mother-in-law for turning Dodge against her; the suit was settled out of court for a reported $9 million.

Then, in 1965, Sherwood Dodge married 27-year-old Dennis Moran, a one-time New York City police officer and Barbara Rockefeller bodyguard, in a lavish wedding at St. Patrick's Cathedral in New York. During their 13-year marriage, the two went through all the Dodge millions on spending sprees that featured round-the-world flights in private jets and parties that cost tens of thousands of dollars each.

By 1967, the couple was living in as 28-room, $400,000 Palm Beach, Florida mansion with son Johnny, according to a Feb. 22, 1967, *Milwaukee Journal* story by Lois Hagen. The household also included up to six Viszlas dogs. Apparently, Hagen noted, Zsa Zsa Gabor had given Johnny Dodge the first dog and soon after his parents bought a mate, they had four puppies.

Hagen also reported that the couple had just sold a house in Beloit, bought one in Connecticut, and had an apartment in Palm Beach for Sherwood Dodge's mother.

In addition, the one-time model reportedly organized Palm Beach's first Heart Ball, raising thousands of dollars for the Heart Association, and helped to found Girls Town Inc., a nonprofit residence and school for underprivileged girls ages 11-18, which was run by an order of nuns. Her latter charitable effort earned the praise of former U.S. first lady Eleanor Roosevelt.

In a *New York Times* article by Janet Arpe, John Francis Dodge said that while he missed his father, he loved his stepfather and life in Florida. "I loved my father, who died when I was 10. He taught me wisdom. My stepfather Denny … taught me patience. He was terrific and I loved him too. My mother was always there," he said.

Life was not all glamorous and generous at the Moran house. In 1968, Moran shot and killed a busboy trying to sneak into a bedroom window, according to an April 24, 1988, Associated Press story, "Owners of Helmsley Mansion Have Had a Long Run of Bad Luck."

In 1977, the former police officer killed himself.

For all the Morans had given away, the couple had spent tenfold. According to bankruptcy reports from 1978, the former Dodge wife who started with $9 million to $11 million in 1962 was $3.5 million in debt by 1978.

In 1979, Sherwood Dodge was arrested for grand larceny after embezzling money from her son's $8 million trust fund. She pleaded guilty to taking $434,000 from her son, including $75,000 taken from a New York bank.

To help pay off the debts, U.S. District Court Judge Thomas C. Britton, who accepted Dodge's guilty plea, authorized an auction of the Dodge family belongings from Palm Beach and apartments on Long Island and Fifth Avenue, according to a 1979 *New York Courier* article by Malcolm Balfour titled "From Rags to Riches: Dodge's Widow, Ex Showgirl Loses It all in Sale to Pay Debits."

"As some 200 bargain hunters sifted through the remnants of the Dodge fortune, Johnny Dodge, his attorney, and sheriff deputies worked to stop the sale of some items including a $12,000 Patek Phillipe pocket watch, photo albums, and a mounted blue-nosed dolphin (the first fish he caught)," Balfour noted.

Johnny Dodge, who reportedly paid his mother's $100,000

bond, later said that it was the financial advisors and trustees who were most to blame for the missing funds. Since then, the former Beloit showgirl's life has quieted down considerably. Now 79, Gregg Sherwood Dodge still lives in Palm Beach and tries to stay out of the limelight she once craved. When *Capital Times* columnist Doug Moe tracked her down in late 2001, Dodge said she'd prefer not to talk about her tumultuous days, and especially about the struggles she and Moran had, saying only, "I spit fire. I always have, and I always will."

ON SCREEN

There aren't many opportunities to catch the on screen performances of Beloit native Gregg Sherwood Dodge, but you can spot her in the following films:

The Girl Next Door (1953)
The Merry Widow (1952) (uncredited)
Iron Man (1951) (uncredited)
The Golden Gloves Story (1950)
The Naked City (1948) (uncredited)

FRED MACMURRAY

A sick relative brought Fred "Bud" MacMurray to Hollywood from Beaver Dam, Wisconsin, in 1929. Talent, charm, and a little luck, let him stay, and shine, there for more than fifty years.

The man who performed in more than a hundred movies, including many of Walt Disney's best, was born August 30, 1908, by way of his father Fredrick's concert violinist tour schedule, in Kankakee, Illinois. But MacMurray always called Beaver Dam home.

The south central Wisconsin city was the hometown of his mother, Maleta Martin MacMurray, daughter of one of the area's most prominent families. Though her family objected to the musician their daughter met when his tour stopped in Beaver Dam, Maleta eloped with the violinist to Chicago. She endured MacMurray's grueling road tours, even while pregnant with their son. With baby in tow, however, the schedule eventually proved too much, and mother and son returned to Beaver Dam. According to Fred MacMurray historian Robert Noll of Beaver Dam, the young family was not fully accepted back into the grand Martin home and lived in the front room, not the main quarters, where they were expected to largely provide for themselves.

The Beaver Dam boy who would become one of TV's favorite dads on *My Three Sons* grew up without one of his own. His father last visited when MacMurray was 5, leaving his son only, though significantly, a love for and talent in music.

Nicknamed "Bud," MacMurray was most influenced by his mother, grandfather and the small town life of Beaver Dam. He was a talented athlete, earning as many as twelve varsity letters in high school as he competed in basketball, track, baseball, and football (as one of the state's top fullbacks and punters). He earned an American Legion medal for having the best athletic and academic record.

When he wasn't playing sports or musical instruments, especially the saxophone, MacMurray was helping make ends meet for his mother, working at canning factories and a funeral home. The young saxophonist played with the American Legion and school orchestra bands and even teamed with friend Mynie Bartell for nightly gigs in the area.

Bud MacMurray continued to play for his supper with local band Tom Joy's Gloom Chasers and his own Mac's Melody Boys, earning enough, with a football scholarship, to enroll at Carroll College in Waukesha, Wisconsin, where another famous movie star, Dennis Morgan, would enroll one year later.

Young Fred MacMurray and friend Randall McKinstry enjoy a Wisconsin winter. Photo courtesy of Wisconsin Center for Film and Theater Research. Image No. WCFTR-3751.

MacMurray is listed in the school's 1927 *Hinakaga* yearbook (which covered the years of 1925-26) as playing the baritone in the college band in addition to playing football. Hollywood releases later would state that MacMurray also sang in the college choir.

One of the few lasting things that MacMurray took away from Carroll College was a lifelong friendship with fellow musician Les Paul, who was later known for developing the electric guitar.

MacMurray, it seemed, loved his music more than his studies. In an October 1925 letter to his good friend Randall McKinstry (collected by Noll), the freshman confessed that he was not hitting anything hard but the football field and the keys on his saxophone.

"We have a lot of fun in the house where I'm staying but I haven't done any studying yet. I haven't even any books yet. I'll have to get busy pretty soon."

Years later he explained to the *Waukesha Freeman* newspaper (as quoted in his obituary) that, "I didn't even think of dramatics at that time. ... I was playing football or blowing a sax with a band in a nightclub six nights a week, until 4 or 5 each morning. I had little chance to do anything else — even study."

And it showed. In 1926, MacMurray quit school and took his horn to Chicago's nightclubs.

One of MacMurray's aunts had connections to Chicago's big band crowd and got her nephew an audition. A shy young man, MacMurray did not do well enough to make a top band but did land a gig with Jack Higgins' Royal Purples, a band composed largely of Loyola University students who performed in Twin Lakes, Wisconsin, in the summer and Chicago in the winter.

Though MacMurray loved music, he also liked to eat on occasion. By the late 1920s, the former wasn't paying enough for the latter. So, the shy musician tried selling vacuum cleaners door-to-door, though he rarely made it past the introductions. For a while, the mediocre salesman took art classes at night, thinking he could work as a commercial artist.

Nothing was panning out in any grand direction and so, when his mother and aunt Hazel needed to visit a sick relative in California, MacMurray offered to drive them. It was the most important decision of his life.

The Wisconsinite soon found work in Hollywood orchestras. His musical talents earned him "preferred status" on the new talking movie sets where he sometimes lent his horn to the soundtrack. He played with the George Olsen Band and Gus Arnheim Orchestra and eventually recorded three vocals for RCA Victor.

Central casting departments soon considered MacMurray a movie extra. By late 1929, the 6-foot 3-inch musician found small parts in three Warner Bros. films: *Girls Gone Wild*, *Tiger Rose,* and *Why Leave Home.*

A Hollywood director spotted MacMurray in a crowd shot in *Girls Gone Wild* but, according to Noll, the actor's shyness again got the best of him when the director asked if MacMurray would be interested in a speaking part.

"He responded 'NO!' ... and it looked like his chance to advance in pictures had just been lost forever to shyness," Noll reports.

MacMurray continued to be more interested in music than movies anyway and was excited to join the California Collegians band on a tour of New York. Once in New York, MacMurray found his way into such Broadway revues as *Three's a Crowd* and the musical *Roberta*.

Most significantly, MacMurray found the love of his life on stage. That love was no act; it was actress Lillian Lamont.

In the middle of their courtship, Paramount scouts spotted MacMurray in *Roberta* and liked what they saw. They signed him to a film contract in 1935, and the musician left his love in New York to pursue his dreams in California.

Lillian was always on his mind, however, and MacMurray reportedly lived with his mother and saved all his checks so he could bring the actress to California, return to New York or even move them both back to Beaver Dam, where the actor had arranged a possible shoe factory job so he'd be ready regardless of which way this movie business went.

MacMurray had small roles in his first few films in 1935 such as when he was loaned out to RKO for *Grand Old Girl*, in which he played a delivery truck driver.

Though driving brought MacMurray to Hollywood in the first place it was the actor's ability to eat and talk at the same time that made him a star, according to Noll.

Paramount was having great difficulty finding an actor who could talk to star Claudette Colbert while chewing popcorn in a scene for *The Gilded Lily*. Then, a casting director noticed MacMurray's scene in *Grand Old Girl* in which he discusses an ongoing football game while eating popcorn. MacMurray got the part.

Starring with Colbert brought MacMurray instantly into the Hollywood spotlight — a spotlight he would share with Colbert in seven more movies over the next 30 years.

It was a different leading lady that MacMurray had his eyes on in 1936, however. That spring, the actor eloped with Lillian to Las Vegas for a June 20, 1936, wedding. In the years to come they would adopt two children, Robert and Susan.

His love for Lillian knew no bounds and neither seemingly did his career. By 1942, MacMurray was the highest paid Hollywood actor and had one of the ten highest salaries in the United States. He had also reportedly starred with more A-list leading ladies than any other actor of the time.

In 1940, he and his wife returned to Beaver Dam so she could meet his friends and relatives. In 1941, they returned again so MacMurray could be grand marshal of the Beaver Dam Centennial Parade.

In fact, Noll insists, MacMurray mentioned his hometown at every opportunity and returned, generally without fanfare, as often as possible. Several of MacMurray's movies reference Beaver Dam or his family in some way, such as his high school graduation picture hanging in the backdrop of *Remember the Night* (1940). Beaver Dam was front and center in *Pardon My Past* (1946), a movie MacMurray produced, that features the travels of two newly discharged Army men on their way to open a mink farm in Beaver Dam. And, when the Beaver Dam American Legion Band came to Hollywood in 1938, MacMurray showed the group around Paramount Studios and arranged a star-studded lunch.

Perhaps no other stories illustrate just how far MacMurray was willing to go for his hometown than the tale of how he returned to be the parade grand marshal in 1941.

"Fred was working on a movie and ... asked the director, cast and crew if they would all work overtime for a few days," explains Noll, who adds that MacMurray wasn't sure he could attend until the day before. "He spent all night on a plane from Los Angeles into Chicago. From there, relatives drove the four hours down, picked him up early in the morning and drove him four hours back to Beaver Dam so that he could participate in the parade that afternoon."

By the 1940s, MacMurray was finding it more and more difficult to get away to anywhere, let alone his hometown.

He was a bonafide Hollywood star, having costarred in the first all-outdoor Technicolor movie *Trail of the Lonesome Pine* (1936) and dozens of other films such as *Swing High, Swing Low* (1937), *The Forest Rangers* (1942), and *No Time for Love* (1943).

Somewhere in between, and unbeknownst to MacMurray, the star was reportedly the inspiration for the first "Captain Marvel" comic book illustrations.

Though his movies were plentiful, MacMurray's appeal as the perpetual nice guy, comedy hero, and love interest was waning a bit.

In 1944, he made a daring move to the dark side and took Billy Wilder up on an offer to play a bad-guy insurance man in *Double Indemnity*. The movie was a hit, earning Oscar nominations for best picture, script, direction, music score, and actress (Barbara Stanwyck). Though he was slighted for a nomination himself, MacMurray gained much from the picture's success and he had proven his depth as an actor.

MacMurray played the bad guy in three subsequent films, *The Caine Mutiny* (1954), *Pushover* (1954) and *The Apartment* (1960) and got laughs as the salesman to a band of murdering hillbillies in the 1945 black comedy *Murder, He Says*. MacMurray also performed in some war effort films, such as narrating *The Last Will and Testament of Tom Smith* (1943). He also continued to play less notorious lead characters in such films as *The Egg and I* (1947), *An Innocent Affair* (1948), and *The Miracle of the Bells* (1948).

While his career took off yet again, his love suffered, not for the lack of it but because his wife Lillian was increasingly ill and often bedridden for weeks. When Lillian died the night of the couple's seventeenth wedding anniversary in 1953, her husband was inconsolable.

Only the couple's children kept him going until he took his friends' advice and returned to work, filming *The Caine Mutiny* in Hawaii.

As 1950s movie tastes turned to Westerns, a genre MacMurray struggled to fit into in movies like *At Gunpoint* (1955), *Quantez* (1957), and *Good Day for a Hanging* (1959), the actor tested a new audience in television.

In the early 1950s, MacMurray appeared with guest host and Broadway friend Bob Hope on NBC's *All-Star Revue* as well as on *The Jack Benny Show*. He also appeared regularly on his friend George Gobel's variety show and worked for a time on a radio show with Irene Dunne.

While he was still getting his television feet wet, MacMurray was offered another venue to escape the Westerns. Walt Disney Studios cast him as the father in 1959 movie, *The Shaggy Dog*, beginning the fourteen-year relationship that featured such Disney hits as *The Absent Minded Professor* (1961) and its sequel *The Son of Flubber* (1963), and launched MacMurray's image as a lovable father figure.

Art, for MacMurray, was imitating life. As he played dad in the movies, he became one again in real life.

MacMurray found the second love of his life, June Harver, eighteen years his junior, at a party thrown by John Wayne, and the two were married June 28, 1954. By this time his two children were all but grown and MacMurray was looking forward to being a grandfather someday in the not too distant future.

His new wife had other ideas and soon convinced the 40ish actor to become a dad again, adopting twin girls Katie and Laurie on May 7, 1956. Soon after the adoption, MacMurray reportedly returned home to Beaver Dam to introduce his new family to his old one.

Though he enjoyed working in movies, MacMurray was a family man at heart and often turned down roles if they interfered too much with family time.

He could afford to be choosy. MacMurray had invested his early acting earnings wisely in everything from factories to a working California cattle ranch that raised prized Angus and doubled as a MacMurray family retreat. By this time, the Beaver Dam alum was one of the richest men in Hollywood.

When he wasn't investing his acting gains, MacMurray was playing. He often invited Beaver Dam chums along on hunting and fishing trips and was an expert skeet shooter, said to be the best in Hollywood at the time, and regularly scored 90 out of 100. "It seems that rabbit hunting back in Beaver Dam proved to be his fertile training ground," Noll said.

MacMurray was also a top Hollywood golfer, the chosen partner of many celebrity golfers such as Bing Crosby and Bob Hope in events like the Bing Crosby PRO-AM and the Bob Hope Desert Classic.

Harking back to his long-ago Chicago thoughts of being a commercial artist and a sketching contest he reportedly won as a child, MacMurray also enjoyed painting. And he liked the cooking, especially his family's traditional sauerkraut, and even took gourmet cooking classes.

With all that and a young second family to keep him busy, MacMurray wasn't overly interested in grueling production schedules that stretched on for months.

So when ABC's Don Fedderson approached MacMurray about playing a father role on a new television series, the actor turned him down in favor of time with his own family.

Fedderson felt MacMurray so right for the role that he adjusted the show's entire schedule to accommodate the family man's priorities. MacMurray worked three months at a time, shooting all of his scenes, and then cast members would be called back to film the rest. The deal was sealed when he learned that his friend William Frawley would play the grandfather housekeeper to his widower-father Steve Douglas in a show called *My Three Sons*. When Frawley died four years later, he was replaced by William Demarest as Uncle Charlie.

The format worked for MacMurray — and for the TV audience. The show first aired in 1960 and was a twelve-year hit, earning a

Golden Globe in 1962.

Toward the end of its run, as the pipe-smoking TV dad struggled with triplets for grandchildren, the real MacMurray was struggling with cancer. In 1970, the actor was diagnosed with throat cancer, but aggressive treatments sent the disease into remission.

After *My Three Sons* ended its stellar run, MacMurray all but retired from performing, though he visited a few talk shows and made a few movies for Disney such as *Charley and the Angel* (1973) and *Herbie Day at Disneyland* (1974) and did a non-Disney film, *The Swarm* (1978).

On June 19, 1987, MacMurray was inducted into the Wisconsin Performing Artists Hall of Fame in Milwaukee, saying to the crowd, "Gee, I'm glad I came."

His wife, June, told the audience how nice it's been "to have this dad around the house" and then asked MacMurray if he'd "love me just the same" now that he was in the Hall of Fame.

The night saw the meeting of Wisconsin's newest moviemakers with one of movie's most celebrated veterans when 1986 inductee, movie producer Jerry Zucker of Shorewood, introduced the MacMurrays. True to his "fried" style of comedy, Zucker teased MacMurray and the audience saying he'd received a letter from then-president Ronald Reagan, who commended MacMurray "for this honor bestowed on him by the Minnesota Hall of Fame," the *Milwaukee Sentinel* reported.

MacMurray was inducted into the Hall of Fame for not only his role as one of TV's favorite dads and Disney's most recognizable nice guys but also for his fifty years of Hollywood success.

Even MacMurray struggled to explain the incredible acting successes of a musician like himself. He once told the *Milwaukee Journal* (in quotes reprinted in his November 6, 1991, obituary) that it wasn't some great actor sweating to portray some intricate character on the screen that you saw in MacMurray's performance. It was just a guy from Beaver Dam playing a part.

"I don't have any of those deep thoughts (as other actors do about their work). I'm just myself. That's what I'm hired for," MacMurray said, first noting in a *Saturday Evening Post* article quoted by the *Journal* that the scenes he was hired for were often of the boy-meets-girl variety. "Sometimes a writer writes a scene for people who just say 'hi' to indicate they're in love. I play those scenes very well."

America lost one of its fathers — and Wisconsin one of its favorite sons — on November 5, 1991, when MacMurray succumbed

Fred MacMurray in a publicity photo for *Men with Wings*. Photo courtesy of Wisconsin Center for Film and Theater Research. Image No. WCFTR-3750.

to pneumonia in Santa Monica, California. He was buried at Holy Cross Cemetery in Culver City, California.

In 1997, the Beaver Dam School Board voted to create a wall of fame for all its distinguished alumni and MacMurray's name is first on the list. That same year, his widow June Harver and two children visited Beaver Dam for a weekend that included showing two of the actor's movies *Murder, He Says* and *Double Indem-*

nity. MacMurray would have loved the hometown party.

"There are hundreds of stories about his decency to family, friends and strangers. And, specifically, to Beaver Dam residents," Noll told Tom Heinen of the *Milwaukee Journal Sentinel* July 13, 1997, adding that what impressed the historian most was the way the Beaver Dam native handled the success he found. "He didn't sacrifice his dignity, or his humbleness or his high moral character."

Nor did MacMurray ever forget the hometown that taught him how to be the man he became.

ON SCREEN

Find America's dad and Beaver Dam's famous son in the following films:

A Salute to Billy Wilder (1986) (TV)
The Walt Disney Comedy and Magic Revue (1985)
A Salute to Frank Capra (1982) (TV)
The Swarm (1978)
Joys (1976) (TV)
Beyond the Bermuda Triangle (1975) (TV)
Herbie Day at Disneyland (1974) (TV)
The Chadwick Family (1974) (TV)
Charley and the Angel (1973)
The Walt Disney Story (1973) (uncredited)
Walt Disney: A Golden Anniversary Salute (1973) (TV)
Sotto a chi tocca! (1972)
The Happiest Millionaire (1967)
Follow Me, Boys! (1966)
Kisses for My President (1964)
Son of Flubber (1963)
Bon Voyage! (1962)
The Absent-Minded Professor (1961)
My Three Sons (1960) TV Series
The Apartment (1960)
The Oregon Trail (1959)
Face of a Fugitive (1959)
Disneyland '59 (1959) (TV)
The Shaggy Dog (1959)
Good Day for a Hanging (1958)
Day of the Bad Man (1958)
Quantez (1957)
Gun for a Coward (1956)
There's Always Tomorrow (1956)
The Far Horizons (1955)
At Gunpoint (1955)
The Rains of Ranchipur (1955)
The "$64,000 Question" (1955) TV Series' substitute host
Woman's World (1954)
Pushover (1954)
The Caine Mutiny (1954)
The Moonlighter (1953)
Fair Wind to Java (1953)
Callaway Went Thataway (1951)
A Millionaire for Christy (1951)
Never a Dull Moment (1950)
Borderline (1950)
Father Was a Fullback (1949)
Screen Snapshots: Motion Picture Mothers, Inc. (1949)
Family Honeymoon (1948)
An Innocent Affair (1948)
The Miracle of the Bells (1948)
On Our Merry Way (1948)
Singapore (1947)
The Egg and I (1947)
Suddenly, It's Spring (1947)
Smoky (1946)
Pardon My Past (1946)
Captain Eddie (1945)
Murder, He Says (1945)
Where Do We Go from Here? (1945)
Practically Yours (1944)
Double Indemnity (1944)
And the Angels Sing (1944)

Famous Wisconsin Film Stars

Standing Room Only (1944)
Show Business at War (1943)
The Last Will and Testament of Tom Smith (1943) (uncredited narrator)
Above Suspicion (1943)
Flight for Freedom (1943)
No Time for Love (1943)
Star Spangled Rhythm (1942)
The Forest Rangers (1942)
Take a Letter, Darling (1942)
The Lady Is Willing (1942)
Popular Science (1941) (uncredited)
Virginia (1941)
New York Town (1941)
Dive Bomber (1941)
One Night in Lisbon (1941)
Rangers of Fortune (1940)
Screen Snapshots Series 19, No. 5: Hollywood at Home (1940)
Too Many Husbands (1940)
Little Old New York (1940)
Remember the Night (1940)
Cafe Society (1939)
Invitation to Happiness (1939)
Honeymoon in Bali (1939)
Men with Wings (1938)
Sing You Sinners (1938)
Coconut Grove (1938)
Exclusive (1937)
True Confession (1937)
Swing High, Swing Low (1937)
Maid of Salem (1937)
Champagne Waltz (1937)
The Princess Comes Across (1936)
The Texas Rangers (1936)
Thirteen Hours by Air (1936)
The Trail of the Lonesome Pine (1936)
Grand Old Girl (1935)
The Bride Comes Home (1935)
Men Without Names (1935)
Hands Across the Table (1935)
Alice Adams (1935)
Car 99 (1935)
The Gilded Lily (1935)
Why Leave Home? (1929)
Tiger Rose (1929)
Girls Gone Wild (1929)

DON AMECHE

Did you know that the telephone was named for a Kenosha-born movie star? Well, that was the long-standing joke in Hollywood anyway, when Americans started referring to telephones as "Ameches," after actor Don Ameche portrayed the telephone's inventor in the 1939 movie *The Story of Alexander Graham Bell.*

Of course, Felix and Barbara Amici had little idea on May 31, 1908, that their newborn son Dominic Felix Amici would one day be a household name, let alone famous movie star Don Ameche.

The family shortened their son's name to "Dom" when he was a toddler, and friends were soon calling him "Don." Amici's last name first began to change to Ameche in school records from Frank Elementary School in Kenosha.

According to an article by Don Jensen of the *Kenosha News,* Don Ameche's family went through more than a few changes in the southeast Wisconsin town. They lived in several homes throughout Kenosha's Italian district while Don was growing up and finally settled on 22nd Avenue (Howland Avenue).

In 1915, Don Ameche welcomed the newest of his seven siblings, Jim, who also grew up to play Alexander Graham Bell in a movie, *The Story of Mankind,* eighteen years after his brother. In addition, Jim Ameche became a popular New York radio star and played Jack Armstrong in the *Jack Armstrong — The All American Boy* radio program, in which brother Don also starred.

The Ameche boys grew up in a strong family, though not an especially loving one, Don Ameche recalled in a 1980 interview with Mary Kimbrough for *Friendly Exchange.*

"Neither of my parents ever told me they loved me," he said. "But I just learned to live with it. When I got to be 40, I just thought things out and said, 'This is what mama is and this is what papa is.' As I grew older, there have come to me a tolerance and understanding that they both did the best they knew."

Family morale wasn't helped any after Prohibition was enacted in 1919. Their father lost the tavern he'd built into financial success, and the strain forced the Ameches' eight children to fend for themselves, and each other, where their futures were concerned.

"By 1930, I had to take over the whole family. I educated every one of my sisters and brothers," said Ameche, the second oldest, to *Detroit Free Press* reporter Shirley Eder for an Oct. 15, 1988 article.

A lack of money wasn't the only burden weighing on young Don Ameche as a grade schooler in Kenosha. He and his siblings were teased a lot by other kids because of their heritage.

"Being born Italian in a city like Kenosha, Wisconsin, was a brutal time. They really looked down on us because Kenosha then was Sicilian. Early in my life, this hurt the hell out of me," he told Eder.

Ameche stayed in Kenosha through his elementary school years but went to boarding school at Columbia Academy in Dubuque, Iowa, for his further education. It was in Dubuque that Ameche met his future wife Honore Prendergast, whom he married in 1932 and eventually had six children, two adopted daughters Bonnie and Connie as well as four sons, Ronald, Dominic, Thomas and Lonnie.

Ameche followed his father's wishes and entered college to become a lawyer, first at Marquette University in Milwaukee, then at Georgetown University in Washington, D.C., and finally at University of Wisconsin in Madison.

Once the law student got to Madison, thoughts of a legal career dimmed fast in the limelight of university stages. Ameche first became passionate about acting when he joined the university's Wisconsin Players theater group and performed at the Garrick Theater, the stage that also launched the acting career of his future costar Ralph Bellamy. Ameche worked in Madison area summer stock companies as well, including the Al Jackson company, where he acted with fellow UW law student Tom Ewell (then Yewell Tompkins). When Ameche took the lead in the Wisconsin Players' 1929 production of *Lillion*, Ewell had created the scenery and met him on stage in a bit part. Ewell later starred with Marilyn Monroe in *The Seven Year Itch* (1955).

The two met again on the streets of New York City when both had been in movies and Ewell was performing on stage. An August 12, 1951 article in the *Wisconsin State Journal* by Earl Wilson describes how the two stars met when Ewell approached Ameche on the street asking if he remembered Yewell Tompkins, Ameche told the Wisconsin reporter. "I said, 'of course, I remember Tom Ewell!' This is a man who is a big hit in Hollywood but he comes up to me and asks whether I remember him."

Ewell and other UW classmates had seen Ameche's first professional performance years earlier in Madison when an accident and timing combined to give him his first paid lead role.

Ameche got that big break one day when he'd gone to the stock company ticket office just to buy a ticket for that night's performance. According to Wilson, the "distraught theater manager — who had just learned that his leading man was in an accident and couldn't go on — remembered Don as a student actor. Within hours, Don was backstage learning his lines and, that afternoon, made his professional debut. He never went back to law school."

Despite his success, Ameche told reporter Eder that he continued to run up against those who thought less of him because he was Italian.

"I went to ... the University of Wisconsin to earn a law degree. Even though I was living in a law fraternity, I didn't get one bid to any fraternity, including the one I lived in," he noted. "When I got the lead in the play *The Devil's Disciple*, the day after opening, I got bids from eight fraternities. I turned them all down. But what it made me do was really read a history of Italy and her contribu-

Don Ameche, 10, with his junior basketball team at Franklin School in Kenosha. Photo courtesy of Wisconsin Center for Film and Theater Research. Image No. WCFTR-3743.

tions to the world. Then I had no problems with it at all."

With boosted confidence from his stage success and a new pride in his heritage, Ameche left for New York and Chicago theater circles in 1929.

He found stage work with Fisk O'Hara and Texas Guinan in vaudeville shows that toured the United States.

Soon Ameche earned a role in the Chicago production of *Illegal Practice,* where costars encouraged the promising actor to take his baritone speaking and singing voice to upcoming auditions for the national radio program *The Empire Builders.*

The radio directors liked what they heard, and Ameche began a radio acting and hosting career that lasted most of his professional life.

That career started with lead roles on such programs as *First Nighter* and *Grand Hotel.* He also played Bob Drake on *Betty & Bob*, Pasquale on *The Edgar Bergen & Charlie McCarthy Show,* and Capt. Hughes on *Jack Armstrong, the All-American Boy.*

Ameche had appeared in a short subject Chicago film, *Beauty at the World's Fair* in 1933, and Hollywood came calling for radio work in the mid-1930s.

California airwaves couldn't hold Ameche for long. In 1935, the Wisconsin actor landed a small role as a prisoner in *Clive of India* and another part in *Sins of Man* (1936). Ameche signed a long-term contract with 20th Century Fox Studios soon after.

The actor's first big romance movie came in 1936 when he was cast as an American Indian with Loretta Young in *Ramona.* Ameche often played the nice guy and the suave suitor in upbeat films and comedies, as he did singing to ice skater Sonja Henie in her first skating film *One in a Million* (1936). Other hit films featuring Ameche included *The Three Musketeers* (1939), *Moon Over Miami* (1941), and *A Wing and a Prayer* (1944).

Sonja Henie was just one of many stars Ameche courted and serenaded on screen. He also made six movies with Alice Faye, including *In Old Chicago* (1938), *Hollywood Cavalcade* (1939), and *Lillian Russell* (1940).

He broke the good-guy typecast to threaten one starlet, Claudette Colbert, in 1948's *Sleep My Love* and played the not-so-wonderful Henry Van Cleve, who recounts his past to the devil in the 1943 hit comedy *Heaven Can Wait.*

Ameche's contract with 20th Century Fox ended in the 1950s and, though Fox's Darryl Zanuck offered the star a three-year contract with no options, Ameche and his agent turned it down to enable the star to freelance. "I'm well aware it was a mistake," he told Shirley Eder of the *Detroit Free Press* in an Oct. 15, 1988, article. "When I went freelance, I never made a total failure but I never made one picture that made a lot of money."

One of Ameche's most famous lines was said off screen about his controversial boss Zanuck — who had a reputation as a womanizer and cut-throat businessman: "Zanuck never did anything but nice to me. Oh yeah, maybe he chased Alice Faye around, but a lot of people chased Alice Faye around."

Starlet chasing is something Ameche may have joked about, but it's largely reported that he took no part in the Hollywood shenanigans of his day. He rarely, if ever, drank, and he spent his spare time collecting paintings or breeding horses and often betting on horses. Ameche was described as a legendary bettor, reportedly losing nearly a million dollars at the tracks, according to David Ragan in his book, *Movie Stars of the 1930s* (1985).

Ameche was by all accounts a solid family man who supported not only his wife and six children but also helped many of his siblings and extended family members.

And while the star worked to ensure that his children never wanted for the necessities and love he had needed as a child, they also knew that they would have to make their own way someday.

Despite all the money he amassed as a movie star, Ameche told *Motion Picture* and *Hollywood Magazine* reporter Alice Canfield in 1944 that his children "earn their spending money... I think that's a sound lesson — that you have to work for what you get."

Their father certainly worked hard for all they had.

Ameche was as active on network radio as he was on screen. He found his most enduring role in a national radio program when he played John Bickerson, the husband of actress Frances Langford (Blanche Bickerson) on the hit comedy *The Bickersons*.

The program, which first aired in 1946 and ran for eight years on radio, featured the married couple constantly battling over everything from their relatives to their cat to John Bickerson's obnoxious snoring. The show was so popular that the actors portrayed *The Bickersons* in commercials and on TV through the 1950s and '60s, and the programs are often repeated even today. On TV, *The Bickersons* were featured six times each on *The Steve Allen Show* and *Sid Caesar's Show of Shows* and five times on *The Perry Como Show* from 1955 to 1960. In the early 1950s, Langford and Ameche had their own TV series and when the show became just

The Frances Langford Show (1960), Ameche still guest-starred.

By the 1960s, Ameche's movie career had faded. Still, the star continued to act on stage, emceed the popular *International Showtime* series, was a panelist on *To Tell the Truth* in 1956, and hosted or guest starred on occasional television shows — including *Take a Chance* (1950), *Holiday Hotel* (1950), *Julia* (1968), and in later years *The Love Boat* and *The Golden Girls*.

A publicity photo of Don Ameche. Photo courtesy of Wisconsin Center for Film and Theater Research. Image No. WCFTR-3742.

By 1970, Ameche was essentially retired from screen work.

As he looked back on his decades of movie stardom, the Wisconsin actor enjoyed the glamour of his chosen profession, he told Robert Higgins for his April 24, 1965, article, "He Has Moved Out of the Center Ring."

"I can see romance and glamour in most anything," Ameche said. "I can understand why an architect must have an impelling urge to build, why a doctor will travel hours to mend a broken body ... or why any worker will completely lose himself in his work ... There's hidden glamour and beauty in practically everything, but it's bad that so few people will take the pains to find them."

The actor added that he remained as star-struck with the movie business as ever, and that he was more impressed with the work of others than his own.

"As you grow older, you realize how important it is to do things well. I may never do anything significant, but I'm awestruck by those who have," Ameche told Higgins.

Yet, just when the actor thought he'd put his work behind him, Ameche discovered he had significant things left to do.

To the pleasant surprise of film fans, Ameche staged one of the sweetest comebacks in movie star history. At the age of 75, he teamed with fellow UW-Madison alum Ralph Bellamy to play a pair of wealthy, conniving stock traders in the 1983 hit *Trading Places*.

Hollywood fell in love with Ameche all over again and soon began sending movie roles his way.

In 1985, Ameche turned in one of the best performances of his career as Art Selwyn in the mega-hit *Cocoon* — a performance good enough to earn the one-time radio star an Academy Award for Best Supporting Actor.

After playing the revitalized senior again in *Cocoon: The Return* in 1988, Ameche acted in a string of films — including *Things Change* (1988), *Coming to America* (1988), *Folks!* (1992), and *Homeward Bound: The Incredible Journey* (1993) as the voice of the wise old dog "Shadow" — that lasted until his December 6, 1993, death from prostate cancer.

Ameche had just wrapped up his scenes as Grandpa Harry in *Corrina, Corrina* (1994) a few days before he died. Though he died in Arizona, Ameche requested that he be buried in the Resurrection Catholic Cemetery in Dubuque, Iowa, near where he had spent so much of his youth at boarding school.

He was later inducted into the Wisconsin Performing Artists Hall of Fame.

ON SCREEN
Discover Don Ameche in the following films:

Corrina, Corrina (1994)
Homeward Bound: The Incredible Journey (1993) (voice)
Sunstroke (1992) (TV)
Folks! (1992)
Our Shining Moment (1991) (TV)
Oscar (1991)
Oddball Hall (1990)
The 1930's: Music, Memories & Milestones (1988) (Video)

Things Change (1988)
Cocoon: The Return (1988)
Coming to America (1988)
Harry and the Hendersons (1987)
Pals (1987) (TV)
A Masterpiece of Murder (1986) (TV)
A Salute to Billy Wilder (1986) (TV)
Cocoon (1985)
Trading Places (1983)
Gidget Gets Married (1972) (TV)
Shepherd's Flock (1971) TV Series
Columbo: Suitable for Framing (1971) (TV)
Suppose They Gave a War and Nobody Came? (1970)

Famous Wisconsin Film Stars

The Boatniks (1970)
Shadow Over Elveron (1968) (TV)
Picture Mommy Dead (1966)
Rings Around the World (1966)
A Fever in the Blood (1961)
International Showtime (1961) TV Series
The Frances Langford Show (1960) TV Series
Junior Miss (1957) (TV)
To Tell the Truth (1956) TV Series
Fire One (1954) (TV)
Phantom Caravan (1954)
Coke Time (1953) TV Series
The Frances Langford-Don Ameche Show (1951) TV Series
Holiday Hotel (1950) TV Series
Star Time (1950) TV Series
Take a Chance (1950) TV Series
Slightly French (1949)
Sleep, My Love (1948)
So Goes My Love (1946)
That's My Man (1946)
Guest Wife (1945)
It's in the Bag! (1945)
Greenwich Village (1944)
A Wing and a Prayer (1944)
Happy Land (1943)
Heaven Can Wait (1943)
Something to Shout About (1943)
The Magnificent Dope (1942)
Girl Trouble (1942)
The Feminine Touch (1941)
Confirm or Deny (1941)
Kiss the Boys Goodbye (1941)
Moon Over Miami (1941)
That Night in Rio (1941)
Down Argentine Way (1940)
Four Sons (1940)
Lillian Russell (1940)
Swanee River (1939)
Hollywood Cavalcade (1939)
The Story of Alexander Graham Bell (1939)
Midnight (1939)
The Three Musketeers (1939)
Gateway (1938)
Josette (1938)
Alexander's Ragtime Band (1938)
Happy Landing (1938)
In Old Chicago (1937)
Love Under Fire (1937)
You Can't Have Everything (1937)
Fifty Races to Town (1937)
Love Is News (1937)
One in a Million (1936)
Sins of Man (1936)
Ladies in Love (1936)
Ramona (1936)
Dante's Inferno (1935) (uncredited)
Clive of India (1935) (uncredited)
Week End In Hollywood (uncredited)
Beauty at the World's Fair

PAT O'BRIEN

One would imagine that an actor named Patrick O'Brien must have been born on the Emerald Isle. In fact, Hollywood was content to let fans believe just that, perpetuating the Irish roots of the star who often portrayed Irish characters in their films.

Truth be told, O'Brien *was* Irish — Milwaukee Irish.

William Joseph O'Brien was born November 11, 1899, in a small apartment over O'Donnell's Saloon, at the corner of 13th and Clybourn streets in Milwaukee, to Gimbel's department store manager William "Tip" O'Brien and his wife Margaret. In honor of his grandfather, who was killed trying to break up a fight over a gun in his tavern, O'Brien later changed his name to William Patrick Joseph O'Brien, shortened to Pat O'Brien for movie credits.

O'Brien's life and career read almost like a Hollywood who's who list of friends and acquaintances. He grew up fighting in the streets alongside a future Wisconsin state senator, Irving "Stuts" Mehigan, and a Jesuit priest, "Cyclone" Mehigan. He joined the Navy with school chum and future Hollywood megastar Spencer Tracy, and learned the finer points of acting in stock company productions with actors and friends Bill Boyd and Frank McHugh. The Irish boy costarred with a future U.S. president and also enjoyed close friendships with actors James Cagney, Bing Crosby, Wisconsinite Dennis Morgan and University of Wisconsin graduate Ralph Bellamy.

O'Brien started down this star-studded path one block from his home, at the Gesu Catholic Church's parochial school.

While he was still in elementary school, the O'Briens moved a few blocks "uptown" to a coal-heated house on 15th and Sycamore streets that featured only a water closet and required Margaret O'Brien to give Patrick and his brothers Edward and Robert their weekly washings in a giant tin tub. The family later moved to a fourth floor apartment five blocks further uptown, at 14th and Prairie streets, which boasted the first electric lights the family household enjoyed.

Though O'Brien's childhood was clouded by the deaths of his brothers at early ages — events the actor rarely discussed — grow-

> "While working at the Milwaukee railroad yards, every train whistle kept singing its dirge, teasing me about the city I longed to be in — New York."
>
> — Pat O'Brien

ing up was an otherwise happy time for the Irish boy. His Milwaukee days were often filled with the usual boyhood adventures, from hopping freight cars to throwing snowballs and from enjoying Saturday picnics at West Park to roasting potatoes called "Mickies' at a nearby corner lot.

O'Brien served as an altar boy at the Gesu Catholic Church, where he learned Latin. In his 1964 autobiography (*The Wind at My Back*), the man who one day played his fair share of priests in movies, fondly recalled his childhood priest, Father Murphy, as the kind of parochial school principal, "who would hand out chocolate drops and tell the kids to try to be a good boy."

A Catholic upbringing meant a great deal to the actor, he added. "I learned to pray at my mother's side, and it has always been my solace when I thought my dreams had tumbled."

All of O'Brien's prayers and altar boy good deeds did not keep him out of trouble completely, however.

O'Brien and the Mehigan brothers caroused in a kid gang, called the Tory Hill Gang, and were known to rumble grade school style with boys from the 16th Street Gang, among others. "We were not goodie, goodie boys, and the priest and nuns had their hands full with us," he wrote.

From an early age, O'Brien showed a gift for acting in class plays and elocution contests. He also took Irish dancing lessons and spent time making facial expressions in a mirror, imagining himself to be a pirate or an Indian.

Other talents took the Irish scrapper some time to develop. "My football career got off to a poor start. I broke my collarbone in scrimmage. Then, in the first game (of the following season), they carried me off the field limp and pale with two broken ankles," O'Brien wrote.

The would-be sportsman fared a bit better in baseball and organized a neighborhood team called the Bullet Stoppers. When the name wouldn't fit on team sweaters, the kids simply abbreviated it as B.S., and thus "evoked many a snide remark," O'Brien recalled.

O'Brien played baseball well into his Hollywood days, though he pitched for a only short time as a Milwaukee youth. He gave up pitching after accidentally knocking out his friend Frank Mehigan at the plate with an errant pitch. "The sound of that ball striking the skull filled the school grounds. I never pitched a ball again," he wrote.

By 1913, O'Brien and his friends found work preparing the football field at Marquette University. "I got a job pouring whitewash on the Marquette field to mark yard lines in the morning. (About noon) dad came and passed newspaper wrapped sandwiches over the fence. Then, we'd sit around and watch the game," O'Brien noted.

The job had special significance years later when O'Brien played the inspirational Notre Dame football coach in the 1940 movie *Knute Rockne, All American*, which starred Ronald Reagan as Notre Dame halfback George Gipp. After all, it had been a 13-year-old O'Brien who poured the whitewash that Rockne ran across in 1913 when he was a Notre Dame end battling Marquette.

Though not poor, O'Brien long knew that attending a private Catholic secondary school like the Marquette Academy, let alone college, would take more than just desire.

The Ancient Order of Hibernians annually gave a full ride to the academy, so O'Brien put his skills — more of the performing kind than studying variety — to work to win the scholarship, he explained in his autobiography.

"I was fully confident that I could never answer the majority of the questions (on the scholarship test). I hit upon a desperate Machiavellian plan. Emotion, not wisdom, might do the trick. I wrote a vast composition ... then tied up the pages with a beautiful green ribbon from a candy box and drew, in emerald chalk, a Shamrock on the title page."

O'Brien's efforts paid off. He enrolled in Marquette Academy (now Marquette High School) in Milwaukee on scholarship, where he played in such school productions as *The Prince & The Pauper* and *The Importance of Being Earnest*. In 1917, he befriended a new enrollee, Spencer Tracy, who like O'Brien was tossing around the idea of becoming a priest.

However, with World War I still raging in Europe, the two friends decided to put any such dreams on hold and leave school to serve their country. They enlisted in the Navy.

"We fought the battle of the Great Lakes (at Great Lakes Naval Station in Chicago)," the actor quipped, adding that serving stateside during wartime was no great adventure, though the seaman spent time playing on the station's football team.

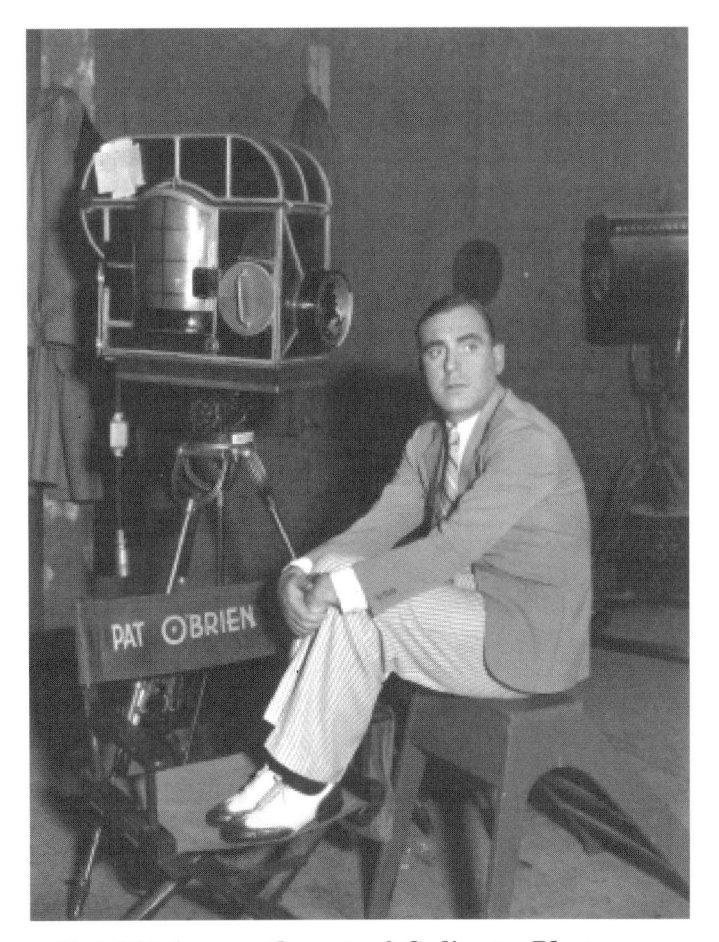

Pat O'Brien on the set of *Caliente*. Photo courtesy of Wisconsin Center for Film and Theater Research. Image No. WCFTR-3754.

The boys' service didn't last long. The war ended on O'Brien's 19th birthday, November 11, 1918, and they were discharged. O'Brien returned to Milwaukee to finish high school. At that time, Marquette Academy had an ROTC program, complete with its own uniforms. According to the Naval Institute Press's 1997 book *Stars in Blue*, O'Brien bucked the system and insisted on wearing his U.S. Navy Seaman First Class blues instead.

After graduation, O'Brien enrolled at Marquette University to pursue a law degree. The future star was less interested in law than he was in football, girls and acting. He played second string to All-American Red Dunne, acted in such plays as *Charley's Aunt*, and courted Milwaukee beauties like Norma Head, the future mother of Robert Head, a childhood friend of Whitefish Bay movie star Jeffrey Hunter.

O'Brien insisted that above all his college pursuits, it was acting that "hovered uppermost" in his thoughts.

He listened to those thoughts in the early 1920s when his Uncle Charlie sent the family $300 so Patrick and his mother could visit him and his Union Club in New York.

O'Brien loved New York and decided to stay on with relatives living in New Jersey, commuting via a three-cent ferry to Manhattan in search of acting jobs.

Desire may have brought O'Brien to New York, but it was his feet that carried him to the stage when the Irish dancing lessons he took as a child helped the actor land his first professional stage role, as a dancer in the musical *Adrienne*.

Just as he was starting his acting career, O'Brien received word that his father was seriously ill in Wisconsin. The would-be actor returned home and, though his father soon recovered, O'Brien re-enrolled at Marquette University.

The performer in O'Brien wouldn't endure the student life for long, however. He soon began dabbling in local theater productions, writing, producing and directing the Junior League's play *Fanciful Follies*, which opened at the Pabst Theater, as well as taking on the job of directing a cast of 1,000 in the city's *Pageant of Progress*.

In between, he worked a long string of jobs, in blacksmith, railroad and city of Milwaukee workshops. "While working at the Milwaukee Railroad yards, every train whistle kept singing its dirge, teasing me about the city I longed to be in New York."

O'Brien set out on a plan to return to New York and looked up his old buddy Spencer Tracy to share his idea of attending the Sargent School of Theater in New York on the servicemen's World War I enrollment allowance.

When O'Brien asked Tracy if he would join him in the New York adventure, the future star reportedly said, "Can a shamrock be anything but green?"

The friends moved to New York and rented what O'Brien called a "mouse nest of a room" at 98th and West End Avenue.

The two shared more than dreams and living quarters, O'Brien noted. "I had a prized pongee shirt. I would wear it proudly for three days and then would rest it in the dresser drawer. Spence would then put it on and wear it for the next three days."

The friends got their first Broadway break together, when they were both cast as $15 a week robots in the futuristic play *R.U.R.* After a few weeks, Tracy was awarded a one line speaking part and earned $20 a week.

Added to the $30 a month each received as an ex-serviceman, the two had almost enough to sustain their apartment and themselves on a pretzel and water diet. "We used a shirt until it frayed away, ... and always wore our aging limp hats with the brim turned down or up at a sharp angle and ... acted at all times as if we had just returned to Broadway from a great success," O'Brien recalled.

Truly great success would take Tracy a few more years, and O'Brien nearly a decade, to achieve.

After leaving the theater school in 1923, both men went to summer stock companies, O'Brien playing first in Plainfield, New Jersey, in such productions as *Gertie's Garter, St. Elmo, Turn to the Right* and *Little Old New York.*

His summer stock debut hardly went much better than that first scrimmage on the Milwaukee football field years before when O'Brien reportedly got locked in a trunk that he was supposed to pop out. His less-than-headline-making performance may have been due to the fact that his heart wasn't in New Jersey. It was back in Milwaukee, in the hands of a girlfriend named Lorraine.

His love was so strong that O'Brien again left New York at her request and went to work in Milwaukee. While back home, the actor wrote, he would often hang out backstage at Jimmy Gleason's stock company performances in the Davidson Theater in Milwaukee. "Out of the kindness of his heart, Jimmy would let me stand in the wings and watch the performance ... and play bit parts in a couple of shows." In the meantime, O'Brien tried to hold down a string of "traditional" jobs that went nowhere.

Nowhere was the same direction O'Brien's love affair was headed, so the struggling actor returned to his New Jersey relatives and tried to work his way back into the spotlight.

He soon landed a role in a tour company production of *Broadway*, which brought him to Chicago in the mid-1920s.

O'Brien's parents came down from Milwaukee to see the show and as the actor entered the stage, he heard his mom yelling, "That's my boy!" followed by great audience applause. "I had never gotten a hand on my entrance," he joked.

But Margaret's son was far more interested in what was on stage than off, especially where his costar Eloise Taylor was concerned. "Everyone who met Eloise wanted to romance this doll from Des Moines," O'Brien wrote, noting he was no exception and spent several years trying to convince the actress to marry him. During their lengthy and often long-distance courtship — since both were touring at times with different stock companies — O'Brien underwent a tonsillectomy back in Wisconsin. The recovery did not go well, and the actor nearly bled to death when he hemorrhaged in the night. Eloise rushed to his side from New York, and "I heard my mother say, 'Never mind the doctor, get the priest,'" he recalled.

Perhaps inspired by a second chance at life, O'Brien finally saw his dreams come true.

On January 23, 1931, the actor sealed the deal with Eloise on the marriage he'd been proposing for so long forming a lifelong union that would soon produce a daughter, Kathleen Brigid. The couple also adopted three children, Mavouneen, Sean, and Terence Kevin.

That same year, Hollywood noticed the Wisconsin actor.

Since his near death experience, O'Brien had been back on Broadway. By 1930, he was starring as Walter Burns in *Front Page* when Hollywood producer Howard Hughes called to ask if he'd be interested in playing the lead role of reporter Hildy Johnson in a *Front Page* movie. The actor later discovered that the producer had mistakenly offered the role to him, thinking O'Brien was the man who played Johnson in the Broadway production.

O'Brien never mentioned the flub to the studio. Instead, he took full advantage of it and launched a movie career from 1931's *Front Page* that endured through more than twenty years and a hundred films, in which he most often starred as the stereotypical Irishman.

According to movie critic Leonard Maltin in an Internet Movie Database biography, "no other leading man of the 1930s and 1940s played as many cops, servicemen or priests."

And, Maltin adds, few actors then or since could match the speed with which the Milwaukee-born Irishman could deliver dialogue. He was "arguably the fastest-talking actor of his day (only Lee Tracy could deliver dialogue at the same rat-a-tat-tat pace)," the critic noted.

After starring and costarring in such films as *Flying High* (1931) and *Final Edition* and *Airmail* with friend Ralph Bellamy (both in 1932), the freelance actor had signed with Warner Bros. Studios for a relationship that lasted seven years. Many of O'Brien's most memorable roles were captured on Warner Bros. film.

By 1940, O'Brien was one of Hollywood's top performers, starring in such films as 1935's *Oil for the Lamps of China* and *Stars Over Broadway*, 1936's *China Clipper*, 1937's *Slim* and *The Great O'Malley*, 1938's *The Cowboy from Brooklyn*, 1939's *Kid From Kokomo* and 1940's *'Til We Meet Again*, among dozens of others.

The actor gained much notoriety as the responsible sidekick to James Cagney, who became one of the closest friends in his life, in seven films including such movies as *Here Comes the Navy* (1934) and *The Irish in Us* (1935). Most memorably, O'Brien played the priest to Cagney's gangster in 1938's *Angels With Dirty Faces* and played the famous real-life priest, Father Duffy, to Cagney's street-wise soldier in *The Fighting 69th* (1940), which also starred Wisconsin's Dennis Morgan as Lt. Ames.

Then, in 1940, he was cast in his most acclaimed and remembered role as the inspirational pep-talking Notre Dame football coach Knute Rockne in *Knute Rockne, All American,* which costarred Ronald Reagan as the Gipper. O'Brien's performance was so riveting that he was often asked to repeat Rockne's famous locker room speech, asking the boys to "win one for the Gipper," as the actor did before a crowd of 1,100 at the National Pro Football Hall of Fame banquet in Canton, Ohio, in 1965.

When Hollywood turned toward World War II concerns on screen and off, beginning in 1941, so did O'Brien. He played heroic figures in such war films as *Flight Lieutenant, Two Yanks in Trinidad,* and *The Navy Comes Through,* all in 1942. In 1943, he again played an Irish hero in *Bombardier* as Col. Patty Ryan.

O'Brien joined dozens of actors performing for U.S. servicemen stationed in the Caribbean, North Africa, and Burma and lent his name and time to war bond fundraisers. He was especially active in events his wife organized as director of women's activities for eight Western states under the direction of the Women's Division of War Finance. At the same time, he was said to lean to the far right politically and even supported Generalissimo Francisco Franco in the Spanish Civil War.

As the war came to a close, O'Brien was cast as a murderous lawyer in RKO's 1945 hit *Having a Wonderful Crime*, which costarred tragic Wisconsin beauty Carole Landis and teamed with Wisconsin star Dennis Morgan in *My Wild Irish Rose* (1947). Though now working again as a freelance actor, O'Brien starred in several RKO films in the 1940s, including *Man Alive* (1945), *Riffraff* (1947), and *Fighting Father Dunne* (1948). He also portrayed the friend in 1948's *The Boy With Green Hair*, directed by La Crosse native Joseph Losey.

As the 1940s came to a close, movie demand for O'Brien began to wane. Though his boyhood friend Spencer Tracy reportedly lobbied Hollywood on his friend's behalf — securing him a costar lead with Tracy in *The People Against O'Hara* in 1951 — O'Brien was no longer making several movies a year, though he still played memorable movie roles in such 1950s films as *Okinawa* (1952).

Most significantly, O'Brien costarred in director John Ford's political masterpiece *The Last Hurrah* (1958), which also featured his friends Spencer Tracy and Frank McHugh as well as Wisconsin actor Jeffrey Hunter.

After a cameo role in the 1959 hit *Some Like It Hot*, O'Brien began to dabble in television, starring in a short-lived series *Harrigan and Son* in 1960-61. He also guest starred on such shows as *The Virginian* (1962), *Bob Hope Presents the Chrysler Theater* (1963), as Uncle Joe on *Happy Days* (1974), and as Col. Buchanan on *WKRP in Cincinnati* (1978). In 1964, the actor wrote his autobiography.

Periodically, O'Brien returned to film with roles in such movies as *Town Tamer* (1965), *Billy Jack Goes to Washington* (1977) and *The End* (1978). And, the actor enjoyed the accolades when the Catholic Actors Guild named him their man of the year in 1973.

However, O'Brien spent most of his later years working on stage alongside his favorite costar, his wife Eloise.

The couple returned to Milwaukee's Swan Theater in 1962 to costar in *Father of the Bride* and to Madison and Milwaukee in 1963 to costar in *Showboat* with fellow Wisconsin star Dennis Morgan. They last appeared together on stage in the play *On Golden Pond* in 1983, when O'Brien was 83.

Eloise was never far for long from O'Brien's side, and the actor often took her — and when possible the children — to film locations. For example, at the height of his career in 1946, the couple traveled to England.

The Wisconsin Irishman was so popular that he was invited to meet King George VI and Queen Elizabeth of England. However, according to the playbill from a later performance of *Showboat* in Milwaukee, O'Brien ruffled a few royal feathers by refusing to meet with the queen unless his wife was allowed to accompany him. The queen bent to the American's wishes and O'Brien presented the queen of his life to Her Royal Majesty.

O'Brien always spent much time as well with the "second banana" of his life, his best friend James Cagney. So, it was only fitting that it was Cagney who last shared the silver screen with O'Brien when the friends costarred in *Ragtime* in 1981.

Cagney was also one of the last actors to speak to O'Brien when he called the star to ask his opinion on a movie role Cagney had been offered. They spoke three days before O'Brien died of heart failure at St. John's Hospital in Santa Monica, Oct. 15, 1983, not long after the Milwaukee Irishman had been inducted, with Dennis Morgan and Jack Carson, into the Wisconsin Performing Artists Hall of Fame in Milwaukee.

Though O'Brien had his vices in his day — with a preference for Cutty Sark, some say a little too much, and horse racing (he cofounded with Bing Crosby the Del Mar Race Track in California) — the actor died well respected in Hollywood as a professional team player on the job and as a solid family man.

In his autobiography, O'Brien confessed that staying grounded and raising a family in Hollywood's spotlight was a constant challenge — and one he was only able to handle thanks to his Wisconsin upbringing and his faith.

"It was my home and my church that saved me in Hollywood," he wrote. "I joined in the prayers with a little private one I added to the others, 'Per Christum Dominum Nostrum ... Let me be as I was.'"

ON SCREEN

Viewers can enjoy Milwaukee Irishman Pat O'Brien's performances in such films as:

James Cagney: That Yankee Doodle Dandy (1981) (TV)
Ragtime (1981)
The Kennedy Center Honors (1980) (TV)
Scout's Honor (1980) (TV)
The End (1978)
Billy Jack Goes to Washington (1977)
Kiss Me, Kill Me (1976) (TV)
The Sky's the Limit (1975)
Adventures of Nick Carter (1972) (TV)
Welcome Home, Johnny Bristol (1972) (TV)
The Phynx (1970)
The Over-the-Hill Gang (1969) (TV)
Town Tamer (1965)
Harrigan and Son (1960) TV Series
Some Like It Hot (1959)
The Last Hurrah (1958)
Kill Me Tomorrow (1957)
Inside Detroit (1955)
Screen Snapshots: Hollywood Beauty (1955)
Ring of Fear (1954)
Jubilee Trail (1954)
Okinawa (1952)
Screen Snapshots: Memorial to Al Jolson (1952)
The People Against O'Hara (1951)
Criminal Lawyer (1951)
The Fireball (1950)
Johnny One-Eye (1950)
A Dangerous Profession (1949)
Screen Snapshots: Motion Picture Mothers, Inc. (1949)
Screen Snapshots: Hollywood's Happy Homes (1949)
The Boy with Green Hair (1948)

Fighting Father Dunne (1948)
Riffraff (1947)
Crack-Up (1946)
Screen Snapshots Series: Famous Fathers and Sons (1946)
Perilous Holiday (1946)
Having Wonderful Crime (1945)
Man Alive (1945)
Secret Command (1944)
Marine Raiders (1944)
His Butler's Sister (1943)
The Iron Major (1943)
Bombardier (1943)
Flight Lieutenant (1942)
Two Yanks in Trinidad (1942)
Broadway (1942)
The Navy Comes Through (1942)
Escape to Glory (1940)
Torrid Zone (1940)
Knute Rockne All American (1940)
Flowing Gold (1940)
'Til We Meet Again (1940)
Castle on the Hudson (1940)
The Fighting 69th (1940)
Slightly Honorable (1940)
The Night of Nights (1939)
Indianapolis Speedway (1939)
The Kid From Kokomo (1939)
Off the Record (1939)
Swingtime in the Movies (1938) (uncredited)
Angels with Dirty Faces (1938)
Garden of the Moon (1938)
Boy Meets Girl (1938)
Cowboy from Brooklyn (1938)
Out Where the Stars Begin (1938) (uncredited)
Women Are Like That (1938)
Submarine D-1 (1937)
Tim Tyler's Luck (1937)
Back in Circulation (1937)
San Quentin (1937)
Slim (1937)
The Great O'Malley (1937)
I Married a Doctor (1936)
Public Enemy's Wife (1936)
Stars on Parade (1936)
China Clipper (1936)
Ceiling Zero (1935)
Devil Dogs of the Air (1935)
A Dream Comes True (1935) (uncredited)
Stars Over Broadway (1935)
Page Miss Glory (1935)
The Irish in Us (1935)
Oil for the Lamps of China (1935)
In Caliente (1935)
I Sell Anything (1934)
The Personality Kid (1934)
A Trip Thru a Hollywood Studio (1934) (uncredited)
Flirtation Walk (1934)
Here Comes the Navy (1934)
Twenty Million Sweethearts (1934)
Gambling Lady (1934)
I've Got Your Number (1934)
The World Gone Mad (1933)
Laughter in Hell (1933)
College Coach (1933)
Bombshell (1933)
Flaming Gold (1933)
Bureau of Missing Persons (1933)
Destination Unknown (1933)
The Strange Case of Clara Deane (1932)
Airmail (1932)
Virtue (1932)
American Madness (1932)
Hollywood Speaks (1932)
Scandal for Sale (1932)
Final Edition (1932)
Hell's House (1932)
Flying High (1931)
Consolation Marriage (1931)
Personal Maid (1931)
The Front Page (1931)
Compliments of the Season (1930) (uncredited)

FREDRIC MARCH

In one moment he is a serene and gentle researcher; in the next, he's a grotesque and violent man. Both faces of Dr. Jekyll and Mr. Hyde belonged to the same actor, stage and screen star Fredric March.

The actor who terrified movie audiences with that 1936 portrayal — and the man movie critic Leonard Maltin would later call, "one of the finest actors who ever worked on screen" — was born Ernest Frederick McIntyre Bickel, the youngest of Racine Hardware Manufacturing Company president John and his wife Cora (Brown Marcher) Bickel's four children. He was born August 31, 1897, in Racine, Wisconsin.

The middle-class family enjoyed a few of the finer things in the early 20th Century. The children had a pony to ride for a while and were able to attend productions at the town's Orpheum Theater when they weren't attending classes at Winslow Grammar School.

The youngest Bickel graduated from Racine High School in 1914, shortly after his school friend Jimmy died of spinal meningitis. Bickel had planned to marry his high school sweetheart, Julia, after he got a college education, but his love didn't like the wait and she married someone else.

John Bickel had hoped to send his son to college in 1915, but a business setback delayed those plans and his youngest son took a $75 a month teller job at Manufacturers Bank in Racine to help earn his tuition.

Though teller work spurred March's thoughts of a banking career, the bank and his time as a Sunday school teacher also provided endless fodder for characters he entertained his family with at night. In her book *Fredric March: Craftsman First, Star Second*, Deborah C. Peterson records that "Fred would stomp around the parlor, sparing no gestures, mimicking whoever impressed him at the bank that day."

The educational delay wasn't all bad because staying in Racine gave Bickel the chance to act in his first professional "performance" when he played a waving car passenger in a Chicago film company's movie, *A Summer Day in Racine*, in 1915.

Young Frederic March performs in a church pageant with another child. Photo courtesy of Wisconsin Center for Film and Theater Research. Image No. WCFTR-3765.

By the fall of 1916, college was again in the young banker's plans, and Bickel enrolled in the University of Wisconsin's School of Commerce, joining his Racine friends Chuck Carpenter and Jack Ramsey on the Madison campus.

The trio immediately pledged a fraternity, Alpha Delta Phi, a place Bickel would return to as movie star Fredric March for reunions in years to come.

Bickel entertained his new family as he had his old with impersonations of famous people like Teddy Roosevelt or just the people he'd met that day. Peterson writes, "Fred would strike dramatic poses and go through various contortions of pantomime that sent his brethren into gales of laughter."

The Racine undergrad was by all accounts a good student and a meticulous planner who could somehow juggle his long list of college activities. Bickel was a football team manager, accountant for the *Badger Annual*, honor member in the Sophomore Society of the Skull and Crescent, and eventual first sergeant in the university's Corps of Cadets.

Bickel also excelled at oratory. He won first place in the 1917

Open Freshman Declamatory contest by performing "Invective Against Cory," a piece he'd performed in high school.

Still fully intending to become a banker, Bickel joined the Edwin Booth Society drama club merely as a side interest. The society was the newer of two male drama clubs on campus, the other being the famed Haresfoot (which Bickel never acted in outside of competing in the annual Haresfoot Follies). As part of the club, Bickel also competed in the annual Union Vodvil at the Fuller Opera House; he played a surgeon in the drama club's 1918 entry, *The Unseen Host*.

Bickel wasn't acting only on stage and in his fraternity house living room. According to Peterson, the future star apparently gave a few great performances in non-theatrical classes as well.

"One day she (his English professor) called for Fred Bickel to read his theme in class. Fred stood up, read from some papers in his hands, and promptly received an 'A.' However, when he sat back down, it was noticed by his classmates that he had not done his homework, for there was not a word written on those papers. He made it up as he went along!"

In between classes and his many other activities, the good-looking freshman found success as a part-time magazine model. He somehow found time to date often, before falling in love his sophomore year with ladies' drama club actress Aline Ellis from Indiana.

Love and studies were put on hold in 1918, however, when the economics student volunteered to fight in World War I and enlisted in the U.S. Army. Bickel was commissioned a second lieutenant after officers candidate school and eventually served stateside as an equestrian instructor, despite the fact that he admitted to knowing no more about riding horses than he learned on the back of a pony he had as a child, Peterson notes, adding that while Bickel taught soldiers, Ellis nursed them back to health as an Army nurse.

Shortly after the war ended, the two returned to the University of Wisconsin in Madison for the 1919 spring semester. The couple went to the prom in 1920 and became engaged that same year. Bickel's list of activities only grew as he took on the role of class president, went out for track, continued to manage the football team and still found time to date Ellis and perform in drama club and university productions.

In 1919, Bickel had teamed up with Carpenter to win third place in that year's *Union Vodvil* competition with an act called *The*

Undertones.

Outside of the drama club, the university at that time offered its own theatrical performances only to students in their junior or senior year of college. Since Bickel now qualified, he began acting, nearly always in the lead role, in university productions of such plays as *The Romancers.*

After graduation, Bickel returned to work at a Racine bank until he took a job as a bank teller in New York City. While the Racine banker toiled by day in the New York financial district, the then still "hobby actor" continued to dabble in the theater world. He was cast as an extra in some of the silent films being produced in New York at that time, including 1921's *The Devil.*

After nearly dying during an emergency appendectomy, Bickel reset his priorities. He gave up banking to pursue his true love of acting. The banker debuted on stage in Baltimore as Frederick Bickel in *Duburau* and traveled to New York with the production, where he acted for the next several years in various New York and touring stock company productions.

On New Year's Day, 1924, Bickel announced that he would from then on be known as Fredric March, creating the stage name from his middle name and his mother's maiden name. According to Peterson, March actually sent out printed announcements that read: "This is 1924. I won't be Bickel any more. Fredric March is now my name. Wishing everyone the same. Happy New Year!"

That year, 1924, proved a year of announcements for the new Mr. March as he was soon notifying family and friends of his marriage to actress Ellis Baker (reportedly the new stage name for Aline Ellis). Despite the fanfare, the marriage was a short one. The couple was divorced by 1927.

It was his work in traveling tour companies that changed March's personal and professional life forever.

In 1926, March was playing in a Denver stock company where he was often paired with the company's leading lady Florence Eldridge, a former Broadway chorus girl, in such productions as *The Swan.* The two paired up off stage as well and were married in Mexico in 1927, the same year March divorced Baker.

The couple returned to New York where March starred in what proved to be his last Broadway production for more than ten years, *The Devil in the Cheese* in 1927.

For the next year, the newlyweds toured the country with the Theatre Guild, taking the role March originated as Tony Cavendish in *The Royal Family* to California theaters.

Paramount Studios scouts liked what they saw when March performed the role in Los Angeles in 1928 and offered the actor a movie contract through 1934.

One of March's first official movie parts was as Trumbull Meredith in the 1929 film, *The Dummy*, which premiered with much hype. However, the film and March received little praise. A critic from *Variety* wrote that March "doesn't get a single close up and remains a zero throughout."

March got better reviews in 1929's *The Studio Murder Mystery* — which costarred his new wife Florence — and 1930's *Laughter*. The Racine actor soon had Hollywood critics literally writing his praises when he brought his stage role of Tony Cavendish to film in the 1930 picture, *The Royal Family of Broadway* and earned his first Academy Award nomination for the effort.

March would win his first Oscar less than two years later for that spine chilling, split-personality performance in *Dr. Jekyll and Mr. Hyde* (1932). It was a role another Wisconsin actor, Spencer Tracy, would perform to critical acclaim in a 1941 version of the film.

That same year, March celebrated a personal honor when he became a father to his adopted daughter Penelope. He celebrated fatherhood again two years later when he and Florence adopted a son, Anthony.

In between, March played a Roman soldier who converts to Christianity in *The Sign of the Cross* (1932), Grim Reaper Prince Sirki in *Death Takes a Holiday* (1933) and Cellini in *Affairs of Cellini* (1934).

After his Paramount contract ended, March signed a two-picture contract with Fox Studios that paid the star a reported $125,000 and featured very liberal terms for its time, including the right to work for other studios, showing how big a screen presence the Racine native had already become.

Incidentally, after that agreement expired, March stayed away from studio contracts and worked only as a freelance actor — one of the few to do so at the time. It was perhaps this desire for personal freedom as an actor that in part led Hollywood insiders to whisper that that star was "difficult." In his 1970 book, *The Movie Stars*, Richard Griffith notes that Fredric March was "never particularly popular in Hollywood" circles and that he had an "ungregarious" reputation as someone who could clash with a director.

Difficult or not, Fredric March was a popular Hollywood commodity by the mid-1930s.

In 1935, he was cast with Greta Garbo in *Anna Karenina* and shared the screen with his wife in *Les Miserables*. Meanwhile, March's wife continued to make some movies of her own, including appearing as Queen Elizabeth in Katharine Hepburn's 1936 film *Mary of Scotland*.

Her husband's next blockbusters came in 1937 when March gave an Oscar-nominated performance as the fading, drunken star husband (Norman Maine) to Janet Gaylord's rising star wife Esther in *A Star Is Born* and played the reporter who makes a supposedly dying Carol Lombard into a star in the classic comedy *Nothing Sacred*.

By the end of that year, March's own star was shining brighter than nearly any other in Hollywood and he was reported to be one of the five richest men in America, earning up to a half million dollars per year.

March invested some of that money in a six-bedroom Beverly Hills home, complete with a screening room, tennis court and wine cellar, which was bought more than sixty years later by modern day film couple Jennifer Aniston and Brad Pitt.

The Marches reportedly used the tennis court often and also enjoyed swimming and horseback riding. March himself was an avid hobby photographer. Over the years, the pair also lent their names to charitable causes and remained active in the Democratic Party.

In 1934, March hosted a post-election Democratic get-together at his home where, according to an October 31, 1993, *Los Angeles Times Press* article by Greg Mitchella, the liberals "complained bitterly about the smear campaign, which included some of the country's first attack ads disguised as newsreel films directed at the defeated Democratic candidate for governor of California, muckraking author Upton Sinclair.

"No one knew who had created the outrageous films ... finally, Irving R. Thalberg, the revered MGM producer, stepped forward, admitting he made the shorts." The admission shocked the party's host who, Mitchella reported, shouted, "It was a dirty trick! ... The damndest unfair thing I've ever heard of," which earned Thalberg's famous reply, "Nothing is unfair in politics."

Yet, for all their political interests, it was acting that always drove the Marches' true passions and life.

Though the two had costarred in some movies together since coming to Hollywood in 1928, they missed acting on stage and being on stage together.

So, in 1938, the two took a break from Hollywood to appear on Broadway in *Yr. Obedient Husband*. The play flopped and according to the 1979 book, *Hollywood Album: Lives & Deaths of Hollywood Stars From the Pages of the New York Times,* it "failed so resoundly" that the Marches took out an ad in a New York newspaper that featured a trapeze artist missing his partner and read, "Oops! Sorry!"

Despite the setback, the Marches didn't give up. After all, to stop working would have been to quit breathing for Fredric March. "I'd keep acting even if I had to get on the back of a truck. I'd act wherever there was a group of people," March says in the *Hollywood Album.*

They took to the stage together again to greater acclaim in such productions as *The American Way*, and in 1939 confirmed their commitment to the East Coat stage by buying a 40-acre farm in New Milford, Connecticut, to go with their California home and New York apartment. At the same time, March brought his resonating voice to the radio airwaves, narrating documentaries and performing in the *Lux Radio Theatre* on air.

All their stage success did not pull the Marches away from movies. The couple soon became dual coast stars — on stage in New York and on set in Hollywood.

In his *Hollywood Album* chapter, March says he loved the stage and movies equally, gaining much from working in both. "It has been my experience that work on screen clarifies stage portrayals and vice versa. You learn to make face expressions more in making movies and in working in the theater, you have a sense of a greater freedom."

Frederic March shovels Wisconsin snow. Photo courtesy of Wisconsin Center for Film and Theater Research. Image No. WCFTR-3767.

March did cut back on the number of films he was taking on, picking and choosing his roles carefully and scheduling his dual efforts with the precision he was known for back in college.

Though he had been vice president of the Screen Actors Guild and was well known and respected in Hollywood, March came under the scrutiny of the witch hunt for communists and sympathizers in the American movie business.

The Marches were among those called before the U.S. House Un-American Activities Committee in 1938. Though the couple denied the allegations to the committee, it didn't stop the *Counter-Attack* magazine from bringing up the subject. In 1948, the Marches won a libel suit against the magazine over the communist charges it had made.

March tried to combat what he saw as the congressional lynching of his peers by running unsuccessfully against the House Committee on Un-American Activities chairman, Rep. Martin Dies, in 1940.

A longtime Democratic Party activist, March said he ran to oppose Dies's accusations, calling them "scatter shot, unfair and ill advised." According to the *Hollywood Album*, Dies was angered by March's challenge and "vowed to look into March's politics but later apologized and put (March) on his list of the 'politically clean.'"

In the midst of these battles, March kept on working in such movies as *Susan and God* (1940), *One Foot in Heaven* (1941), *I Married a Witch* (1942), and *The Adventures of Mark Twain* (1944), and volunteered in Hollywood's World War II efforts, from entertaining troops overseas with the USO to working at the Stage Door Canteen.

In 1946, March turned in one of his most memorable and celebrated performances as World War II veteran Al Stephenson struggling to adjust to his postwar life in the year's Best Picture, *The Best Years of Our Lives*.

Actor Ed Asner of Lou Grant fame was a longtime fan of the film and its star, he told Pulitzer Publishing Company in an August 25, 1995, wire service survey of actor's favorite films. "I pick *The Best Years of Our Lives*. I go nuts watching Fredric March, he was just so good," Asner said.

March won his second Best Actor Oscar for his poignant *Best Years of Our Lives* portrayal, making him one of only two Wisconsin actors to win two Best Actor Oscars, the other being Spencer Tracy.

In a 1947 ceremony, the star pulled off a remarkable accomplishment. March won a Tony Award for his 1946 work in *Years Ago*, becoming the first actor to win both a stage Tony Award and movie Oscar in the same year.

After costarring with his wife in the films *Another Part of the Forest* and *An Act of Murder*, both in 1948, and playing Christopher Columbus in the 1949 film of that name, March again turned in an Academy Award nominated performance. This time he played the tragic salesman Willy Loman in the 1951 movie version of Arthur Miller's stage classic, *Death of a Salesman*.

March leapt at the chance to play the classic character on screen, in part because he had passed up the opportunity to launch the role on stage years before — a move he often referred to as the biggest mistake of his professional career. He made the most of his second chance and earned another Academy Award nomination for Best Actor.

Five years later, March won his second Tony Award for Best Actor when he starred in the 1956 production of Eugene O'Neill's *Long Day's Journey Into Night*, again sharing the Broadway stage with his wife. It was one of several 1950s productions the couple costarred in, including: *Now I Lay Me Down To Sleep* in 1950 and *An Enemy of the People* and *The Autumn Garden*, both in 1951. March was nominated for another Tony for his 1962 performance in *Gideon*.

March earned his fifth and last Oscar nomination playing William Jennings Bryan opposite fellow Wisconsinite and two-time Best Actor Oscar winner Spencer Tracy's Clarence Darrow in *Inherit the Wind*, a 1960 film about the Scopes monkey trial, in which Florence March played Bryan's wife.

By this time in his career, March had accomplished perhaps his greatest feat — one which few actors master. He successfully aged on screen without diminishing his star quality as he moved from young, good looking leading man to top-performing character actor.

In the 1960s March continued to turn in powerful screen performances in such films as *The Young Doctors* (1961), *The Condemned of Altona* (1962) and *Hombre* (1967). In 1964, he played the president of the United States in *Seven Days in May*, a film about a military attempt to overthrow the U.S. government.

Occasionally, the Marches appeared in television, hosting or making guest appearances. In 1954 and 1958, the Racine native played *A Christmas Carol's* Scrooge among other parts in a TV series he hosted, called *Fredric March Presents Tales from Dickens*. He also hosted the *Tribute to John F. Kennedy From the Arts* special in 1963.

The Kennedys had paid tribute to the Marches by asking March to present a dramatic reading during a White House dinner honoring Nobel Prize winners in 1962. A few years earlier, March had read Lincoln's Gettysburg address before Congress in honor of the 150th anniversary of Lincoln's birth. In addition, the government sent the Marches abroad to perform for foreign dignitaries throughout the 1960s.

Frederic March as Freddy Bickel, photographed on the steps of his Madison fraternity house. Photo courtesy of Wisconsin Center for Film and Theater Research. Image No. WCFTR-3766.

For all the applause he received throughout the world, March was reportedly most touched when his alma mater named its play circle theater after the one-time economics student. March returned to the UW-Madison campus in 1971 for the official dedication of the Fredric March Theater.

The celebrated Wisconsin actor made just two movies in the 1970s, *tick...tick...tick...* in 1970 and *The Iceman Cometh* in 1973 as he struggled with prostate cancer. March reportedly filmed his *Iceman Cometh* scenes between cancer treatments.

March died on April 14, 1975, at Mount Sinai Hospital in Los Angeles, where he'd been admitted nine days earlier.

He remains won of the most celebrated and honored actors not just in Wisconsin — having been inducted into the Wisconsin Performing Artists Hall of Fame — but also as one of the most respected actors in the world. To date, only seven men have won two Academy Awards for Best Actor: March, Tracy, Tom Hanks, Jack Nicholson, Dustin Hoffman, Marlon Brando, and Gary Cooper.

No other actor reportedly has matched March's double-crown victory of winning an Oscar and Tony for different lead performances within the same year.

ON SCREEN

See why Fredric March is considered one of America's most talented actors in his performances in the following.

The Iceman Cometh (1973)
...tick...tick...tick... (1970)
Hombre (1967)
Seven Days in May (1964)
A Tribute to John F. Kennedy from the Arts (1963) (TV)
I, Sequestrati di Altona (1962)
The Young Doctors (1961)
Inherit the Wind (1960)
Middle of the Night (1959)
Tales from Dickens (1958) TV Series
The Winslow Boy (1958) (TV)
Albert Schweitzer (1957) (voice)
Island of Allah (1956)
Alexander the Great (1956)
The Man in the Gray Flannel Suit (1956)
The Desperate Hours (1955)
Shower of Stars (1954) TV Series
The Bridges at Toko-Ri (1954)
A Christmas Carol (1954) (TV)
Executive Suite (1954)
Man on a Tightrope (1953)
Death of a Salesman (1951)
It's a Big Country (1951)
The Titan: Story of Michelangelo (1950) (voice)
Christopher Columbus (1949)
An Act of Murder (1948)
Another Part of the Forest (1948)
The Best Years of Our Lives (1946)
Tomorrow the World! (1944)
The Adventures of Mark Twain (1944)
I Married a Witch (1942)
Lake Carrier (1942)
Bedtime Story (1941)
One Foot in Heaven (1941)
So Ends Our Night (1941)
Victory (1940)
Susan and God (1940)
Lights Out in Europe (1940) (voice)
The 400 Million (1939)
Trade Winds (1938)
There Goes My Heart (1938)
The Buccaneer (1938)
Nothing Sacred (1937)
A Star Is Born (1937)
Anthony Adverse (1936)
Mary of Scotland (1936)
The Road to Glory (1936)
Anna Karenina (1935)
The Dark Angel (1935)
Les Miserables (1935)
The Barretts of Wimpole Street (1934)
Good Dame (1934)
We Live Again (1934)
The Affairs of Cellini (1934)
Death Takes a Holiday (1934)
All of Me (1934)
Design for Living (1933)
The Eagle and the Hawk (1933)
Tonight Is Ours (1933)
The Sign of the Cross (1932)
Smilin' Through (1932)
Make Me a Star (1932) (uncredited)
Merrily We Go to Hell (1932)
Strangers in Love (1932)
Dr. Jekyll and Mr. Hyde (1931)
My Sin (1931)
Night Angel (1931)
Honor Among Lovers (1931)
The Royal Family of Broadway (1930)
Laughter (1930)
Manslaughter (1930)
True to the Navy (1930)
Ladies Love Brutes (1930)
Paramount on Parade (1930)
Sarah and Son (1930)
The Marriage Playground (1929)

Footlights and Fools (1929)
Jealousy (1929)
Paris Bound (1929)
The Studio Murder Mystery (1929)
The Wild Party (1929)
The Dummy (1929)

The Great Adventure (1921) (uncredited)
Paying the Piper (1921) (uncredited)
The Devil (1921) (uncredited)
The Education of Elizabeth (1921) (uncredited)

COLLEEN DEWHURST

She grew up the tomboy daughter of Canadian football star Fred Dewhurst and wanted more than anything in high school to follow Amelia Earhart into the sky.

Though she never became the aviatrix of her dreams, Milwaukee's Colleen Dewhurst certainly reached the stars.

The actress who would one day win two stage Tonys and four television Emmys was born June 3, 1924, in Montreal, Quebec. After her father retired from the Canadian Football League, he moved the family around the East Coast of the United States in search of work. Dewhurst spent most of her early years in Massachusetts, where she quickly learned to fight back when teased as the grade school outsider.

The young tomboy had her father's sports talents and often played baseball with the boys and was captain of the girls' baseball team. She also loved to swim with her mother during the family's frequent summer car trips back to Canada.

When her father lost his job after Dewhurst finished eighth grade, the family moved to Milwaukee, where the pre-teen started an awkward high school career as an outsider in Whitefish Bay.

Soon after, Dewhurst's parents split up, a reality weighing on the freshman's mind when a senior asked Dewhurst to the prom. It was only after they arrived at the dance that Dewhurst realized her date was on Prom Court and, therefore, so was she, the actress recalled in *Colleen Dewhurst: Her Autobiography*.

"Our dates had been asked to pick out a song for the band to play as each of us (in the court) came down the stairs. ... Jack (no last name given) had chosen 'Charming Scatterbrain.' Jack and I spun out amid gales of laughter," she recalled.

By all accounts, Dewhurst enjoyed her time at Whitefish Bay and was an average, though independent, student.

In her autobiography, the actress relates difficult encounters with the dean of women, including a time she was caught among a group of girls smoking in the bathroom. Though Dewhurst insists she was not smoking, the dean called her — and only her — into the office, saying she could avoid four days of after school detention if she ratted out her friends. Dewhurst refused to play the stool pigeon, though it bothered her that the other girls would "stick their head into the office where I was sitting out the hour (detention) and wave. But never did any of them volunteer to take her own hour."

Dewhurst took the blame in another incident a short time later when she and some friends were taking out street lights with snowballs. Dewhurst confessed that she took part. Thanks to the good arm she developed playing baseball, the tomboy "led with the greatest number of hits."

When the police investigated, the other girls insisted Dewhurst had taken out all the lights, and her mother had to pay the village of Whitefish Bay for the damage.

"Probably, the reason I remember both these incidents so well is that in each case, I was involved with close friends who, for reasons that I don't understand to this day, would never take even partial responsibility," she wrote, adding that she also remembered how her mother stood up for her in both cases.

Her mother was less supportive just weeks later when Dewhurst — still too young for a driver's license — disobeyed her and got behind the wheel of a friend's car.

"We drove a block or two before I made a right turn and lost control of the car, running over the sidewalk and into the yard of a house, hitting a tree," she recalled.

This time, it was her mother who called the police and made her daughter report what she'd done.

After a week recovering from a sore ankle caused by the crash, Dewhurst returned to high school and the friendly teasing of her classmates, who called her "Crash Dewhurst" for the rest of the year.

That summer, Dewhurst and her mother moved to the Milwaukee suburb of Shorewood, forcing another school change. After she completed her junior year at Shorewood High School, the two moved again, and Dewhurst finished high school at Milwaukee's Riverside High in 1941.

Always being the new kid in school was difficult, especially during high school, Dewhurst recalled in her autobiography.

"This was absolute agony," she writes. "Each time I entered the scene, all the girls had their cliques and groups of friends already set since grade school."

To top it off: "Shorewood was, of course, the sworn enemy of Whitefish Bay High School … and Riverside High School was the sworn enemy of Shorewood. … Riverside High played both Whitefish Bay and Shorewood. ... This left me rather unsure of just where I should sit at basketball and football games," she said.

It was at Riverside High that Dewhurst got her first taste of drama, and she didn't like it. Needing one English credit to graduate, the teenager took a speech class to fill the requirement. For the final exam, she had to present a monologue before the entire class, and the thought of getting up alone before an audience nearly paralyzed her with fear.

"I was always a class clown and rather loud (but) I could not speak in front of people. I was a terrible blusher," she wrote.

The teen may have been embarrassed, but it never showed. Dewhurst's final exam speech from *Dulcy* was so well presented that her teacher insisted she compete at the state level, a competition that was "a blur of horror."

A high school stage debut as Olivia in Shakespeare's *Twelfth Night* didn't make Dewhurst feel any better about acting when she left the stage in an embarrassed blush still struggling to get a veil off, to hoots of audience laughter.

"This one moment is all I can remember from what, I guess, must be acknowledged as the first time I ever appeared in a play. And, as far as I was concerned, ... it would be the last," she wrote.

It was her mother who convinced Dewhurst to further her education in college before becoming the female pilot of her dreams. She encouraged her only daughter to compete for an English scholarship at Lawrence University in Appleton, Wisconsin.

Though she didn't get the scholarship, Dewhurst had such a good time at a fraternity party on her one weekend on campus that the future actress knew she wanted to further her education after all.

Fate intervened, however, when her father couldn't come up with his half of the tuition money, so the Dewhursts enrolled their daughter at Milwaukee's Downer College. The idea of attending the all-girl college did not appeal to the fun-loving Dewhurst. "(It) was a definite step down (from Lawrence)," she wrote. "For if there was one place I did not wish to be, it was at an all-girls college!"

Dewhurst's college career didn't get off to, nor end, on a very good note. Her first day of classes, the Riverside High grad noticed that her name was the only one listed on a posted notice of probationary freshmen. "It was a mystery to me ... but somehow, perhaps because I had registered so late, or due to my 'unenthusiastic' 85 percent (average in high school), ... someone saw me coming," she wrote.

Once the tomboy in Dewhurst realized that to play on the school's baseball and field hockey teams she needed to get good grades, she excelled in her studies, at least during sports seasons.

Good grades meant Dewhurst could partake in other extra activities as well. Her freshman year, she volunteered to write the skit for the school's annual theater competition between classes. The play featured classmates acting as each of the twelve months of the year, with Dewhurst eventually moving from the page to the stage by casting herself as one of the months.

Though she believes that her script was "dreadful," it was good enough to win the freshman class its first ever first prize in the competition.

"Flush with success, … that night, I informed my mother … I wanted to be an actress," Dewhurst wrote, adding that her mother was less than convinced that the profession was a good choice until the two attended some Milwaukee and Chicago plays.

It was her mother, then, who suggested Dewhurst enroll in the American Academy of Dramatic Arts in New York.

But, it was Downer College that suggested the budding actress do so before finishing her college studies. After a semester that featured an 'A' in creative writing and an 'F' in chemistry, the college's president Lucia Briggs wrote the Dewhursts a letter, essentially kicking their daughter out of school.

According to Dewhurst, she wrote: "With the knowledge that Colleen is leaving Milwaukee Downer for the American Academy at some time in the future, she is at this time, officially asked to leave as of now."

Ironically, the all-girls school Dewhurst attended merged into the one she wanted most to attend, Lawrence University, in 1964. In 1972, the actress was invited to Appleton to accept an honorary doctorate in fine arts from the university where she only spent a weekend.

When she rose to accept the degree, the university presenter merely noted that the actress had attended Downer College "for some time," Dewhurst recalled in her autobiography. "I can only assume that my real academic records were never found (or perhaps they were), and that somewhere Lucia R. Briggs was spinning in her grave."

If that's true then Biggs may have been sitting up in her grave in 1983, when the school awarded Dewhurst the Lucia R. Biggs Distinguished Achievement Award.

Dewhurst's love for Lawrence University extended well beyond the weekend she spent there. The actress once served on the college's board of trustees and returned in 1977 to address the graduating class, saying "All right, my darlings, all I can say is that life is a joy. This is what it's about. Don't waste your time. For there will never be enough."

Dewhurst returned again to the university in 1985 to present a convocation class, titled "Theater: An Extension of Life." In addition, the actress's youngest son, Campbell Scott, also a movie and stage star, graduated from Lawrence University in 1983 and now serves on the college's 42-member board.

Before Dewhurst could start down the road that led to that honorary degree — and six more she received from other universities — she would work as a saleswoman, elevator operator, and dental assistant.

Her mother insisted that the recent college dropout work for a year before attending the New York acting academy. Dewhurst dutifully got a job in a Milwaukee department store — a position she was fired from in just a few days.

A friend soon invited the actress to move to Gary, Indiana, where Dewhurst worked first as an elevator operator and then as a dental assistant.

Dewhurst may not have found much satisfying work in Gary, but she found the first serious love of her life and was soon engaged to a recently discharged soldier, though the engagement didn't last once Dewhurst moved to New York a year later.

Instead, Dewhurst met actor Joseph Vickery in New York and married him in 1947. Their marriage lasted until 1960, when she divorced Vickery to marry the costar of many of her New York productions, actor George C. Scott (the later Oscar-winning star of the movie *Patton*). They had two sons, Alex and Campbell, before divorcing in 1965 after infidelities on Scott's part. The acting pair reconciled and married again in 1967, only to have the union fall apart when Scott confessed to straying yet again with actress Trish Van Devere, whom he later married.

The future stage and television legend began fulfilling her New York dreams when she won the tryout to enter the American Academy of Dramatic Arts in the mid-1940s by presenting a dramatic piece she had written herself.

"I played a woman saying goodbye to her lover. As he goes out the door, she is casually laughing. Closing the door, she leans against it and proceeds to realize, very dramatically, that each and every piece of furniture is laughing at her. I had written dialogue with each chair. Finally ... she ends up in a heap on the floor, sobbing uncontrollably. The premise was that this woman laughed her way through every experience, never facing that she was in any way affected by the great loss," Dewhurst recalled in her autobiography.

The academy was impressed by its new student's talents, and the student was soon impressing theater audiences as well.

Dewhurst began her theatrical career playing in summer stock companies and off Broadway shows. She worked in New York Shakespeare Festival productions, where Dewhurst learned how to handle anything the stage threw her way — including a pantless toddler wandering up on stage and staring at her to the delight of the audience during an outdoor performance of *Taming of the Shrew*, the actress recalled in her autobiography.

Shakespeare led Dewhurst to celebrated American playwright Eugene O'Neill. Her first Broadway appearance was in O'Neill's 1952 *Desire Under the Elms*. By the end of her career in 1991, Dewhurst had appeared in so many O'Neill plays she joked that the headline on her obituary would read, "O'Neill Actress Dies Somewhere."

Though the stage made Dewhurst famous, she also ventured to Hollywood, appearing in a dozen or so Hollywood films and many made-for-TV movies and television series.

Her first performance on screen was in the TV movie *The Count of Monte Cristo* in 1958. In 1959, she made the move to the big screen in two films, first as a psychopath in *The Nun's Story*, starring Audrey Hepburn, and then as Helen Benson in *Man on a String*.

Dewhurst returned to television and stage performances for most of the 1960s in TV shows like *I, Don Quijote* and in Broadway plays like *All The Way Home*, for which she won her first Tony in 1961. In all, Dewhurst was nominated for eight Tony Awards for her work in *Great Day in the Morning* (1962), *The Ballad of the Sad Café* (1964), *More Stately Mansions* (1968), *All Over* (1972), *Mourning Becomes Electra* (1973), and *Who's Afraid of Virginia Woolf?* (1977). She won her second Tony Award in 1974 for her performance as farm girl Josie Hogan in *A Moon for the Misbegotten*.

Dewhurst loved the theater best and said in her autobiography that she never acted in a bad play, at least while she was making them. "When you're involved, plays, like lovers, are a wonderful experience."

As she was having and raising two sons with Scott in the 1960s,

Dewhurst stuck to the theater. She had time for just a few film roles such as the 1966 movie *A Fine Madness*.

The actress spent most of her non-theatrical time with her family at the South Salem, New York, home, called The Farm, which she and Scott bought in 1962 (in addition to a summer home she kept on Prince Edward Island in Canada).

The Farm was a warm, slightly chaotic place that friends, stars and passersby liked to visit. In addition to being a home for the Scott family, The Farm was a menagerie including peacocks, sheep, cats, a donkey named Nicholas and a goat called Buckle.

In the early 1970s, the stage star jumped back into movies in three successive films, *The Last Run* in 1971, *The Cowboys* in 1972 and *McQ* in 1974. During the filming of *McQ*, Dewhurst, who had starred with such acting notables as George C. Scott, Lillian Gish, Ben Gazzara, and Ingrid Bergman, was especially impressed by her love interest in the film, John Wayne. In her autobiography, Dewhurst calls the cowboy star, "one of the best actors I've ever worked with."

Colleen Dewhurst. Photo courtesy of Wisconsin Center for Film and Theater Research. Image No. WCFTR-3763.

The same year the actress addressed Lawrence University graduates, Dewhurst showcased her acting talents as Diane Keaton's mother in the Oscar-winning movie *Annie Hall* (1977). She graced the screen again two years later in the 1979 hit *Ice Castles*.

Dewhurst did not return to Hollywood movie sets until 1983 when she made *The Dead Zone*. By this time, she was working heavily in television, starring in *The Blue and The Gray* miniseries (1982) as well as the critically acclaimed series *Anne of Green Gables* (1985).

In 1988, she was cast in a recurring guest star role as the mother of TV sitcom news reporter *Murphy Brown*. It was a small role for which Dewhurst will be forever remembered in a big way. Dewhurst earned two of her four Emmy awards for her portrayal of Avery Brown Sr. In all, the actress was nominated for thirteen Emmy Awards, winning Emmys twice for *Murphy Brown* and twice as a Best Supporting Actress in a Mini Series, in 1986 for *Between Two Women* and in 1989 for *Those She Left Behind.*

In between filming, Dewhurst served from 1985 to 1991 as president of the Actors' Equity union and worked for more than ten years with Tom Viola on her autobiography — a book Viola completed and published in 1997. In addition, the actress was a dedicated coach of the Lewisboro, N.Y., girls softball team, the Fireflies, and volunteered her services at the Northern Westchester Center for the Arts, which renamed its venue the "Colleen Dewhurst Theater" in 2001.

While still appearing on the *Murphy Brown* series, Dewhurst continued her stage performances and once again took to the movie screen. In 1989, she filmed two Canadian movies released after her death, *Termini Station* and *Bed and Breakfast*. In 1990, Dewhurst lent her trademark gravely voice to the character of Satan in *The Exorcist III.*

Then in 1991, after being diagnosed with cervical cancer while touring with the play *Love Letters*, the 64-year-old actress joined her son Campbell Scott on the movie screen in the ironically titled *Dying Young*, starring Scott and Julia Roberts.

"I'm so grateful to have had the chance to work with her," said her son Campbell, in an April 27, 1998 *Milwaukee Journal Sentinel* article by Renee Graham, adding that he also acted with his mother on stage in *Long Day's Journey Into Night* in 1986. "I learned a lot from her and she was a pro. She was delightful."

As the daughter of a Christian Scientist mother, the 1984 Wisconsin Performing Artists Hall of Fame inductee refused cancer surgery. She died August 22, 1991, two days before winning her fourth Emmy and her second as Murphy Brown's mother.

Dewhurst's legacy of acting greatness lives on not only through her work that the camera captured. In late 1991 her ex-husband George C. Scott played the supporting role of Gramps in *On Borrowed Time*, a Broadway comedy performed in her memory.

And, the actress's sons have taken to the stage in their mother's footsteps, albeit walking in their own unique directions. Alex works as an actor, writer and stage manager. Campbell is a stage and independent film star.

Campbell and Alex Scott share their mother's Wisconsin ties. Campbell graduated in 1983 with a degree in theater and performing arts from Lawrence University and Alex graduated from Lawrence two years later.

In an article for the Nov. 9, 2001, *Milwaukee Journal Sentinel*, Campbell Scott noted that the idea of an acting career was far from his mind when he entered Lawrence as a history and then English major. It wasn't until his junior year that he discovered his passion and talent for acting.

"My brother and I weren't the kind of kids who put on skits to entertain our parents or their friends," he told Randall King of the *Winnipeg Sun* for a Nov. 29, 1999, article. "Neither my brother nor I ever talked about being actors but, through osmosis, we got a feeling for the profession."

That feeling got stronger for Campbell Scott at Lawrence when he tried out for plays his junior year, he explained to *Appleton Post Crescent* writer Jim Lundstrom for a May 6, 2002, article.

"I love the theater department. It was tiny. It's still tiny. But I love that. It was a safe place to be very comfortable," noted the actor when he returned to campus to serve as one of ten alumni on the university's board of directors.

Scott recently wrote, produced, and codirected a version of *Hamlet* with fellow alum Eric Simonson. According to the *Post-Crescent*, Scott hired Lawrence graduate Gary DeMichele to compose the music for the production. The film reportedly cost $4.5 million to make, a shoestring budget by Hollywood standards.

Hamlet is just one of the many smaller, independent films Scott has been acting in and producing for the past several years, after breaking from Hollywood mega-productions.

Though he shared movie sets with stars like Jodie Foster in *Five Corners* (1987), and Julia Roberts and his own mother in *Dying Young* (1991) — and earned critical acclaim for his portrayal of Willy in *Longtime Companion* (1990) — the one-time Appleton resident prefers the flexibility and independence of smaller films and theater work. He's acted in such smaller films like *Roger Dodger* (2002), *Delivering Milo* (2000), *The Spanish Prisoner* (1997), *Big Night* (1996), and *Mrs. Parker and the Vicious Circle* (1994).

He last worked in a big Hollywood movie project when he costarred with Bridget Fonda in Cameron Crowe's 1992 movie, *Singles*.

Singles was one of the dozens of big films that Wisconsin born assistant director Jerry Ziesmer had a hand in creating. Ziesmer noted that on the set in Seattle, Washington, he and Scott discovered how much they each enjoyed their time in the Badger State.

"Once he heard that (my wife) Suzanne Ziesmer and I were from Wisconsin, we couldn't get him away from us," the assistant director reports, smiling. "He was full of stories about the north side of Milwaukee (Brown Deer) where his friends and their family lived, and about his years at Lawrence College in Appleton."

Scott recalled his Wisconsin memories in the *Post-Crescent* article. "I had a good time in my four years here ... I met the mother of my (pre-school age) child here. My best friend still lives in Milwaukee."

And, like his mother before him, Scott continues to enjoy the life's work he first developed a passion for in Wisconsin.

Campbell Scott told the *Milwaukee Journal Sentinel* in 1998 that he likes his life as an independent film and stage actor, saying that the thoughtful independent films he's starred in and produced in recent years keep him in the profession he loves and yet grant him the flexibility work in the theater, "support a family and make me happy as well."

In other words, the son is living up to his mother's charge to other Lawrence graduates some twenty-five years before. "Life is a joy. This is what it's all about."

ON SCREEN

View Milwaukee graduate Colleen Dewhurst's performances in the following productions:

Bed & Breakfast (1992)
Dying Young (1991)
"Road to Avonlea" (1990) TV Series
Lantern Hill (1990) (TV)
Kaleidoscope (1990) (TV)
"The Civil War" (1990) (mini) TV Series (voice)
The Exorcist III (1990) (uncredited)
Termini Station (1989)
Those She Left Behind (1989) (TV)
Murphy Brown (1988) TV Series
Obsessed (1988)
Anne of Green Gables: The Sequel (1987) (TV)
Hitting Home (1987) (TV)
Bigfoot (1987) (TV)
Johnny Bull (1986) (TV)
Sword of Gideon (1986) (TV)
The Boy Who Could Fly (1986)
As Is (1986) (TV)
Between Two Women (1986) (TV)
Eugene O'Neill: A Glory of Ghosts (1985) (TV) (interviewee)
Ingrid (1985) (interviewee)
Anne of Green Gables (1985) (TV)
A.D. (1985) (mini) TV Series
You Can't Take it with You (1984) (TV)
The Glitter Dome (1984) (TV)
The Dead Zone (1983)
Alice in Wonderland (1983) (TV)
The Blue and the Gray (1982) (mini) TV Series
Between Two Brothers (1982) (TV)
A Few Days in Weasel Creek (1981) (TV)
Tribute (1980)
Final Assignment (1980)
Baby Comes Home (1980) (TV)

Famous Wisconsin Film Stars

A Perfect Match (1980) (TV)
The Women's Room (1980) (TV)
Guyana Tragedy: The Story of Jim Jones (1980) (TV)
Escape (1980) (TV)
Death Penalty (1980) (TV)
Mary and Joseph: A Story of Faith (1979) (TV)
When a Stranger Calls (1979)
And Baby Makes Six (1979) (TV)
"Studs Lonigan" (1979) (mini) TV Series
Silent Victory: The Kitty O'Neil Story (1979) (TV)
Ice Castles (1978)
The Third Walker (1978)
Annie Hall (1977)
A Moon for the Misbegotten (1975) (TV)
The Story of Jacob and Joseph (1974) (TV)
McQ (1974)
The Cowboys (1972)
The Last Run (1971)
The Price (1971) (TV)
The Crucible (1967) (TV)
A Fine Madness (1966)
Focus (1962) (TV)
I, Don Quixote (1959) (TV)
Burning Bright (1959) (TV)
Man on a String (1959)
Medea (1959) (TV)
The Nun's Story (1959)
The Count of Monte Cristo (1958) (TV)

You can see Lawrence University graduate Campbell Scott in the following:

The Secret Lives of Dentists (2002)
Roger Dodger (2002)
The Pilot's Wife (2001) (TV)
Follow the Stars Home (2001) (TV)
Delivering Milo (2000)
Hamlet (2000) (TV)
Other Voices (2000)
Lush (1999)
Spring Forward (1999)
Top of the Food Chain (1999)
Hi-Life (1998)
The Impostors (1998)
The Tale of Sweeney Todd (1998) (TV)
The Love Letter (1998) (TV)
LIBERTY! The American Revolution (1997) TV Series
The Spanish Prisoner (1997)
The Daytrippers (1996)
Big Night (1996)
Let It Be Me (1995)
Would You Kindly Direct Me to Hell?: The Infamous Dorothy Parker (1994) (TV)
Mrs. Parker and the Vicious Circle (1994)
The Innocent (1993))
Singles (1992)
Dead Again (1991)
Dying Young (1991)
The Perfect Tribute (1991) (TV)
Ain't No Way Back (1990)
Longtime Companion (1990)
The Sheltering Sky (1990)
The Kennedys of Massachusetts (1990) TV Series
From Hollywood to Deadwood (1989)
Five Corners (1987)

JAMES & TYNE DALY

Wisconsin Rapids native Jim Daly started down his road to Hollywood fame on a bicycle, with just $10. Born October 23, 1918, in Wisconsin Rapids, Daly had just graduated from Lincoln High when he and his older sister "Mel" (Mary Ellen) pedaled for Iowa City, Iowa, some 260 miles away.

The two had lost their father, Percifer, owner and manager of Daly Ice & Coal Co, in a 1935 car crash, and their goal was to catch up with their mother, Dorothy, and new stepfather, Ray Mullen, who were moving to Iowa by car.

"After we were all packed in with brother David, sister Cynthia, and grandma, it just didn't look like there would be room in the car for Jim and me. So, we volunteered to bike to Iowa City instead, and our mom let us do it," Mel Daly said in a 2002 interview.

"We were riding those old bikes, and we had to really pump the pedals. But it was fun, an adventure, to us," she recalls. "When we got tired, we'd just stop and rest in some field. Because we didn't have a lot of money, we stayed at boarding houses" — raising the occasional eyebrow as a young man and woman of unknown marital status traveling together.

The pair had $10 between them, which Mel kept tucked in a shirt pocket. After one stop, she noticed the money was gone and the siblings had to retrace their route to find the bills, which were lying in a field where they'd rested.

The best-friend brother and sister team reached their destination after six days and soon both enrolled in college. Mel became the first woman drum major in the Big Ten at the University of Iowa while Jim pursued studies at Cornell College in Mount Vernon, Iowa, graduating from there in 1940. Years later, the college would grant Daly an honorary doctorate in fine arts.

Mel Daly says that it was their upbringing at their Third Street home in Wisconsin Rapids that gave her brother the determination, work ethic, and skills needed to catch up to his dreams.

"We were very lucky to have good parents and grow up where we did. Wisconsin Rapids was really a great place to grow up; we had so many opportunities to play," she says. "We played outside all the time, skiing, skating, swimming you name it. I even learned how to fence. We walked miles in the pine woods through the years."

The siblings were artistic from the start.

In high school, Jim participated in plays and oratorical contests from sophomore through senior year and was the junior prom chairman.

He and Mel also played in the band all through high school, Jim on oboe and Mel on flute. They were both talented enough to make the 1933 all-Wisconsin band traveling to the World's Fair that year. However, after their arrival in Madison for the band's formation, Jim Daly's appendix ruptured. Though he survived the life-threatening event, Daly was so heartbroken about missing out on the great adventure that his mother took him to the fair herself.

Their mother enjoyed the theater, and encouraged her children to participate in the arts, attend circuses when they came to town, and watch Saturday movies at the Grand Theater in Wisconsin Rapids.

"We liked to do shows in the back yard," Daly recalls. "For one, *The Forty Thieves*, we slid down the coal chute into our basement, put on different clothes and came back up as a new thief."

It was Mel who led her brother, younger by 15 months, into acting, she insists. "I actually acted more in high school than Jimmy did. He caught the bug from me I guess, and we both wanted to be actors when we grew up."

Jim Daly wrote scenes for his sister to perform after the *Daily Tribune* hired her to pitch their children's feature by putting on performances around town. "It was comedy and funny stuff. The girls were always tied to the railroad tracks and the hero would run in screaming and hollering," Mel recalled in a 1988 history book *River City Memoirs* by Dave Engel.

The brother and sister acting team also spent a lot of time acting up. Mel said they were known to cut school in favor of Ma Freschette's candy store.

Perhaps their most infamous escapade happened one Halloween when the two, along with cousin John Roberts, took a man-size dummy door-to-door to scare the neighbors. "Then we'd walk in front of a car and drop the dummy casually and, of course, the brakes would screech," she told Engel.

The night ended with two of the three dummy-toting pranksters, Jim and John, in the local jail to "think about what they'd done." They'd been arrested after carrying the prank too far and throwing the dummy off the Woolworth building on Grand Avenue as Mel stood below feigning a horrified scream.

"I felt so guilty that they were down at the jail that I turned myself in," she told Engel.

The two hoped to be professional actors together some day. It was Mel who made it to Hollywood first, though it would be Jim who would make it in show business.

Tired of an unchallenging academic life, the one-time drum major worked as a radio announcer in Minnesota before heading to California and an advertising and public relations job at the *Los Angeles Times*. Mel Daly married a P-38 fighter pilot in 1942 and though they were divorced in 1947, the union brought Daly into military service — a job she stayed in until retiring as a lieutenant colonel in the Air Force in 1968.

Meanwhile, her little brother Jimmy was doing his own part to serve his country.

"Jimmy had been drafted into the Army and volunteered for the Army Air Corps right out of college in Mount Vernon, Iowa. This was about two years before World War II. He said he'd served in the 'broomstick army' because there weren't even enough rifles to go around and they had to practice drills with broomsticks!"

After his discharge, Jim married Hope Newell and followed his acting ambitions. He was performing with fellow Wisconsinite Alfred Lunt and his wife Lynn Fontanne in *There Should Be No Night* when the Japanese bombed Pearl Harbor on December 7, 1941. "Jimmy went right down and enlisted in the U.S. Navy, chasing submarines on a destroyer, the U.S.S.

Mel and Jim Daly on a bicycle. Photo courtesy of the South Wood County Historical Society.

Winslow."

While he chased Nazi subs and ducked Japanese zeros, the rest of Daly's family also was serving the war effort. In addition to Mel's service in the Army air corps, sister Cynthia enlisted in the WAVES, brother David went into the Army, and their mom joined the O.S.S. (the predecessor of the Central Intelligence Agency).

"Mom didn't retire from the CIA until she was 70," Mel Daly notes.

After his second discharge, in 1945, Jim Daly returned for a time to Wisconsin, studying and teaching at the University of Wisconsin and working at a Madison packing company.

On February 21, 1946, the Dalys welcomed the second of four children, a daughter Ellen Tyne Daly. Their family also included eldest daughter Peggy and siblings Mary Glynn and future movie and TV star Timothy (who costarred with Wisconsinite Tony Shalhoub on the hit TV show *Wings*).

Soon after the family moved to New York, Jim Daly landed a role as an understudy in *Born Yesterday* and found continual work on and off Broadway stages for the next thirty years, acting in such Broadway classics as *Who's Afraid of Virginia Woolf*, *The Glass Menagerie* and *Billy Budd*.

Daly also was a Hollywood movie star. He broke into movies in an uncredited role as an intern in the 1950 movie, *The Sleeping City*, before landing bigger roles in such films as *The Court Martial of Billy Mitchell* (1955), *The Young Stranger* (1957), *Wernher von Braun* (1959), *Planet of the Apes* (1968), and *The Five Man Army* (1969).

Daly is also remembered for his work as the famous Camel cigarettes spokesperson who said, "I'd walk a mile for a Camel."

In a 1997 interview with Frank Rizzo of *The Los Angeles Times*, Tyne Daly said she "got the riot act" when she once told her dad she thought he was selling cigarettes so he'd have enough money to maintain control over what roles were handed his way.

"You're selling Camels so you can pick and choose wonderful scripts when they come in so you won't have to do the crappy ones," Tyne recalled telling her father when she was about 15. He replied "'You silly, patronizing piece of... How many great scripts do you think are lying around the house?'"

In other words, actors like her father and herself, she told the *Times*, seldom have control over what they are offered. "If you have to put shoes on the children's feet, you go and do *Conan the Librarian*," she said.

In a March 1970 interview with *TV Guide* writer Carolyn See, "Nothing Personal," Jim Daly admitted that he did the cigarette ads not so he could "pick and choose parts" but so that he could afford to work on stage. "(Camel) was very good to me. It was the one way I could work in the theater and be rich at the same time."

A Midwest work ethic and love for acting, especially stage acting, pushed Jim Daly to take the roles that came his way and keep working in a cutthroat business.

The hard work paid off, and Daly became a well-known actor in American households, gaining his greatest fame from roles he played on television from the mid-1950s to mid-1970s.

In all, Daly had more than six hundred roles on TV including as Michael Powers (1953-54) in the TV series *Foreign Intrigue* and as the lead, Dr. Paul Lochner, in the long-running TV drama *Medical Center* from 1969 to 1976. He won an Emmy in 1966 for his television performance of Dr. O'Meara in *Eagle in a Cage*.

As his Hollywood star glowed brighter and brighter, Daly got quieter and quieter about his personal life. He generally refused any interviews at his house and, when he divorced Hope after twenty years of marriage, Daly's only comment to reporters, as noted in See's article, was "a marriage of many years broke up. That's all."

Daly explained to See that his personal life was no one's business because "personal lives are pretty much the same; everyone has one. Because they're often dull. Because ... everyone knows too much of that sort of thing about each other, but maybe what they know is the least important part."

Yet, Daly's personal life, especially his four children, meant the most to the actor. He was proud of his sister Mel's lieutenant colonel rank, as well as his mother's work in the CIA, his brother's work as an FBI agent and his sister Cynthia's accomplishments as a speech pathologist, and mentioned it often in interviews.

And he was loyal to his Midwest roots, returning occasionally to Wisconsin. In 1958, Daly came to the University of Wisconsin in Madison to speak about "actors, authors and their proponents" at a seminar sponsored by the UW's speech and education departments. In addition to his presentation, Daly, who was a Civil War buff, provided a kinescope presentation of his newest work in *Lee at Gettysburg*.

Daly also returned to Wisconsin Rapids incognito at least once, reports Mel Daly. "He took his son Tim back with him to show him his old stomping grounds and Tim got a big kick out of it.

They saw that the old high school had been tore down and saw a duplicate of Grandfather Daly's logging raft, which Jim wanted to buy but they wouldn't sell."

Much of the actor's free time was spent in his New York State home, where family often visited.

"They had a beautiful home there and, when I wasn't stationed somewhere, having moved thirty times in thirty-three years, I was playing with the kids, dancing with them as babies to the Victrola, and spending time with Jimmy. We may have fought like the devil when we were kids, but we were very close," Mel Daly recalls.

Mel Daly lost her best friend and the world lost one if its fine actors abruptly in 1978. At age 59, Daly suffered a fatal heart attack July 3 in Nyack, N.Y., while on his way to star with son Timothy in a Connecticut production of *Equus*.

Two of the Wisconsin actor's children, Ellen Tyne Daly and Timothy Daly, both have achieved star status, and Tyne Daly's daughter Kathryne Dora Brown also shows promise in following in her famous family footsteps as a regular on the TV show *Promised Land*.

Like her movie and TV star father, Tyne Daly also has Wisconsin roots. She was born in Madison on February 21, 1964, while her father was teaching at the University of Wisconsin.

The actress didn't stay long in Wisconsin, however. By the time her brother Tim was born, the family was living in New York where the four Daly children grew up.

Tyne Daly attended the American Academy of Dramatic Arts in New York and began her acting career on stage and television in the late 1960s, when she moved to Los Angeles.

The actress' first film role was as Hilary in 1969's *John and Mary*, and she followed with roles in such films as *Angel Unchained* (1970) and *Play It As It Lays* (1972).

In between, Daly also appeared on several TV shows, including with her father on *Medical Center* and in such shows as *Ironside*, *Barnaby Jones* and *Quincy*. She also appeared on *The Rookies*, which starred her husband, George Stanford, whom she married in 1966. The interracial couple had three daughters, Kathryne, Alisabeth and Alyxandra before they divorced in the early 1990s. Soon after her divorce, on February 14, 1991, Daly pleaded no contest to driving under the influence, paid a fine of $927.50 and participated in a 90-day alcohol education program.

Daly continued to gain supporting roles in Hollywood movies in the 1970s. Most significantly, she was cast as police officer Kate

Moore in 1976's *The Enforcer* and as a CIA agent, like her real-life grandmother, in 1977's *Telefon*.

Having played two law enforcement characters back to back, Daly was reluctant at first glance to take on the part of female cop Mary Beth Lacy in a TV pilot called *Cagney & Lacy*. Though the show was cancelled in 1983, a letter campaign by viewers brought it back for many more years and several TV movies based on the show in the mid-1990s. Daly's performance as Lacy won the actress four Emmys. She won a fifth Emmy in a supporting role on the TV series *Christy* (1994).

Daly's accolades weren't limited to Emmys, however. The talented actress continued to earn praise on stage as well, and won a Tony in 1990 for her portrayal of Mama Rose in *Gypsy*.

That same year, Daly guest starred on her brother Tim's hit TV show *Wings*.

The actress continues to star in TV movies and shows, appearing on *The Nanny* (1993) and *Veronica's Closet* (1997), and lent her voice in 1994 to the character of Dr. Tennelli on the educational cartoon *The Magic School Bus*.

She also starred in many made-for-TV movies and mini series, including: several *Cagney & Lacy* TV movies and *Columbo* murder mystery specials in the 1990s as well as in TV movies *Bye Bye Birdie* (1995), *The Perfect Mother* (1997), and *The Wedding Dress* (2001).

Today's TV audiences surely recognize the actress as social worker and mother/grandmother Maxine Gray on the hit series *Judging Amy*, which debuted in 1999.

In a May 2000, *TV Guide* article, the "take-me-as-I-am" actress and outspoken feminist told Michael Logan that she likes playing a blunt, older lady on TV.

"I'm interested in playing old ladies because I am becoming one," she said. "To display my actual face, my actual belly, my real legs, my real hair in television is doing some kind of service in a world where women are constantly being told there's something wrong with us."

Daly added that she always works hard to give an audience as great a performance as she can. "I was raised to be in service to something larger than myself," she noted. "A lot of actors concentrate on what they will get out of the profession, rather than what they can offer it."

As for other details about her upbringing, the Los Angeles actress remains, like her father, largely guarded about personal details, though she answers questions with a sometimes biting but often gracious sense of humor.

For example, when Kevin D. Thompson of Fox News Service asked the actress about her brother Tim's starring role in the then upcoming (but ultimately short-lived) TV show *The Fugitive*, Daly said in the December 5, 2000, *Spokesman Review*, "There are posters of Tim everywhere. I asked my mom, aren't you proud of your son? He's wanted all over the country!"

Noting that more and more people are recognizing that the two stars are related, Daly added that she was waiting for some producer to propose a cross-over show between the two series. "Yeah, we are waiting for a headline to read the 'Daly Double,'" she quipped.

ON SCREEN

Catch TV star Jim Daly's movie performances in the following pictures:

Roots: The Next Generations (1979) (TV Mini Series)
The Storyteller (1977) (TV)
Wild in the Sky (1972)
The Resurrection of Zachary Wheeler (1971)
Medical Center (1969) (TV Series)
The Big Bounce (1969)
U.M.C. (1969) (TV)
The Five Man Army (1969)
Rose rosse per il fuehrer (1968)
Treasure of San Bosco Reef (1968)
Planet of the Apes (1968)
An Enemy of the People (1966) (TV)
Eagle in a Cage (1965) (TV)
Give Us Barabbas (1961) (TV)
Wernher von Braun (1959)
The Young Stranger (1957)
To Tell the Truth (1956) (TV Series)
The Court-Martial of Billy Mitchell (1955)
Lady in the Dark (1954) (TV)
Foreign Intrigue (1951)
The Sleeping City (1950) (uncredited)

Fans can view Tyne Daly in the following Hollywood and TV movies:

The Wedding Dress (2001) (TV)
A Piece of Eden (2000)
The Simian Line (2000)
Absence of the Good (1999) (TV)
Intimate Portrait: Michele Lee (1999) (TV)
Execution of Justice (1999) (TV)
Judging Amy (1999) TV Series
Three Secrets (1999) (TV)
Autumn Heart (1999)
Vig (1998) (Video)
The Perfect Mother (1997) (TV)
Tricks (1997) (TV)
The Lay of the Land (1997)
Cagney & Lacey: The View Through the Glass Ceiling (1995) (TV)
Cagney & Lacey: Together Again (1995) (TV)
Cagney & Lacey: True Convictions (1995) (TV)
Bye Bye Birdie (1995) (TV)
Cagney & Lacey: The Return (1994) (TV)
Columbo: Undercover (1994) (TV)
Christy (1994) TV Series
Christy (1994) (TV)
The Forget-Me-Not Murders (1994) (TV)

Scattered Dreams (1993) (TV)
On the Town (1992) (TV)
Columbo: A Bird in the Hand (1992) (TV)
Face of a Stranger (1991) (TV)
The Last to Go (1991) (TV)
Stuck with Each Other (1989) (TV)
Kids Like These (1987) (TV)
Intimate Strangers (1986) (TV)
The Aviator (1985)
Destination Nicaragua (1985)
Movers and Shakers (1985)
Your Place... or Mine (1983) (TV)
Cagney & Lacey (1982) TV Series
Zoot Suit (1981)
Cagney & Lacey (1981) (TV)
A Matter of Life and Death (1981) (TV)
The Women's Room (1980) (TV)
Better Late Than Never (1979) (TV)
Telefon (1977)
Speedtrap (1977)
Intimate Strangers (1977) (TV)
The Enforcer (1976)
The Entertainer (1976) (TV)
The Law (1975) TV Mini Series
Larry (1974) (TV)
The Adulteress (1973)
The Man Who Could Talk to Kids (1973) (TV)
Play It As It Lays (1972)
Heat of Anger (1971) (TV)
A Howling in the Woods (1971) (TV)
Angel Unchained (1970)
In Search of America (1970) (TV)
John and Mary (1969)

STANLEY & JOHN BLYSTONE

Movies were a family affair for the Blystone clan of Northern Wisconsin, back in the early days of silent and talking movies.

Three brothers — Stanley, John and Jasper — traveled west to Hollywood in the 1920s to help create motion picture classics with silent film legends Tom Mix and Buster Keaton, as well as comedians Laurel and Hardy and the Three Stooges, and many others. Among them, the brothers took part in more than 400 films, though few film biographers, nor even their hometown historical societies and libraries, have recorded much at all about the Blystones.

John G. Blystone, born December 2, 1892 in Rice Lake, Wisconsin, likely brought his brothers into the movie trade when he tried his hand at acting in silent films after graduating from the University of Wisconsin in Madison in 1914.

The oldest brother, also known as J.G. or Jack Blystone, did land a few small movie roles in such 1914 productions as *A Wife on a Wager*, *Passing of the Beast*, *Cupid Incognito*, and *The Wheel of Life*.

However, the fledgling Wisconsin performer found he had more interest and talents on the other side of the camera. In 1916, he began working in production crews, mostly as a property man and film supervisor on such films as *Murder by Mistake* (1916), *Rough Stuff* (1917), and *Beach Nuts* (1917).

By 1918, John Blystone was producing and, by 1923, directing films. Among his early directorial efforts were Buster Keaton's *Balloonatics* and *Our Hospitality* in 1923. That same decade, he also directed some twenty films, including *Ladies to Board* (1924), *Hard Boiled* (1926), *Sharp Shooters* (1928), and *Thru Different Eyes* (1929), and was soon under contract with Fox Studios.

Blystone quickly developed a reputation as the kind of director who made stars look good without stepping on their toes. According to *All Movie Guide* biographer Hal Erickson, John

Blystone's reputation caught the attention of such stars as Will Rogers, his cowboy star and friend Tom Mix and comedians Laurel and Hardy. In 1938, the Wisconsin movie maker was hired to direct the Laurel and Hardy films *Swiss Miss* and *Block-Heads*, "with the understanding that Blystone would merely yell 'action' and 'cut' and leave the comedians to their own devices in between," Erickson said.

The Laurel and Hardy films were the popular director's last. Blystone died of a heart attack Aug. 6, 1938, at age 45.

Blystone's younger brother William Stanley lasted longer in films. Though Stanley very rarely worked under his brother's direction on screen, it was the older Blystone who introduced Stanley to Hollywood when his brother joined him there in the early 1920s. Over the years several biographers have confused the two, crediting Stanley with some of John's early work.

Incidentally, John and Stanley also got their younger brother Jasper (born October 30, 1899) into the movie industry. Jasper worked for decades as a second unit (assistant) director at Fox Studios and eventually directed *The Reluctant Dragon: Behind the Scenes at Walt Disney Studio* in 1941. He died in 1965.

The most prolific film star among the brothers — and one of the busiest film actors of any era — William Stanley Blystone, was born August 1, 1894, in Eau Claire, Wisconsin, while the family was reportedly living there for a short time before returning to Rice Lake.

By 1924, movie credits were beginning to list the 30-year-old Stanley Blystone (or William Blystone or William Stanley as he was sometimes called) as a supporting cast member.

His first film appearances were in small parts and bit roles in such films as 1924's *Excitement* (Stanley's first film), 1927's *The Jolly Jitter* and 1928's *The Circus*. Most notably, he appeared as the shady ringmaster with cowboy Tom Mix in *The Circus Ace* in 1927.

Though rarely if ever a leading man, Stanley Blystone carved out a solid career for himself as a freelance actor playing shady characters, authoritarian bosses, or just outright villains for film studios like RKO and Columbia.

By the 1930s, the husky actor found recurring work as villains or supporting characters in several of the Three Stooges' movies and shorts, playing a cement layer in *Three Little Beers*, mean-spirited Sgt. McGillicuddy in *Half Shot Shooters* (1936), a ventriloquist in *Even as I.O.U.* (1942), a circus owner in *Three Little Twirps*

(1943), and a bad guy in *Out West* (1947).

He played Paulette Goddard's father Sheriff Couler in Charlie Chaplin's *Modern Times* in 1936 and appeared in two Charlie Chan movies in 1937, *Charlie Chan at the Opera* and *Charlie Chan at the Olympics*.

Stanley Blystone also had an uncredited role with Laurel and Hardy in one of his brother John's final films, *Swiss Miss*, in 1938. The actor had previously worked with the comedy duo on such films as *The Laurel-Hardy Murder Case* (1930), where Blystone played the detective.

In the 1940s and '50s, Blystone was a recognizable bad guy in many Hollywood westerns, but as his career tapered off a bit, Blystone also filled uncredited and smaller roles as bartenders, store clerks, cops, townspeople and the like in dozens of films, such as: *Square Dance Katy* (1950), *Fly-By-Night* (1942), *Vacation in Reno* (1946), *The Spider Returns* (1941), *Policeman My Favorite Spy* (1951), and *Pardners* (1956). He also shared the screen with other Wisconsin actors, playing the detective in Carole Landis's *I Wake Up Screaming* (1941) and appearing with Pat O'Brien in *Fighting Father Dunne* (1948).

The supporting actor's final film appearance was much like his first, an uncredited role as Longhorn Pete in 1960's *Stop! Look! and Laugh!*

As his movie career wound down, Blystone was working to kick start a career in television and appeared in several episodes of *The Lone Ranger* from 1949 to 1951 as well as on TV shows like *The Cisco Kid* (1950), *Stories of the Century* (1954), and *The Adventures of Champion* (1955).

Stanley Blystone died July 16, 1956, of a heart attack suffered on his way to a TV studio.

Though he had no top film or leading man roles to his credit, the Northern Wisconsin actor left more than just supporting roles and bit parts to remember him by.

Stanley Blystone lives on in more than 350 Hollywood films — nearly *three times* the movie appearances of any other Wisconsin actor.

ON SCREEN

Spot supporting actor and Northern Wisconsin native Stanley Blystone in the casts of the following 367 movies:

Stop! Look! and Laugh! (1960) (uncredited)
Ghost of Zorro (1959)
Pardners (1956)
You're Never Too Young (1955) (uncredited)
A Lawless Street (1955) (uncredited)
Nobody's Home (1955)
Living It Up (1954) (uncredited)
Destry (1954) (uncredited)
Pals and Gals (1954) (uncredited)
Calamity Jane (1953) (uncredited)
Abbott and Costello Go to Mars (1953) (uncredited)
The Great Sioux Uprising (1953) (uncredited)
A Perilous Journey (1953) (uncredited)
Jack McCall Desperado (1953) (uncredited)
The Great Adventures of Captain Kidd (1953) (uncredited)
Carson City (1952) (uncredited)
The Duel at Silver Creek (1952) (uncredited)
The Lawless Breed (1952) (uncredited)
Road Agent (1952)
Rancho Notorious (1952) (uncredited)
Colorado Sundown (1952) (uncredited)
A Missed Fortune (1952) (uncredited)
Santa Fe (1951) (uncredited)
My Favorite Spy (1951) (uncredited)
Overland Telegraph (1951)
Flight to Mars (1951)
Honeychile (1951)
Yellow Fin (1951) (uncredited)
Hot Lead (1951) (uncredited)
Silver Canyon (1951)
Gunplay (1951) (uncredited)
Wedding Yells (1951)
Mrs. O'Malley and Mr. Malone (1950) (uncredited)
Trail of Robin Hood (1950) (uncredited)
Let's Dance (1950) (uncredited)
Slap Happy Sleuths (1950)
Sunset in the West (1950) (uncredited)
Triple Trouble (1950) (uncredited)
Desperadoes of the West (1950)
County Fair (1950)
Atom Man Vs. Superman (1950) (uncredited)
House About It (1950)
Covered Wagon Raid (1950) (uncredited)
Please Believe Me (1950) (uncredited)
Six Gun Mesa (1950)
Kill the Umpire (1950) (uncredited)
Square Dance Katy (1950)
Singing Guns (1950) (uncredited)
The Nevadan (1950) (uncredited)
Range Land (1949)
Powder River Rustlers (1949)
Let Down Your Aerial (1949)
Wha' Happen? (1949)
Mary Ryan, Detective (1949)
Samson and Delilah (1949) (uncredited)
Deputy Marshal (1949)
Navajo Trail Raiders (1949) (uncredited)
Calamity Jane and Sam Bass (1949) (uncredited)
Ghost of Zorro (1949) (uncredited)
Rustlers (1949)
Ride, Ryder, Ride! (1949)
Rose of the Yukon (1949) (uncredited)
The Paleface (1948) (uncredited)
Loaded Pistols (1948) (uncredited)
Station West (1948) (uncredited)
El Dorado Pass (1948)
The Strange Mrs. Crane (1948)
Eyes of Texas (1948)
I, Jane Doe (1948) (uncredited)
I Wouldn't Be in Your Shoes (1948)
Fighting Father Dunne (1948) (uncredited)

Famous Wisconsin Film Stars

Smart Woman (1948) (uncredited)
Tex Granger (1948) (uncredited)
Big City (1948) (uncredited)
The Bride Goes Wild (1948) (uncredited)
Pardon My Clutch (1948)
Shivering Sherlocks (1948) (uncredited)
Her Husband's Affairs (1947) (uncredited)
Jack Armstrong (1947) (uncredited)
Road to Rio (1947) (uncredited)
Brick Bradford (1947)
Under Colorado Skies (1947)
Key Witness (1947) (uncredited)
Joe Palooka in the Knockout (1947) (uncredited)
The Sea Hound (1947)
The Perils of Pauline (1947) (uncredited)
Killer at Large (1947)
Too Many Winners (1947)
That's My Gal (1947) (uncredited)
Out West (1947) (uncredited)
Hit Parade of 1947 (1947) (uncredited)
Shoot to Kill (1947)
Fright Night (1947) (uncredited)
Backlash (1947) (uncredited)
Suddenly, It's Spring (1947) (uncredited)
The Thirteenth Hour (1947) (uncredited)
Criminal Court (1946) (uncredited)
The Hoodlum Saint (1946) (uncredited)
The Scarlet Horseman (1946)
That Brennan Girl (1946) (uncredited)
San Quentin (1946) (uncredited)
Vacation in Reno (1946) (uncredited)
Magnificent Doll (1946) (uncredited)
King of the Forest Rangers (1946)
Moon Over Montana (1946)
Six Gun Man (1946)
The Navajo Kid (1945)
Roger Touhy, Gangster (1944) (uncredited)
Action in the North Atlantic (1943) (uncredited)
Adventures of Smilin' Jack (1943)
City Without Men (1943) (uncredited)
A Gem of a Jam (1943) (uncredited)
Phantom of the Opera (1943) (uncredited)
Three Little Twirps (1943)
Back From the Front (1943) (uncredited)
I Spied for You (1943)
Spook Louder (1943)
A Blitz on the Fritz (1943)
His Wedding Scare (1943)
Born to Sing (1942) (uncredited)
Fly-By-Night (1942) (uncredited)
Lady Bodyguard (1942) (uncredited)
My Favorite Spy (1942) (uncredited)
Ice-Capades Revue (1942) (uncredited)
Piano Mooner (1942)
Even as I.O.U (1942)
Carry Harry (1942) (Uncredited)
The Old Homestead (1942) (uncredited)
Timber (1942) (uncredited)
Powder Town (1942) (uncredited)
In Old California (1942) (uncredited)
Gang Busters (1942)
Jesse James, Jr. (1942)
True to the Army (1942) (uncredited)
Mr. Wise Guy (1942) (uncredited)
Roxie Hart (1942) (uncredited)
Pardon My Stripes (1942) (uncredited)
Arizona Terrors (1942) (uncredited)
Appointment for Love (1941) (uncredited)
I Wake Up Screaming (1941) (uncredited)
Pacific Blackout (1941)
Tall, Dark and Handsome (1941)
West of Cimarron (1941) (uncredited)
Holt of the Secret Service (1941)
Sea Raiders (1941)
King of the Texas Rangers (1941)
Sunset in Wyoming (1941)
The Spider Returns (1941) (uncredited)
Country Fair (1941) (uncredited)
Lady from Louisiana (1941)

Mutiny in the Arctic (1941)
Sky Raiders (1941) (uncredited)
Back in the Saddle (1941) (uncredited)
Buck Privates (1941) (uncredited)
Remedy for Riches (1940) (uncredited)
Little Men (1940) (uncredited)
Pony Post (1940)
Captain Caution (1940) (uncredited)
Charlie Chan at the Wax Museum (1940) (uncredited)
Dance, Girl, Dance (1940) (uncredited)
Stranger on the Third Floor (1940) (uncredited)
The Tulsa Kid (1940)
Those Were the Days (1940) (uncredited)
Pop Always Pays (1940) (uncredited)
Grandpa Goes to Town (1940) (uncredited)
Johnny Apollo (1940) (uncredited)
Ma, He's Making Eyes at Me (1940) (uncredited)
Framed (1940) (uncredited)
A Chump at Oxford (1940) (uncredited)
Young Tom Edison (1940) (uncredited)
The Invisible Man Returns (1940) (uncredited)
Emergency Squad (1940) (uncredited)
Mandrake the Magician (1939) (uncredited)
The Big Guy (1939) (uncredited)
Crashing Thru (1939)
Tower of London (1939) (uncredited)
Mr. Moto Takes a Vacation (1939) (uncredited)
Allegheny Uprising (1939) (uncredited)
Torture Ship (1939)
The Day the Bookies Wept (1939) (uncredited)
Full Confession (1939) (uncredited)
When Tomorrow Comes (1939) (uncredited)
Way Down South (1939) (uncredited)
They Shall Have Music (1939) (uncredited)
Charlie Chan in Reno (1939)
Three Texas Steers (1939)
Man of Conquest (1939) (uncredited)
The Rookie Cop (1939) (uncredited)
They Made Her a Spy (1939) (uncredited)
Twelve Crowded Hours (1939) (uncredited)
The Lone Ranger Rides Again (1939)
Flying G-Men (1939) (uncredited)
Drifting Westward (1939)
Trigger Pals (1939)
Disbarred (1939) (uncredited)
Red River Range (1938)
California Frontier (1938)
Cipher Bureau (1938)
Touchdown, Army (1938) (uncredited)
King of Alcatraz (1938) (uncredited)
Room Service (1938) (uncredited)
Fugitives for a Night (1938) (uncredited)
The Stranger From Arizona (1938)
Valley of the Giants (1938) (uncredited)
The Affairs of Annabel (1938)
Crime Ring (1938) (uncredited)
Saint in New York (1938) (uncredited)
The Devil's Party (1938) (uncredited)
Blind Alibi (1938) (uncredited)
Swiss Miss (1938) (uncredited)
Flat Foot Stooges (1938) (uncredited)
Vivacious Lady (1938) (scenes deleted)
Dangerous to Know (1938) (uncredited)
Maid's Night Out (1938) (uncredited)
Bringing Up Baby (1938) (uncredited)
Spirit of Youth (1938) (uncredited)
The Jury's Secret (1938) (uncredited)
The Buccaneer (1938) (uncredited)
Music for Madame (1937)
Radio Patrol (1937)
Tim Tyler's Luck (1937)
Headin' East (1937)
High Flyers (1937)
Edgar & Goliath (1937)

Famous Wisconsin Film Stars

Second Honeymoon (1937) (uncredited)
Stand-In (1937) (uncredited)
Boots and Saddles (1937)
The Life of Emile Zola (1937) (uncredited)
Bury the Hatchet (1937)
Windjammer (1937)
The Toast of New York (1937) (uncredited)
Galloping Dynamite (1937)
Goofs and Saddles (1937) (uncredited)
Love in a Bungalow (1937)
Armored Car (1937)
Charlie Chan at the Olympics (1937) (uncredited)
King of Gamblers (1937) (uncredited)
New News (1937)
Bars and Stripes (1937) (uncredited)
Two Wise Maids (1937)
You Only Live Once (1937) (uncredited)
Charlie Chan at the Opera (1937) (uncredited)
Ace Drummond (1936)
Here Comes Trouble (1936)
Little Miss Nobody (1936) (uncredited)
Pennies from Heaven (1936)
She's Dangerous (1936) (uncredited)
Smartest Girl in Town (1936) (uncredited)
Come and Get It (1936) (uncredited)
End of the Trail (1936) (uncredited)
The Three Mesquiteers (1936) (uncredited)
The Vigilantes Are Coming (1936) (uncredited)
False Alarms (1936)
Human Cargo (1936) (uncredited)
The Riding Avenger (1936)
The Last Outlaw (1936) (uncredited)
Ex-Mrs. Bradford (1936) (uncredited)
Half-Shot Shooters (1936)
The Little Red Schoolhouse (1936) (uncredited)
The Prisoner of Shark Island (1936) (uncredited)
Hell-Ship Morgan (1936) (uncredited)
Modern Times (1936)
Strike Me Pink (1936)
Captain Hits the Ceiling (1935)
The Farmer Takes a Wife (1935) (uncredited)
Smart Girl (1935) (uncredited)
Another Face (1935) (uncredited)
Show Them No Mercy! (1935) (uncredited)
Gallant Defender (1935) (uncredited)
Three Little Beers (1935) (uncredited)
The Fighting Marines (1935)
A Night at the Opera (1935) (uncredited)
The Three Musketeers (1935) (uncredited)
Bad Boy (1935) (uncredited)
His Family Tree (1935) (uncredited)
The Public Menace (1935) (uncredited)
Page Miss Glory (1935) (uncredited)
Trail's End (1935)
Rainbow's End (1935)
Ginger (1935) (uncredited)
The Roaring West (1935) (uncredited)
Ladies Crave Excitement (1935) (uncredited)
Saddle Aces (1935)
Code of the Mounted (1935)
Justice of the Range (1935) (uncredited)
Fighting Pioneers (1935)
Men of the Hour (1935)
'G' Men (1935) (uncredited)
Vagabond Lady (1935) (uncredited)
Les Misérables (1935) (uncredited)
I'll Love You Always (1935)
The Revenge Rider (1935) (uncredited)
In Spite of Danger (1935) (uncredited)
The Phantom Empire (1935)
The Whole Town's Talking (1935) (uncredited)
Restless Knights (1935) (uncredited)
Carnival (1935) (uncredited)
When a Man's a Man (1935) (uncredited)
Mystery Man (1935) (uncredited)

Annie Oakley (1935) (uncredited)
The Ivory-Handled Gun (1935)
Burn 'Em Up Barnes (1934)
Hell in the Heavens (1934) (uncredited)
Such Women Are Dangerous (1934) (uncredited)
The Chases of Pimple Street (1934) (scenes deleted)
Broadway Bill (1934) (uncredited)
In Old Santa Fe (1934) (uncredited)
We Live Again (1934) (uncredited)
The Lemon Drop Kid (1934) (uncredited)
The Case of the Howling Dog (1934) (uncredited)
The Party's Over (1934) (uncredited)
Bachelor Bait (1934) (uncredited)
The Hell Cat (1934) (uncredited)
Murder at the Vanities (1934) (uncredited)
Manhattan Melodrama (1934) (uncredited)
We're Not Dressing (1934) (uncredited)
Hips, Hips, Hooray! (1934) (uncredited)
Moulin Rouge (1934) (uncredited)
Infernal Machine (1933) (uncredited)
The Wolf Dog (1933)
Sons of the Desert (1933) (uncredited)
Roman Scandals (1933) (uncredited)
Dancing Lady (1933) (uncredited)
Rhapsody in Brew (1933)
Crossfire (1933)
Before Dawn (1933) (uncredited)
The Fighting Parson (1933)
Picture Snatcher (1933)
Strange People (1933)
The Nuisance (1933) (uncredited)
Phantom Thunderbolt (1933) (uncredited)
Man of Action (1933)
The Trial of Vivienne Ware (1932) (uncredited)
Wild Girl (1932) (uncredited)
The Golden West (1932) (uncredited)
Lucky Larrigan (1932)
Sunkissed Sweeties (1932)
Hold 'Em Jail (1932)
Miss Pinkerton (1932) (uncredited)
Honor of the Mounted (1932)
Doctor's Orders (1932)
Galloping Thru (1931)
Sundown Trail (1931)
The Man from Death Valley (1931)
Dancing Dynamite (1931)
Men On Call (1930) (uncredited)
Noche de duendes (1930)
The Laurel-Hardy Murder Case (1930)
The Fighting Legion (1930)
Young Eagles (1930)
Parade of the West (1930)
Waltzing Around (1929)
Thru Different Eyes (1929)
Synthetic Sin (1929)
Always a Gentleman (1928)
His Maiden Voyage (1928)
Ladies Preferred (1928)
Wildcat Valley (1928)
Four Sons (1928) (uncredited)
The Circus (1928) (uncredited)
Smith's Surprise (1927)
The Circus Ace (1927)
Cured in the Excitement (1927)
The Jolly Jilter (1927)
Under the Rouge (1925)
Darwin Was Right (1924)
Excitement (1924)

ON SCREEN

John Blystone directed more than 50 Hollywood movies in the 1920s and 30s. He is credited as a director of the following films (unless otherwise noted):
Block-Heads (1938)
Swiss Miss (1938)
Music for Madame (1937)
Woman Chases Man (1937)
23 1/2 Hours Leave (1937)
Gentle Julia (1936)

Famous Wisconsin Film Stars

Great Guy (1936)
Little Miss Nobody (1936)
Magnificent Brute (1936)
Bad Boy (1935)
The County Chairman (1935)
Hell in the Heavens (1934)
Change of Heart (1934)
Coming-Out Party (1934)
My Lips Betray (1933)
Shanghai Madness (1933)
Hot Pepper (1933)
Amateur Daddy (1932)
Too Busy to Work (1932)
The Painted Woman (1932)
She Wanted a Millionaire (1932)
Charlie Chan's Chance (1932)
Mr. Lemon of Orange (1931)
Young Sinners (1931)
The Big Party (1930)
Men On Call (1930)
Princess and the Plumber (1930) (uncredited)
Tol'able David (1930)
So This Is London (1930)
The Sky Hawk (1930)
Thru Different Eyes (1929) (producer)
Captain Lash (1929)
Mother Knows Best (1928)
Sharp Shooters (1928)
Pajamas (1927)
Slaves of Beauty (1927))
Ankles Preferred (1927)
Wings of the Storm (1926)
The Family Upstairs (1926)
Hard Boiled (1926)
My Own Pal (1926)
The Best Bad Man (1925)
The Everlasting Whisper (1925)
Dick Turpin (1925)
The Lucky Horseshoe (1925) (producer)
The Last Man on Earth (1924)
Teeth (1924)
Oh, You Tony! (1924)
Ladies to Board (1924)
Our Hospitality (1923)
Soft Boiled (1923)
A Friendly Husband (1923)
Hey, Doctor! (1918) (producer & actor)
Ambrose and His Widow (1918) (producer)
Ambrose, the Lion Hearted (1918) (producer)
Ambrose's Icy Love (1918) (producer)
Balloonatics (1917) (producer & director)
A Wife on a Wager (1914) (actor)
Passing of the Beast (1914) (actor)
Cupid Incognito (1914) (actor)
The Wheel of Life (1914) (actor)

GENA ROWLANDS

Though she played dysfunctional characters in her most famous movies, Gena Rowlands's own upbringing in the American heartland was happy and secure.

Born June 19, 1930 (or 1934 by some Hollywood records), in Cambria, Wisconsin, Virginia Cathryn "Gena" Rowlands spent her childhood being loved and pampered, she said in a December 8, 1996, interview with Andrew Billen of *The London Observer*. "I was a sickly little kid and everyone is nice to a sickly little kid. So, there was a lot of love around me ... and my parents were crazy about each other and had a long marriage."

The future actress added that she enjoyed the freedom and security of growing up in a small town like Cambria. "There was a lot of safety in small towns, so I grew up in a very permissive atmosphere of love," she explained.

The young girl showed artistic interests early, inspired no doubt by her mother Mary Ellen, a talented artist. She also developed an understanding of the world and the plight of people in it from her father E.M. Rowlands, a Welsh-speaking U.S. representative from Wisconsin.

While Rowlands was still in primary school — for some years at the Nakoma School in Madison — the political family moved first to Wauwatosa, Wisconsin, and then to Washington, D.C., where her father eventually worked as head of the U.S. Office of Price Administration. It was there that Rowlands graduated from high school and decided to return to her home state for college.

Rowlands started acting in school and community plays when she was 14 and won a scholarship to the Jarvis Repertory Theatre while in Washington, D. C.

The actress came back to her Midwest roots to further her education, however. She enrolled at the University of Wisconsin in Madison in 1947, where she continued to pursue acting and occasionally ventured north to see old family friends in Cambria.

By her junior year, the aspiring actress decided she wanted to be closer to Broadway. Rowlands left the UW and moved to New York City to attend the American Academy of Dramatic Arts.

It was on stage as an academy student in 1954 that she first caught the eye of actor John Cassavetes. The future movie director wasn't as interested, at first sight, in Rowlands' impressive acting skills as he was in her mesmerizing charm and beauty.

Rowlands related in the *The London Observer* interview, that the then Broadway assistant stage manager decided by intermission that he wanted to marry Rowlands. The two began a whirlwind courtship and married four months later. They eventually had three children — Nick (a film producer in his own right), and two daughters: professional singer Alexandra "Xan," and comedy writer Zoe.

Meanwhile, Rowlands was finding herself in brighter and brighter Broadway lights. One of the Cambria native's first professional New York roles was as an understudy in *The Seven Year Itch* on Broadway. She eventually took over the role, and her performance led to other Broadway opportunities, such as when she was cast with Edward G. Robinson in the 1956 production of *Middle of the Night*.

Later in the 1950s, Rowlands and Cassavetes decided to try their luck in movies. Rowlands first landed a role as Powell in the 1955 TV series *Top Secret* and got her first Hollywood film break when she appeared in 1958's *The High Cost of Living*.

After work in another TV series *Staccato*, which her husband directed in 1959, Rowlands caught Hollywood's attention for good when she appeared as Jerry Bondi with Kirk Douglas in *Lonely Are The Brave* in 1962.

By this time, Rowlands and her sometimes actor, mostly director husband were living in their first Pacific Palisades house with first child, Nick, born in 1959. In a September 13, 1959, *Wisconsin State Journal* article, Cassavetes said that he left the decorating of their new home up to his wife. "Gena's an excellent artist, so naturally she loves color. I told her to choose whatever shade she wanted for the carpeting. She sure did — it's red throughout!"

Not long after, in 1963, John Cassavetes was cast out of Hollywood directing circles after he punched producer Stanley Kramer for re-cutting his film, *A Child Is Waiting* — in which Cassavetes filmed actual retarded children instead of using actors and cast his wife as a star. Cassavetes was furious because, after he had finished with his own director cuts, Kramer had reportedly gone in and re-edited the film.

That argument was a turning point in the lives of Cassavetes and Rowlands, sparking their determination to find success in making independent films apart from the Hollywood crowd. While Rowlands remained at work in Hollywood movies and television, Cassavetes stayed home with the children and wrote screenplays for the films they later produced.

The couple often made their movies in and around their home, with Cassavetes directing and Rowlands costarring with talented actors and friends like Peter Falk, Seymour Cassel, and Ben Gazarra, and often casting family members like their children and Rowlands's mother in smaller parts.

Gena Rowlands in *A Woman Under the Influence*. Photo courtesy of the Wisconsin Center for Film and Theater Ressearch. Image No. WCFTR-3756.

The innovative and often gritty dramatic films Cassavetes produced — in a style similar to the French New Wave cinema releases of the time — earned him international respect as the "European American director." While the action and dialogue of the films seemed improvisational, they proved very powerful on screen.

Rowlands later said that though his movies appeared improvised, her husband and the actors were always working from a screenplay that Cassavetes had written. The improvisation came in the director's fondness for letting the action roll and his being comfortable with actors not always following the script.

"You never stopped a take, whatever happened. If you dropped something, you would just carry on," she noted in a March 2, 2001, interview in *The Guardian* newspaper in London. "It gave such a natural feeling to the film that people thought they were improvised."

The couple worked production schedules around, and right through, family life, Rowlands noted in a September 2, 1997, article in the *Milwaukee Journal Sentinel*, saying her children were raised among cameras and movie film.

"We made half our movies in our house. When (the kids) came out of their bedrooms with toothbrushes, they'd fall over a cable or the sound man would say, 'Everybody stop for room tone.' I think they thought everybody lived like that," the actress explained. She further noted that her husband and director "John would have a thing like a coat rack with strips of film hanging on it."

Their son Nick, who first appeared in a movie at age 11 when his dad bribed him with the promise of a new toy if he'd play with his old ones in a scene for *Husbands* in 1970, remembered the film especially well in a June 28, 1997, interview with Richard Williams in *The Guardian*.

"All the strips of film were hung in my room and (Dad) would get me to find bits for him. He'd say, 'Don't tell your mother I'm waking you up, but find me that piece of film where she holds her head in a certain way,'" the now Academy Award nominated movie director said of his childhood indoctrination into the movie business.

The son also remembered his mother's flair for fun and her interest "in everything," he detailed in a May 14, 2000, article he wrote for the *Los Angeles Times*.

"Mom was hip. God, she was beautiful. With her skinny little legs and her Ungaro outfits and the big Jackie O sunglasses. And the hair. Dad used to call her Golden Girl," Nick Cassavetes wrote.

"That's the way it was with Mom. You could do anything," he added. "You'd come home from school, she'd have a costume party prepared. Or a treasure hunt. Or she'd read to you from the encyclopedia. (She read Encyclopaedia Britannica from A to Z to her children). That's the thing I like about Mom. She's interested in absolutely everything."

Nick didn't see as much of his mom when she was acting away from home, a reality the family lived with to make ends meet and keep making the movies they wanted.

Rowlands and Cassavetes personally financed the ten independent pictures they made through movie and TV acting jobs, with occasional help from costars like Falk.

"When we ran out of money, which was all the time, we would stop and each take a movie," Rowlands told *The Guardian*. To that end, in the late 1960s, Rowlands played Adrienne Van Leyden on TV's *Peyton Place* and appeared on the *Nick Quarry* TV show, while her husband earned an Oscar nomination for his performance in 1967's *Dirty Dozen*. The money they made from these projects helped finance their first independent movie the critically acclaimed *Faces*, a 1968 film about marital infidelity.

Faces was one of the first independent movies to be well received by mainstream audiences and earned Cassavetes an Oscar nomination for Best Original Screenplay.

From the beginning, distributing the independent films they made was often the most difficult aspect, Rowlands noted in her *Guardian* article. It was so difficult that one night John "went to a late-night newsstand and bought all the out-of-town papers ... to see which cinemas were playing the sort of films they liked. He would then ring them and ask if they would take his movies. Sometimes it even worked."

As they sought more venues to showcase their work, the pair continued to work on new projects, producing *Minnie and Moskowitz* in 1971. Then, in 1974, Cassavetes cast his wife as disturbed housewife Mabel Longhetti in the movie he'd written, *A Woman Under the Influence*.

The film brought the director and star wide acclaim and earned each of them an Oscar nomination, Cassavetes for best director and Rowlands for best actress.

When Oscar night came in the spring of 1975, Rowlands's hometown was holding its breath, hoping that the shy girl they remembered would win, noted Don Davies in an April 6, 1975, *Wisconsin State Journal* article. After all, the small Wisconsin town knew not only the nominated actress but also her mother, Mary Ellen, who played a role in the film.

Cambria Mayor Jay Williams predicted that at least 750 Cambrians would be glued to their TV sets during the awards show, Davies noted.

"Win or lose, a bouquet of roses from Cambria will be presented to Miss Rowlands at a party to be held right after the awards ceremony," Davies wrote, adding that more than a hundred Cambria residents donated to a fund to buy the flowers.

Though the actress didn't win the Oscar, her hometown was no less proud of her accomplishments, noted family friend Mrs. Arvon Sanderson of Cambria.

"They all want her to win, but we want her to know how we feel (about her), win or lose," Sanderson told Davies. She added that she and others in Cambria still kept in touch with Rowlands through the actress's mother, who was known to return to town from time to time with two of the Cassavetes children in tow.

Meanwhile, the Cassavetes' movie-making marriage continued to blossom. The couple starred in the 1976 thriller *Two Minute Warning* and then produced and starred in the 1977 film *Opening Night*, in which Rowlands plays an alcoholic actress who falls apart the first night of her new play, after a fan dies trying to meet her.

In 1980, Cassavetes again cast his wife in an Oscar-nominated role, this time as a mobster's girlfriend in *Gloria*.

To help finance future projects, Rowlands starred opposite her husband in 1982's *The Tempest* and took roles in TV movies like *Thursday's Child* (1983) and *Rapunzel* (1981).

Though they had their arguments like any married couple, both agreed to — and did — keep personal issues off the movie set, Rowlands insists. Still, they had their private disagreements, Cassavetes said in a 1963 *Playboy* article.

"I believe that any two people who disagree should really go as far as they can, and I think we do; screaming, yelling, petty acts of hostility and cruelty, but it's all meaningless ... if that essential love is there," Cassavetes noted. "Like a rubber band that you stretch out, no matter how far you pull it, and even if it stings snapping back, it returns; the love reappears."

But, their love and respect for each other as husband and wife and performers shines through on screen, especially in their last collaboration, *Love Streams*, a 1984 movie about a loving brother and sister that featured Cassavetes playing his wife's brother.

"Jon Voight (who played the brother on stage with Rowlands) was supposed to do it but at the last minute he couldn't and John said, 'Oh, hell, I'll do it,'" Rowlands said in her *Guardian* article. "I'm so glad that he did do it," she adds. "Not that I don't love Jon Voight, but because that was our last film together."

Last because Cassavetes had been diagnosed with cirrhosis of the liver, a fatal disease that claimed his life in 1989.

Six years before he died, Cassavetes told *Playboy* magazine how great it was to work, and keep learning better ways to work, with his wife and friend. "We keep learning how to play together, so that I can step on her toes gently and she can step on mine gently and we can make a lot of noise," he said, adding that the dance didn't mean the couple didn't have its disagreements — artistic, professional, and personal.

For a while, Rowlands was lost without her personal and professional partner — without the other half that filled and challenged her. Though she doesn't speak often about their thirty-five-year love affair, saying the loss of it remains too painful to discuss publicly, in 1997, the actress did tell *Toronto Sun* writer Bob Thompson that she was "a zombie for a couple of years" after her husband died. "It takes a lot of strength to deal with all that, just when you don't have any strength to spare," she said.

To survive, Rowlands returned to the arms of her other great love: acting.

Rowlands had won an Emmy for her 1987 portrayal of Betty Ford in the TV movie, *The Betty Ford Story* (1987) and carried that success, and her two Oscar nominations, into a long list of film roles, including 1995 films *The Neon Bible* and *Something to Talk About*, starring Julia Roberts, and winning another Emmy for her role in the TV movie *Face of a Stranger* (1991). In 1993, the actress received a career achievement award at the Sundance Film Festival, which showcases independent filmmakers.

In 1996, her film director son Nick revived his father's innovative genius and completed the film John Cassavetes worked on before his death, casting his mother as the widow Mildred Hawks who befriends a single mother (Marisa Tomei) and her son in *Unhook the Stars*.

Rowlands's son cast his mother in another of his father's unfilmed screenplays, *She's So Lovely*, in 1997. The actress played a therapist in the film, which featured Sean Penn.

In the years since, the Cambria native has starred with Sean Connery in the romantic drama *Playing By Heart* (1998), with Green Bay, Wisconsin, native Tony Shalhoub in *Paulie*, with actress Sandra Bullock in *Hope Floats*, and with Brooke Shields in *The Weekend* (1999). Most recently, the 70-plus-year-old movie star plays as Mrs. Ritchie in *The Incredible Mrs. Ritchie* (2002) and Virginia in *Hysterical Blindness* (2002).

Though she's had the privilege of some wonderful Hollywood-generated roles over the years, Rowlands remains steadfast that she loved the characters her husband wrote for her most. "The best parts I have ever had, John wrote," she told *The Times* of London July 3, 1997. "If an actress has two roles in her lifetime that are really exceptional, she's a lucky woman. I've had seven or eight."

And, unlike many of those characters, the American heartland actress who portrayed them remains happy in her adulthood.

Show business "is a dazzling life to look at, but it's got a lot of

Famous Wisconsin Film Stars

really difficult things emotionally," Rowlands said in 1997. Her advice? "Don't waste your time doing (anything) unless it makes you happy. Which happens a lot...."

After all, she and Cassavetes wasted no time in producing the movies that made them happiest.

ON SCREEN

Find Cambria native Gena Rowlands's many screen performances in the following movies:

The Incredible Mrs. Ritchie (2002)
Charms for the Easy Life (2002) (TV)
Hysterical Blindness (2002)
Wild Iris (2001) (TV)
Intimate Portrait: Brooke Shields (2001) (TV)
The Color of Love: Jacey's Story (2000) (TV)
Ljuset håller mig sällskap (Light Keeps Me Company) (2000)
AFI's 100 Years... 100 Stars (1999) (TV)
The Weekend (1999)
Playing by Heart (1998)
Grace and Glorie (1998) (TV)
The Mighty (1998)
Hope Floats (1998)
Paulie (1998)
Best Friends for Life (1998) (TV)
She's So Lovely (1997)
Unhook the Stars (1996)
Cassavetes: Anything for John (1995)
The Neon Bible (1995)
Something to Talk About (1995)
Parallel Lives (1994) (TV)
Silent Cries (1993)
Crazy in Love (1992) (TV)
Ted and Venus (1991)
Face of a Stranger (1991) (TV)
Night on Earth (1991)
Once Around (1991)
Montana (1990) (TV)
Another Woman (1988)
The Betty Ford Story (1987) (TV)
Light of Day (1987)
An Early Frost (1985) (TV)
Love Streams (1984)
Thursday's Child (1983) (TV)
Tempest (1982)
Rapunzel (1981) (TV)
Gloria (1980)
Strangers: The Story of a Mother and Daughter (1979) (TV)
The Brink's Job (1978)
A Question of Love (1978/I) (TV)
Opening Night (1977)
Two Minute Warning (1976)
Columbo: Playback (1975) (TV)
A Woman Under the Influence (1974)
Minnie and Moskowitz (1971)
Faces (1968)
Nick Quarry (1968) (TV)
Intoccabili, Gli (Machine Gun McCain) (1968)
Tony Rome (1967)
Peyton Place (1964) TV Series
A Child Is Waiting (1963)
Lonely Are the Brave (1962)
The Spiral Road (1962)
87th Precinct (1961) TV Series
Staccato (1959) TV Series
The High Cost of Loving (1958)
Top Secret (1955) TV Series

NICHOLAS RAY

Central High School in La Crosse, Wisconsin, boasts not one but two famous movie directors — Joseph Losey and Nicholas Ray. Besides sharing the same hometown and high school, both directors battled their own demons and creative genius to become cutting edge directors with controversial lives.

Both also supported communist ideals to varying degrees and each endured the communist hunts of the early 1950s that left many Hollywood stars blacklisted from American cinema.

Yet, for two men who grew up only a couple years and a few city blocks away from each other, Ray and Losey reportedly never formed a deep friendship. They certainly didn't hang out together as children.

Joseph Losey's sister Mary, who was the same age in school as future director Nicholas Ray, remembered Ray only vaguely as a "pestiferous (and) a rather unattractive boy whom I had no desire to know," noted La Crosse author Rick Harsch in his January 14, 1996, *La Crosse Tribune* article, "Nicholas Ray: From La Crosse to Hollywood."

The "pestiferous" boy went on to become the director of one of Hollywood's most famous movies, *Rebel Without a Cause*.

Nicholas Ray was born Raymond Nicholas Kienzle August 7, 1911 (or 1912 depending on the source), in Galesville, Wisconsin, to Mr. and Mrs. Raymond L. Kienzle — the only boy in their six-child household.

By 1919, architect Raymond Kienzle had moved his family to 226 West Avenue North in La Crosse, where the future director did most of his growing up. Ray showed interest in drama early on and participated in an area stock company run by Guy Beach, whom Ray later thanked by finding the bit-part actor roles in many of his films. Ray also was featured on La Crosse radio programs and remained friends with Russell Huber, the eventual music director of WKBT-WKBH.

Presumably in part to support the rebel image he personified in Hollywood, the director often claimed he was kicked out of high school many times, but Ray reportedly did graduate in 1929.

His teenage years were tumultuous enough, however. The director's father died November 11, 1927, when his son was just 16. Some say Ray developed the remote father figure and discontented adolescent tone in *Rebel Without a Cause* (1955) from his experiences with his own father.

In a 1996 *La Crosse Tribune* article, Rick Harsch writes about memories Ray shared about his alcohol- and drug-addicted dad's final days. "One night at 16, my father could not be found. I went hunting for his mistress and found her in a speakeasy across from a brewery my father had built. She led me to a motel room. He was lying in sweat and puke ... I took him home and nursed him through the night. In the morning Doc Rhodes came. I went to the S & H Pool Hall ... (My father) was dead when I got home."

Ray never left his father's demons behind completely and took some of them on for himself. He began drinking in high school and eventually developed his own addiction to alcohol.

The La Crosse boy also developed a creative thirst that could never be quenched.

Ray left La Crosse to channel his creativity into an architectural career in 1930-31. He studied first at the University of Chicago, where he also performed in summer stock company productions and reportedly befriended writer Thornton Wilder, before returning to Wisconsin to study with legendary architect Frank Lloyd Wright at his Taliesin studio in Spring Green, Wisconsin, from 1933 to 1934.

In between, Ray married Jean Evans, and they had a son Anthony before they divorced in 1940. Ray is also said to have married a woman named Betty Utey.

Ray and Jean moved from Spring Green to New York so the talented Wisconsinite could continue his architectural studies. However, Ray soon discovered that he loved creating theater more than buildings. He began to look for work in New York's theater circles.

Two of his early friends and mentors were theatrical directors Elia Kazan and John Houseman. Nicholas Ray, as he was soon calling himself, started working in government-sponsored Works Progress Administration theater productions, many of which were produced by Houseman and Wisconsinite Orson Welles. Houseman also hired Ray to oversee the production of Voice of America radio programs in more than twenty languages.

Ray can thank Houseman for his start in Hollywood as well. Houseman gave the aspiring director, who had worked as an assistant director on such films as *Tuesday in November* in 1945, the TV production *Sorry, Wrong Number* in 1946, and his first feature film directing opportunity in *They Live by Night*, starring Cathy O'Donnell and Farley Granger.

Though it was a low-budget, black and white production, other Hollywood producers took notice of the new director's visual artistry, and Ray soon had film proposals rolling in. He made films like *Born to Be Bad* with Robert Ryan in 1950, *The Flying Leathernecks* World War II movie with John Wayne in 1951 and the modern-day rodeo film, *The Lusty Men*, with Robert Mitchum in 1952.

It was his work for, and relationship with, Howard Hughes that probably saved Ray from the fate of his fellow Central High alum Joseph Losey, who was blacklisted from Hollywood productions in 1951 after being named a communist before the U.S. House Un-American Activities Committee. Ironically, though Losey had radical political beliefs, it was Ray who had been the actual card-carrying member of the Communist Party for a time. Yet Hollywood insiders overlooked this detail in their up and coming star director's life and kept him working on one hit film after another.

As Ray's Hollywood star was rising, the director married actress Gloria Grahame, June 1, 1948, while she was pregnant with their son Timothy (born November 12, 1948). Grahame was perhaps best known for her role as the tempting Violet in the 1946 film *It's a Wonderful Life*.

Life wasn't so wonderful in the Ray household, however. Ray cast his wife in the lead with Humphrey Bogart in 1950's *In a Lonely Place*, but the marriage lasted less than five years and ended in divorce in 1952. According to The Associated Press, Grahame appeared at the divorce hearings wearing "a black dress as low-cut as any court attachés could remember."

Ray's love life went from sad to bizarre when his former wife married Ray's 23-year-old son Tony (her stepson) May 13, 1960, and had two more children Anthony Jr. and James, in addition to the son Tim that she had with Nicholas Ray (now the stepson and half brother of her husband) and a daughter Marianna that she had in a 1954 marriage to Cy Howard. Grahame's marriage to her stepson lasted longer than her other attempts at matrimony. They divorced in 1976 after sixteen years of marriage.

Despite the turmoil in his private life, which included bouts of manic depression, Ray's ability to paint emotional urgency into lasting and innovative visual images impressed his peers then and continues to inspire directors today. French audiences and filmmakers, like Francois Truffaut, were especially fond of Ray's style.

Ray once said of the work praised by so many that, "I am the best damn filmmaker in the world who has never made one entirely good, entirely satisfactory film," quotes Harsch in his 1996 retrospective story for the *La Crosse Tribune*.

As in life, Ray liked to push the limits in his films. On screen, he challenged artistic and social norms, often urging his color-film peers to shoot movies in black and white, as he sometimes did for effect. "Let's get rid of the idea that black and white are not colors," the director urged in his autobiography *I was Interrupted*, edited and published after his 1979 death by his last wife, Susan Ray.

It was audiences that Ray threw for a loop in his 1954 film noir-style Western *Johnny Guitar*, when the film showcased two women — Joan Crawford and Mercedes McCambridge — shooting it out in a Western mining town.

Ray was also one of the first directors to tackle the subject of drug addiction on screen in his 1956 film *Bigger Than Life*, starring Barbara Rush, James Mason, and Walter Matthau.

It was Ray's portrayal of dysfunctional families that drew the most audience and critical acclaim, especially where his most famous picture, 1955's *Rebel Without a Cause*, is concerned. The director was nominated for an Academy Award for Best Story for the picture. It was one of several screenplay stories Ray wrote or cowrote in his career. Others included such films as: *Swing Parade of 1946* (1946), *The Savage Innocents* (1959), *Circus World* (1964), *The Murder of Fred Hampton* (1971), and *Lighting Over Water* (1980).

Rebel Without a Cause starred Hollywood wild boy James Dean as the rebellious teenage son of a dysfunctional middle-class family, along with Natalie Wood as his girl Judy and Sal Mineo as his pal "Plato." It also featured the director himself, as the man standing in the last shot of the film. It was not the first time Ray worked himself into small parts in his own movies; he played a bakery clerk in *A Tree Grows in Brooklyn* (1945), and a U.S. minister in *55 Days at Peking* (1963).

For all the upheaval on screen, Ray created a bit of his own when the 43-year-old director had a brief affair at the famous Chateau Marmont with 17-year-old Wood, the then girlfriend of actor Dennis Hopper, who played a goon in the film, reported Jay

McInerney in a November 21, 1996, story about the California hotel for *The Observer* in London.

Along with praise and popularity, violence and tragedy followed the film's principals as its director (Ray) battled depression and its three top stars died young — Dean died in a car crash, Wood drowned while boating off Catalina Island, and Mineo was murdered in his apartment.

Still, Ray's star continued to shine and he turned out many more movies in the 1950s, including: *Bigger Than Life* (1956), *Winds Across the Everglades* (1958), and *The Savage Innocents* (1959).

Ray challenged himself further by taking on the most well-known story and character of all time — the life of Jesus — in his 1961 Biblical epic *King of Kings*, starring Jeffrey Hunter as the Messiah.

Like most actors of the day, Hunter jumped at the chance to work with the great director with a reputation for respecting his actors and crews. He had worked with Ray in the 1957 film *The True Story of Jesse James* along with one-time Wisconsin school teacher Agnes Moorehead, whom Ray later hired to be a dialogue coach on *King of Kings*.

"Ray is a man who, like (director John) Ford, has a great ability to communicate ideas concisely," Hunter noted in an Actor's Choice article for *Films and Filming,* April 1962. "Ray is a quiet man; he's not bombastic on the set and if he has something he wants to tell you he tells you alone. ... (He) doesn't try to act out the part for you. He watches you act it out and he reacts to what you do. ... Consequently, the many observers who sit in the audience of his daily work of filmmaking, miss I'd say 90 percent of his performance."

Ray also had a reputation for taking extra time to ensure visual details, visiting locations many times before shooting. According to the book, *Metro Goldwyn Mayer Presents Samuel Bronston's Production King of Kings,* Ray drove five hundred miles around the Spanish countryside, compiled 7,000 extras, set up eighty-one different cameras and laid 160 feet of camera track to shoot the movie's Sermon on the Mount scene alone.

The movie got mixed reviews. Some audiences were thrown that their western and rebel movie director would make a Biblical movie. And, though Ray had actually met with Pope John XXIII to review the script for religious authenticity, critics were upset that the movie skipped many of Jesus's most well-known miracles, didn't like that a divorced Hollywood heartthrob played such a deeply religious figure and were critical of Hunter's acting abilities. One *Time* magazine critic dubbed the film "I Was a Teenage Jesus," and the nickname stuck.

Critic Edwin Jahiel later noted that the criticism may well have had more to do with the film's timing than its merits. "The movie came after a spate of youth-centered pictures such as Nicholas Ray's own classic *Rebel Without a Cause* (1955), and after silly titles like *I Was a Teen-Age Frankenstein* or *I Was a Teen-Age Werewolf*. So the wags dubbed it *I Was a Teen-Age Jesus* — a good jest had the movie deserved it. But it didn't. The joke was unfair to the film, its makers and Jeff Hunter," he wrote.

Still, Hollywood paid attention to the criticism, and Ray made only one more star-studded feature, *55 Days at Peking* (1963), with Charlton Heston and Ava Gardner. In 1964, he wrote the story for the lesser film *Circus World* and then faded from Hollywood.

Ray began teaching film at New York University and married his last wife, Susan. The celebrated director helped his students make independent films, like *You Can't Go Home Again* (1973).

Ray also returned to La Crosse in 1970, sporting an eye patch thanks to an infection and visiting the Losey Memorial Arch, named for the family of his fellow director, the *La Crosse Tribune* reported May 7, 1970.

It was not the first time Ray had revisited his roots. The director came to Wisconsin several times to see his mother and sister, Mrs. Ernest Hiegel, as well as friends like Bill Freise and Ed Schaefer.

During a July 1954 visit, the director took a motorboat cruise up the Mississippi River with his brother-in-law and Schaefer, commenting to the *La Crosse Tribune* July 13, 1954, how nice it was to be home again.

"Wisconsin has never been so beautiful. I flew in from Chicago, and I've seen the state from the air, the land and the water. There's a lovely warmth and a special quality in the landscape," he said.

In what was probably his last public visit to La Crosse, in 1970, Ray filmed his old radio friend Russell Huber walking through familiar scenes for a future movie, though Ray refused to disclose which movie to the local paper. Many such movie efforts the director made in the 1970s never materialized or came to screens as small independent films.

In 1977, German director Wim Wenders asked Ray to play a small part in his film *The American Friend*. His German friend returned to Ray's side when the Wisconsin director was dying of cancer in 1979.

Together they filmed a documentary about Ray's death called *Lightning Over Water,* in which Ray talks about his struggles not only with cancer but with alcohol and drug addiction and manic depression. Ray died June 16, 1979. The documentary proved Ray's final painting upon the silver canvas. It was released in 1980.

ON SCREEN

In all, Nicholas Ray directed more than twenty films, including:

Lightning Over Water (1980)
Marco (1978)
We Can't Go Home Again (1976)
Wet Dreams (1974)
55 Days at Peking (1963)
King of Kings (1961)
The Savage Innocents (1959)
Wind Across the Everglades (1958)
Party Girl (1958)
Bitter Victory (Amère victoire) (1957)
The True Story of Jesse James (1957)
Bigger Than Life (1956)
Hot Blood (1956)
Rebel Without a Cause (1955)
Run for Cover (1955)
Johnny Guitar (1954)
Androcles and the Lion (1952) (uncredited)
The Lusty Men (1952)
Macao (1952) (uncredited)
On Dangerous Ground (1951)
The Racket (1951) (uncredited)
Flying Leathernecks (1951)
Born to Be Bad (1950)
In a Lonely Place (1950)
They Live by Night (1949)
Roseanna McCoy (1949) (uncredited)
A Woman's Secret (1949)
Knock on Any Door (1949)

DENNIS MORGAN

From early on, everyone who'd every heard Stanley Morner sing knew he'd be a star. His college newspaper even predicted that, "In years to come (we) will no doubt be proud to claim as one of (our) sons the famous Stanley Morner, world's greatest tenor."

Years later they were proud to claim him as a famous alum, though never as the "world's greatest tenor." Instead, the singer, whose "voice flowed as easily as water from a pitcher" according to a 1928 Waupaca newspaper review, became one of the biggest stars in American cinema of the 1940s. Stanley Morner became Dennis Morgan.

Morgan was born Earl Stanley Morner in Prentice, Wisconsin, a town his great grandfather reportedly founded, on December 10, 1910 (or December 30, 1910 or even December 20, 1908, depending on the source). His singing talent was recognized early in the Presbyterian church choir where he often soloed, and voice lessons improved his range.

Though singing was his first love, Morner also enjoyed the stage and reportedly first appeared in a barn theater near the Jump River. He attended high school in Marshfield and won the Wisconsin State High School Singing Contest at the University of Wisconsin's Bascom Hall his senior year. That same year he fell in love with Lillian Vedder, a Marshfield High School junior.

Morner had thoughts of attending Lawrence University in Appleton before he fell for Vedder. The beautiful and fun loving Vedder quickly persuaded him to join her at Carroll College in Waukesha instead.

After high school graduation in 1926, Morner began his freshman year at Carroll College thinking he would study business and keep his singing voice primed by participating in the schools men's glee club, Ye Carroll Troubadours.

Morner also tried out for the school's winter play, *The Goose Hangs High,* and was immediately cast as Hugh Ingals. He performed "two very well-sung solos" December 1-4, 1926, according to the college newspaper, the *Carroll Echo.*

Business school was quickly forgotten and Morner focused

most of his efforts on singing and acting, under the tutelage of the college's renowned drama teacher and director Ms. Rankin. Though he hadn't learned of her reputation for producing spectacular shows and stars (like Alfred Lunt) before he enrolled at Carroll, the teacher quickly impressed her new student.

"Ms. Rankin had tremendous flare. She believed in good and sometimes unusual staging. I remember that for, that time and era, it was quite a set. I can still see it. ... She was also a stickler for enunciation. She had a great deal to do with (my success) because she gave me the feeling that I had the ability" to succeed as an actor, Morner told Marquette University graduate student Marilyn William Linley in a 1969 interview for her thesis.

In addition to drama department recitals and Theta Alpha Phi (drama) fraternity plays, such as *The Valiant* in January of 1930, Morner appeared in all of Rankin's college productions from 1926 to 1930, taking the lead in most of them.

He played Richard in *Smiling Through* in June 1927 and Oliver Winslow in *The Youngest* December 8-10, 1927. Based on just these performances, the *Carroll College Bulletin* listed Morner as among those "who have made their names in Carroll's roll of honor on the stage."

Morner earned further acclaim as Viscount Charles Deeford in a June 1928 production of *Disraeli* and as Adam West in *Wake Up Jonathon* December 6-9, 1929.

He starred as King Eric VIII in the June 1929 production of *The Queen's Husband,* a performance that earned him the praise of a *Carroll Echo* reviewer who said, "Stanley Morner again won the hearts of the audience by his brilliant, easy going manner of acting."

While his performance was something to celebrate, the show proved to be the last that Rankin directed personally. The legendary drama teacher had an accident while preparing the play and thus had to produce Carroll College plays from her home, using guest directors — including famous Wisconsin stage star Alfred Lunt. She died March 2, 1931, from an illness that resulted from the June 1929 commencement play accident. Morner later donated $1,000 to her memorial fund.

It was under the direction of theater great Lunt that future movie great Morner performed his final role at Carroll College, playing Torvald Helmer in the June 1930 commencement production of *A Doll's House.*

Morner's performances were nearly always flawless, though

Dennis Morgan visits Carroll College and washes dishes at Goff's Restaurant, his former workplace, with Mrs. Goff. Photo courtesy of Wisconsin Center for Film and Theater Research. Image No. WCFTR-3752.

he later admitted in a 1945 Warner Bros. news release that one of the most embarrassing moments of his career occurred during a Carroll College drama department performance of *Romeo and Juliet* at a local Waukesha school. "I'll never forget the night I was playing Romeo. My tights split, and we had to do a quick sewing job in the wings (between scenes). I rushed on stage with the needle and thread still dangling behind."

While the 6-foot, 2-inch actor performed flawlessly by the audience's standards, costars like his future wife Lillian — who earned college praise for her realistic Theta Pi Delta presentation of *Peter Pan* during a May 1930 drama department production — knew differently. "He would not study his lines and often fluffed them, much to the discomfiture of the rest of the players," she told the *Milwaukee Journal* in a 1948 interview.

Morner also was a member of a college singing quartet and the Ye Carroll Troubadours Glee Club for most of his college career. The glee club toured the state, traveling by bus and staying in homes, colleges and even basements, from Sheboygan to Neenah and Green Bay to Madison. Morner performed as the group's first tenor in 1928 and as lead tenor in 1929 and 1930, when he also was the club's manager.

Wisconsinites statewide soon learned of his musical talents. A Waupaca newspaper noted after the club's 1929 performance in town that when Morner sang the Irish ballad, "Kerry Dance," he "sang with a clearness and feeling that is seldom found away from the operatic stage."

One place the singers performed was at the Rotary Club in Baraboo, Wisconsin, according to the actor's friend Don Philips — who later became an American Airlines pilot. Philips played the piano as Morner sang. In the middle of "The Garden of Tomorrow," Philips got stage fright, quit playing and left. "Stan didn't even look at me, he just went right on singing," he told writer Maxine Arnold in her 1947 *Milwaukee* magazine piece "Badger Boy."

The glee club ended its 1929 tour with a bit of campus mischief, according to the *Carroll Echo*. After the club's end-of-tour concert, "at an hour when all good college girls should have been soundly sleeping, the Glee Boys (including Morner) serenaded the (women's) dormitory."

Morner serenaded the Midwest in 1929 as well when he won the state radio singing contest and went on to perform at the district level in Chicago, placing in the Top 10 as a representative from Marshfield. WTMJ Radio in Milwaukee carried the competition live on the air for all of Morner's college classmates to hear.

His musical talents were so impressive that the radio station hired him his senior year to sing as their "prince of song" in a half-hour musical program.

Performing wasn't Morner's only talent, however. He was a star, 200-pound tackle on the college football team from 1926 to 1929 and played on two championship teams. In December of 1983, Morner told Jason Methou of *The New Perspective* that the greatest victories he remembered from his football days were when Carroll College upset the then powerhouse Northwestern University.

His wife also recalled the times Morner played against Lawrence University and her old high school boyfriend, Olin Jesup. "After a game, he'd rush into the dressing room and pile on street clothes as fast as he could so as to get back to where I was before Olin appeared," recalled Lillian in a March 14, 1948, *Milwaukee Journal* article.

Somewhere between the football field and the stage, Morner also found time to be president of his sophomore class from 1927 to 1928, a member of the national dramatic fraternity Theta Alpha Phi, a member of Beta Pi Epsilon fraternity, and an Inter-fraternity Council representative his senior year. Meanwhile, his wife and high school sweetheart Lillian was vice president of the Student House Government Association, according to the college's *Hinakaga* yearbooks.

When he wasn't performing, Morner was working in Waukesha, either dishing up ice cream at Mike Zoler's Sweet Shop on South Street or washing dishes at Goff's Restaurant at 800 Clinton Street, or stopping there with Lillian after plays for milk toast. Every time he returned to Milwaukee, Morgan is reported to have stopped in to see his old bosses, who were more like his Waukesha family. He is also known to have kept in touch with old college friends like Fred Zickerick, Les Smith, Lee Larson and Joe Adams.

According to the 1948 *Milwaukee Journal* article, Zoler remembered Morner for his big heart and big appetite. "That boy! He works 50 cents worth and eats $3 worth!"

 "We used to like to have Stan around. While he never put in any extra hours, he'd come over the house. Mr. Goff would get his cello out and my daughter Betty and Stan would sing duets," Mrs. Goff added in the 1945 Warner Bros. publicity release.

Still, Morner was living on a shoestring and his piano teacher and other friends were often known to gladly give the singer a few dollars now and then so he could take his girlfriend out on a proper date.

One time, the couple had gotten permission to keep Lillian out past the women's curfew for such a proper date to see *The Beggar's Opera* in Milwaukee. "But we skipped off and took in a movie. Someone talked and, as a punishment, I had to give a complete report on the opera before all the girls at a special meeting called by Dean Perkins," Lillian told the *Milwaukee Journal* in 1948.

Stanley Morner graduated from Carroll College in 1930 with a certificate in literary interpretation and worked at WTMJ while he waited for Lillian to graduate in 1931 and join him.

While Morner continued to perform on WTMJ, Lillian taught school for a few years in Shawano, Wisconsin, until the couple married on September 5, 1933.

While working for WTMJ, Morner often bumped into radio actor and future Hollywood and stage star Dave Willock, a University of Wisconsin alum. One of Willock's good friends was Jack

Carson — a future movie star then selling insurance in Milwaukee. Willock introduced Carson to Morner at a restaurant near the radio station. The two new friends got together "often to discuss their futures with mugs of root beer and shooting the pinball machines," noted writer Maxine Arnold in a 1947 *Milwaukee* magazine story "Badger Boy." Carson and Willock soon formed a popular vaudeville act while Morner moved to Chicago with his new bride and into national radio, and eventually, Hollywood.

Morner's work on WTMJ caught national ears in the early 1930s, and he was signed to do a coast-to-coast program with the "Silken Strings" of the Chicago Symphony Orchestra. Meanwhile, he continued to improve his voice at the Chicago Music College.

By 1935, Morner was a Ted Weems Orchestra vocalist at Chicago's Palmer House, sang the lead in the *Xerxes* opera at the University of Chicago and gave concerts at the Bohemian Club. When opera star Mary Garden heard his singing in *Xerxes*, she asked the Wisconsin performer to star with her in *Carmen*. When production plans fell through, Garden got Morner into a screen test for MGM Studios instead.

That same year, Morner returned to his alma mater to sing "Ich Hatte Viel Bekummernis" in the School of Music's Bach Music Festival May 27, 1935, and sing several numbers in a college recital that June.

Using Stanley Morner, or a new variation of his name Richard Stanley, the actor signed an MGM contract in 1936, and spent his first year in Hollywood playing bit parts in such movies as *Suzy* (1936), *Navy Blue and Gold* (1937), and *King of Alcatraz* (1938). His first credited role was in 1936 in *I Conquer the Sea,* which reportedly took just eight days to make.

His biggest early role was as a soloist in MGM's famous musical *The Great Ziegfeld* (1936). However, the role was also one of the singer's most frustrating since the studio used Allan Jones's voice as Morner's.

Morner subsequently broke the contract and joined the Los Angeles Civic Light Opera Company where he sang in *The Student Prince.* That performance led to an offer from Paramount Studios in 1938.

In 1939, Morner returned to Chicago to make a record-breaking appearance in the Palmer House's Empire Room during the World's Fair. He then went to Milwaukee's Riverside Theater where he was reportedly singing when he got an offer from Warner Bros. Studio to take a screen test for a new film *The Desert Song.*

He took the offer and changed his name to Dennis Morgan.

Though *The Desert Song* wasn't made for two more years, Warner Bros. kept their new star busy. In all, he performed in forty films for the studio. His Warner Bros. career began with B movie leads in such films as 1939's *Waterfront* and 1940's *River's End* and A movie supporting roles in such films as 1941's *Affectionately Yours*.

Morgan proved his star potential by playing the love interest of Ginger Rogers, who won an Academy Award for her role in RKO's 1941 hit *Kitty Foyle*. Rogers once said that of all the hundreds of stars she had danced with, only a handful rated in her top 10; Morgan was among them, along with Jimmy Stewart, Cary Grant, and Fred Astaire. In Morgan's 1994 obituary in the *Milwaukee Journal*, Rogers, with whom he also starred in 1950's *Perfect Strangers*, was quoted saying, "Just because a person dances well on the stage doesn't automatically mean he is delightful on the dance floor." Morgan was delightful.

Warner Bros. liked what they saw, too. The studio moved Morgan up to star status, beginning with the delayed *The Desert Song* in 1943, where the college tenor and one-time opera star was finally getting major, un-dubbed, singing roles.

By the mid-1940s, Morgan had become the highest paid actor in Hollywood. He starred in such movies as *The Hard Way* and *Thank Your Lucky Stars* (1943), *Shine on Harvest Moon* and *The Very Thought of You* (1944), *Christmas in Connecticut* and *God is My Co-Pilot* (1945), *One More Tomorrow* (1946), and *Cheyenne* (1947).

Most fans believed Morgan was an Irishman. Though he sang many Irish tunes, could carry the accent well, and played an Irishman in such films as *Three Cheers for the Irish* (1940) and *My Wild Irish Rose* (1947) — which also featured his then 8-year-old daughter Kristin — Morgan and his clan never hailed from the Emerald Isle. The closest his lineage came, in fact, was Scotland, Sweden and the Netherlands.

More than with any leading lady, Morgan was most often paired with his old Milwaukee friend Jack Carson, who provided the comedic sidekick to Morgan's romantic lead. The two starred together in *The Hard Way* in 1942, *One More Tomorrow* in 1946, and *The Time, The Place and The Girl* (1947). They also toured military bases and hospitals off screen during World War II and spent a lot of free time enjoying each other's company and families at Morgan's 500-acre California ranch in Ahwahnee.

By this time, Warner Bros. was bent on making the pair a more permanent act in the hope that the friends would rival Paramount's popular Bob Hope and Bing Crosby road-trip films.

Though they never reached Hope-Crosby status, Morgan and Carson did put their home state on the Hollywood map with the 1947 movie *Two Guys from Milwaukee*. The movie is actually set in New York with Morgan playing a European prince disguising himself as a man from Milwaukee to find out how the average American lives. He meets and befriends New York cab driver and actual Milwaukee native Buzz Williams, played by Carson. The friendship is tested when the prince falls in love with the cabbie's Brooklyn girlfriend Connie, played by Joan Leslie.

The exciting part of this film for most Wisconsinites was not its plot, nor its title. It's that the movie premiered in Milwaukee, with the two Wisconsin natives returning home for the gala, staged as one of the many events during Milwaukee's Centurama centennial celebration in 1946.

In a November 3, 1995, article "Premieres Here Nothing New," *Milwaukee Journal Sentinel* writer Jackie Loohauis, relates that:

"The pair made a glamorous, comic entrance into our city by water in a tiny white rowboat, that was 'rescued' by the Coast Guard and finally escorted to a landing while sirens wailed, yachts gave an honor guard and a fire boat hosed streams of water in the air. Fifteen thousand citizens watched the spectacle (after which) … police escorted Carson and Morgan through a crowd of fans estimated at 100,000 (to the Warner Theater)."

Two years later the team produced *Two Guys from Texas* (1948) to less fanfare. Then, in 1949, the friends costarred in a unique movie, *It's a Great Feeling*, a comedy in which each actor played himself: Carson as an actor/director trying to recruit a cast for a movie and Morgan as the star he's trying to win for the lead.

In between, Morgan continued to star and costar in movies through the 1940s, including *One Sunday Afternoon* in 1948.

As Hollywood moved toward westerns in the 1950s, Morgan moved away from movies. He did make a few cowboy films in the early 1950s, such as *Cattle Town* (1952), *The Nebraskan* (1953), *The Gun That Won the West* (1955), and *Uranium Boom* (1956). And, Morgan tried his talents on the small screen too, starring in the 1959 television series *21 Beacon Street*.

Essentially the film star was retired, devoting himself even more to his wife Lillian and their three children Stan, Kristin, and Jim, and living off the substantial earnings he'd wisely invested from his movie career. Morgan was often seen singing in his church's choir or sitting in the bleachers at La Canada public schools, cheering on his children.

Morgan said he loved the role of father and husband the best, though he struggled to maintain a normal life for his Hollywood family. "It's not the easiest thing in the world to be a success in Hollywood and still be the ordinary husband and father," he often lamented.

He lived modestly and spoiled himself only with the luxury of a summer home in the state he loved most — Wisconsin.

In his 1994 *Milwaukee Journal* obituary, his nephew David Foster said his uncle "went to Wisconsin every chance he got. He was always a very practical fellow, a good Midwesterner. He didn't buy a new car every year, even at the peak of his career. He always had enough wood for his fires."

Morgan and Lillian returned to their Lac du Flambeau home for six weeks or more every year to hunt and fish. Though Lillian often dressed in flannel and accompanied her husband into the woods and duck blinds, it was his old childhood and college friends who most often traveled along on Morgan's outdoor adventures.

"Dennis makes a swell Boy Scout when he goes along on fishing trips. He does all the dirty work, gets up early, makes the fires and you've never eaten such fish as he can cook," said Morgan's old singing teacher, Mario Silva, to writer Maxine Arnold for her mid-1940s *Milwaukee* magazine "Badger Boy" story.

Silva's student could still carry a beautiful tune too. As often as Morgan returned to Wisconsin for recreation, he returned to perform for old friends and/or help his alma mater or hometowns raise money.

Morgan was the featured singer in a patriotic concert at Milwaukee's Washington Park in 1941 for the national American Legion convention and set the Washington Park attendance record at 40,000 when he starred in a 1945 *Music Under the Stars* production.

The actor returned to the Badger State during World War II to help sell war bonds, attending a 1942 Carroll College rally that raised $181,000 worth of bonds and singing at the Rex Theater, where he used to watch westerns as a boy, for a war stamp fundraising performance. Morgan also returned to help his alma mater where fundraising was concerned, visiting in 1948 to boost a building fund campaign.

The actor was so dedicated to Carroll College that he served as the alumni association's president from 1961 to 1962 and gave the 1963 commencement speech, saying "Carroll is our own. We alumni must never let her down."

They were words Morgan lived as well as he spoke.

Morgan had his Carroll College pictures and diplomas displayed prominently in his California home. And, over the years, the actor donated and raised money for the college and returned to his alma mater for many special occasions.

In 1946, Morgan attended the college's centennial celebration where he was presented with an honorary doctorate degree in fine arts and serenaded homecoming queen Cora Sue Pepin at halftime of the football game.

That same year, Morgan suited up to play on the alumni basketball team, reassuring the crowd that it was good he chose acting and not basketball as a profession. According to a 1983 *Waukesha Freeman* article, the actor was "far from the star of the game. The team couldn't let the man play without scoring one point, so they trucked out a stepladder, which he climbed to sink his shot. At that, he almost missed."

Morgan returned for homecoming in 1961 where he crowed the queen, visited his old Beta Pi Epsilon fraternity house and attended his wife's 30th class reunion.

In 1963, the singing actor returned with fellow Wisconsinite and film star Pat O'Brien to perform *Show Boat* in Madison and Milwaukee. Pat O'Brien played Capt. Andy, his wife Eloise O'Brien played Parthy Ann Hawks, and Dennis Morgan played Gaylord Ravenal.

During the show's performance in Madison, the two stars reportedly took turns presenting the news and sports on Madison TV station WKOW, according to retired University of Wisconsin journalism professor Blake Kellogg, who was working for the station at the time. The TV man also recalled seeing the stars drinking on State Street after their performance and watched a tipsy O'Brien slide into a phone booth to call a friend in northern Wisconsin.

Morgan came back to Milwaukee in 1967 to help the radio station that gave him his start celebrate its 40th anniversary and to host the *Music Under the Stars* program again.

In 1974, the actor took some skilled swings in the Vince Lombardi Memorial Golf Classic at North Hills County Club and then attended a private party thrown by William Pabst at the Oconomowoc Lake Club. Morgan's college roommate, Gerald

Sivage, president of Marshall Field & Co. in Chicago, also attended. And, the *Milwaukee Journal* reported July 1, 1974, the talented tenor "joined the band for a round of Irish tunes and guests stopped dancing to join in."

In between special appearances, the actor spent his time raising money for worthy causes, especially the American Cancer Society.

"My best Hollywood pals were killed by cancer, including Jack Carson, my Wisconsin buddy ... It was Jack's death (in 1963) that helped get me involved so much with the ACS," he told the *Milwaukee Journal* July 23, 1978.

In fact, fundraising and old friends were the only things that pulled the one-time Hollywood star back onto the screen of any size. "I don't go on talk shows very much because I don't have anything to sell. ... Except now and then, when the cancer people say it will help," he told the *Journal*.

In 1980, his friend Jane Wyman convinced Morgan to appear in an episode of *The Love Boat* with her, and he was talked into appearing as a tour guide in the flop *Won Ton Ton, the Dog Who Saved Hollywood* (1976), his last movie.

Morgan never slowed down, however. He enjoyed his 500-acre ranch in the Hollywood hills and his Wisconsin summer home into the 1990s.

In January of 1983, he and Lillian were seriously injured when their station wagon "plunged down a ravine and caught fire near Tracy, California," The Associated Press reported. Lillian was partially crippled in the accident and the actor suffered head and chest injuries, reportedly losing sight in one eye.

The injuries didn't stop the couple, then married fifty years, from returning to their home state later that year to watch Morgan and his friend Jack Carson be the first inductees into the Wisconsin Performing Artists Hall of Fame in Milwaukee. (Carson was inducted posthumously.) While in town, Morgan also accepted a Distinguished Alum Award from Carroll College.

Wisconsin's star singer died of respiratory failure ten years later on September 7, 1994, in Fresno, California, two days after his 61st wedding anniversary.

In his later years, Morgan had guest-starred in University of Wisconsin-Marshfield and Wood County Players summer productions such as *The Pleasure of his Company* and *Paint Your Wagon*. He reportedly worked only for his expenses and used his presence to help add thousands of dollars to the troupe's scholarship

Jack Carson and son John with Dennis Morgan and son Jimmy at Carson's San Fernando Valley Ranch. Photo courtesy of Wisconsin Center for Film and Theater Research. Image No. WCFTR-3745.

fund.

Morgan especially enjoyed his northern Wisconsin performances, he told the *Milwaukee Journal* in 1978. "Working with the players is fun to do and it isn't really a star situation ... Let me tell you, there are fine people in that group."

Some of the players were so talented that the star had to wonder why he made it big and they didn't.

"Don't let anybody ever tell you this business isn't a matter of luck," he added. "Why it hit for me and not for some others, I'll never know."

Famous Wisconsin Film Stars

ON SCREEN
Find Carroll College alum and Wisconsinite Stanley Morner as Hollywood Star Dennis Morgan in the following:

Won Ton Ton, the Dog Who Saved Hollywood (1976)
Busby Berkeley (1974)
That's Entertainment! (1974)
Rogues' Gallery (1968)
21 Beacon Street (1959) TV Series
Uranium Boom (1956)
Pearl of the South Pacific (1955)
The Gun That Won the West (1955)
Cattle Town (1952)
This Woman Is Dangerous (1952)
Painting the Clouds with Sunshine (1951)
Raton Pass (1951)
Pretty Baby (1950)
Hollywood Goes to Bat (1950)
Perfect Strangers (1950)
The Lady Takes a Sailor (1949)
It's a Great Feeling (1949)
One Sunday Afternoon (1948)
Two Guys from Texas (1948)
To the Victor (1948)
Let's Sing a Song From the Movies (1948)
Always Together (1948)
My Wild Irish Rose (1947)
Cheyenne (1947)
One More Tomorrow (1946)
Two Guys from Milwaukee (1946)
The Time, the Place and the Girl (1946)
Christmas in Connecticut (1945)
God Is My Co-Pilot (1945)
Shine On, Harvest Moon (1944)
The Very Thought of You (1944)
Hollywood Canteen (1944)
Road to Victory (1944)
The Desert Song (1943)
Thank Your Lucky Stars (1943)
The Hard Way (1942)
Wings for the Eagle (1942)
In This Our Life (1942)
Captains of the Clouds (1942)
Kisses for Breakfast (1941)
Bad Men of Missouri (1941)
Affectionately Yours (1941)
Kitty Foyle: The Natural History of a Woman (1940)
River's End (1940)
Flight Angels (1940)
Tear Gas Squad (1940)
Three Cheers for the Irish (1940)
The Fighting 69th (1940)
The Singing Dude (1939)
The Return of Doctor X (1939)
Ride, Cowboy, Ride (1939)
No Place to Go (1939)
Waterfront (1939)
Persons in Hiding (1939) (as Richard Stanley)
Men with Wings (1938) (as Richard Stanley)
Illegal Traffic (1938) (as Richard Stanley)
King of Alcatraz (1938) (as Richard Stanley)
Navy Blue and Gold (1937) (as Stanley Morner)
Song of the City (1937) (as Stanley Morner)
Mama Steps Out (1937) (as Stanley Morner)
I Conquer the Sea! (1936) (as Stanley Morner)
Annie Laurie (1936) (as Stanley Morner)
Old Hutch (1936) (uncredited)
Piccadilly Jim (1936) (uncredited)
Suzy (1936) (as Stanley Morner)
The Great Ziegfeld (1936) (uncredited)

JACK CARSON

There were few, if any, show business venues that actor Jack Carson didn't play. He started in vaudeville, acted on America's top stages, starred on radio, lit up the silver screen, tested freelance films, and pioneered television variety shows.

All the while, the diverse actor never forgot his home state. He often worked Wisconsin references into scripts and returned many times to perform, raise war bond money, visit friends in Milwaukee, or just relax in Door County or Northern Wisconsin.

Though Jack Elmer Carson considered himself a Milwaukee boy at heart, the actor was born in Carman, Manitoba, on October 27, 1910.

He was only 2 when his insurance salesman father, John "Jack" Elmer Carson, followed a job to Milwaukee and eventually settled his family on the East Side. Carson and his brother Robert, who also grew up to be an actor, attended Hi-Mount and Hartford Avenue grade schools before enrolling at St. John's Military Academy in Delafield. The brothers also both attended Carleton College in Northfield, Minnesota.

Though always a bit of a ham as a child, Carson didn't pursue acting as a career until he returned from college. At first he tried to follow in his father's path, selling insurance in Milwaukee.

But, his love of entertainment was too hard to fight. Within a year, Carson had formed a vaudeville act with his friend and future movie actor Dave Willock, a WTMJ radio personality in Milwaukee, who would later play characters on Jack Carson's radio program. In between, Carson met promising singer and actor Dennis Morgan, with whom he would also star one day, and formed a friendship that lasted on and off screen through four Hollywood decades.

For five years, the comedic and musical duo of Willock & Carson played the Riverside Theater in Milwaukee and toured America's vaudeville circuit, enjoying public and critical acclaim.

By 1934, Carson had settled in Kansas City, taking a job as the singing master of ceremonies at the Tower Theater. It was a two-week job that the theater persuaded Carson to hold for two years.

His performances drew enough attention that, in 1936, Carson went west for a Hollywood screen test. It did not go well, and the actor returned to performing, this time with a theater group run by Milwaukee actor Ben Bard.

It was his brief work in Bard's group that finally caught Hollywood's eye and director George Stevens invited him back for another screen test in 1937. This time, Carson's test went well enough to earn him roles as a contract extra for RKO Studios. He had a bit part in *It Could Happen to You*, played a reporter in *Toast of New York* and was a gas station attendant in *You Only Live Once*, all in 1937. He was an uncredited "roustabout" in the hit *Bringing Up Baby* in 1938 and gradually grew into bigger roles.

As his movie career edged ahead, Carson married Elizabeth Lindy in 1938. The marriage was short lived even by Hollywood standards and the couple divorced the following year.

Carson had small but recognizable parts as Jack Tyndall in *Destry Rides Again* and Stanley Brown in *The Kid From Texas*, both in 1939, and worked in other RKO comedies and westerns until 1941. The actor then moved to Warner Bros. in hopes of sparking a more diverse movie career.

The move was a good one, and Carson was soon landing better supporting, even costarring, roles. The 6-foot 2-inch, 200-pound actor most often played "big, lumbering dopes ... and (had) few equals in the portrayal of obstreperous, obnoxious, often dull-witted lunkheads," Leonard Maltin wrote in a *Movie Encyclopedia* biography on the actor.

By the early 1940s, moviegoers began recognizing Carson, not only from his size, but also from his trademark double takes, complete with wrinkled forehead and bulging eyes.

Warner Bros. began to recognize the actor as a versatile hard worker they could use in most any movie. Beginning with *Navy Blues* and *The Strawberry Blonde*, both in 1941, Carson spent the next ten years as one of the studio's go-to supporting actors.

Also beginning in 1941, Carson formed a partnership with singer Kay St. Germaine in a marriage that lasted nine years and produced two children, John and Germaine Catherine.

Though Carson had memorable roles in some Warner Bros. dramas — as Realtor Wally Fay in *Mildred Pierce* (1945) and Officer Pat O'Hara in *Arsenic and Old Lace* (1944) — he was probably best as a comedy actor and best remembered as the nice guy who never got the girl. Case in point was one of his earlier Warner Bros. movies, *The Hard Way* (1942), which paired the actor with his Milwaukee friend Dennis Morgan. Carson played a good-natured entertainer named Albert who loses his love to his shrewd partner played by Morgan.

"I'm best at making people laugh," Carson once said as quoted in the book *Star Quality: The Great Actors and Actresses in Hollywood* (1974). The actor further acknowledged that he was probably never leading man material. "They don't want me for the morbid, over-sexed stuff Hollywood is turning out nowadays."

Warner Bros. did want the chemistry Carson brought alive on screen with Morgan, however, and paired the actor friends often in films with the hopes that they would become the studio's version of the popular Bing Crosby and Bob Hope movies.

Though they never gained anywhere near the popularity of Crosby-Hope movies, Carson and Morgan did make movie memories together and developed a deep friendship off screen, teaming up to visit military bases during World War II and getting together as families to ride horses at Carson's San Fernando Valley ranch. The two were so

Jack Carson, 10, with a hat and walking cane. Photo courtesy of Wisconsin Center for Film and Theater Research. Image No. WCFTR-3744.

close that when they were inducted into the Wisconsin Performing Artists Hall of Fame in 1983, as the hall's first inductees, the bronze busts of the two actors reportedly were done as one depicting both friends.

Morgan and Carson's first pairing as "road-trip" movie stars was in the appropriately titled 1946 film, *Two Guys From Milwaukee*. In a case of life imitating art, or vice versa, the two actors traveled to Milwaukee to premiere the film July 25, 1946, during the city's month long "Centurama" extravaganza celebration, which featured daily plays, a sky-shaking performance by soon-to-be-legendary pilot Chuck Yeager, and thirty-one nights of fireworks. According to reporter John Gurda in a June 7, 1998, *Milwaukee Journal Sentinel* article remembering the event, the duo was "mobbed by 100,000 adoring fans" as they paraded their way through town to the movie's premiere.

Along the way, Gurda reports, the two "appeared at the Centurama to present Mayor John Bohn with the key to Warner Bros. Studios."

Jackaboy, as Carson was known to friends, teamed with Morgan for similar Hope-Crosby pairings in *Two Guys From Texas* (1948) and *It's a Great Feeling* (1949), in which Carson plays himself.

In the musical Hollywood spoof, Carson is looking for a director for his new film and conning would-be actress Judy Adams to help him con Dennis Morgan (also playing himself) into being in the film. When the lies are discovered Carson and Morgan follow Adams as she returns to her hometown of Gerky Corners, Wisconsin, to marry her childhood love, who turns out to be Errol Flynn.

The film was the third that paired Carson with another screen star, Doris Day, who played Adams in the movie. The two had previously starred together in *Romance on the High Seas* (1948) and *My Dream is Yours* (1949).

Day wasn't the only leading lady Carson was paired with. In the mid-1940s, he starred in a handful of films with Jane Wyman such as *Make Your Own Bed* (1944). But Day was the only leading lady Carson was paired with off screen as well. The two reportedly dated for a time after his 1950 divorce from St. Germaine.

A different actress soon caught Carson's eye. In 1952, the actor married Lola Albright, an actress ten years his senior who costarred with Kirk Douglas in *Champion* (1949) and was the nightclub singer Edie Hart on the *Peter Gunn* TV series. They divorced in 1961, and Carson then married stage actress Sandy Tucker. Though Carson has more than a hundred films to his credit, he is probably better known for his starring roles *off* of the silver screen.

In the 1940s, Carson gained wide popularity as host of his own Jack Benny-style radio program for CBS, *The Jack Carson Show*. His comedic style was so popular that he often did stand-up comedy in Las Vegas. Wisconsinite Dave Willock guested as a variety of characters on the show, which often incorporated Wisconsin sites and themes in its skits. For example in his December 20, 1944, show, Carson created an old-fashioned Milwaukee Christmas; and on his June 26, 1946, program, he and Dennis Morgan traveled back to Milwaukee. In addition to his own show, Carson joined such stars as Roy Rogers in *Command Performance*, a weekly radio program for World War II servicemen.

Carson's radio success led him directly into a new acting medium in the 1950s — television. On the small screen, he gained prominence as a variety show host. He began by rotating a host position with Danny Thomas, Ed Wynn, and Garry Moore on NBC's *Four Star Revue* from 1950 to 1952 and then helped host *The U.S. Royal Showcase* in 1952. From 1954 to 1955, the comic actor was his own host on *The Jack Carson Show*.

In between he played himself in several Hollywood studio *Screen Snapshots* and made guest appearances on TV shows, including as a car salesman who couldn't lie as long as he owned his Model A on *The Twilight Zone*.

Carson continued to costar in movies as well. Though fewer in number than his 1940s run, Carson's later films often provided the actor with a wider variety of roles. Most memorably, he had the lead in *The Good Humor Man* in 1950, played a morally-challenged publicity man in the 1954 classic *A Star is Born*, and starred with Paul Newman in *Cat on a Hot Tin Roof* in 1958. Carson last appeared on movie screens in the 1961 film *King of the Roaring Twenties*.

It was not, however, his final performance. Carson completed a TV comedy for Walt Disney in 1962 called *Sammy the Way Out Seal* and continued to star in stage productions from time to time.

In fact, one of Carson's last official performances, ironically and appropriately enough, was in Milwaukee. In 1962, he starred in *Make a Million* and *Petrified Forest* at Milwaukee's Swan Dinner Theater before traveling to other American stage venues. On August 26, 1962, the actor collapsed on stage during a dress rehearsal in New Jersey.

Until just a few weeks before his death, not even Dennis Morgan, Dave Willock, or any of Carson's other close friends knew the real reason for the actor's collapse. Carson had stomach cancer (and/or, according some reports, liver cancer). The 52-year-old actor underwent unsuccessful surgery in November of 1962 and died January 2, 1963, in Encino, California.

Though he died in California, Carson's heart remained in Wisconsin. "Stan (Dennis Morgan) and I are still country boys in the Holly Woods," he once told writer Maxine Arnold. "You can only transplant so far, you know."

ON SCREEN

Catch Carson's famous double take and other roles in the following films:

Sammy the Way Out Seal (1962) (TV)
King of the Roaring '20s - The Story of Arnold Rothstein (1961)
The Bramble Bush (1960)
Rally 'Round the Flag, Boys! (1958)
Cat on a Hot Tin Roof (1958)
The Tarnished Angels (1957)
The Tattered Dress (1957)
Fabulous Hollywood (1956)
Magnificent Roughnecks (1956)
The Bottom of the Bottle (1956)
Screen Snapshots: Playtime in Hollywood (1956)
Ain't Misbehavin' (1955)
Screen Snapshots: Hollywood Plays Golf (1955)
Screen Snapshots: Hollywood Cowboy Stars (1955)
The Jack Carson Show (TV Series Host) (1954-55)
Phffft! (1954)
A Star Is Born (1954)
Red Garters (1954)
Dangerous When Wet (1953)
Screen Snapshots: Hollywood's Pair of Jacks (1953)
The U.S. Royal Showcase (TV Series Host) (1952)
Mr. Universe (1951)
The Groom Wore Spurs (1951)
Four Star Revue (TV Series Alternate Host (1950-1952)
Hollywood Goes to Bat (1950)
Bright Leaf (1950)
The Good Humor Man (1950)
The Soundman (1950)
My Dream Is Yours (1949)
John Loves Mary (1949)
It's a Great Feeling (1949)
April Showers (1948)
Two Guys from Texas (1948)
Romance on the High Seas (1948)
Let's Sing a Song From the Movies (1948)
Always Together (1948)
Love and Learn (1947)
So You Want to Be in Pictures (1947)
One More Tomorrow (1946)
Two Guys from Milwaukee (1946)
The Time, the Place and the Girl (1946)
Roughly Speaking (1945)
Mildred Pierce (1945)
The Doughgirls (1944)
Make Your Own Bed (1944)
Shine On, Harvest Moon (1944)
Hollywood Canteen (1944)
Arsenic and Old Lace (1944)
Road to Victory (1944)
Princess O'Rourke (1943)
Thank Your Lucky Stars (1943)
The Hard Way (1942)
The Male Animal (1942)

Gentleman Jim (1942)
Wings for the Eagle (1942)
Larceny, Inc. (1942)
The Strawberry Blonde (1941)
Blues in the Night (1941)
Navy Blues (1941)
The Bride Came C.O.D. (1941)
Love Crazy (1941)
Mr. & Mrs. Smith (1941)
Sandy Gets Her Man (1940)
Young as You Feel (1940)
Love Thy Neighbor (1940)
Parole Fixer (1940)
Lucky Partners (1940)
Queen of the Mob (1940)
Girl in 313 (1940)
Alias the Deacon (1940)
Typhoon (1940)
Shooting High (1940)
Enemy Agent (1940)
The Honeymoon's Over (1939)
I Take This Woman (1939)
The Kid From Texas (1939)
Destry Rides Again (1939)
Legion of Lost Flyers (1939)
Mr. Smith Goes to Washington (1939)
The Escape (1939)
5th Ave Girl (1939)

Crashing Hollywood (1938)
Go Chase Yourself (1938)
Law of the Underworld (1938)
Mr. Doodle Kicks Off (1938)
Carefree (1938)
Having Wonderful Time (1938)
This Marriage Business (1938)
The Saint in New York (1938)
Picketing for Love (1938)
Vivacious Lady (1938)
Condemned Women (1938)
Maid's Night Out (1938)
Night Spot (1938)
Bringing Up Baby (1938)
Everybody's Doing It (1938)
Music for Madame (1937)
She's Got Everything (1937)
Too Many Wives (1937)
Quick Money (1937)
High Flyers (1937)
A Rented Riot (1937)
Stand-In (1937)
Stage Door (1937)
You Only Live Once (1937)
Reported Missing (1937)
The Toast of New York (1937)
On Again Off Again (1937)
It Could Happen to You (1937)

EDUARD FRANZ

Eduard Franz wanted to be a commercial artist, had to be a chicken farmer, and still became a well-known character actor in some fifty Hollywood films.

Franz was born Eduard Franz Schmidt October 31, 1902, in Milwaukee, knowing from an early age that he wanted to be an artist. He decided he could best make a living as a commercial artist and was well on his way toward fulfilling his career goals at the University of Wisconsin in Madison when he joined the university's new student theater group, the Wisconsin Players Theater, for its 1922-23 season. The acting experience was enough to persuade Franz to set aside his easel and pursue a stage career.

Franz performed for the Coffer-Miller Players in Chicago from 1924 to 1925 and then headed to New York. He soon dropped his last name and performed with the Provincetown Players in Greenwich Village as Eduard Franz. The would-be commercial artist found steady stage work until 1930, when the Great Depression halted his dreams.

Franz and his young wife made their way to Texas where they scratched out a living raising chickens on an inherited farm. The chicken business did not last long though, and by the early 1930s, Franz and family returned to Wisconsin where the actor taught art. While he taught for a paycheck, Franz never gave up acting and continued to perform in regional theater productions, including with the Wisconsin Players.

By 1936, Franz had returned to the national stage spotlight, appearing in plays from New York to Los Angeles. A talented singer as well as actor, Franz starred from 1944 to 1947 in operettas with the St. Louis Municipal Opera.

Always skirting the edges of acting fame, Franz moved to California in 1947 to give motion pictures a try. It was a good move, and Franz found regular work for the next thirty years as a character actor for every major film studio.

Franz's first role was a bit part in the 1947 film *Killer at Large* but he found a more memorable role the next year as Frederick Muller in *The Scar* (also called *Hollow Triumph*), a movie about a fugitive impersonating a psychiatrist he killed.

Though most of Franz's roles were of the supporting, B movie, or bit-part variety, he had several noteworthy film performances, mostly in the 1950s and early 1960s. In the 1953 version of *The Jazz Singer*, Franz played the cantor father whom singer Jerry Golding (played by Danny Thomas) defies. Two years later, he starred with Charlton Heston in *The Ten Commandments* (1956), playing Jethro, the Jewish elder Moses (Heston) stays with after being banished to the desert. Then, in 1962, Franz played Orsini in MGM's version of *Beauty and the Beast* and starred in several popular westerns of the era, including *White Feather* (1955), *The Indian Fighter* (1955), and *The Last of the Fast Guns* (1958).

Franz continued to perform on stage as well, and in the 1950s followed the wave of actors testing television waters. He appeared on such shows as *Gunsmoke* and *The F.B.I.*, and had a recurring role as Gregorio Verdugo on *Zorro* in 1957. In 1963 he starred in the TV series *Breaking Point*.

By the 1970s, Franz was appearing almost exclusively on television series and in made-for-TV movies, in addition to his theater performances. He guest-starred on such shows as *Hart to Hart*, *Vega$*, *The Bionic Woman* and *The Waltons* and appeared in TV movies such as *The Brotherhood of the Bell* (1970) and *The Secret Life of T.K. Dearing* (1975).

Franz's final film role was as an old man in the motion picture *Twilight Zone: The Movie*, released in 1983, the year he died. That same year, the one-time commercial artist and chicken rancher was inducted posthumously into the Wisconsin Performing Artists Hall of Fame in Milwaukee.

ON SCREEN

Fans can spot Milwaukee actor Eduard Franz in the following:

Twilight Zone: The Movie (1983)
The Secret Life of T.K. Dearing (1975) (TV)
Panic on the 5:22 (1974) (TV)
The Sex Symbol (1974) (TV) (voice)
Johnny Got His Gun (1971)
The Brotherhood of the Bell (1970) (TV)
The President's Analyst (1967)
Cyborg 2087 (1966)
Breaking Point (1963) TV Series
Beauty and the Beast (1962)
Hatari! (1962)
Francis of Assisi (1961)
The Fiercest Heart (1961)
The Story of Ruth (1960)
The Four Skulls of Jonathan Drake (1959)
The Miracle (1959)
A Certain Smile (1958)
The Last of the Fast Guns (1958)
Day of the Bad Man (1958)
Zorro (1957-58) TV Series
Man Afraid (1957)
The Burning Hills (1956)

Operation Cicero (1956) (TV)
The Ten Commandments (1956)
Three for Jamie Dawn (1956)
The Indian Fighter (1955)
Lady Godiva (1955)
Man on the Ledge (1955) (TV)
White Feather (1955)
The Last Command (1955)
Sign of the Pagan (1955)
Living It Up (1954) (uncredited)
Beachhead (1954)
Broken Lance (1954)
Latin Lovers (1953)
Sins of Jezebel (1953)
Dream Wife (1953)
The Du Pont Story (1952)
Everything I Have Is Yours (1952)
The Jazz Singer (1952)
One Minute to Zero (1952)
Because You're Mine (1952).
The Desert Fox: The Story of Rommel (1951)
Shadow in the Sky (1951)
The Thing From Another World (1951)
Unknown Man (1951)
The Great Caruso (1951)
Emergency Wedding (1950)
Francis (1950)
The Goldbergs (1950)
Magnificent Yankee (1950)
The Vicious Years (1950)
Oh, You Beautiful Doll (1949)
Outpost in Morocco (1949)
Whirlpool (1949)
Madame Bovary (1949)
Wake of the Red Witch (1948)
The Iron Curtain (1948)
Hollow Triumph (1948)
Killer at Large (1947)

BRIAN DONLEVY

It's rare that the actor playing an American hero actually is one in real life. But, in the case of Brian Donlevy, his real-life heroics may well have outshined those of all the tough guys he played on screen.

The life of Waldo Bruce "Brian" Donlevy reads more like a movie script than a biography. Donlevy was reportedly born in Cleveland on February 9, 1901, though some sources say 1899. Hollywood biographers perpetuated the story that he was born in Portadown, County Armagh, Ireland, where they said he was christened Grosson Brian Boru Donlevy.

Either way, Donlevy was in America by the age of 10 months and was still a toddler when his family moved from Ohio to southeastern Wisconsin. They lived, at least for a time, in the Delafield, Wisconsin, area where Donlevy was enrolled in St. John's Military Academy.

When he was 14 or 15 (accounts vary), Donlevy ran away and convinced U.S. Army Cavalry recruiters in Wisconsin that he was of age. The young boy, who was big for his age, soon found himself among General Pershing's troops invading Mexico in pursuit of Pancho Villa, the Mexican guerilla fighter who had invaded Columbus, New Mexico, and killed 16. Donlevy served as a bugler in the Army during the raid. His actual service was brief and he soon returned to school, reportedly in Cleveland.

He didn't toil long in book studies, however, before lying about his age again. This time, Donlevy went to France to fly with the famed Lafayette Escadrille during World War I. As a sergeant, he flew combat missions as a bi-wing bomber pilot through the entire war and was wounded twice.

After the war ended in November 1919, Donlevy returned to America a decorated French war hero and began pilot and military training at the U.S. Naval Academy in Annapolis, Maryland.

It was here that a war hero found the side interest that became the great passion of his life: acting. After two years in Annapolis, where he performed in academy plays, Donlevy decided not to sign up again for military life and to try his luck on Broadway instead.

His success came slowly, and Donlevy supplemented his income by posing for Arrow Collar and cigarette ads and trying to sell his poetry and writing. Then, with help from actor Louis Wolheim he landed a small part as Corporal Gowdy in the Broadway play *What Price Glory* in 1924.

Though the play was a hit, Donlevy continued modeling and acting in other Broadway shows, such as *Milky Way* and *Hit the Deck*. Broadway work got steadier from 1927 to 1932 as he landed bigger and bigger roles in such productions as *Rainbow, Queen Bee* and *The Inside Story*.

In between, Donlevy tried his acting hand at the newer medium of silent movies. He had bit parts in *Jamestown* (1923), *School for Wives* (1925), *Gentlemen of the Press* (1929), and *Mother's Boy* (1929). His first sound film role was as the chauffeur in *A Modern Cinderella* (1932).

Donlevy's Hollywood break didn't come until 1935. Just when the pilot-turned-actor was thinking of flying back to Broadway, he finally got a role as tough guy Knuckles Jacoby in United Artist's *Barbary Coast*. It was the beginning of a long line of villainous and tough guy roles, including Gil Warren in *Old Chicago* (1938), Kent in *Destry Rides Again* (1939) and, most memorably, the sadistic Sgt. Markoff in *Beau Geste* (1939). By 1936, he was under contract with 20th Century Fox and filmed as many as seven movies in one year, flipping back and forth between A and B movie hero and villain roles.

Donlevy's wicked performance of Sgt. Markoff — an evil yet resourceful soldier with the French Foreign Legion who leads the defense of Fort Zinderneuf in Africa — earned him an Oscar nomination for Best Supporting Actor.

However, he paid the price for such a good role, physically. In one battle scene, Ray Milland was to stab Donlevy in the shoulder with his bayonet but missed and hit Donlevy in the ribcage, reportedly giving him a lifelong scar.

Donlevy collected his share of "scars" off the set as well. In 1928, he had married New York showgirl Yvonne Grey. They divorced in 1936 and he married singer Marjorie Lane that same year. The two had a daughter, his only child.

According to biographer J. Byron Dean, Donlevy's divorce from his second wife in 1947 was particularly unpleasant. Donlevy filed for divorce after a detective he hired found Marjorie in a "hotel room in a compromising position." The news was dragged through the tabloids and, though Donlevy eventually got custody of their daughter Judy, the father-daughter relationship was forever strained. In fact, Dean adds, "It was reported that Judy stopped contact with her father when he refused to give her some money that she asked for."

In the midst of his personal turmoil, Donlevy continued as the likable tough guy in film after film. He played a series of soft-sided tough guys in the 1940s such as the homeless man who becomes governor thanks to the mob in the *The Great McGinty* comedy, Captain Mercer in *I Wanted Wings*, and Major Geoffrey Caton in *Wake Island*.

Tough though he naturally was, making Donlevy the "dashing actor" took a bit of work, noted movie reviewer Leonard Maltin in the *Movie Encyclopedia*. Donlevy "was an unlikely leading man. Short (he wore platform shoes), stocky (he wore a girdle), with wavy brown hair (he wore a toupee), flashing smile (he wore false teeth), and piercing blue eyes (*those* were real)."

While his physical "flaws" probably kept him from leading man roles, Donlevy's acting ability and on-screen persona carried him well in Hollywood. He played in nearly a hundred films from the 1920s until his last film, *The Winner (Pit Stop)*, in 1969. He took to the small screen in the 1950s, starring as Steve Mitchell in the *Dangerous Assignment* TV show and was a guest on such shows as *Rawhide*, *Wagon Train*, *Perry Mason*, and *Family Affair*.

The man who survived a Mexico raid, countless combat missions, and all that Hollywood could dish out, nearly became one of those "fate-crossed stars who died too young" when the plane he was

Brian Donlevy in uniform. Photo courtesy of Wisconsin Center for Film and Theater Research. Image No. WCFTR-3764.

Famous Wisconsin Film Stars

piloting near Solvang, California, crashed into a hillside on January 11, 1950. Fortunately, Donlevy's war-tested piloting skills remained quite sharp all the years after the war and he was able to walk away from the crash.

It wasn't many years later that reports of Donlevy's heavy drinking began to make the Hollywood circuit. In the last twenty years of his life, it became physically apparent that drinking was taking a toll on his health, aging the actor quicker than the years. Still, Donlevy continued working into the late '60s. He married for a third time in 1966 when he wed Lillian Lugosi, the former wife of actor Bela Lugosi, who was famous for portraying *Dracula* in the 1931 Universal Studios picture.

He officially retired from acting in 1969 and spent his remaining years gold mining and writing poetry and short stories. Donlevy died of throat cancer at Motion Picture County Hospital in Woodland Hills, California, in April 1972. His ashes were reportedly spread over Santa Monica Bay.

ON SCREEN

You can spot Brian Donlevy on the big screen in the following movies:

The Winner (1969)
Rogues' Gallery (1968)
Arizona Bushwhackers (1968)
Five Golden Dragons (1967)
Hostile Guns (1967)
Waco (1966)
Curse of the Fly (1965)
The Fat Spy (1965)
Daikaijū Gamera (1965)
How to Stuff a Wild Bikini (1965)
MGM's Big Parade of Comedy (1964)
The Pigeon That Took Rome (1962)
Girl in Room 13 (1961)
Errand Boy (1961)
Never So Few (1959)
Juke Box Rhythm (1959)
Cowboy (1958)
Escape From Red Rock (1958)
Quatermass 2 (1957)
A Cry in the Night (1956)
The Quatermass Xperiment (1955)
The Big Combo (1955)
The Woman They Almost Lynched (1953)
Dangerous Assignment (1952) TV Series
Ride the Man Down (1952)
Hoodlum Empire (1952)
Slaughter Trail (1951)
Fighting Coast Guard (1951)
Kansas Raiders (1950)
Shakedown (1950)
Impact (1949)
The Lucky Stiff (1949)
A Southern Yankee (1948)
Command Decision (1948)
Killer McCoy (1947)
The Trouble with Women (1947)
Unusual Occupations (1947) (he played himself with daughter Judy)
Heaven Only Knows (1947)
Kiss of Death (1947)
The Beginning or the End (1947)
Song of Scheherazade (1947)
Our Hearts Were Growing Up (1946)
Two Years Before the Mast (1946)
Canyon Passage (1946)
The Virginian (1946)
Duffy's Tavern (1945) (he played himself)
The Miracle of Morgan's Creek (1944)

An American Romance (1944)
The City That Stopped Hitler: Heroic Stalingrad, (1943) (narrator)
Stand by for Action (1943)
Hangmen Also Die (1943)
Nightmare (1942)
The Remarkable Andrew (1942)
Two Yanks in Trinidad (1942)
The Great Man's Lady (1942)
The Glass Key (1942)
Wake Island (1942)
A Gentleman After Dark (1942)
Birth of the Blues (1941)
South of Tahiti (1941)
Hold Back the Dawn (1941)
Billy the Kid (1941)
I Wanted Wings (1941)
Brigham Young - Frontiersman (1940)
When the Daltons Rode (1940)
The Great McGinty (1940)
Union Pacific (1939)
Destry Rides Again (1939)
Allegheny Uprising (1939)
Beau Geste (1939)
Behind Prison Gates (1939)
Jesse James (1939)
Sharpshooters (1938)
We're Going to Be Rich (1938)
Battle of Broadway (1938)
In Old Chicago (1937)
Midnight Taxi (1937)
Born Reckless (1937)
This Is My Affair (1937)
36 Hours to Kill (1936)
High Tension (1936)
Crack-Up (1936)
Human Cargo (1936)
Half Angel (1936)
Thirteen Hours by Air (1936)
The Milky Way (1936)
Strike Me Pink (1936)
Mary Burns, Fugitive (1935)
Another Face (1935)
Barbary Coast (1935)
A Modern Cinderella (1932)
Mother's Boy (1929)
Gentlemen of the Press (1929)
A Man of Quality (1926)
School for Wives (1925)
Monsieur Beaucaire (1924)
Damaged Hearts (1924)
Jamestown (1923)

RAY "CRASH" CORRIGAN

It wasn't Johnny Weissmuller wrestling those alligators in the Tarzan movies of the 1930s, and those weren't real gorillas chasing the Three Stooges around. It was a Milwaukee boy named Ray.

If there was vine swinging, horse falling, cliff leaping, starlet scaring or just plane monkeying around to do, Hollywood directors called Ray.

Well, not exactly Ray. Anyone who knew Ray called him Crash.

Hollywood stuntman and cowboy movie star Ray "Crash" Corrigan was born Ray Benard on Valentine's Day of 1902 in the caretaker's cottage at the Schlitz brewery grounds in Milwaukee.

After a few years growing up on the brewery grounds where his father, Bernard A. Benard, worked as a caretaker, Ray, his dad, and mom Ida moved to Denver, a more fitting setting for a future cowboy.

By 1922, Corrigan was heading to Hollywood not to chase dreams of movie stardom but to find a famed naturist, Bernarr McFadden, who might help him build his physique enough to hide a double curvature of the spine that plagued him. Within a year, Benard was transformed from a slightly stooped young man into a 1930s-style Arnold Schwarzenegger.

McFadden was a trainer to the stars. He worked with Metro-Goldwyn-Mayer studios and helped the likes of Joan Crawford and Dolores del Rio keep their figures marketable. He took Benard in as a trainer.

Stars were soon talking not only about the results of Benard's training, but about the incredibly built man himself. It wasn't long before MGM art director Cedric Gibbons made the trainer a Hollywood stuntman, and he eventually stunted for thirty-one MGM movies alone. The one-time trainer is said to have been the first to accomplish vine swinging in jungle movies and was also the stuntman brave enough to fall from the ship's high yardarm in MGM's *Mutiny on the Bounty* (1935) after another man died trying the stunt.

The Milwaukee native's stunt career coincided with the popularity of jungle adventure movies, like the Tarzan series, and Benard donned handmade gorilla suits and other costumes to play primates and other monsters in a wide variety of movies, especially in the 1940s and '50s. To make his portrayals more believable, Benard spent time studying gorilla mannerisms at the San Diego Zoo.

Audiences thought his performance believable enough when, for example, Corrigan dressed as the gorilla Zamba in the movie of the same name (1949) and rescued then 6-year-old actor Beau Bridges from the jungle.

While all that monkey business helped pay the bills, Corrigan rarely was listed in the credits as "ape," thinking fans would not believe him a credible actor if they knew he was the guy in the gorilla suit. In fact, while Corrigan's name appears in the credits of *Come On, Cowboys* (1937) and *Three Texas Steers* (1939), in which he costarred, his appearances as apes in both films remained uncredited.

Corrigan had established himself as an actor by the mid-1930s, using the stage names Ray Corrigan, Ray "Crash" Corrigan, Crash Corrigan, and even just his nickname, Crash.

His acting career began with bit parts in action movies such as *Undersea Kingdom* (1932). In 1936, he began the *Three Mesquiteer* cowboy adventure series of films — twenty-four in all by 1939 — starring as Tucson Smith. Later, the cowboy actor starred in twenty of the twenty-four *Range Busters* films from 1940 to 1943 and had supporting and lead actor roles in B movies and other serials. Along the way, Corrigan began wearing the tall 10-gallon Stetson hat that became one of his trademarks.

While filming a western on the Iverson Movie Ranch in Chatsworth, California, Corrigan reportedly took a hunting break with Clark Gable and came across some nearby ranch land where he envisioned building a movie ranch of his own. He paid $1,000 down on the Simi Valley land and paid $1,000 a month until the $11,354 sale price was paid, according to an April 18, 1999, "perspective on local history" story by William Ehrheart of the *Los Angeles Times* and author of the book, *The World's Most Famous Movie Ranch: The Story of Ray 'Crash' Corrigan and Corriganville.*

Most of his *Range Busters* movies were filmed on the ranch he called Corriganville, as were at least 750 other movies and 2,750 TV episodes.

In 1949, Corrigan opened the ranch's gates to the public on weekends — the only one of Southern California's dozens of movie

Ray "Crash" Corrigan, at right, pauses for a Coke. Photo courtesy of Wisconsin Center for Film and Theater Research. Image No. WCFTR-3746.

ranches and studios to do so. Thus, Crash swung open the doors to what quickly became one of the state's biggest tourist attractions, where weekend casts acted out the gunfight at the OK Corral and Billy the Kid's jailbreak. For a while, stagecoaches, wagons and horses galloped through the town each weekend, but that was eliminated due to liability concerns in the 1960s.

Tourists could also meet western stars who served as grand marshals of the Corriganville rodeo parade. Visitors often met Corrigan himself, who welcomed them wearing one of his tall cowboy hats and shouting a friendly "Howdy, pardners."

One fan who was greeted at the ranch by a personable Corrigan remembered the 1958 encounter fondly in a Sept. 7, 2000, article in the *Los Angeles Times*, "The Handsome Actor in the White Stetson."

"I had my movie camera, the old 8-mm one, with me, and asked him if he would pose for me," Doris E. Gill recalled. "Instead, he took the camera from me, handed it to a bystander, put his arm around my waist and said, "Now walk toward the camera!" The handsome actor in his white Stetson and me, both smiling, still young, will live forever in that roll of film, even though now he is gone and I have become a senior citizen. What a wonderful day it was!"

In the midst of its popularity, Corriganville and the Corrigan family became entangled in the shooting death of another screen star, Carl Switzer, who played Alfalfa in the *Our Gang* comedies and worked as a bartender and hunting guide at Corriganville.

Switzer was shot to death January 21, 1959, by Moses S. "Bud" Stiltz, a Corriganville mechanic and welder — and one time bodyguard for Corrigan himself — who was then the husband of Corrigan's ex-wife Rita. (Corrigan was then married to bit actress Elaine DuPont.)

Corrigan's son Tom, then 14 and living on the ranch with his mother and stepfather, told Scripps Howard New Service correspondent Colleen Cason that his stepfather shot Switzer after a long-heated argument over who would pay the $50 needed to get one of Stiltz's dogs — which disappeared when Switzer had borrowed it for a hunting trip — out of the dog pound.

"It was more like murder," the now 57-year-old Tom Corrigan, told Cason in her January 28, 2001, story, "42 Years Later, Witness Says Alfalfa Was Murdered."

The young Corrigan said he was only feet from the actor and longtime family acquaintance he called "Alfie" when his stepfather met the allegedly drunk and argumentative Alfie at the door of their home with a .38-caliber revolver.

Standing a few feet away in the living room, Tom watched as the two men fought over the gun. It discharged and Tom was grazed by flying plaster when the bullet hit a wall. As his two sisters ran to a neighbor's to call police and he stepped just outside the front door, Stiltz shot Switzer. Tom Corrigan told the reporter that he turned in time to see Alfie — "a surprised look on his still-freckled face — sliding down the wall. He had been shot in the groin." Alfie was holding a closed pocketknife at his side.

Stiltz argued that he acted in self defense because Switzer had come after him with a knife, and a corner's inquest agreed.

The scandalous tragedy was the start of hard times at the ranch. By the mid-1960s, attendance had waned enough that Corrigan sold the park to Bob Hope for some $3 million.

Before Hope could reopen the once popular ranch and movie set as "Hopetown," many of the buildings were destroyed by fire. The ranch was eventually turned over to the local park district and city of Simi Valley, which reopened it as a 225-acre nature preserve that still features western skits.

There is little of the old movie sets for visitors to see, though the old "hangin' tree" is still visible as is a large basin studio crews filled with water to film scenes for *The African Queen*.

Ray "Crash" Corrigan did not live long enough to see his ranch restored. He suffered a fatal heart attack August 10, 1976, in Brookings Hollow, Oregon.

ON SCREEN

You can ride into the sunset with cowboy Ray "Crash" Corrigan in his many Western films listed below. Or, try to find him in one of uncredited roles. Remember, if the movie listed wasn't a Western, Corrigan probably had a bit role or, more likely, was playing the ape or monster in the film.

Sharad of Atlantis (1966) (TV)
It! The Terror from Beyond Space (1958)
The Domino Kid (1957)
Zombies of Mora Tau (1957)
Apache Ambush (1955)
The Great Adventures of Captain Kidd (1953)
Killer Ape (1953)
Trail of Robin Hood (1950) cameo appearance
The Adventures of Sir Galahad (1949)
Zamba (1949) (uncredited)
Unknown Island (1948) (uncredited)
Renegade Girl (1946)
The Monster and the Ape (1945)
White Pongo (1945) (uncredited)
The White Gorilla (1945)
Nabonga (1944) (uncredited)
She's for Me (1943)
Bullets and Saddles (1943)
Black Market Rustlers (1943)
Captive Wild Woman (1943)
Cowboy Commandos (1943)
Land of Hunted Men (1943)
Texas Trouble Shooters (1942)
Dr. Renault's Secret (1942) (uncredited)
Arizona Stage Coach (1942)
Boot Hill Bandits (1942)
The Strange Case of Doctor Rx (1942)
Rock River Renegades (1942)
Thunder River Feud (1942)
Tumbledown Ranch in Arizona (1941)
Underground Rustlers (1941)
Tonto Basin Outlaws (1941)
Saddle Mountain Roundup (1941)
Fugitive Valley (1941)
Wrangler's Roost (1941)
The Kid's Last Ride (1941)
Trail of the Silver Spurs (1941)
The Range Busters (1940)
Trailing Double Trouble (1940)
West of Pinto Basin (1940)
The Ape (1940) (uncredited)
New Frontier (1939)
Wyoming Outlaw (1939)
Three Texas Steers (1939)
The Night Riders (1939)
Red River Range (1938)
Santa Fe Stampede (1938)
Overland Stage Raiders (1938)
Pals of the Saddle (1938)
Heroes of the Hills (1938)
Riders of the Black Hills (1938)
Outlaws of Sonora (1938)
Call the Mesquiteers (1938)
Purple Vigilantes (1938)
Wild Horse Rodeo (1937)

The Trigger Trio (1937)
Heart of the Rockies (1937)
Range Defenders (1937)
The Painted Stallion (1937)
Come on Cowboys (1937)
Gunsmoke Ranch (1937)
Hit the Saddle (1937)
Join the Marines (1937)
The Riders of the Whistling Skull (1937)
Roarin' Lead (1936)
Country Gentlemen (1936)
Ghost-Town Gold (1936)
The Three Mesquiteers (1936)
The Vigilantes Are Coming (1936) (uncredited)
Kelly the Second (1936) (uncredited)
Undersea Kingdom (1936)
The Leathernecks Have Landed (1936)
Darkest Africa (1936), his last known credit with his real name Ray Benard, before becoming Ray "Crash" Corrigan
The Singing Vagabond (1935)
Mutiny on the Bounty (1935) (uncredited)
Dante's Inferno (1935) (uncredited, he played the Devil)
She (1935) (uncredited)
The Night Life of the Gods (1935)
The Phantom Empire (1935) (uncredited)
Tomorrow's Youth (1935)
Tomorrow's Children (1934) (uncredited)
Romance in the Rain (1934) (uncredited)
Tarzan and His Mate (1934) (uncredited)
Mystery Ranch (1934) (uncredited)
Murder in the Private Car (1933) (uncredited)

CHARLES WINNINGER

Charles Winninger was born into show business as Karl Winninger in the far-from-Hollywood location of Athens, Wisconsin, May 26, 1884.

By all accounts, the Winningers remained in northern Wisconsin until Charles was about 9. Then, he quit school and joined the family vaudeville act on the road.

Though Winninger spent years in stage productions throughout America, including on Broadway, where he originated the role of Captain Andy in the 1927 premiere of *Show Boat* and earned lead billing in the *Ziegfeld Follies,* Winninger didn't make it big on the silver screen until he was in his mid-40s.

The vaudeville comedian and singer turned movie character actor had been featured in some short and silent films in the 1920, such as *September Mourning* (1916) and *Summer Bachelors* (1926), before landing the role of Otto Schmidt in the 1930 Three Stooges feature *Soup to Nuts*.

Winninger got his biggest Hollywood break in 1936 when he revised his *Show Boat* captain role for the movie version and performed what many critics, including Leonard Maltin in a 1994 biography, deemed the "greatest performance of his career."

The mid- to late-1930s proved the busiest and most successful time for the new Hollywood film star. Winninger was featured in such hits as *Three Smart Girls* (1936), *Nothing Sacred* (1937) in which fellow Wisconsinite Fredric March costarred, *Every Day's a Holiday* (1937) with Mae West, and *You Can't Have Everything* (1937) where Winninger was able to show off his boisterous singing voice. In 1939, he starred in the musical *Babes in Arms* and then played drunken banjo player Washington Dimsdale, alongside Badger State native Brian Donlevy as "Kent" and upcoming Milwaukee raised actor Jack Carson as Jack Tyndall, in *Destry Rides Again*.

Winninger's biggest hit of the 1940s was most likely *State Fair* (1945). Though he had been considered for but didn't get the role of the wizard in the *Wizard of Oz*, Winninger did costar with Oz actress Judy Garland in the 1940 musical *Little Nellie Kelly*. He also appeared in such movies as *Ziegfeld Girl* (1941), the musical

Give My Regards to Broadway (1948) and *Father Is a Bachelor* (1950).

In 1953, legendary director John Ford complimented Winninger's acting talents by asking him to star in a special movie project of his, *The Sun Shines Bright*, a remake of Will Rogers' *Judge Priest*. Winninger starred as the old judge, clinging to his glorious Civil War past, in a turn-of-the-century Kentucky town.

His movie career had begun to wane by this time, however, as had his marriage to actress Blanche Ring, which ended in divorce in 1951 when she was 73 and he 67. (His first marriage to bit actress and screen writer Gertrude Walker had also ended.)

Though Winninger acted in a few more movies — his last in the 1960s, *Raymie*, about a barracuda fishing trip — he turned to television for more work in the 1950s and early '60s, returning to his vaudeville roots for a guest appearance as Fred Mertz's old vaudeville partner on an *I Love Lucy* episode and as the father on *The Charlie Farrell Show* in 1956.

Charles Winninger's performances faded away as the 1960s wore on, and he died January 27, 1969, in Palm Springs, California. He was posthumously inducted into the Wisconsin Performing Artists Hall of Fame.

ON SCREEN

Watch Charles Winninger's performances in the following movies:

Raymie (1960)
The Charles Farrell Show (1956) TV Series
Las Vegas Shakedown (1955)
Champ for a Day (1953)
The Sun Shines Bright (1953)
A Perilous Journey (1953)
Torpedo Alley (1953)
Father Is a Bachelor (1950)
Give My Regards to Broadway (1948)
The Inside Story (1948)
Living in a Big Way (1947)
Something in the Wind (1947)
Lover Come Back (1946)
She Wouldn't Say Yes (1945)
State Fair (1945)
The Two-Way Street (1945)
Sunday Dinner for a Soldier (1944)
Belle of the Yukon (1944)
Broadway Rhythm (1944)
Hers to Hold (1943)
Flesh and Fantasy (1943)
A Lady Takes a Chance (1943)
Coney Island (1943)
Friendly Enemies (1942)
Mister Gardenia Jones (1942)
My Life with Caroline (1941)
The Get-Away (1941)
Ziegfeld Girl (1941)
Pot o' Gold (1941)
Little Nellie Kelly (1940)
If I Had My Way (1940)
Beyond Tomorrow (1940)
My Love Came Back (1940)
Destry Rides Again (1939)
Barricade (1939)
Babes in Arms (1939)
Three Smart Girls Grow Up (1939)
Hard to Get (1938)

Goodbye Broadway (1938)
You're a Sweetheart (1937)
Every Day's a Holiday (1937)
Nothing Sacred (1937)
You Can't Have Everything (1937)
The Go Getter (1937)
Cafe Metropole (1937)
Woman Chases Man (1937)
Three Smart Girls (1936)
White Fang (1936)
Show Boat (1936)
The Social Register (1934)
Children of Dreams (1931)

Flying High (1931)
Husband's Holiday (1931)
The Sin of Madelon Claudet (1931)
Night Nurse (1931)
God's Gift to Women (1931)
Gun Smoke (1931)
The Bad Sister (1931)
Fighting Caravans (1931)
Soup to Nuts (1930)
Summer Bachelors (1926)
The Canadian (1926)
Pied Piper Malone (1924)
A September Mourning (1916)

JOSEPH LOSEY

John Ford. Francis Ford Coppola. Orson Welles. Steven Spielberg. Nicholas Ray. Joseph Losey. ... Who? Most American moviegoers don't recognize the last name on that list of Hollywood directors, though European film fans remember the American director Joseph Losey well.

That's because the La Crosse, Wisconsin, native made most of his films overseas after the Hollywood establishment blacklisted him in 1951 for being a communist.

Losey was well on his way to becoming a top Hollywood film director when the blacklisting occurred, and though he made some critically and publicly popular films in Europe — many of which were shown in America — he never found Hollywood's brightest spotlights.

The director was born January 14, 1909, into a prominent La Crosse pioneer family, for whom Losey Boulevard in the town is named. His father, a Burlington Railroad agent, died around the time his son and namesake graduated from Central High School in La Crosse in 1925, the same high school fellow moviemaker and La Crosse area native Nicholas Ray — director of *Rebel Without a Cause* — would graduate from a few years later.

In addition to being an acolyte at LaCrosse's Episcopal church, Losey kept busy in high school where he later said he had felt alienated. According to David Caute in *Joseph Losey — A Revenge on Life,* the future director was a competing orator, "played the saxophone and served on the editorial committee of the school annual, the Booster." He was also a member of the Falstaff Society and performed in a few high school productions, including *The Manicure Shop, The New Poor* and *Adam and Eva.* Losey's graduation epitaph read, "inebriated with the exuberance of his own verbosity," according to Caute.

Losey was an unhealthy child, suffering the mumps several times, enduring appendicitis, scarlet fever and a host of other ailments. When he wasn't ill, the upper-middle class boy enjoyed time at his Aunt Mary Losey Eaton's palacious home, which featured a bowling alley, greenhouse and carriage house. Losey remembered going canoeing and boating in his "Aunt Mer's exquisite boat house," on the Mississippi, Caute notes.

After graduation, Joseph Walton Losey left Wisconsin to become a doctor, earning a bachelor's degree from Dartmouth College and a graduate degree in English literature from Harvard University before dropping out of medical school to pursue his literary and theatrical interests.

Losey moved to New York and reviewed plays for the *New York Times* and *New York Herald-Tribune,* among other publications, to make ends meet. By 1932, he was a stage manager at Radio City Music Hall and directed his first play, *Little Ol' Boy,* before taking directing jobs with political theater groups.

Five years later, Losey was hanging out in New York with playwrights Harold Pinter and Bertolt Brecht — whom he met while studying with Sergei Eisenstein in Moscow on a theater tour of Russia and Scandinavia in 1935.

In 1938, the stage director made the first of sixty documentary films for the Rockefeller Foundation and soon filmed a short series for MGM.

He was working as an NBC radio drama director, when America entered World War II. The director was eventually drafted and reportedly went to some lengths to get out of military service, such as sleeping with two cats to spark an allergic reaction the night before his medical exam, according to author David Caute in his book *Joseph Losey: A Revenge on Life* (as reviewed by Ian McIntyre in *The Times*, London, 1994). Losey's eventual service in America's armed forces didn't last long, and he received a medical discharge.

After he returned to New York, the future moviemaker directed Brecht's *Galileo Galilei* in 1947.

The acclaim Losey received for his stage direction drew Hollywood's attention. In 1948, he directed his first major film, *The Boy With Green Hair* about an ostracized war orphan, starring Wisconsinite Pat O'Brien as one of the boy's only friends.

Losey enjoyed analyzing social issues in film and did so in his 1950 movie *The Lawless* about Southern California fruit pickers.

Common in Losey's films were characters whose self-destructive behavior led to their own downfalls, such as in his 1951 film *The Prowler,* with disgruntled cop character Webb Garwood.

But just as his Hollywood movie career was picking up speed and praise, and shortly after his completion of the movie *M* in 1951, Losey and his wife, Louise, were publicly "outed" as communists by screenwriter Leo Townsend in his testimony before the U.S. House Un-American Activities Committee. Eventually the Hollywood establishment blacklisted hundreds of movie talents.

Though producers thought enough of Losey's often gritty, intellectual film style to reportedly consider him to direct the eventual hit *High Noon*, Hollywood offers ended as soon as the communist allegations broke.

Not that Losey hadn't given the committee reason to suspect he was a communist.

Though he eventually signed a statement denouncing communism in 1960, Losey was reportedly a longtime fan of Soviet leader Joseph Stalin and publicly claimed to be a socialist as well as a Marxist. Losey also had a reputation for being a womanizer who was reported to have shared mistresses with one of his sons, an alcoholic, a political radical and just plain rude, according to Caute. In fact, the FBI had been investigating the director's loyalties since 1943, and kept him under surveillance through 1966, amassing a 750-page report, which hinted at the director's possible links to Soviet spies, Caute revealed.

Regardless of whether there was truth in the accusations, the results of Losey's communist status were the same: He was effectively banned from making films in America.

Losey was reportedly filming *Stranger on the Prowl* in Italy at the time the accusations surfaced on Capitol Hill and opted not to respond to the committee's summons.

Instead, the director moved first to Canada and then to England, reportedly leaving behind his wife and son, so he could continue to make films. Though the blacklist controversy eventually faded into history, the American director never returned to film in his birth country, according to a documentary about his life, *Joseph Losey: The Man With Four Names* by Japanese filmmaker Hideo Tanaka, profiled in a June 2, 1998, article in Tokyo's *Daily Yomiuri*.

When Losey began directing in Great Britain, he did so under assumed names like Andrea Forzano, Terence Hanbury, Victor Hanbury or Joseph Walton in order to avoid further U.S. investigations. In his first years of exile, the director created mediocre films such as *Stranger on the Prowl*, finally released in 1953, and *Finger of Guilt* (1956). Losey continued to weave political statements, as well as themes about betrayal, into his films as in *Time Without Pity*, a 1956 movie that takes on capital punishment.

By the 1960s, time and Losey's directorial talents had worn away at the communist stigma and Losey was able to direct films under his real name, several written by his old friend and playwright Harold Pinter. The La Crosse son found fame in his new home in London with such thrillers as *Blind Date* in 1959 and *Eva* in 1965.

In 1963, he directed one of his most acclaimed films, *The Servant*, which explored the difficulties of transcending the class system. It was a theme that recurred in his movies like *King and Country* (1964), *Accident* (1967), and *The Go-Between* (1971). Other films included *The Romantic Englishwoman* (1975), *Mr. Klein* (1976) and *Don Giovanni* (1979).

Most significantly in his later years, Losey directed Elizabeth Taylor and Richard Burton in *Boom!* in 1968 and American actress Jane Fonda to critical acclaim in *A Doll's House* in 1973.

Not long after, Losey moved to France, where he directed three films in French. Losey returned to England for his final film, *Steaming*, movie about women in a Turkish bath, written by his fourth wife Patricia.

Losey died in London on June 22, 1984. There was reportedly no eulogy given at his funeral, notes Ian McIntyre in the 1994 *The Times* article.

ON SCREEN

See Joseph Losey's work in the following films:
Steaming (1985)
La Truite (1982)
Boris Godunov (1980) (TV)
Don Giovanni (1979)
Roads to the South (Les Routes du sud) (1978)
Mr. Klein (1976)
Galileo (1975)
The Romantic Englishwoman (1975)
A Doll's House (1973)
The Assassination of Trotsky (1972)
Figures in a Landscape (1970)
The Go-Between (1970)
Secret Ceremony (1968)
Boom (1968)
Accident (1967)
Modesty Blaise (1966)
King & Country (1964)
The Servant (1963)
Eva (1963)
The Damned (1962)
The Criminal (1960)
First on the Road (1959)
Blind Date (1958)
The Gypsy and the Gentleman (1958)
Finger of Guilt (The Intimate Stranger) (1956)
Time Without Pity (1956)
A Man of the Beach (1955)
The Sleeping Tiger (1954)
Stranger on the Prowl (Imbarco a mezzanotte) (1951)
M (1951)
The Big Night (1951)
The Prowler (1951)
The Lawless (1950)
The Boy with Green Hair (1948)
Galileo (1947)
A Gun in His Hand (1945)
A Child Went Forth (1941)
Youth Gets a Break (1941)
Pete Roleum and His Cousins (1939)

CHARLOTTE RAE

Nobody knows the facts of life better than Shorewood High School graduate Charlotte Rae Lubotsky. After all, the actress spent more than seven years getting intimately acquainted with those words as the star of the hit TV show named for that phrase.

Long before Charlotte Rae played girls' school housemother Edna Garrett, the character actress was sharing the local stage with fellow aspiring actor and future movie star Jeffrey Hunter. While both were studying at their respective Milwaukee area high schools, the two acted in Port Players summer stock productions in Whitefish Bay, were featured on Milwaukee community radio programs and in children's theater, and later both performed at Northwestern University, where Rae graduated in 1948 and Hunter in 1949.

She also befriended community actress Charlotte Zucker, the mother of future Hollywood directors David and Jerry Zucker. "I remember her very fondly, and she's Milwaukee through and through. She's a very good and real person," Mrs. Zucker recalled. "She is sweet, generous and warm. I've seen her do some serious work on stage and she's a superb actress."

Born April 22, 1926, as the middle daughter of a Russian-Jewish immigrant who ran a Milwaukee tire business, Rae dreamed of being a star from an early age, she told Dwight Whitney of the *TV Guide Review* for his Dec. 8, 1979, profile "Plain is Beautiful." Always a serious and insecure girl, Rae explained that she thought, "If I could just be a big star I'd feel like somebody too."

It was her Milwaukee grade school teacher, Miss Knight, who was the first to officially recognize and encourage the young girl's dreams, Rae said: "A bunch of us kids sang 'Hi ho, it's off to work we go.' She singled me out and it felt really good. I sensed I had the talent, and I grasped onto it like a drowning person onto a life raft."

Her high school yearbook confirmed Rae's talents and desires, noting that she sang in the mixed choir her first two years of high school and joined the drama club as a junior. The yearbook reports that she was an "outstanding member," who performed in such school productions such as *Quality Street*, where she stole the show with her portrayal of Susan. "She follows her hobbies of singing, dancing and dramatics very seriously," one yearbook editor noted.

Little did her classmates know just how "very seriously" she would pursue her talents.

Rae honed her skills in Northwestern University's theater department where she met lifelong friend and actress Cloris Leachman and began her career as a character actress in such university performances as *The Three Penny Opera* in which she played Mrs. Peachum, a role she later took to the Broadway stage.

In between classes, Rae acted and performed on Chicago radio programs. It was a soap opera radio program director who convinced the actress to drop her last name because " Lubotsky" simply wouldn't grab a national audience's attention.

Though itching to take her acting and singing talents to New York, Rae followed her parents' wishes and graduated from college before she and Leachman moved to the Big Apple and shared an apartment while chasing their dreams.

To help make ends meet, Rae took a job at the Sawdust Trail bar where she would sing tunes like "Can't Help Lovin' That Man."

"Sometimes a drunk would give me 50 cents," she recalled in the 1979 *TV Guide* article, adding that her Midwest parents didn't approve of the way their daughter was making ends meet. "My father came in once and nearly died. With tears in his eyes he told me the cigarette girl had tried to hustle him."

It was her voice that brought Rae to the sunnier side of Broadway. She was soon opening for singer Richard Dyer Bennett at the Village Vanguard, where she met and eventually married composer John Strauss. They had two sons, Larry and Andy (who was autistic), and divorced in the mid-1970s.

By the 1950s, Rae was getting regular work on Broadway, thanks to some added training from drama coach Mary Tarcai. Her first Broadway appearance was in the flop musical *Three Wishes for Jamie* in 1952. Regardless of the show's failings, Rae relished her first opening night on Broadway, she told Whitney. "It was kinda nice. … My father was so proud when we walked into Sardi's and everyone applauded," the actress recalled.

Despite the awkward start, Rae was soon a Broadway name. She created "Mammy Yokum" in the 1956 musical *Lil' Abner* and was eventually nominated for two Tony Awards — once each for her performances in *Pickwick* and *Morning, Noon and Night*.

Beginning in the late 1950s, Rae began splitting her talents between the Broadway stage, the television box and the movie screen. She got her small screen break with a part in the 1959 TV show *The World of Sholom Aleichem* and then appeared in such TV series as *From These Roots* (1958) and *Car 54, Where Are You?* (1961). The actress also took her turn at commercials, selling Excedrin to headache sufferers with Charles Nelson Reilly and gaining audience recognition "squeezing the Charmin" in the toilet paper commercials.

Charlotte Rae's high school picture. Photo courtesy of Shorewood High School.

Rae has always continued to act on stage as well. And, though it took decades, the insecure Milwaukee girl finally caught her Hollywood star when Norman Lear liked her Los Angeles performance as a tourist in *Time of the Cuckoo*. He cast her as the mother in the short-lived TV series *Hot L Baltimore*. That role led her to the hit show *Diff'rent Strokes*, where she first played the character Mrs. Garrett until 1978.

Her TV performances drew movie directors' attention, and Rae was cast in several Hollywood films. She first played Myrtle Ruth in *Hello Down There* and Bella Star in *Jenny*, both in 1969. In 1971 she was Mrs. Mellish in *Bananas* and then played Ma Murch in the diamond heist movie *The Hot Rock* in 1972. She also appeared as Cousin Claire in 1978's *Rabbit Test*, as a party guest in 1979's *Hair* and, most recently, as the fortune teller in 1997's *Nowhere*.

Audiences may well recognize her voice as well as her face in movies, since Rae also lent her vocal talents to such cartoon characters as Aunt Pristine Figg in *Tom and Jerry: The Movie* (1992) and the nanny in *101 Dalmatians* (TV series, 1996).

Others may recognize her from a long list of TV movies, including *Crime in Connecticut: The Story of Alex Kelly (1999)*, *Save the Dog! (1988)*, and *The Worst Witch (1986)* — and her many guest appearances on such shows as *The Love Boat*, *Barney Miller*, and

All in the Family. Rae also played Molly the Maid on *Sesame Street* from 1972 to 1973 and, most recently, guest starred on *Diagnosis Murder* (2000).

For all her roles, however, the talented character actress will forever be known as the housemother character, Mrs. Edna Garrett Gaines, on *The Facts of Life* TV show, which first aired in 1979. In 1982, Rae won an Emmy for Outstanding Lead Actress in a Comedy Series for her portrayal of the stern but cool and loving Mrs. Garrett. She also was inducted into the Wisconsin Performing Artists Hall of Fame.

Through Mrs. Garrett, Rae often worked Wisconsin, her friends, and family into the show. For starters, Rae created her housemother character, who was born and raised on a farm near Appleton, as a morally upstanding person who, like Rae, didn't like to hear people swear. The show's Natalie character was named for one of the actress's friends, and the character of Andy for her autistic son. When Rae ended her character's role by having Mrs. Garrett marry and join the Peace Corps, she was replaced by Cloris Leachman as Mrs. Garrett's sister, and new housemother, Beverly Ann (a character named for Rae's real sister).

And, if you ever doubted Rae's singing talents first noticed in that Milwaukee grade school, listen to the show's theme song. That's Rae singing "… it's the facts of life, the facts of life."

It took a few decades, but the Milwaukee girl had finally made it big. Even today, Rae is recognized everywhere she goes as Mrs. Garrett. "I can't even go to Barbados without people wanting to hug me and say 'Oh, Mrs. Garrett,'" she's quoted as saying in an Internet Movie Database biography.

It's the kind of recognition and acceptance she sought so eagerly as an insecure girl, the now 76-year-old grandmother and continual stage actress once told Whitney. "When strangers put their arms around you and tell you how much they love you it somehow makes it all worthwhile."

ON SCREEN

Check out Charlotte Rae's screen performances in the following:

The Facts of Life Reunion (2001) (TV)
Biography: Kim Fields: A Little Somethin' Somethin' (2001)
Intimate Portrait: Kim Fields (2001) (TV)
Al Lewis: Forever Grandpa (2000) (Video)
Another Woman's Husband (2000) (TV)
Crime in Connecticut: The Story of Alex Kelly (1999) (TV)
Nowhere (1997)
101 Dalmatians: The (TV) Series (1996)
Tom and Jerry: The Movie (1992) (voice)
Save the Dog! (1988) (TV)
The Worst Witch (1986) (TV)
Words by Heart (1985) (TV)
The Facts of Life Goes to Paris (1982) (TV)
Beanes of Boston (1979)
The Facts of Life (1979-1986) TV Series
Hair (1979)
The Triangle Factory Fire Scandal (1979) (TV)
A Different Approach (1978)
Rabbit Test (1978)
Diff'rent Strokes (1978-1979 & 1984) TV Series
Sidewinder 1 (1977)
Our Town (1977) (TV)
The Rich Little Show (1976) TV Series
Queen of the Stardust Ballroom (1975) (TV)
Hot L Baltimore (1975) TV Series
In Fashion (1974) (TV)
The Hot Rock (1972)
Sesame Street (1969, 1972-1973) TV Series
Bananas (1971)
Hello Down There (1969)
Jenny (1969)
The Journey of the Fifth Horse (1966) (TV)
Car 54, Where Are You? (1961) TV Series
From These Roots (1958) TV Series
The World of Sholom Aleichem (1959) (TV)

TOM HULCE

Wolfgang Amadeus Mozart was born in Salzburg, Austria, January 27, 1756. Nearly two hundred years later, on December 6, 1953, Whitewater, Wisconsin, welcomed Thomas Edward Hulce, the man who would one day bring the legend back to life.

In 1984, dressed in a white wig and sporting a maniacal laugh, Hulce turned in an Oscar-nominated performance as the brilliant, funny, conceited, and obnoxious composer.

Mozart was a far cry from some of his other recognizable movie characters, including the "good-boy" fraternity pledge Larry Kroger, "Pinto," in National Lampoon's *Animal House* in 1978.

But then, challenge and variety have been hallmarks of Hulce since he first broke into movies in 1977 as a depressed boy in *September 30, 1955*. A decade later, Hulce portrayed a mentally handicapped man who works as a garbage collector to put his brother through medical school in *Dominick and Eugene*, a 1988 movie also starring Ray Liotta and Jamie Lee Curtis. By 1996, Hulce was lending his voice to that of bell ringer Quasimodo in the Disney feature animation motion picture *The Hunchback of Notre Dame* and its video sequel.

In all, the Wisconsin native's name can be found prominently displayed in the credits of more than twenty motion pictures and television movies, including as a young dreamer in the TV movie *The Rise and Rise of Daniel Rocket* (1986), a gambler in *Parenthood* (1989), and a sleazy lawyer in *Fearless* (1993).

Though still seen on movie sets, Hulce is more likely to be found on stage and has performed in dozens of plays from London to Broadway to Seattle, where he now lives.

What influence Whitewater and the Badger State had on Hulce's talents would be hard to measure, short of simply giving him a good start in life. A few years after he was born, Hulce, his two sisters and older brother moved to Plymouth, Michigan, where Hulce's father had a job with Ford.

Hulce began performing early, singing in the church choir at 5 and attending the National Music Camp at Interlochen, Michigan at 11. He often played "the kid" in Detroit-area productions, and at 13 landed a role in an Ann Arbor recreation department production of *Take Me Along*. In 1967, he played Oliver in the University of Michigan's production of *Oliver!*; the next year he played the snake in the Interlochen Arts Camp's production of *The Apple Tree*.

By 15, Hulce had enough experience to know that he needed more professional acting training and wanted a shot at Broadway.

In a September 5, 1980, *New York Times* article by Anna Quindlen, Hulce said that his parents weren't all that crazy about the idea. Though his mom had been a professional singer and better understood her son's performing desires, "my practical father wanted me to go to the University of Michigan and get a good basic education. I just couldn't do it. I left home at 15 with nothing but potential."

Hulce enrolled in the North Carolina School of the Arts and studied there for the next three or so years, acting in plays from Michigan to Maine and London to Florida. In the early 1970s, as he was dealing with his parents' divorce, Hulce started chasing his acting dreams in New York City, taking work as a shopper/gopher for the New York Shakespeare Festival.

Though Hulce had given himself ten years to make it as an actor, it was just six weeks before he was poised to move from behind the scenes to center stage when he landed a spot as the understudy to Peter Firth in the Broadway production of *Equus*. Originally, Hulce was to be an understudy and play one of the horses in the production about a boy whose love of horses gets in the way of other relationships. However, when Firth left the role, Hulce stepped up to his marks, playing opposite Tony Perkins in New York and Anthony Hopkins in Los Angeles.

Though he had tried his talents on movie screens while an understudy — in *Forget Me Not Lane* for PBS, and in *Emily, Emily* — it was his stage role in *Equus* that drew the attention of Hollywood directors.

Hulce's *Equus* performance caught the eye of director John Landis in Los Angeles, but it took three tries and some debate before Landis gave Hulce the part of Pinto in *Animal House*, Hulce told Quindlen in the *New York Times* interview.

"They saw me in *Equus* and said, 'Oh, this is not what we want,' and then they saw me in *September 30, 1955*, a film I had done with James Bridges and said 'That's not it.' And then I came in and met them, and they said, 'No, that's not it.' Then finally they let me come in and do the part for them. That's what I do, and that's how I got it."

The next year, Hulce returned to Wisconsin for a few weeks to perform the role of Romeo in the Milwaukee Repertory Theater's production of *Romeo and Juliet*, and then starred as Artie in the movie *Those Lips, Those Eyes* in 1980.

Hulce did not return to movies for four years, acting on stage in the title role of *Little Johnny Jones* among others. But when Hulce did return to the Hollywood lights, he shined brightly.

After a grueling audition, in which he beat out Simon Callow, who had played Mozart on the English stage, Hulce was cast by director Milos Forman as the gifted and quirky composer.

As he is known to do with any of his roles, Hulce researched the historic character in depth, learning to conduct an orchestra and play piano as well as listening to all of Mozart's music and memorizing much of it, including "Requiem," the piece Mozart dictated from his deathbed.

His performance was so convincing that the Whitewater native was nominated for both a Golden Globe and an Oscar, and sales of Mozart's music reportedly increased thirty percent after the movie's release.

Hulce told interviewer Don Shewey that he learned of the Oscar nomination while promoting the movie in Singapore when the phone rang in the middle of the night.

At the Academy Awards ceremony itself, Hulce said he was more nervous about the possibility of speaking in front of large and prestigious crowd than about winning or losing the nomination. "When I heard who had won (F. Murray Abraham) my first reaction was one of relief," he said.

Two years later, Hulce returned to a role written for him by playwright Peter Parnell, that of Daniel Rocket in *The Rise and Rise of Daniel Rocket*. He'd been playing Daniel in an off-Broadway production when he learned he got the Mozart part and, in 1986, transformed the story of the young dreamer who could fly into a PBS American Playhouse TV movie of the same name.

Since his astounding success as Mozart in 1984, Hulce has continued to act in movies, most recently as the voice of Quasimodo in Disney's *Hunchback of Notre Dame* animation films. However, his most acclaimed works of recent years have been on stage, including his Tony-nominated performance as Lt. J.G. Daniel Kaffee in the stage production of *A Few Good Men* at The Music Box

Theatre in New York in 1989.

Most recently, Hulce has done much of his stage work in the Seattle area where he has lived for the past eight years. Married to Cecilia Ermini in 1996, Hulce is now divorced and focusing his theatrical talents toward directing. Together with codirector Jane Jones, Hulce brought John Irving's 1985 novel, *The Cider House Rules,* to the stage from 1995 to 1999, with much critical acclaim, in an eight-hour production that took audiences two days to see.

ON SCREEN

In addition to his most well known films *Amadeus* (1984) and National Lampoon's *Animal House* (1978), you can spot Tom Hulce on the big screen in the following movies:

The Hunchback of Notre Dame II, video (2002)
The Brink of Summer's End, documentary (1997)
The Hunchback of Notre Dame (1996)
The Heidi Chronicles, TV (1995)
Wings Of Courage (1995)
Mary Shelley's Frankenstein (1994)
Fearless (1993)
The Inner Circle (1992)
Murder in Mississippi (1990) (TV)
Black Rainbow (1990)
Parenthood (1989)
John Henry (1988) (TV)
Dominick and Eugene (1988)
Shadowman (1988)
Slamdance (1987)
Echo Park (1986)
The Rise and Rise of Daniel Rocket (1986) (TV)
Those Lips, Those Eyes (1980)
Emily, Emily (1978)
September 30, 1955 (1977)
Forget-Me-Not Lane (1975) (TV)

ELLEN CORBY

For many Americans, Racine native Ellen Corby will always be "Grandma." From 1972 to 1979, and for two decades afterward in made-for-TV special movies, Corby portrayed Esther Walton, the matriarch of the close-knit mountain family in the *The Waltons* TV series, for which she won three Emmy awards (1973, '74 and '75) and a Golden Globe in 1974. In 1976, she suffered a stroke and her mumbling speech and slow movements were built into the previously acid-tongued character in its final season and subsequent specials until her death in 1999.

Few fans of the TV series realize how long Corby appeared on motion picture reels before she got caught in the TV spotlight. In all, Corby performed in more than a hundred movies from 1933 to 1972.

Born Ellen Hansen on June 3, 1911 (or 1913 depending on the source) in Racine, Wisconsin, Corby grew up in Pennsylvania and worked for a time as a chorus girl in Atlantic City. In the early 1930s, at the height of the Great Depression, the petite and serious hard worker chased her dreams to California.

The actress didn't exactly make a big splash in Hollywood. She worked as a chorus line dancer and began slowly earning small, uncredited roles in *Rafter Romance* (1933), *The Broken Coin* (1934) and *Speed Limited* (1935), before fading from the screen for nearly a decade.

While she wasn't on camera, Corby was hardly idle. She worked twelve years as a script girl (script supervisor) for RKO Pictures and wrote part of the script for *The Broken Coin*. She later cowrote the script for *Twilight on the Trail* (1941) and wrote the story for *Hoppy's Holiday* (1947). She also worked on her marriage to Francis Corby, whom she married in 1934. Though they divorced ten years later, the one-time script girl kept his last name as she moved on to steady work in dozens of uncredited and minor movie roles and a few lead ones.

She was next seen on the big screen in an uncredited role in *Cornered* (1945). Then, in 1946, she was cast in minor roles in fourteen different films, including *The Truth About Murder* and *In Old San Francisco*. She also played the cleaner who found the body in *The Dark Corner*, and she was the woman Jimmy Stewart kissed on the head after she withdrew only $17.50 during the rush on his Building & Loan in *It's a Wonderful Life*. Corby also acted on stage from time to time in the 1940s, touring in a play called *The Ink Well*.

During World War II, Corby volunteered to entertain troops with the United States Overseas (USO) and was sent to Alaska's Aleutian Islands to perform *The Male Animal*. The ten-actor cast shared two dressing rooms and staged the play with wintry-wet weather as their backdrop.

Corby's biggest motion picture moment came in her portrayal as Aunt Tesh in 1948's *I Remember Mama*, a performance that won her a Best Supporting Actress Academy Award nomination.

For the next three decades, Corby mostly played maids, old-lady gossips and busybodies, in such box office hits as *Shane* (1953), *Vertigo* (1958) and *Hush... Hush, Sweet Charlotte* (1964) and lesser films such as *Rusty Saves a Life* (1949) and *The Ghost and Mr. Chicken* (1966). Three Stooges fans may also remember her as the lady who with Dean Martin gave Larry, Moe and Curly a "triple face slap" in *4 for Texas* (1963).

Though never without work in the fickle Hollywood business climate, Corby earned her greatest fame on television. When she first appeared in her most famous role on *The Waltons*, 1950s and 60s TV fans no doubt recognized the actress from her many guest and serial television appearances.

Corby appeared in episodes of *The Tab Hunter Show, Mr. Terrific,* and *Pride of the Family*. She played Hubcaps Lesh, the leader of a band of car thieves, on *The Andy Griffith Show* and appeared as an acting teacher on the *I Love Lucy* episode where the red-headed comedian met Wisconsin native and Hollywood legend Orson Welles. She had a recurring role in the 1960s as the maid on *Please Don't Eat the Daisies* and as Mother Lurch on *The Addams Family*. She also appeared in several 1950s western TV series, including *Trackdown* and *Wagon Train,* for which she was given a Golden Boot by the Motion Picture and Television Fund in 1989.

Corby's last appearance was as Grandma Walton in the 1997 TV movie, *A Walton Easter*. By the late 1990s, Corby was a partial invalid and spent much of her time in the Los Angeles home that she'd shared since 1976 with her friend of forty-five years, Stella Luchetta, occasionally watching *Waltons* reruns. The 87- (or 86-) year-old actress spent her final weeks in a nursing home and died April 14, 1999.

Ellen Corby as she appears in *Rockabilly Baby*. Photo courtesy of Wisconsin Center for Film and Theater Research. Image No. WCFTR-3747.

Following a small memorial service, Corby was buried at Forest Lawn Cemetery in Glendale, California. There, *The Waltons* executive producer Earl Hamner sealed into her resting place a copy of a final Waltons' scene written especially for "Grandma."

ON SCREEN

You can spot Ellen Corby before (and after) she became Grandma Walton in the following films:

The 51st Annual Primetime Emmy Awards (1999) (TV)
A Walton Easter (1997) (TV)
A Walton Wedding (1995) (TV)
A Walton Thanksgiving Reunion (1993) (TV)
A Day for Thanks on Waltons' Mountain (1982) (TV)
A Wedding on Waltons Mountain (1982) (TV)
All the Way Home (1981) (TV)
The Story of Pretty Boy Floyd (1974) (TV)
Napoleon and Samantha (1972)
The Waltons (1972) TV
The Homecoming: A Christmas Story (1971) (TV)
A Tattered Web (1971) (TV)
Support Your Local Gunfighter (1971)
Cannon (1971) (TV)
Angel in My Pocket (1969)
Ruba al prossimo tuo (1969)
The Legend of Lylah Clare (1968)
The Mystery of Edward Sims (1968) TV Series
The Gnome-Mobile (1967) (uncredited)
Mr. Terrific (1967) TV Series
The Ghost and Mr. Chicken (1966)
The Night of the Grizzly (1966)
The Glass Bottom Boat (1966)
The Family Jewels (1965)
Please Don't Eat the Daisies (1965) TV Series
Hush... Hush, Sweet Charlotte (1964)
The Strangler (1964)
4 for Texas (1963)
The Caretakers (1963)
Saintly Sinners (1962)
Pocketful of Miracles (1961)
Visit to a Small Planet (1960)
As Young as We Are (1958)
Vertigo (1958)
Macabre (1958)
All Mine to Give (1957)
God Is My Partner (1957)
The Seventh Sin (1957)
Rockabilly Baby (1957)
Night Passage (1957)
The Go-Getter (1956)
Stagecoach to Fury (1956)
Slightly Scarlet (1956) (uncredited)
Illegal (1955)
About Mrs. Leslie (1954)
Sabrina (1954)
Susan Slept Here (1954) (uncredited)
The Bowery Boys Meet the Monsters (1954)
Untamed Heiress (1954)
The Vanquished (1953/I)
The Story of Three Loves (1953) (uncredited)
Monsoon (1953)
A Lion Is in the Streets (1953)
Shane (1953)
The Woman They Almost Lynched (1953)
Fearless Fagan (1952)
Big Trees (1952)
Angels in the Outfield (1951)
On Moonlight Bay (1951)
The Barefoot Mailman (1951)
The Sea Hornet (1951)
Here Comes the Groom (1951)
Goodbye, My Fancy (1951)
The Mating Season (1951)
Caged (1950)
Harriet Craig (1950)
Edge of Doom (1950)
Peggy (1950)
The Gunfighter (1950)
Ma and Pa Kettle Go to Town (1950)
Captain China (1949)
The Judge Steps Out (1949) (uncredited)
Madame Bovary (1949)
Mighty Joe Young (1949) (uncredited)
Little Women (1949)
A Woman's Secret (1949)
Rusty Saves a Life (1949)
The Dark Past (1948)
If You Knew Susie (1948) (uncredited)

Famous Wisconsin Film Stars

Strike It Rich (1948)
Fighting Father Dunne (1948) (uncredited)
The Noose Hangs High (1948) (uncredited)
I Remember Mama (1948)
Forever Amber (1947) (uncredited)
Living in a Big Way (1947) (uncredited)
The Long Night (1947) (uncredited)
They Won't Believe Me (1947) (uncredited)
Railroaded! (1947) (uncredited)
Driftwood (1947) (uncredited)
The Bachelor and the Bobby-Soxer (1947) (uncredited)
The Fabulous Joe (1947) (uncredited)
Born to Kill (1947) (uncredited)
Beat the Band (1947) (uncredited)
Cuban Pete (1946)
The Dark Corner (1946) (uncredited)
The Locket (1946) (uncredited)
The Scarlet Horseman (1946)
Sister Kenny (1946) (uncredited)
The Truth About Murder (1946) (uncredited)
It's a Wonderful Life (1946) (uncredited)
The Spiral Staircase (1946) (uncredited)
Crack-Up (1946) (uncredited)
Till the End of Time (1946) (uncredited)
Lover Come Back (1946) (uncredited)
In Old Sacramento (1946)
Bedlam (1946) (uncredited)
From This Day Forward (1946)
Cornered (1945) (uncredited)
Speed Limited (1935) (uncredited)
The Broken Coin (1934) (uncredited)
Rafter Romance (1933) (uncredited)

GENE WILDER

Eccentric candy factory owner Willy Wonka hobbles out on a cane to greet chocolate bar contest winners in the opening scene of the 1971 movie, *Willy Wonka & The Chocolate Factory*. Wonka stumbles. He summersaults. He smiles.

And so did the frizzy-haired actor playing him, Milwaukee native Gene Wilder.

Wilder had refused to do the movie unless he introduced Wonka that way because, from that first moment on, the movie audience would never know for sure if Wonka was being honest or not — essential to the half mad, half genius, half generous benefactor the chocolate guru was.

The comic genius who knew just how to play the sane man pretending to be insane — or was it the insane man pretending to be sane? — was born as Jerome "Jerry" Silberman June 11, 1933, in Milwaukee.

Silberman's father was a Russian immigrant who imported and manufactured novelties like tiny beer bottles. In fact, the *Milwaukee Journal Sentinel* noted July 23, 1996, Schlitz Brewery actually once sued the future star's dad when he created miniature outhouses that featured a tiny Schlitz beer bottle inside.

The young boy's life changed forever when his mother, Jeanne, was incapacitated by a heart attack she suffered when Silberman was in elementary school.

"The night she came home from the hospital, the doctor said two things to me: 'Don't get angry with your mother because you might kill her,' ... (and) the second was to change my life. He said, 'Make her laugh,'" Wilder recalled in an August 12, 1996, interview by Cassandra Jardine of *The Daily Telegraph*, London.

Making his mother laugh by calling to her in a thick German or Yiddish accent, or imitating stars like Danny Kaye and Sid Caesar, "gave me confidence that others might laugh too," he noted, adding that the fear of killing his mother had an impact on Wilder from a young age as well. "When I felt loud inside, I couldn't let it out. Like many very shy people, I am terribly aggressive but I cannot show it, so when I get nervous I pretend I am Mel Brooks and make a joke. It's like putting on a mask, except that it is also part of me," he told *The Daily Telegraph*.

From then on, greater family responsibilities fell upon the young boy, and he put it on himself to cheer up his mother in any way possible, often improvising skits to entertain her.

His parents eventually sent Silberman to school at the Black-Foxe Military Institute in Los Angeles, though his studies there didn't last long. He returned to Milwaukee and graduated from Washington High School in 1951. Years later, the high school added Gene Wilder to their Alumni Hall of Fame, which includes Sen. Herbert Kohl, former Wisconsin Governor Lee Dreyfus, and baseball commissioner Bud Selig. Wilder has also been inducted into the Wisconsin Performing Artists Hall of Fame.

Silberman performed beyond his living room as a teenager, following his older sister who had taken drama lessons before him. He studied with Herman Gottlieb in Milwaukee and made his stage debut as *Romeo and Juliet*'s Balthazar in the Milwaukee Playhouse in 1948.

Though he loved to make people laugh, Silberman turned toward serious acting after catching a Broadway performance of *Death of a Salesman* in 1949. High education was paramount to chasing dramatic dreams, however, and the Silberman's son soon enrolled at the University of Iowa. When he wasn't hitting the books, Silberman was reading scripts for student and summer stock productions he performed in throughout his college career.

While there, Silberman also formed a lifelong relationship with the Alpha Epsilon Pi fraternity, and, in 2001, donated a collection of his movie scripts, including the final version of one he wrote himself, *The World's Greatest Lover* (1977), to the fraternity that started him down the road to fame.

After graduating from the University of Iowa in 1955, Silberman studied drama at the Bristol Old Vic Theatre School in England where he also became a top fencer, winning the school's championship.

The actor took a break from the stage during a two-year stint in the U.S. Army from 1956 to 1958, where he volunteered to serve on the neuropsychiatric ward at Valley Forge Hospital in Pennsylvania, thinking it would provide neurotic characters that he could later draw from as an actor. Even in the Army, Silberman continued his dramatic studies, taking weekend classes at the Herbert Berghof Studio in New York.

After his discharge, Wilder went to New York, where he married playwright and actress Mary Mercier, July 22, 1960, taking in her daughter Katherine Anastasia as his own. Katherine died when she was 22, a story "too sad to go into," Wilder told Larry King when he was interviewed on the TV talk show May 2, 2002.

In 1967, the Wilders divorced. It wasn't long, however, before Wilder married Mary Joan Schutz October 27, 1967, a union that would last until 1974 when they, too, divorced.

A year later, when he was 26, the aspiring actor took the professional name of Gene Wilder, basing it reportedly (though accounts vary) on Eugene Gant, the character in Thomas Wolfe's *Look Homeward Angel* and on his idol Thornton Wilder.

Like many a Wisconsin actor before him, Wilder broke through the thespian curtain on Broadway stages in 1961, appearing first in an off-Broadway show, *Roots*, and then as a valet in *The Complaisant Lover*. Wilder joined Kirk Douglas in the 1963 Broadway production of *One Flew Over the Cuckoo's Nest* and Helen Hayes in the 1964 production of *The White House*.

During his early years, the one-time fencing champ reportedly helped make ends meet by teaching fencing, including as fencing choreographer for the Cambridge, Massachusetts Drama Festival productions of *Twelfth Night* and *Macbeth* in 1959.

As the saying goes, "it's always who you know" ... and in Wilder's case, it was who he knew on *stage* that made the difference in his career. In 1963, the future movie star performed with Ann Bancroft in *Mother Courage and Her Children*. At the time, the actress was dating director Mel Brooks, who eventually asked Wilder to join his stock company's stage productions.

Wilder's first movie role was not in a Brooks film, however. He played the undertaker in *Bonnie and Clyde* in 1967. That same year, Brooks finally cast Wilder in a movie about a Broadway show producer who tries to scam investors by selling 25,000 percent of stock in a new play that's destined to bomb. Of course, the scam play was an instant hit as was the movie about it, *The Producers*, in which Wilder plays frantic accountant Leo Bloom.

The Producers earned Wilder a Best Supporting Actor Oscar nomination and brought movie star status to the actor with a genius flare for comedic roles.

After starring as French "twins" Claude and Philippe in *Start the Revolution without Me* (1970), Wilder was cast as the world's chief candyman in the now classic *Willy Wonka & The Chocolate Factory* (1971). The role earned him his first Golden Globe Best Motion Picture Actor in a Musical/Comedy nomination and propelled the movie's theme song "Candyman" into the No. 1 spot on

Billboard's Top 100 list in 1972.

Wonka was a role Wilder would have passed up had producers not let him include the stumbling cane scene as Wonka's introduction, he explained in an interview posted on the *Willy Wonka Facts* Internet site. "We all grew up on movies with scenes where the actor is lying and (we) know he's lying, but he wants to make sure you know it's a lie so he overacts and all but winks at you. ... I wanted to do the opposite (in Willy Wonka), to really lie, and fool the audience ... I wanted people to wonder ... so that you wouldn't really know until the end ... what Willy's motivations were."

When Wilder wasn't pulling the truth over the audience's eyes in *Willy Wonka*, the actor was working in a different kind of children's venue on television as the voice of The Letterman on public television's *The Electric Company*, from 1972 to 1977.

One year after memorializing himself as Wonka, Wilder earned more adult laughs as a Woolite drinking doctor in love and in bed with a sheep in Woody Allen's *Everything You Always Wanted to Know about Sex*. "That's not an easy task, being in bed with a sheep," Wilder told King in 2002, "especially if you make the sheep nervous."

Mel Brooks again called Wilder when he needed a frazzled-looking, "sane" man to play his alcoholic gunslinger, the Waco Kid in a cowboy Western spoof, *Blazing Saddles* in 1974, a screenplay Brooks cowrote with Wilder. The movie was predicted to make about $2.5 million at the box office; in its first year, the movie brought in well over $40 million and continues to be a comic favorite.

Though he would like to play serious roles, Wilder recognizes that his best talents lie in playing soft-spoken but comedic characters who walk a tight line between determined and neurotic, between championing a right over a wrong and obsessing about righting that wrong.

"There's fourteen other guys who will always do (serious roles) better than me. But, if it's a comedy, it's a different story," he told King in 2002.

Wilder earned his second Oscar nomination for his screenwriting talents with Mel Brooks on the 1974 hit *Young Frankenstein*, in which Wilder played a California Frankenstein family descendant who had to travel back to Transylvania to inherit the family's castle.

Wilder came up with the *Young Frankenstein* story himself,

Gene Wilder peers through a camera lens. Photo courtesy of Wisconsin Center for Film and Center Research. Image No. WCFTR-3761.

which he and Brooks brought to the screen as the comedic pair's third hit together.

One day, "after lunch, I took a yellow legal pad and a blue felt pen and I wrote 'Young Frankenstein' on the top. Then for two pages, I thought what could happen to me if I suddenly found out I was an heir to Beaufort von Frankenstein's whole estate in Transylvania ... I wrote two more pages," Wilder told Larry King.

Riding the success of such a string of popular movies and the even bigger success he'd encounter with his next comedic partner, Richard Pryor was both exhilarating and unnerving, Wilder admitted to King. "Success is a terrible thing and a wonderful thing. If you can enjoy it, it's wonderful. If it starts eating away at you, and they're waiting for more from me, or what can I do to top this, then you're in trouble."

In 1975, Wilder tried out the directors' chair for his next film, *The Adventure of Sherlock Holmes' Smarter Brother*, which costarred other Mel Brooks' stars Madeline Kahn and Marty Feldman.

As an actor, he also earned critical acclaim and audience approval as the Western rabbi to Harrison Ford's cowboy in *The Frisco Kid* (1979).

Then, when the actor couldn't find the funny-sad roles he preferred to play, Wilder wrote his own.

In addition to *Young Frankenstein*, Wilder created and played Sigerson Holmes, the title character in the detective drama spoof, *The Adventure of Sherlock Holmes' Smarter Brother* (1975). He also wrote and starred in *The World's Greatest Lover* (1977), where Wilder played a neurotic baker from Milwaukee named Rudy Valentine. The baker with the romantic sounding name traveled to Hollywood to compete with 1920s heartthrob Rudolph Valentino. As he did with other movies, Wilder also wrote a song for the film, and acted as its producer, scriptwriter, director and star. The one-time Milwaukee living room performer also reportedly wrote a scene into the movie in honor of childhood mentor, Charlie Chaplin, where the baker gets trapped on a cake conveyor belt.

For all his movies, Wilder remains best known for his pairings with two legendary comedians: stand-up comic and actor Richard Pryor and *Saturday Night Live* TV comedian Gilda Radner.

Wilder first paired with Pryor in the 1976 commercial hit *Silver Streak*, in which he played a man wrongly accused of murder — a theme in several Wilder films. Wilder's performance earned the actor his second Golden Globe nomination for Best Motion Picture Actor in a Musical/Comedy. The two also starred in the 1980 hit *Stir Crazy*. Watching Pryor's and Wilder's antics on screen is like watching a well-executed comedic waltz, where the laughter keeps the beat.

Wilder told King that though he can't really explain the how or why of the success of the on-screen pairings, he and Pryor did make hilarious comedy together.

"I hope this comes out right, but (our relationship) is a little bit like sex," Wilder told King. "When you meet someone and the chemistry is there, you don't know why, you don't know how, but it's there. … (When) we did the first scene and he said something and I something, and it wasn't in the script… it all went very well. And he said, 'did you know you were going to say that?' I said, 'no. Did you know you were going to say that?' He said, 'no.' I never improvised in a film before … but with him, I always improvised."

As a team Pryor and Wilder earned both rave and critical reviews equally for their third movie together, the somewhat controversial comedy about a blind and a deaf witness to a crime in *See No Evil Hear No Evil* (1989), for which Wilder wrote the screenplay.

They paired up again for a less-well received movie, *Another*

You, in 1991, while Pryor was obviously stricken with multiple sclerosis.

When the Kennedy Center honored Pryor in a 1998 tribute, the actor thanked the comedian for being one of his greatest teachers. "I learned more from you than from the greatest artists. ... I love you Richard," Wilder said.

It was Pryor's unavailability for a 1982 role in *Hanky Panky* that caused the first pairing of Wilder and Radner on screen, after the Pryor role was rewritten for Radner. That movie led to real love for Wilder and Radner and eventually to the altar when they married in 1984.

The couple appeared in two more films together, including *The Woman in Red* (1984), which Wilder directed and cowrote, and *Haunted Honeymoon* (1986), before Radner was diagnosed with ovarian cancer.

In 1988, one year before Radner died, assistant film director Jerry Ziesmer and his film production assistant wife Suzanne went to see *A Fish Called Wanda* in Los Angeles. Throughout the movie, Ziesmer recalled in his book, *Ready When You Are Mr. Coppola, Mr. Spielberg, Mr. Crowe*, the Ziesmers could hear the hearty laughs of another couple sitting behind them — the only others in the theater. When they left the theater the Ziesmers realized that other couple was Gene Wilder and Gilda Radner, who was then ill from cancer treatments.

When Gilda excused herself and went into the ladies' room, Wilder grinned and said she wasn't feeling well. "All the tears were held behind his eyes, and nothing was coming out," Ziesmer wrote. "Suzanne and I smiled. I had worked briefly with (Gilda) a couple years ago on the comedy *It Came From Hollywood* (1982). She was so alive back then, and so frail now.

"We looked at him as if maybe there was something Suzanne and I could do to help. 'Don't worry,' he said, 'We'll be fine.' He smiled again, and I was the one holding back the tears," Ziesmer continued. "I nodded. Suzanne squeezed my hand and we began to leave. When (Gilda) left the ladies' room and rejoined him, we heard their laughter begin again. Gilda Radner and Gene Wilder were good at laughing together."

Their laughter stopped when Radner died in 1989. Wilder dedicated himself to completing an unspoken promise to his wife to help build the kind of cancer support group centers that Radner had longed for when she was ill.

He spent four years helping to raise the money and interest in building Gilda's House sites, which feature a play room for children and an "It's Always Something Room" relaxation area. The first center opened in New York in 1991 and there now are more than a dozen centers, including one on Oakland Avenue in Shorewood, Wisconsin. Another center is planned for Madison.

"Since Gilda died, everything in my life has changed," the actor said in a 1996 *Variety* article. In a *The Daily Telegraph* article that same year, he said in the years since he lost Radner, he has found a peace with her death. "She's at peace now, and I'm at peace finally," he said. "When I do think about Gilda it's like noticing something pleasant, such as the color of the sky. In that respect she's here all the time."

Helping Wilder heal from the loss was a new love he found with the speech pathologist who had coached him for his role as a deaf man in *See No Evil, Hear No Evil* in 1989.

Several months after Radner's death, pathologist Karen Boyer asked Wilder's help on a research grant video she was producing. Eventually Wilder asked Boyer to dinner. On September 8, 1991, they were married.

Boyer was so supportive in launching the Gilda's House sites, that Wilder put his wife center stage with Radner when he awarded Karen "The Gene Wilder Unconditional Love Award for the rest of her life" for "living with Gilda all these years" at a 1995 dinner ceremony for the Gilda clubs.

"For years, I have thought about Gilda and cancer every day," he told the crowd. "The time has come for me to rejoin the human race."

Since his marriage, Wilder has seldom ventured onto the silver screen, preferring to write or star in television movies and on stage in England.

In 1994, he launched a TV show, *Something Wilder*, which went nowhere. Then, in 1996, Wilder got better reviews as he toured Great Britain in *Laughter on the 23rd Floor*, in which he played TV writer Max Prince, a character based on the comic genius he once imitated as a kid, Sid Caesar.

More recently, Wilder has returned to writing screenplays, so far for TV movies such as 1999's *The Lady in Question* and *Murder in a Small Town*, in which he also played the role of Larry Carter. Wilder appeared as Mock Turtle in the 1999 *Alice in Wonderland* TV movie and, in 2001, gave the okay for a TV movie to be made on the life of Gilda Radner called *It's Always Something,* based on a book Radner cowrote while she was dying.

Ten years after Wilder had lost Radner to ovarian cancer, the comic actor was tossed into a cancer fight of his own when he was diagnosed with non-Hodgkin's lymphoma. Wilder underwent stem cell transplant treatments using his own blood as well as traditional chemotherapy treatments to beat it into remission. Though he lost his trademark frizzy hair for a while and had to put acting on hold for many months, Wilder told Larry King he feels lucky to have been granted more time to enjoy life.

In 2002, Wilder planned to return to movie screens in a screenplay he'd written about a psychiatric patient who is convinced that he is a female Hollywood star.

Though he keeps his talents in the Hollywood pool, Wilder today is more apt to be enjoying a game of tennis or setting up his easel to paint watercolors in the "Jewish Buddhist Mormon life" he's carved out for himself in the Connecticut home he and Boyer share.

His quieter, more structured real life contrasts the soft-spoken neurotics he usually played on screen. Though, Wilder admitted to Jardine in *The Daily Telegraph*, that he still "loses it" on occasion.

So the audience remains puzzled. Is Wilder the soft-spoken man of most of his interviews or is that a wild spark we still see in his eyes … still teasing at the truth with his audience?

"My quiet exterior used to be a mask for hysteria," he admitted in a July 20, 1970, *Time* magazine article. "After seven years of analysis, it just became a habit."

ON SCREEN

Wilder's neurotically funny characters are always easy to spot on screen, such as in the following movies:

The Lady in Question (1999) (TV)
Alice in Wonderland (1999) (TV)
Murder in a Small Town (1999) (TV)
Something Wilder (1994) TV Series
Another You (1991)
Funny About Love (1990)
See No Evil, Hear No Evil (1989)
Haunted Honeymoon (1986)
The Woman in Red (1984)
The Making of 'The Woman in Red (1984) (TV)
Hanky Panky (1982)
Stir Crazy (1980)
Sunday Lovers (1980)
The Frisco Kid (1979)
The World's Greatest Lover (1977)
Silver Streak (1976)
The Adventure of Sherlock Holmes' Smarter Brother (1975)
The Little Prince (1974)
Young Frankenstein (1974)
Thursday's Game (1974) (TV)
Blazing Saddles (1974)
Rhinoceros (1973)
Everything You Always Wanted to Know About Sex (1972)
The Scarecrow (1972) (TV)
The Electric Company (1971) TV Series (voice)
Willy Wonka & the Chocolate Factory (1971)
Quackser Fortune Has a Cousin in the Bronx (1970)
Start the Revolution Without Me (1970)
The Producers (1968)
Bonnie and Clyde (1967)
Death of a Salesman (1966) (TV)

WILLEM DAFOE

He's been a war hero, a vampire and a savior, a poet and a thug, all with a kind of chilling realness that makes audiences wonder where the person Willem Dafoe is hiding within the character he so convincingly portrays.

While today's movie audiences recognize the Wisconsin-born actor as action hero nemesis the Green Goblin in the 2002 hit *Spider-Man*, folks around Appleton still see him as "Billy," the young child star of the Attic Theater there.

Dafoe was born the sixth of eight children to Dr. William and Muriel Dafoe July 22, 1955, in Appleton, Wisconsin.

While his parents worked as a gastrointestinal surgeon and nurse for more than thirty-five years in Appleton (with an office at 1602 N. Meade Street), the Dafoe children were expected from an early age to gain the independence and self-reliance they needed to hold their own in the busy household and in the world itself.

"I grew up in a pretty free-wheeling household. We never ate together and everyone was pretty independent. There was pride in family, but I didn't have those Beaver Cleaver rituals," Dafoe told Lori J. Smith in an October 1988 *Center Stage* story.

The sheer number of family members provided Dafoe with an early audience, however, and boosted his desires to perform, he told the *Appleton Post-Crescent* newspaper November 30, 1985. "Coming from a large family had something to do with how my personality developed. I tried to catch everybody's attention by acting out a bit."

Dafoe did a lot of pretending as a child, playing the cop to someone's robber and writing and producing little historical dramas for neighborhood kids to act out with him in the family's wood-paneled basement, he told the *Milwaukee Journal*'s Cindy Pearlman in a March 5, 1995, interview. "The plays would always have grand titles like *Gold Rush*. The neighborhood kids would play my victims and I wouldn't settle for anything less than grandeur," he said, noting later on that acting is really just an extension of those early pretending games.

As an actor, "you're always approached with a 'what if I am

this guy' and it forces you to imagine. ... That activity reminds me most of when you're a child," Dafoe relayed to *The Observer* reporter Jonathan Romney in a November 8, 1998, article for the London newspaper.

When Dafoe wasn't playing hero in his basement, he attended Huntley Grade School and then Einstein Junior High School in Appleton, where he was known as Billy. Movie production assistant Susanne Ziesmer taught at the grade school for years before moving to Hollywood in 1982. Though she never taught Dafoe herself, she reports that other teachers at the school remembered Billy as a good student.

Dafoe might have liked many of those teachers, but he hated being called Billy, or worse Junior, since his father was William Sr. As an alternative, Dafoe came up with "Willem" in high school, and the new nickname stuck, although writers continue to misspell it, most often as William.

"If I had to do it over again, I think I'd be just 'Bill,' with no last name, like Cher or something," Dafoe told the *Appleton Post Crescent* February 1, 1986.

He was still called Billy when he made his professional "pretending" debut in the town's Attic Theater production of *A Thousand Clowns*. It was the beginning of a childhood theatrical relationship that provided the future star sound stage training. Dafoe also reportedly wrote at least one play for the group, which was performed on a nearby Lawrence University stage.

Dafoe's talents showed early on in the Attic productions and Appleton East High School plays, noted then drama director John Svejda in a November 30, 1985, *Appleton Post Crescent* story.

"My biggest problem was not in developing Bill but in developing everybody else so I would not have a one-man show," Svejda said of the young actor he directed in such productions as *The Crucible, Little Mary Sunshine, The Matchmaker,* and *My Fair Lady.*

Actor Tom Callaway, who starred with Dafoe in the Attic Theater production of *A Thousand Clowns* among others, remembers the "chubby cheeked" actor's talents well, he said in an August 21, 1988, *Post-Crescent* article. "When the Attic needed a child, we said, 'let's get Billy Dafoe. He's obnoxious, he'd be perfect," Callaway recalled. "I knew Billy from diapers on ... he's very extroverted, constantly doing stand-up comedy and sight gags for family and friends."

James Auer, who knew Dafoe since the future star was about 12, recalls that Billy was an "inquisitive and mischievous" young actor who was never late for rehearsal and had an "eagerness to please ... He always knew his lines the first day and accepted the director's suggestions but improved on them," he noted in an April 9, 1989, *Wisconsin State Journal* magazine article.

Dafoe carried his talents to Appleton East High School as well.

It was in high school that Dafoe's "pushing the envelope" artistic vision first butted heads with "the establishment" when he got kicked out of school after officials closed down a video project he was working on, alleging that it was "pornographic."

"I interviewed three students (for a high school magazine show he was doing) who were all outsiders — a drug dealer, a Satan worshipper and a nudist," Dafoe explained to Romney in 1998. "I never got to finish it because somebody came into my editing room when I went for lunch and they saw the rough footage.

"Now, I never intended to use some of this stuff that I shot but they got a little upset and when I got back, the door was locked and I was told to go home. ... My parents called me at home and said you're making pornography (but) it wasn't true," Dafoe stressed.

In a February 16, 2001, article, Dafoe told *Washington Post* writer Sharon Waxman that though he quickly moved on from the incident, the school's criticism of his work troubled him. "Something snapped in me. I saw the narrowness of people," Dafoe noted.

The future star graduated from Appleton East High School in 1973, actually completing the one credit he was short his senior year at Lawrence University.

Dafoe moved to Milwaukee to pursue a college degree, studying fine arts at the University of Wisconsin-Milwaukee for two years.

Though he continued to enjoy acting and had a "very driven" personality, Dafoe told Blake Green of *Newsday* in March 31, 1997, that being an actor for the rest of his life "as a goal was never articulated for me. I just gravitated to things that interested me and had some luck. Now I think somewhat pridefully, 'maybe that's the way to live.'"

While at the university, Dafoe became involved in an experimental theater group, Theater X in Milwaukee, where he appeared in such productions as *Razor Blades* and *The Unnamed*.

One costar, Flora Coker, who played with Dafoe in *The Wreck: a Romance* and *A Fierce Longing*, recalled in the *Wisconsin Journal* magazine that Dafoe had an obvious talent and a tremendous work ethic at Theater X. "He's one of the hardest workers in the world, always working, always thinking."

Dafoe agreed in a 1997 interview in the *Bergen County* (New Jersey) *Record*. ""I will not lie; I think I've got something. But I think (my success) has more to do with who am I than what I do. ... I'm not a terrifically clever actor but I'm good at committing to something as if my life depended on it."

In 1977, Dafoe packed up his talent and drive and hopped a bus for New York, hoping to find a bigger venue for the theatrical future that he had now committed himself to.

The Appleton native quickly found work at an experimental theater company called the Wooster Group. Though he started as a set carpenter at a former car shop turned theater called the Performing Garage, Dafoe was quickly cast in the group's avant-garde performances, often "made-from-scratch" productions that incorporate film and video into stage performances.

Dafoe remains at home in experimental theater, always pushing the envelope as he did back in high school and building a well-respected name for himself on stage without ever starring in a Broadway production.

Broadway, he told the *Wisconsin State Journal* in 1989, is a venue he tries to avoid. "I'm suspicious of what immense production costs can do to (a production's) integrity," he said, adding that while "I don't thumb my nose at Broadway theater, it's just not for me. It's too set in cement."

Dafoe remains committed to the freer forms of Wooster Group and especially to the group's director, Elizabeth LeCompte, his live-in companion since 1977, with whom he has a grown son, Jack.

Wooster Group remains intensely creative because of her vision and drive, Dafoe told Bob Irvy of the *Record* June 8, 1997. His "fierce, brave and rigorous" companion is "great not just for what she does but for how she approaches her work," Dafoe noted. "The moment it ceases to be alive for her, she changes it, destroys it or transforms it."

Though the two share a deep love and mutual respect and passion in each other's work, the couple will probably never marry, he told *People* magazine May 15, 1989. "I sometimes call her my wife for simplicity's sake," Dafoe noted, though "I don't believe in the institution (of marriage). It still smacks of possession."

Three years into his relationship with LeCompte and Wooster Group, Dafoe tried acting in a more conventional medium — Hollywood movies.

He worked as an extra in the 1980 movie *Heaven's Gate* and then played Vance in the independent film, *The Loveless*. Following a string of smaller roles, Dafoe was cast as a tough biker, the Bombers' leader Raven Shaddock, in *Streets of Fire* and then in the bigger role of counterfeiter Rick Masters in *To Live and Die in L.A.*, a violent film but one that showed Dafoe's acting depths to the world.

Muriel Dafoe told the *Appleton Post Crescent* November 30, 1985, that she didn't care for the film's violence but was very proud of her son's "debut" performance. "I thought he did very well with the character, ... but as a mother, I would have chosen a different role for him."

Still, it was a violent setting — the Vietnam War — that brought her son his first, and perhaps most famous role, that of saint-like Sergeant Elias in 1986's Oscar-winning epic *Platoon*.

To get the film's actors more into their soldier characters, a then virtually unknown Hollywood director, Oliver Stone, enrolled his cast in a two-week mini boot camp with the Marines. "(Stone) had a terrific stake in a certain kind of realism and a certain kind of commitment on the part of the actors," Dafoe told Romney in 1998. The boot camp experience "helped root everything that we did. It gave us a relationship to our clothes, to our bodies, to our weapons, so all those things became automatic when you played the scene."

Life nearly reflected art too much when Dafoe first arrived in the Philippines where *Platoon* was being shot. The actor arrived the night before the Philippines revolution of the mid-1980s. "When I woke up, I opened the curtains of my room and there were tanks out in the street. ... Sure enough, there was a revolution and (as one of the first actors to arrive) I was stranded there ... That was an interesting way to start a movie."

The reaction to Dafoe's performance as the "good" Sgt. Elias was overwhelmingly positive. He received an Oscar nomination as Best Supporting Actor, and Appleton residents soon boasted that a native son's face graced the cover of *Time* magazine.

Within two years, that same son was again on the famous cover, though this time under more controversial circumstances.

Dafoe had taken on the job of portraying Jesus in 1988's modern-day biblical story *The Last Temptation of Christ*. When he accepted the role, Dafoe became the second Wisconsin actor to play Jesus in a movie. Whitefish Bay's Jeffrey Hunter played Jesus in the 1961 movie *The King of Kings*, which was directed by Wisconsinite Nicholas Ray of La Crosse.

Like Hunter, Dafoe was warned by other actors not to take on the "role of roles."

"Some people warned me against playing Christ. They listed all the actors who played Christ and what happened to them ... and to the movies," Dafoe told the *Chicago Tribune* on August 14, 1988, before the movie debuted. He added in a 1988 interview that he still couldn't "believe I was so brazen to think I could pull off the Jesus role."

To prepare, Dafoe had read different accounts of the Bible to draw better parallels between it and the stories being told through the modern-day script.

Most of those who actually saw the film were impressed by Dafoe's performance — so impressed that he was nominated for an Academy Award for his performance.

The problem was that not as many people saw Dafoe's performance as lined up to criticize his portrayal of a more colloquial Jesus as blasphemous.

The criticism "broke my heart," Dafoe told Romney, "because I think it's a beautiful film and I know the spirit we made it in. In a world where you have very cynical, crass slasher movies ... it blew my mind that somebody makes a movie about love, forgiveness, about this incredibly revolutionary character, and people get nervous.

"The religious right used — and I don't think they even knew what the movie was about — the opportunity as a chance to ... galvanize their political agenda."

"They won," he admitted to Irvy in the 1997 interview with *The Record*. "Without seeing the picture (these religious groups) hounded it into obscurity. It's never going to be shown on cable, never going to be shown on network TV, it's hard to find in the video store, isn't shown in retrospectives. It's a hot potato. I understand what happened, but it's so misguided."

The movie wasn't even shown in the actor's hometown when it first debuted. In reaction to religious group concerns over Dafoe's humanized portrayal of Christ, the Midwest's Marcus Theater Corporation refused to show the film in any of its theaters, including those in Appleton. Fox River Baptist Church preacher Rev. Marion Adams was elated the theater chain took such a bold step, he told the *Minneapolis Star Tribune* August 14, 1988, noting that he was asking ban supporters to "write thank you letters to Marcus Corporation."

Three months after *The Last Temptation of Christ* opened in theaters nationwide, the movie finally opened in its star's hometown when an Essaness-owned theater in the Fox River Mall agreed to show it.

"It's about time," Dafoe's father told the *Appleton Post Crescent* October 20, 1988. "We have seen the film and thought it powerful, so powerful that I forgot it was my son up there."

As the controversy swirled, Dafoe was earning praise for his other, less controversial, 1988 performance as straight-laced FBI agent Ward in *Mississippi Burning*.

After playing an imprisoned boxer in *Triumph of the Spirit* (1989), a paralyzed veteran in *Born on The Fourth of July* (1989), a pilot in *Flight of the Intruder* (1991), an undercover cop in *White Sands* (1992), a lawyer too easily tempted by Madonna (his client) in *Body of Evidence* (1993), and a mercenary in *Clear and Present Danger,* Dafoe tackled poetry as famous poet T.S. Eliot in the 1994 British film *Tom & Viv*.

Dafoe told Pearlman in 1995 that it was a role he was reluctant to take until he discovered that Eliot had been a midwesterner. "I'm a Midwesterner. He had a certain puritanical upbringing. I had the same thing. I started to make connections," he explained.

Dafoe moved from poet to spy to villain in movies over the next two years. The Appleton actor portrayed spy Caravaggio in the hit World War II drama *The English Patient* (1996) and jumped into the world of Hollywood action blockbusters as the villain in *Speed 2: Cruise Control* (1997).

In between, Dafoe has remained loyal and excited about performing with the Wooster Group, taking the lead in such productions as *The Hairy Ape* and most recently, *To You, the Birdie!* The actor insists that switching between stage and screen helps feed his curiosity, which in turn fuels his enthusiasm for always-different roles in both venues.

"I love it when I can go back and forth (between the stage and the movie set). It feeds different parts of you and exercises different muscles," he told *The Observer*'s Romney.

When he's not working hard, which isn't often, Dafoe practices yoga. He also hasn't forgotten his hometown, donating a jacket he wore in his role as the Green Goblin in *Spider-Man* to the Attic Theater for a fundraiser.

Especially since his parents retired to Florida, the actor hasn't visited his old stomping grounds very often, and Dafoe ruffled some hometown feathers when he appeared on a national talk show in April 1992 and repeated a joke that he said had circulated in Appleton when he was a kid. "We'd say: 'You know what (fellow Appleton native and world-famous magician) Harry Houdini's greatest escape was? Leaving Appleton.'"

After "telling that joke on a talk show once ... I can never go back there," Dafoe later told Romney in the 1998 *Observer* story, adding, "It doesn't break my heart; it's okay with me."

Still Dafoe travels through Appleton a lot — on screen anyway.

More recently, movie fans have recognized Dafoe as Rolfe Whitehouse in 1997's *Affliction*, Detective Donald Kimball in 2000's *American Psycho*, and John Carpenter in 2002's *Auto Focus*.

© Rufus F. Folkks/CORBIS
Willem Dafoe

If it weren't for the credits, few fans would have recognized the actor underneath large wax ears, elongated fingers and eerie makeup in *Shadow of a Vampire* (2000), however.

Dafoe played creepy vampire Max Schreck in the movie, which tells the story of a silent film era producer who hires real vampire Schreck to portray a vampire in his movie and then offers up the beautiful costar as a sacrifice to bloodthirsty Schreck. Dafoe's portrayal was so twistedly absorbing that the actor earned yet another Academy Award nomination as Best Supporting Actor.

"I like bending myself to the character," not bending the character to them "as other Hollywood actors do," he often says.

In 2002, Dafoe again earned praise for his ability to bend himself into twisted characters, this time into Norman Osborn, the Green Goblin, in the 2002 mega-hit *Spider-Man*.

Osborn is the kind of interesting, split-personality, in-the-margins character Dafoe likes to play most.

"I'm always looking for characters that (have) an ambiguity ... an ambivalence," Dafoe told Romney in 1998, noting he likes characters that depict the gray line between right and wrong. "At what point does the really, really bad guy come out on the other side. When does the really good guy come out on the other side?" In other words, he told Waxman for her 2001 *Washington Post* article, "I get excited in a movie when I think, 'Oh, you jerk!'"

ON SCREEN

Check out the variety of characters, sinners and saints, which Appleton native Willem Dafoe has portrayed in the following films:

Once Upon a Time in Mexico (2003)
Finding Nemo (2003) (voice)
Auto Focus (2002)
Spider-Man (2002)
Bullfighter (2001)
The Reckoning (2001)
Edges of the Lord (2001)
The Directors: Martin Scorsese (2000) (Video)
Pavilion of Women (2000)
Film-Fest DVD: Issue 5 - Cannes 2000 & SXSW (2000) (Video)
Shadow of the Vampire (2000)
Animal Factory (2000)
American Psycho (2000)
The Boondock Saints (1999)
eXistenZ (1999)
Conundrum (1998)
What Is Yoga? (1998) (Video, narrator)
New Rose Hotel (1998)
Lulu on the Bridge (1998)
Affliction (1997)
Speed 2: Cruise Control (1997)
The English Patient (1996)
Basquiat (1996) (Build a Fort, Set It on Fire)
Victory (1995)
The Night and the Moment (1994)
Tom & Viv (1994)
Clear and Present Danger (1994)
In weiter Ferne, so nah! (Faraway, So Close!) (1993)
Body of Evidence (1993)
White Sands (1992)
Fishing with John (1991) TV Series
Light Sleeper (1991)
Flight of the Intruder (1990)
Wild at Heart (1990)
Cry-Baby (1990)
Born on the Fourth of July (1989)
Triumph of the Spirit (1989)
Off Limits (1988)
Mississippi Burning (1988)
The Last Temptation of Christ (1988)
Dear America: Letters Home from Vietnam (1987) (TV) (voice)
Platoon (1986)
To Live and Die in L.A. (1985)
The Communists Are Comfortable (1985)
Roadhouse 66 (1984)
Music Videos and Inside 'Streets of Fire' (1984) (TV))
Streets of Fire (1984)
New York Nights (1984)
The Hunger (1983)
The Loveless (1982)
Heaven's Gate (1980) (uncredited)

BILL REBANE

Giant spiders, frog monsters, Big Foot, and Tiny Tim all roamed the woods near Gleason, Wisconsin, thanks to B-movie producer Bill "Ito" Rebane, whose feature film studios operated in Wisconsin's Northwoods for thirty years.

Born in 1937 in Riga, Latvia, the now U.S. citizen discovered Wisconsin and his love of movies via Chicago.

After fleeing the Russian Army in World War II, Rebane immigrated with his parents to Chicago in 1952. The first course of business was to learn English.

"As a child, I watched hundreds of movies to help improve my English. Though I had no movie career plans at the time, I was greatly influenced by the musicals of that time period and my early ambitions were to produce musicals or become a dance and song man ala Donald O'Connor or Fred Astaire, two of my idols," he recalled in a 2002 phone interview.

Still, Rebane did have some interest in entertainment and was soon studying at the Art Institute of Chicago and working as a radio announcer, actor, singer, and tap dancer. By the time he was 20, Rebane had gone to Germany and taken a job as a production assistant and then assistant director first for Baltes Film and then for Bendestorf Film Studios near Hamburg.

"In that capacity, I pretty much became a seasoned film business person and that's where my movie career really was, in the business area of making movies, in the deal making," says Rebane.

Bendestorf Studios hired Rebane to handle their international projects, and the director served as the studio's representative in the United States through the mid-1980s, traveling from his home in Chicago to Hollywood, New York, and Germany to coordinate bringing American studios' film work to Germany. Among the films Rebane brought to Bendestorf were the World War II movie *How I Won The War* (1967), starring singer John Lennon, and the 1974 thriller *The Odessa File*, starring Jon Voight, as well as Columbia Pictures's docudrama *The True Story of The Battle of The Bulge*. Parts of *Chitty Chitty Bang Bang* (1968) were also filmed through the German studio.

Rebane often returned to the United States with film industry ideas and wares as well. "My real contribution to the industry was not really the low-budget movies I made in Gleason, Wisconsin," Rebane noted. "It was the impact of the first 360-degree motion picture process created with one camera (and projected with one projector, on one seamless screen) that I brought over here from Germany in the early 1960s. To this day, I'd say that's one of my most significant accomplishments because it received worldwide recognition. I screened the (sample) experimental movies for industry dignitaries like Walt Disney and the 360-degree process is what led to cinemax efforts in movies."

While still working as a representative for the German studio, Rebane was learning the production side from working on TV shows the studio was producing. He tried his hand at directing and made independent, short subject films — mostly musicals that were distributed through American International Pictures. "They were successful, and that was the genre I was going to work in," he recalls.

Then, in 1965, Rebane made what even he calls "the worst picture ever made," *Monster A Go-Go*. Well, he started making the picture anyway.

"We were making it under the name *Terror at Half Day* but ran out of money, so I sold the footage I had to Herschel Gordon Lewis, a Chicago producer who became known as the 'king of gore.' Well, he massacred the whole thing into *Monster A Go-Go (*about a radiated astronaut who returns to Earth as a monster that chases girls in bikinis)" and distributed it as Sheldon Seymour.

The movie wasn't a complete disaster, however. "It surprisingly got a lot of drive-in theater exposure."

About this same time, Rebane was looking to move his growing family (of then two and eventually four kids) out of the Chicago city life.

"I took a fishing trip to Wisconsin and, on the way back, eighty acres near Gleason (about 25 miles north of Wausau) caught my eye. I came home and informed my wife that I had just bought a ramshackle farm."

Ramshackle it was, but it was a start toward Rebane's goal of providing a rural setting for his children and good movie locations for him.

Rebane says he felt especially drawn to the area and discovered, perhaps, why five years later. "I only discovered after we moved here that Gleason was founded by Estonians and the terrain was very similar to Estonia. Though I left Latvia when I was only 1, perhaps the terrain made me feel like home. Then, after a reporter called about a story on the local church, I discovered that my father's cousin actually founded the first Estonian Church in America ... in Gleason, Wisconsin! That certainly made me feel even more at home with my decision to move here!"

Slowly, Rebane and his wife, Barbara, began building a life in their new community and transforming the farm into a working production studio, called The Shooting Ranch. They funded their efforts by making a series of industrial films for such corporations as State Farm Insurance.

Proceeds from those films gave the Rebanes the financing to build a post-production studio at the farm and maintain a suitable Northwoods lifestyle.

"I enjoyed filming in Wisconsin because of the complete freedom of doing what I needed to do as a filmmaker and being able to operate without Hollywood influences. Wisconsin provided an escape from that Hollywood type of life, and most of all it was a very good place for my kids to grow up."

It wasn't long before Rebane decided to put his growing studio to work on bigger films.

"You could say I got the movie itch again in 1969," Rebane explains of his efforts to produce low-budget feature films in northern Wisconsin.

In 1970, he filmed and produced the documentary *Roar of Snowmobiles*, which featured scenes from the World Powderpuff Championship in Merrill, Sawdust Races in Tomahawk, and world championship races in Eagle River

In 1974, Rebane wrote and decided to film a sci-fi screenplay called *Invasion From Inner Earth*. "As far as I know that was the first feature film made entirely in Wisconsin with a Wisconsin cast and crew," he said.

After the movie enjoyed a "nice theatrical release," Rebane was inspired to continue in the B movie, sci-fi horror genre and aim for distribution in the "wide open drive-in theater market."

In 1975, he produced *The Giant Spider Invasion*, starring former *Gilligan's Island* skipper Alan Hale Jr. as the Marathon County sheriff faced with stopping giant spiders that invaded Earth via a black hole opened by a falling meteor. The spiders devour a farm family, terrorize Merrill and are headed for the big Gleason Days festival before the sheriff's call to NASA finally brings the brain power that devises a way to squash the eight-legged bugs by blowing up the black hole.

The movie is by no means Academy Award material, but *The Giant Spider Invasion* was one of 1975's top moneymakers. It grossed $23 million (against a production cost of $340,000), was a hit at drive-in theaters, enjoyed worldwide distribution, and became a cult classic. The movie was recently re-released on DVD.

In an article for the *Horror-Wood* Webzine, columnist and former Wausau area resident Gene Dorsogna described the experience of being one of the local extras in the low-budget film that had its world premiere at the Grand Theater in Wausau, where it "ran for months."

"*A semi-cab hauling a flatbed trailer rounded the corner and ... there, on the flatbed, was what appeared to be a Volkswagen Beetle wearing a tatty fur coat. There were legs attached to its sides that resembled big, thick pipe cleaners dyed black. The wheels of the bug, indeed the lower several inches of the chassis, were clearly visible. Two globes, the kind of which are used on lamp posts, were on the front of the contraption and had pupils and red thunderbolts painted on them. These "eyes" were placed so that they were over the car's headlights. ...Its pipe cleaner legs wobbled up and down but did not touch the ground. It could not move under its own steam, so lots of burly guys were conscripted to walk real close to it, pushing it along. Then the assistant director urged us to run away from the spider. Most of us did not have to be asked twice. It was in all a moment of delirious, nutty fun.*"

"The Volkswagon bettle was self-propelled with its original engine, however, there were eight kids (one for each leg) inside the body making the legs move. A second version could only be lifted with a crane," Rebane further explained, adding that the spider's eyes were never completed "thanks to a drunk special effects man who made do by simply pasting two half-round plastic globes over the area."

Rebane admits that his films were low budget and marginally acted, often involving local talent, but he preferred making the B-movie features because "they were relatively easy to do, required small crews and were a great way to make a start," he explains, adding that each film's success enabled him to make another and expand his studio.

Eventually the studio/farm became known as the Shooting Ranch Ltd. and grew to two hundred acres. In addition to making movies, the family raised cattle and horses on their acreage.

"For about thirty years, we were the only full-time feature film studio in the Midwest, let alone Wisconsin," he said.

The success of *The Giant Spider Invasion* meant Rebane could continue making low-budget monster movies, such as *Rana: The Legend of Shadow Lake*, a 1975 film about a frog monster; *The Capture of Big Foot* in 1979, *The Alpha Incident* (Gift From a Red Planet) in 1977, and *The Legend of Big Foot* in 1982.

In addition, Rebane produced *The Game*, starring Wisconsin lottery host Lori Monnetti, in 1982 and provided the location for a Hollywood-produced movie, *Devonsville Terror*. The Shooting Ranch also produced *The Demons of Ludlow* in 1983. Filmed in three weeks, Rebane notes that *The Demons of Ludlow* was "the first picture to be made entirely on the large studio built at the Shooting Ranch."

In 1986, Rebane hosted a 1950s nostalgia concert at the Shooting Ranch, inviting Forrest Tucker, Jaye P. Morgan, Bill Halley's Comets and late-1960s hit tulip tiptoer Tiny Tim.

The relationship with Tiny Tim, a falsetto-pitched ukulele player, lasted well beyond the concert and Rebane cast him as the murderous Marvelous Mervo in a 1987 horror film *Blood Harvest*, which features Tiny Tim singing the credits at the end of the film. Rebane and Tim tried to team up again, along with actor-comedian Rex Benson, to produce a one-hour children's TV show *Tiny Tim, His Friends and The Golden Ukulele* in 1992. The show never aired because of conflicts with Benson, and Tiny Tim died in 1996.

Though movie critics pooh-poohed his low-budget efforts, and even Rebane admits to "never looking at any of the pictures again; I'd rather forget most of them," the producer is happy to say that, "at least, I can claim none of my pictures ended up just on a shelf somewhere. They all enjoyed reasonable worldwide distribution."

Wisconsin has benefitted from Rebane's love of movies and his affection for the state where he filmed them. "I call myself a dyed-in-the-wool Wisconsinite and I just believe this state has so much to offer other filmmakers, especially in locations."

Beginning in 1969, Rebane pushed hard to help Wisconsin catch Hollywood's attention, encouraging the state legislature to establish a Wisconsin Film Office that would promote the state to movie studios around the world. Through his Hollywood contacts, Rebane coordinated a meeting to introduce the governor and film office proponents to important Hollywood players.

In 1986, legislation passed that established the film office under the Department of Tourism, a decision that still rubs Rebane a bit the wrong way. "I was happy to see the film office created but in my mind it should have been, and should still be, a function of the Department of Commerce. Attracting a movie to Wisconsin means big business for Wisconsin." Producers for *Back to School,* for example, reportedly spent $50,000 in the state to film just a few scenes for the 1986 movie.

In 1988, Rebane suffered a stroke. The illness and costs incurred led to the closure of the Shooting Ranch.

After he recovered, Rebane returned to Estonia in the early 1990s with hopes of forging a relationship with the fledgling film industry there. "While it was a good trip, it was also depressing to see a city so torn up. I did have some good connections and friends there though and was going to represent the capital's film studio and get some productions under their feet," though no movie cooperation ever saw the big screen.

In the mid-1990s, Rebane moved with his wife, Barbara, to Watersmeet in Michigan's Upper Peninsula, where he helped her operate an antique store and "resorted to writing and freelance work." He wrote and published a book, *Film Funding 2000* through Exploration Press.

Always looking for publicity angles, Rebane proposed the Watersmeet Chamber of Commerce build a 5-foot, 8-inch, glow-in-the-dark, alien statue to attract tourists and direct them to other points of interest. According to the Watersmeet Chamber of Commerce, the statue was built and placed for a time in front of the Rebanes' store, though it was eventually removed.

The Rebanes moved back to Wisconsin in 1999, settling in Hurley, where they ran a hotel as well as a new film production business called Eagle's Nest Productions. Today, Rebane lives in nearby Saxon, where he works as a film industry consultant.

Rebane tried to get a matching grant for Hurley to host a small film festival called the Silver Street Festival, named after the notorious logging town street of the past. When the chamber couldn't come up with all the matching money, Rebane kicked in his own money to ensure the festival went on.

Rebane also has been busy writing a screenplay called *Murder on Silver Street* and working with a couple of producers from Appleton, including William Foersche, who worked at George Lucas' Skywalker Ranch in California, to develop a documentary about Rebane and his studio called *Wisconsin Movie Scrapbook*.

In 2002, the one-time movie producer announced his longshot candidacy for Wisconsin governor as an American Reform Party candidate.

"I know that the chance of an independent getting anywhere is pretty slim," he said. "You have to have just the right gimmick and right press at the right time to have a chance."

Never afraid of small-time longshots, Rebane was more than ready to throw his director's chair into the political ring.

ON SCREEN

Writer, director and producer Bill Rebane created the following movies:

Twisters Revenge (1988)
Blood Harvest (1987)
The Demons of Ludlow (1983)
The Game (1982)
The Legend of Bigfoot (1982)
The Capture of Bigfoot (1979)
The Alpha Incident (1977)
The Giant Spider Invasion (1975)
Rana: The Legend of Shadow Lake (1975)
Invasion from Inner Earth (1974)
Monster a-Go Go (1965)

CHRIS FARLEY

Comedian Chris Farley was equal parts humor and humanity. He was a Wisconsin boy who loved every inch of his home state — from cheese and bratwurst to the Badgers and Packers — and a hyper-energized talent who loved to make others laugh, most often at his own expense.

Christopher Crosby Farley was born February 15, 1964, in Madison, Wisconsin, where his father, Tom, ran the family's Scotch Oil Supply business that sold asphalt throughout the Midwest.

Third of the Farley's five children, Christopher joined a religious and humor-loving Irish family that enjoyed the Badger State's many recreations. Chris Farley was on ice skates when he was still in training pants. Always a physical guy, Farley liked to dance, ski, and play hockey and football and especially show off his often-zany antics.

Farley grew up mostly in affluent Maple Bluff, a suburb of Madison where the family moved in 1963.

Chris Farley's baby photo, courtesy of the Farley family.

An athletic and energetic boy, Farley spent his summers swimming and water skiing and spent his Edgewood and St. Patrick's grade school days doing anything to get attention and make people smile.

"I'll never forget that first laugh," Farley told The Associated Press in a Feb. 4, 1996, article. "The nun came over to my desk to yell at me for something, and I said, 'Gee, your hair smells terrific,' like in that commercial. Well, all the kids laughed hysterically. It was like a revelation."

With the energy of a wind-up doll that can't be stopped, Farley had a hard time sitting still for church, school or much of anything as a kid and often leapt up in class to say or do something funny, like sing a Donny Osmond song.

Even then, the pudgy grade schooler was most often the butt of his own jokes, beating his classmates to the punch line often as a way to deflect other kids' fat jokes.

"Kids made fun of me all through school," Farley once acknowledged to Louis B. Hobson of *The Calgary Sun*. "They called me really degrading names. Of course it hurt. I may be fat but I'm not thick-skinned."

The teasing was the beginning of Farley's lifelong fight against perhaps his greatest opponent: low self-esteem.

Farley's mother enlisted Weight Watchers to help her sensitive son diet, Farley told David Letterman on his *Late Night* TV show March 29, 1995.

"We had Weight Watchers all up and down the refrigerator, and she had the ice cream in there and I'd come home after school, watch reruns of *Gilligan's Island* and take that gallon of Weight Watchers ice cream and eat it. My mom would go, 'Christopher, I know it's Weight Watchers, but it doesn't work when you eat the whole gallon.'"

In third grade, Farley's teachers warned his parents that kids were often laughing *at* their son instead of with him.

When the nun said that, "I thought, 'Who cares? As long as they're laughing,'" Farley once told the *Wisconsin State Journal* in a December 19, 1997, story.

When he was 9, Farley began spending seven weeks each summer at the Red Arrow Camp in northern Wisconsin. It was on the Northwoods stage that Farley got his first taste of performing, in a structured environment anyway. In one of his first skits, Farley played an evil magician and immediately his audience recognized him as a kid who had "that something."

Like his brothers Tom, Kevin, and John and his sister Barbara Ann, Farley continued to attend the camp as a teenager, first working at the camp as a "cookie" in the kitchen and then becoming a counselor. All the while, Farley continued to take part in camp skits, often combining a fine singing voice with a talent for physical comedy and improvised characterizations.

In 1975, Farley began tuning into a new late night comedy program, *Saturday Night Live*, as often as allowed. Through the show, Farley developed an admiration for one of its comedians, John Belushi, a one-time University of Wisconsin-Whitewater student.

Farley's admiration for the pudgy and physical comedian only grew when he saw the star's performance in the college comedy movie *Animal House*.

In 2002, lifelong friend Don Healey told an *E! True Hollywood Story* TV show biographer that the two saw the movie together in 1978, and that his friend "saw himself in the character (Belushi's

Bluto)." Farley also had already taken note of how Belushi made his father, Tom Farley, laugh — something Farley always strived to do.

Farley learned the "fatty falls down" pratfalls he would become most known for while he was a 5-foot 9-inch, 200 pound high school athlete, he told interviewer Bob Fenster January 17, 1997 for a Freedom Communications article that appeared in *The Arizona Republic*.

The comedian developed a thick skin for physical comedy by purposely falling down and sliding around on the football sidelines, he noted, adding that it's "easier to fall down when you're wearing (protective) equipment."

The difficult part was getting used to the idea of being banged up a bit, as the comedian later was when he crashed through tables and ran into, or through, walls. It was something high school athletics prepared Farley for as well, he said. "In football games, I'd be scared but once I got that first hit, I was OK. It's the same thing making a movie. I take that first hit and the butterflies go away."

In high school, Farley continued to go all out to get the biggest laugh possible from his classmates, recalled Edgewood guidance counselor Nick Burrows in a December 23, 1997, *Capital Times* article by Katherine MacDonald. "He would crack up the dean of students, his teacher and other students all of the time, but he never did it at the expense of others."

"He was always on stage, always wanted to be a joke" (whether it was snapping a girl's bra during a choir concert, hopping on chairs like a frog, or making funny faces and comments), confirmed Farley's high school choir director Dennis McKinley in the article. "That's precisely why," the teacher added, "he was seated in the front row."

Occasionally, Farley's attempts went too far, such as when, on a dare, he mooned a girl in class his senior year — for which Farley was expelled and forced to graduate a semester late in 1982.

Whenever his jokes went astray in negative ways, the star always "apologized profusely" because, his family insists, Farley never wanted to hurt anyone physically or emotionally. After all, his salesman father would often tell his kids how important it was to "always build the other guy up and never tear anyone down to make yourself feel better, even for a joke."

Hints of other troubles bigger than a few misguided pranks began to emerge in high school as well. According to his family,

Christopher began drinking with friends on weekends in high school and thus launched a party lifestyle that he never could stop.

His parties took on a wilder tone once Farley found himself away from home and enjoying college life at Marquette University in Milwaukee, where he first took business classes thinking he might some day take over the family business.

Chris Farley and family at his Marquette University graduation. Photo courtesy of the Farley family.

Farley continued to overindulge, not just in food and beer but, increasingly, in drugs, starting with marijuana while still at Marquette.

He also continued to be the zany friend everybody loved, noted Marquette alum Patrick Finn.

Farley was always hamming it up on campus and would do anything to attract attention and make people laugh, including "standing on a professor's desk half-naked, pouring beer foam on his head," he told Jack Norman of the *Milwaukee Journal Sentinel* February 8, 1998. That also included putting "straws up his nose, holding up his rugby shorts like a thong bathing suit to confuse the other team ... running into a snowbank or doing push-ups on the street," he added in a February 9, 1998, *Wisconsin State Journal* article.

Never a star pupil, Farley was always an eager participant. He even took — and reportedly really liked — ballet classes at the university, adding to his natural grace and agility and learning the dancing skills that he'd parlay into comedy routines such as his first *Saturday Night Live* performance as a Chippendale stripper and his last performance as a dancing lunch lady.

The future TV star also performed on stage in several university productions, including *Curse of the Starving Class* (1985), sometimes playing serious roles and proving he had acting abilities well beyond pratfalls.

Farley also played on the university's rugby team, which had an appealing reputation for wild parties.

By his sophomore year, Farley was convinced he was ready to leave school. His parents had other ideas and agreed that, while they wanted Christopher to pursue his dreams, he had to get a college diploma first. So, Farley stayed as a communications major and graduated with a bachelor's degree in 1986.

Once again, however, the comedian's senior year was clouded when he carried comedy a bit too far. Just before he left Marquette, Farley tossed a smoke bomb into a friend's dorm room. He turned himself in, pleaded guilty and was sentenced to thirty hours of community service, which Farley spent telling stories — often dressed in characters like Robin Hood — to Madison grade school children. While fulfilling his community service, Farley sold asphalt for a time with his father. In addition, Farley performed in the ARK Improvisational Theater and eventually founded his own comedy group, "Animal Crackers."

Through it all, his friends say, Farley never lost sight of his dreams of following in John Belushi's footsteps.

His senior year, Farley and some friends signed up to perform a skit in the university's annual variety show, his *E!* biography show noted. When they hadn't even rehearsed by opening night, Farley made up a dating game skit off the top of his head back stage and soon had the show's audience in stitches. As the audience laughed, Farley reportedly said, "We're going to be doing this the rest of our lives."

Even more important than the comedic vision Farley honed at Marquette was the religious faith that grew stronger, he later said. The comedian had never lost the cross his mother gave him as a child, attended Mass at least once a week and spent many additional hours on his knees praying in the chapel. Despite all his struggles with drug and alcohol addiction, Farley never lost his faith — and never stopped asking for God's help to battle his demons, friends and family affirm.

In April of 1996, while at the university to accept the College of Communication Young Alumnus Award, Farley stopped joking to say how important the "university's spiritual emphasis was," the *Milwaukee Journal Sentinel* reported in its coverage of the event. A religious focus not only "makes us stronger and better," Farley said, "but has proven to be the greatest asset I've taken from Marquette into the other side."

Though he was enjoying time with family and friends in Madison after graduation, the comedian inside could wait no longer. In 1987, Farley headed to Chicago and joined the Improv Olympic Theater Company where, after a few weeks of classes, he demanded to be put on stage instead of waiting for the months of training most would-be comics complete.

Management struck a deal with the Wisconsin class clown, the *E!* biography reported. They'd give Farley one chance on stage, but just one. If Farley didn't prove his worth, the Madison native couldn't come back. After just a few minutes on stage, the company knew they'd never want to let this new funny man leave.

By 1988, the 24-year-old Farley had moved up the comedy ladder and was standing in Belushi's spotlight, performing on Chicago's famous Second City main review stage, achieving in one year what it took most three or more years to accomplish.

His costars always noted that although Farley was not the creative idea man for skits, he was a great improviser and remained very committed to any character he was playing. As a case in point, even after breaking his foot by jumping off the stage in Second City's *The Gods Must Be Lazy*, Farley never lost his character. Even his costars didn't realize Farley was injured until the curtain closed.

While at Second City, Farley began to follow Belushi's footsteps down less glorious paths as well, frequenting the Blues Bar where Belushi used to do drugs and sometimes taking drunk and high to un-funny extremes.

Then, in August of 1990, all of Farley's comedic dreams came true.

Saturday Night Live producer Lorne Michaels liked what he saw in Farley's Second City performance so much that he immediately cast Farley on the show.

"He was more than excited. He was elated," recalled his brother Kevin in the *E!* biography. Being on *Saturday Night Live* was what Chris "had always dreamed of."

Within a month, Farley had a Manhattan apartment near the studios and made his first *Saturday Night Live* appearance in late October 1990, playing a dancer in a now famous Chippendales stripping sketch that pitted overweight Farley against muscled dancer Patrick Swayze in a competition to become the next Chippendale.

The former improvisational theater star loved the live TV comedy show atmosphere from the start, he told Fenster. "That live element is like being shot out of a cannon. It gets your adrenaline going."

Farley's career and popularity skyrocketed. Thanks to his comedic portrayals and physical comedy talents, the Wisconsin native quickly became one of the show's audience favorites. Farley showcased his skating skills by keeping up gracefully in a skit with ice skating champion Nancy Kerrigan. He let audiences see some of the real him in his over-the-top portrayal of a vulnerable, shy and self effacing interviewer in The Chris Farley Show, and he let them see the overindulging side of himself as a hyper-enthusiastic fan of "Da Bears."

Perhaps most memorably, Farley created a motivational character named after his college friend and priest Matt Foley. Unlike Foley, Farley's leisure-suit clad, hyperactive, speaker was always warning the audience that if they weren't careful they'd end up, "livin' in a van, down by the river!"

Farley gained press off of the *Saturday Night Live* stage as well when then congressman Scott Klug, who he'd been friends with since they met on vacation in 1990 and Farley campaigned for him in 1996, invited Farley to imitate then U.S. House Speaker Newt Gingrich in a celebration of the speaker's first hundred days in office in April 1995. The photo of Farley and Gingrich smiling side by side ran nationwide.

By now, Farley was certainly a well-known comic celebrity, but he also became respected as the kind of guy who'd always stop and chat and sign an autograph. He explained why to David Letterman during his March 29, 1995, show.

"The chef at a restaurant came up and asked for an autograph and so I signed it. My dad goes, 'what'd you put on there?' and I go, 'Well, he just wanted an autograph, so I signed my name. (Dad) goes, "Oh, for God's sake, make it personal! Folks are coming up there taking a risk in asking you. Make it personal, for God's sake!" Farley recalled.

As he usually did when public talk got too serious, Farley ended the explanation by dumping himself and his chair backward off the platform.

Farley loved his fans, his family says, though he never understood the adulation. A simple wave to fans in a room was never enough. Farley would always sign everything, shake hands and make jokes.

When the comedian came to Planet Hollywood for an interview in Santa Monica with Freedom Communication's Bob Fenster in 1997 (which ran in the *Arizona Republic* January 17, 1997), fans were lined up in the restaurant to greet him. Instead of just waving as he was supposed to, Farley mobbed his fans back. "He shouts ... he cheers .. he mugs," Fenster noted. "He gets them as pumped as he is. He signs everything in sight."

Even when he didn't want to be recognized, he was gracious, recalled two 15-year-old fans from Waupun who met a disguised Farley in a Madison hotel lobby two weeks before his death.

The girls relayed to the *Capital Times* newspaper January 19, 1998, that Farley saw them giggling with excitement at recognizing the star, walked over to them and said, "hello ladies," before sitting down with them on a lobby couch to talk for a while.

When their mother, Debbie Jabas, went looking for the girls she found them in the lobby with Farley and confessed to the star that she wasn't familiar with his work. "Oh, you're probably in bed with a good book by the time my stuff comes on TV," he laughed.

"He was very charismatic," Jabas added. "You were just drawn to him. He could joke with the girls about something and then turn and talk to me too."

"(Fans) make me feel good," Farley then told Fenster. "It's a boost to my low self esteem. They make me want to keep trying to be funny for them."

Farley's fame reportedly never went to his head and he remained a fun-loving, self-effacing and generous guy, according to *Saturday Night Live* costar Al Franken. "Chris was an amazing fan of everybody else (and was) the most generous guy who ever came through the show. ... He thought everyone else was very funny but never appreciated the talent in himself," he told *E!*

Franken added that he was equally impressed by Farley's generous and charitable nature off stage when he visited cancer-stricken children in a New York pediatric oncology unit and volunteered at a New York site for homeless elderly.

"He was the type of guy that felt that (helping others, cheering others up) was why you're on Earth," Franken said.

As aware as the *Saturday Night Live* cast was of their costar's humility and immense talents, they were painfully aware of his problems as well. Virtually every cast member tried to counsel Farley on getting help for his addictions, but to no avail.

Michaels even threatened to fire Farley, hoping to scare him into sobriety before the show lost another of its overweight funny men. As a result, Farley did check into the Hazelton Clinic in Minnesota and went back to the show sober in 1992.

He remained free of drugs for several years, his family has said, but then fell into a cycle of abuse and sobriety that haunted him until his death.

By 1994, friend and fellow comedian Tom Arnold was again concerned about Farley's health. When he asked the *Saturday Night Live* star to appear on his TV show *Tom* in 1994, Arnold did so to get Farley into an intervention confrontation with his friends at Arnold's California home.

The intervention seemed to work. Farley admitted himself to the Daniel Freedman Hospital for 28 days and reported a new commitment to sobriety.

Meanwhile, Farley had already begun making a name for himself in movies.

Michaels cast Farley in his first Hollywood film, giving him a small role as a security guard in the 1992 movie *Wayne's World*, which he followed with a similar performance as Milton in the 1993 sequel *Wayne's World 2*.

"Danged I was scared (about doing that first movie)," Farley admitted to Fenster in 1997. "I was freaking out because I didn't want to screw up. Luckily I was on the set for a day."

Farley proved he could carry his comedy to the screen, however, and Michaels began casting him in other supporting roles. He played Conehead Connie's boyfriend Ronnie in the 1993 movie *Coneheads,* which was based on the popular *Saturday Night Live* skit. He played Officer Wilson in 1994's *Airheads,* and played a bus driver in 1995's *Billy Madison* (1995).

By 1995, Michaels felt Farley was comfortable and good enough for a starring role and cast him with fellow *Saturday Night Live* star and friend Dennis Spade in *Tommy Boy*. Farley played dimwitted but dedicated Thomas 'Tommy' Callahan III who teams up with his dad's uptight assistant Richard Hayden (Spade) to save the family auto parts factory.

Though the movie was scripted, Farley and Spade ad libbed in many of the scenes they filmed in Toronto, Farley told Fenster in 1997. The directors said, "Whatever you want Chris. Play with it. ... (and) I threw a million ideas around. If they pick 10, that's cool with me."

Of course, letting a comedic dynamo like Farley loose on a set meant having to tug on the reins at times. "They say to me, 'You can take it down about 1 million percent, Chris," Farley added.

Farley's performance — often comic and sometimes sweetly

serious — remains the favorite film performance of the Farley family, Kevin Farley told *E!* biographers, noting that their father was especially moved by a scene at the end of *Tommy Boy* where Tommy Callahan is talking to his father. "Dad just welled up. He just loved that movie," Kevin Farley said.

His father's reaction was always most important to the *Saturday Night Live* comedian. "There was always only one guy in Madison, Wisconsin, sitting on a chair that (Chris) wanted to make laugh," Kevin Farley added.

Tommy Boy got Farley's dad rolling, and a lot of moviegoers laughed along. The movie opened No. 1 at the box office in April 1995, grossed some $30 million, and remains a comic cult classic.

Based on its success, Michaels cast Farley and Spade as Mike Donnelly and Steve Dodds in *Black Sheep* (1996), a film that made as much as *Tommy Boy* and propelled the comedians to potential box office stardom.

Things were looking up for Farley in seemingly every direction in 1995. He was sober and thinner than he'd been in years.

That year, he performed in an improvisational group in Madison featuring his brothers Kevin and John at the Funny Business comedy club, his only performance at the Madison club. He also donated a drawing to a Madison Repertory Theater doodle auction that featured a pair of open-mouthed heads.

It was one of many times Farley returned to his hometown for publicity, for charity or for just plain fun. "Farley was known to drop by the UW campus and do his (*Saturday Night Live*) Matt Foley motivational speaker routine to get the football players fired up," noted a posthumous profile in the *Wisconsin State Journal*. When the Badgers went to the Rose Bowl, so did Farley who entertained at the Rose Bowl dinner, cheered at the parade, and visited the players. Farley also reportedly once appeared as a special correspondent at a Wisconsin vs. Northwestern football game.

The comedian loved to come home and go to Badger and Packer games, hang out on State Street and just stay home, his family reports, and "of course, of course," he owned and wore a Cheesehead, donning one for host Jay Leno during a *Tonight Show* appearance.

In 1996, Farley was paid $6 million to star in *Beverly Hills Ninja* and even took martial arts lessons in Chicago to better play the part. After a January 1997 private showing, Farley reportedly hated his performance so much on screen that he cried and vowed he would never do that again.

Though the movie was another financial hit, the disappointment in how he looked started Farley down a self-destructive spiral.

By the time he was shooting the American explorer adventure comedy, *Almost Heroes* with Matthew Perry, and lending his voice to a Dream Works animated featured called *Shrek*, Farley was out of control. Though Farley was especially excited about his role as tracker Bartholomew Hunt because it gave him an opportunity to "broaden his image. ... (bring) his acting out," John told the *Chicago Sun Times* June 12, 1998, producers of both films went to great lengths to keep their star from overindulging in his free time.

During *Almost Heroes* Farley had to attend AA Meetings, reported Ginia Bellafante in a December 29, 1997, article for *Time* magazine. Dream Works "put the comic under 24-hour bodyguard during recording to make sure he remained sober," though studio partner Jeffrey Katzenberg reported that he and his associates "were at times themselves taking drinks out of Farley's hands."

In addition, friends, lawyers, and agents hired counselors for Farley, confronted him, pleaded with him, and took him to rehab.

In 1997 interviews, Farley himself seemed to know he was in a desperate battle to clean up his act.

"I have a tendency toward pleasures of the flesh," he told Fenster. "It's a battle for me ... I try to fight those demons."

That battle had to start with trying to figure out a way to settle down off stage, he noted.

"I'm trying to grow up a little bit and be able to take off the red nose and floppy shoes when I need to," he added in a January 24, 1997, interview with Chris Vognar of the *Dallas Morning News*. Farley noted that he was trying hard not be "on" 24 hours a day, saying he wanted "to be a husband soon, and have a family, (but) when you're wacky and crazy all the time, I don't think you can do both worlds. I'd like to have that other world."

Farley continually tried to find that other, more sober world-checking into rehab clinic after rehab clinic, as many as seventeen in all, for increasingly short periods. However, each time he returned, Farley quickly fell back into excessive alcohol and drug use.

The comedian's friends and family grew desperately concerned.

"I laid into him ... I said it many times, he way playing with death if he did this and look who went before him," Dan Aykroyd told Bellafante of *Time*.

"I can't buy that he wanted to emulate Belushi this much,"

Aykroyd said referring to his friend and Farley's lifelong comedian idol John Belushi, who had also spiraled out of control and died of a drug overdose at age 33 in 1982.

Farley's parents were especially alarmed over their son's health when he sent them a videotape of the house he bought in California from money he made in movies.

Throughout the tape, Farley can be heard wheezing for breath as he walks the house's hallways and stairways. The sounds concerned his parents enough to insist he visit a doctor, which Farley said he did.

As encouragement to straighten out, Michaels invited Farley to host *Saturday Night Live* again, provided he could stay sober. The show aired October 25, 1997. It was the 33-year-old comedian's last TV performance.

Farley died December 18, 1997, in his Chicago apartment from heart failure caused by an accidental opiate (morphine) and cocaine overdose — and three blocked arteries. His death came after a wild four-day binge on alcohol and drugs.

"His last hours were spent around people that weren't his friends. That's what hurts," his brother Tom told *E!* biographers in 2002.

Farley's last movie appearance — in *Almost Heroes* as well as a cameo in *Dirty Work* (1998) — were both released after his death, and his voice role as *Shrek* was recast. At the time of his death, Farley had reportedly been excited about a chance to play silent-film comedian Fatty Arbuckle in an upcoming biography, a chance he never had to show off his more serious acting skills.

Friends and family members say that it was Farley's high speed style — which Klug likened to a motor burning "170 miles per hour, seventeen hours a day" — his desire to please, a lack of self-esteem, and lifelong addictive patterns that snuffed out the star's potential at just 33.

"Everybody loved him but ultimately that wasn't enough because he didn't love himself," former *Saturday Night Live* cast member Rob Schneider told Bellafante after Farley's death.

Farley's death hit his hometown especially hard. WZEE radio program director Jimmy Steele told the *Wisconsin State Journal* December 19, 1997, that the station received more than two hundred calls about Farley within an hour of breaking the news.

As hundreds lined the streets outside, more than five hundred people attended Farley's December 23, 1997, funeral mass at Our Lady Queen of Peace Catholic Church in Madison, including Lorne

Michaels, Dan Aykroyd, John Goodman, Tom Arnold, Chris Rock, Adam Sandler, George Wendt, and Rob Schneider.

Before Farley was buried at Madison's Resurrection Cemetery, the funeral program sent a message about his life and his death. The service contained the "Serenity Prayer," from Alcoholics Anonymous as well as "The Clown's Prayer" that Farley had been keeping in his wallet and no doubt reading to himself from time to time since college.

Since their son's death, the Farleys have established a yearly scholarship in his name at Marquette University.

They've also been working hard to educate kids about the dangers of following their Christopher's self-destructive path. Soon after the funeral, the family distributed a poster to every high school and middle school in the Madison area, which featured a picture of Chris Farley and said, "Drugs and Alcohol Can Kill The Laughter in Anyone."

Though Tom Farley Sr. died of kidney failure one year after burying his 33-year-old son, his wife, Mary Ann, and children continue to push an addiction-fighting message. The family founded the Chris Farley Foundation to support efforts to talk with preteens, high school students and young adults "about the damages of drugs with honesty and credibility ... and, as Chris would have, with humor."

The family also supports the annual efforts of *Comics Come Home*, a local stand-up and improvisational night that raises money for the foundation and keeps Farley's memory alive through laughter.

After all, laughter is what Farley loved most in life. As "The Clown's Prayer" says,

"Dear Lord, as I stumble through this life help me to create more laughter than tears, dispense more happiness than gloom, spread more cheer than despair ...

... And, in my final moment, may I hear You whisper, 'When you made my people smile, you made me smile.'"

Though he may have doubted it himself, Farley's prayer had always come true. After all, the people who loved and knew and saw him laughed *with* him ... and they're smiling still.

ON SCREEN

Smile along with Madison comedian Chris Farley in the following films:

Dirty Work (1998) (uncredited)
Almost Heroes (1998)
Beverly Hills Ninja (1997)
Black Sheep (1996)
Tommy Boy (1995)
Billy Madison (1995) (uncredited)
Airheads (1994)
Wayne's World 2 (1993)
Coneheads (1993)
Wayne's World (1992)

MORE FAMOUS FARLEYS

Christopher isn't the only Farley brother listed in Hollywood credits. His brothers John and Kevin Farley, both actors and improvisational comedians, have appeared in several TV shows and movies.

They began playing bit parts in almost all of their brother's films. For example, John plays a bartender in *Almost Heroes* (1998); Kevin plays a policeman in *Beverly Hills Ninja* (1997). In addition, Kevin played Doug Linus in the MTV boy band series *2gether* in 2000.

"The main thing was that Chris always liked to have us on the set for a while. It made shooting a movie more fun for him, and we always got a kick out of it," Kevin says.

KEVIN FARLEY

Frank McKlusky, C.I (2002)
It's a Secret (2001)
Joe Dirt (2001)
Artie (2000)
2gether: The Series (2000) TV Series
2gether (2000) (TV)
Misguided Angels (1999) TV Series
Love Stinks (1999)
The Straight Story (1999)
The Breaks (1999)
The Waterboy (1998)
Dirty Work (1998)

JOHN FARLEY

It's a Secret (2001)
Corky Romano (2001)
Joe Dirt (2001)
The Animal (2001)
Artie (2000)
Little Nicky (2000)
The Straight Story (1999)
The Breaks (1999)
The Waterboy (1998)

TONY SHALHOUB

Green Bay native Tony Shalhoub launched his screen career as cab driver Antonio Scarpacci on the hit TV series *Wings* from 1991 to 1997. His career in movies has been taking off ever since.

One of ten children in a Lebanese-American family, Shalhoub was born October 9, 1953. His parents and extended family started a grocery chain in downtown Green Bay that, Shalhoub told *Café Arabica* writer Randa Kayalli, his father had hoped the children would one day take over.

"But it didn't really take on. Many of us didn't want to stay in that community, (though) in some ways it would have been nice (to stay). ... There was a strong sense of socializing and people helping each other out," he said of Green Bay.

The city made a lasting impression on Shalhoub as the town where he discovered his passion for acting. He was just 6 years old when one of his older sisters got him a part as an extra in her high school play, *The King and I*. Though he ended his scene on the wrong side of the curtain, the little brother now knew what he wanted to be when he grew up.

Shalhoub attended the University of Southern Maine in Portland before gaining a master's degree from the Yale School of Drama. The Green Bay boy honed his acting skills for four years in Cambridge, Masssachusetts, with the American Repertory Theater and then moved to New York where he established himself on the right side of the Broadway curtain with such performances as his Tony-nominated portrayal of a Jewish man reviewing his life in *Conversations With My Father* in 1992. That same year, Shalhoub married actress Brooke Adams who gained recognition opposite Richard Gere and Sam Shepard in the 1978 movie *Days of Heaven*. Shalhoub and Adams began married life with Adams's daughter Josie, whom the actress adopted in 1989. They soon added to their family with daughter Sophie, born in 1993.

Meanwhile, Shalhoub was adding credits as well. By this time, *Wings* was taking off on TV, and the actor was catching more Hollywood attention.

Though he'd debuted in films in 1990 as a doctor in *Longtime*

Companion and stole the scene from Bill Murray as a foreign cab driver in *Quick Change*, Shalhoub gained more audience recognition as Buddy Walker in *Honeymoon in Vegas* (1992) and as a chess club member in 1993's *Searching for Bobby Fischer*.

He earned critical acclaim, and the National Society of Film Critics' Best Supporting Actor award, for his portrayal of temperamental chef Primo in *Big Night* (1996).

Shalhoub also played an Arab-American federal agent in the eerily foreshadowing movie, *The Siege* (1998), about Arab suicide bombers who strike New York City.

Though the Green Bay native continues to act in a variety of genres, he is probably best known for his comic roles.

Most recently, fans will recognize him as the villain in *Spy Kids* (2001), the homeless prophet in *Life or Something Like It* (2002) and regenerative alien Jack Jeebs in *Men in Black II* (2002), a role he carried from 1997's *Men in Black*.

Shalhoub's directorial debut came in 2002 when he directed his sister-in-law Lynn Adams's screenplay *Made Up*. The film is a true family affair with Shalhoub's wife starring as his love interest Elizabeth and her real sister starring as Elizabeth's sister Kate. Shalhoub's directing talents have already received critical acclaim; the movie won the "audience award" for Best Narrative First Film at the South by Southwest Film Festival in 2002.

Movie fans can expect to see much more from the versatile actor. In 2002, Shalhoub was working on his portrayal of Larocca in *Against The Ropes*, a film also starring Meg Ryan and Timothy Daly, and in Robert Altman's new movie, *Voltage*.

The actor's work doesn't stop on the big screen, however. Shalhoub has also returned to television, starring as a germ-phobic detective in the new cable TV series *Monk*.

ON SCREEN

Fans can see Green Bay native Tony Shalhoub in the following:

Against the Ropes (2003)
Voltage (2002)
Monk (2002) TV Series
Men in Black II (2002)
Life or Something Like It (2002)
Made-Up (2002)
Impostor (2002)
The Heart Department (2001) (TV)
Thirteen Ghosts (2001)
The Man Who Wasn't There (2001)
Spy Kids (2001)
Galaxy Quest (1999)
Stark Raving Mad (1999) TV Series
That Championship Season (1999) (TV)
The Tic Code (1998)
A Civil Action (1998)
The Siege (1998)
The Impostors (1998)
Paulie (1998)
Primary Colors (1998)

Gilpatrick

A Life Less Ordinary (1997)
Gattaca (1997)
Men in Black (1997)
Radiant City (1996) (TV)
Big Night (1996)
I.Q. (1994)
Gypsy (1993) (TV)
Addams Family Values (1993)
Searching for Bobby Fischer (1993)
Honeymoon in Vegas (1992)
Barton Fink (1991)
Longtime Companion (1990)
Quick Change (1990)
Wings (1990-97) TV Series
Money, Power, Murder. (1989) (TV)
Day One (1989) (TV)
Alone in the Neon Jungle (1988) (TV)

DAVID & JERRY ZUCKER

There's probably a cosmic reason why zany and Zucker both start with "Z." When it comes to the Zucker brothers from Shorewood, Wisconsin — writers and directors with Shorewood native Jim Abrahams of such off-the-wall comedy classics as *Airplane!, Police Squad* and *Naked Gun* — it's hard for a writer to know which "Z" to capitalize.

"I guess David and I got thrown together in the same house for a reason," agrees Jerry Zucker, adding that he and his older brother started out "normal" enough as the two brothers in Burton and Charlotte Zucker's three-child household with sister Susan. David was born October 16, 1947, and Jerry on March 11, 1950. Their father had graduated from the University of Wisconsin in Madison and was a Milwaukee real estate businessman who sold and managed office buildings. Their mother was a former New York City radio and stock company actress who earned a master's degree in speech and education from UW in Madison and taught school before raising her children.

Though older sister Susan would team up with David to pick on Jerry from time to time, the Zuckers mostly filled their childhood days creatively, their mother recalls.

"The boys were always very creative. David put out a newspaper when he was very young and wrote a comic book in elementary school, and Jerry was always an excellent writer," Charlotte Zucker notes. "I never imagined they would be in movies. Like any mother, I imagined my sons would grow up to be doctors or lawyers."

They were creative in their play as well, Jerry Zucker adds. "We used to invent endless games, including one with a Frisbee where we'd try to hit the house from across the street. If we hit the roof it was like a home run.

As the future movie directors were growing up, Charlotte Zucker participated in Shorewood area theater productions from time to time, such as in Shorewood Chamber Theater where she played one of the sisters in a production of *Arsenic & Old Lace*. Still, she believes, it was their father Burton's sense of humor that influenced her sons the most.

David Zucker recalled his influences in an interview for this book.

"The Marx Brothers and Woody Allen were influences, but I think the biggest influence was *MAD Magazine*," he said. "My mother remembers me sitting alone in the den, reading *MAD* and laughing out loud."

What he read on those satirical pages helped form the sense of humor he later parlayed into comedy hits like *Naked Gun*, Zucker added. "Basicallly *MAD* would set up familiar situations and then reverse the outcome that readers expected. This is pretty much was we do in our films."

Equally influential were his parents, David Zucker said, agreeing that his dad's dry sense of humor rubbed off on his children and that his mother's love of theater impacted him as well. "She took us, dragged us, to plays and musicals and took us to see the movie *My Fair Lady* by telling us they had a swear word in it, so naturally we wanted to go. The swear word, I still remember, was 'bloomin' arse,' but once we were there, we loved it.

"Also, because Mom was an actress, watching TV with her was watching with a running commentary, so we observed through her not to just accept what was coming off the TV," he said, noting his mother's friend was TV actress Charlotte Rae, also a Shorewood High graduate.

Not all the Zucker fun involved imagination. "My brother had the train schedule and knew all the times the trains were coming by. So, for a good time, we'd ride our bikes down to Dairy Queen and watch the trains. I was a vanilla cone with chocolate dip guy and still am," Jerry Zucker says. Trains are a hobby David Zucker continues to enjoy, and his Ojai, California, ranch boasts a model train track that winds through several rooms.

David Zucker also played guitar in several bands while in high school, including his own band, The Chevelles, which also featured his friend and now famous blues musician John Paris.

Though both brothers participated in drama at Shorewood High School, they and Abrahams (who is three years older than David Zucker) were better known as class clowns.

"We were always entertainers trying to make other kids laugh," Jerry Zucker said in a 2002 interview, adding theirs was a blossoming talent that only a few teachers appreciated or at least tolerated, most memorably, Otis Sweiger, Margaret Sturr, Wally Schneider, Peter Harrington, and drama teacher Barbara Gensler.

Jerry Zucker especially remembers history teacher Chester

Rinka. "Most teachers would reprimand me, but he would just turn around, shake his head and say, 'Jerry, I know one day I'll be paying to see you do this.'"

By 1971, Jerry Zucker was a student teacher finishing his college degree at the University of Wisconsin in Madison, where brother David had just graduated in 1970 and David had dated the sister of famous Wisconsin film star Willem Dafoe, but then it was "Billy" and the family pronounced the name *Day*-foe, not Da-foe, according to Zucker.

While the elder Zucker had been a well-known anti-war demonstrator in college, he also was a film student and once made *The Best Things in Life are Free,* which featured a "desperate" Jerry Zucker running up Bascom Hill in search of a place to relieve himself and finding a solution on the statue of Lincoln at the top of the hill, David Zucker recalled in an October 25, 1996, interview with Tom Alesia, then of the *The Capital Times* in Madison.

After college, David Zucker sent some of his student films to advertising agencies in the Midwest, hoping to land a job writing commercials and had been working a year for his dad as a construction supervisor when a friend invited him to see a unique show in Chicago called *The Groove Tube* that showcased comedy in a new medium: video. "That was the epiphany," David Zucker said.

He soon lit on an idea to form a satirical comedy theater group in Madison called Kentucky Fried Theater and invited his brother and Shorewood friend Jim Abrahams to join in the fun.

Born May 10, 1944, in Milwaukee, Abrahams knew the Zuckers better out of school because Abrahams's father was a business partner with Burton Zucker. Jim Abrahams had attended the University of Wisconsin and was working as a law firm investigator when Zucker approached him with a zany idea. Soon, Abrahams quit his job for a chance to make it big by having fun.

The longtime Zucker family friend remembered that David Zucker first approached him to make some just-for-fun videotape spoofs of TV commercials, Abrahams told *The Independent* in an August 16, 1993 interview. "One day (1970), I ran into David Zucker, who was supervising construction for his father, and he said, 'We have this video equipment (on loan from Shorewood pharmacist Bill Kesselman which featured reel-to-reel tape with a huge camera), do you want to come and play around with it?' ... So we started to videotape spoofs of TV commercials, and scenes from *The Love Story*. It was really just for our own amusement, but even-

Yearbook photos of David, from left, Jerry Zucker and Jim Abrahams. Photos courtesy of Shorewood High School.

tually, we showed it to some of our friends and they laughed, so we decided to take it to the University of Wisconsin," Abrahams recalled. The friends hatched the idea of a spoof-style comedy theater group that would combine their videos with stage performance. They reportedly came up with the name for the group, Kentucky Fried Theater, while munching on fast food chicken during a brainstorming session.

Kentucky Fried Theater opened as sit-down on bleachers kind of theater above the Daisy Cafe near the Capitol, David Zucker told Alesia, but it closed before it opened when the brothers encountered building permit problems.

The Zucker-Abrahams team improvised and moved the performance to the University of Wisconsin Union. "It was a disaster," David Zucker recalled of the group's first night in Alesia's story. "We had no idea what we were doing. We had advertised a 90-minute show, and after 20 minutes, we ran out of material. So we called an intermission. After that one of the troupe, Dick Chudnow, went out and entertained." He saved the show.

Troupe members Chudnow, Lisa Davis, Bill West and Chris Keene soon were performing the improv-video comedies in a theater they built behind the Shakespeare & Company bookstore on Regent Street.

Despite their inexperience, Kentucky Fried Theater got rave reviews for its combination of comedy skits and short, satire-styled movies.

Though they achieved critical success in Madison, the $1 a ticket seats weren't enough to pay the bills. The comedy team decided to move the Kentucky Fried Theater concept to Los Angeles in hopes of making a name and a living for themselves. "We really thought we'd find success even faster than we did," David Zucker recalled. "We were naive I guess. There's a certain innocence in the Midwest and looking back on it when we were in California we were like the little boy in the story, 'The Emperor Has No Clothes.'"

In 1972, the group (now featuring the Zuckers, Abrahams, Chudnow and Davis) turned a former drug rehabilitation center in Los Angeles into a theater, furnished with items from their parents' garages and attics.

"When Jim, Jerry and David left our driveway with that U-Haul full of dreams Burt and I stood in our driveway and waved. I was crying but Burt said, 'don't worry honey, they'll be back in six months,'" recalls Charlotte Zucker.

The three Shorewood friends never looked back, however, and they didn't need to. Their Los Angeles Kentucky Fried Theater performances were such a hit that they were asked onto *The Tonight Show* in 1972. The troupe added pianist Steve Stucker from Los Angeles and performed successfully together for five years. After a year in L.A., Chudnow returned to Madison and later founded the chain of comedy improvisation theaters known as Comedy Sportz.

David Zucker recalled that the rave reviews Kentucky Fried Theater got made him smile for more than one reason. "They would say, 'From Wisconsin of all places comes a feisty, funny troupe,' and we thought, 'from Wisconsin of all places' was exactly why we were funny. We sharpened our wit to survive in high school and came from a place where everyone thinks it's great to laugh at themselves, so that enabled us to laugh at big-city media, something no one had really done before when we started spoofing it."

In the meantime, the Zuckers and Abrahams wrote the screenplay for *Airplane!* but could get no takers. They used the $35,000 they had saved and borrowed to make a 10-minute segment that they could show Hollywood producers in hopes of making a movie based on their Kentucky Fried zaniness.

The United Artists Theater Circuit, a theater chain, liked what it saw enough to fund a low-budget film for about $650,000 that featured a montage of the group's TV and movie parodies. That first film, *The Kentucky Fried Movie*, was directed by John Landis and enjoyed moderate box office success in 1977 and enjoys cult comedy classic status today.

More importantly, the Zucker-Abrahams-Zucker team, ZAZ, now could show Hollywood studios they could make money while people were laughing. In 1980, Paramount Studios backed the trio to write and direct what became a hit disaster-movie spoof called *Airplane!*, in which they cast such actors from original, serious disaster movies as Robert Stack and Lloyd Bridges.

The whole experience of not only writing a movie screenplay but actually directing, as they did for the first time with *Airplane!*, was exhilarating.

"We were all very excited when the reality hit us that we were going to make a movie but we were soon so immersed in the process of getting the film made that we didn't have a lot of time to say, 'Oh boy! Look at us!' Jerry Zucker recalls. "However there certainly were times we'd take a moment — especially when we were making *Airplane!* — and say, 'hey cool! a couple of guys from Milwaukee are making a real Hollywood movie!'"

The Zuckers wanted their family to share in their success as well and cast their actress mother Charlotte, dad Burt and sister Susan — and Abrahams's mother Louise Yaffe — in bit parts in the movie (and many other films).

Of her sons' seventeen productions, Charlotte Zucker says that her *Airplane!* performance as a woman applying lipstick during turbulence remains best remembered by fans. "Though a role I did later in Jerry's *Ghost* is my favorite because it was meatier and had the most lines, I still hear the most about being the lipstick lady," she said, adding that despite her many recognizable film roles, she's not a big movie star. "Yes, I was in seventeen movies but when you blink, you've missed me."

Sister Susan played a ticket agent in the film, but Burt Zucker was initially left out when he stayed back in Milwaukee to work. After returning home, Charlotte and Susan decided that if they were in the movie, Burt should be too. "The boys said, 'we'll fix it' and blew up a big picture of Burt to use in a scene. He's the Employee of the Month hanging on the wall when all the reporters rush to a bank of phone booths and knock it over."

The Milwaukee guys proved they had Hollywood talent with *Airplane!* when the movie became an $83 million grossing hit. The trio returned to Madison to share their success in 1980 when, according to a November 9, 1980, *Wisconsin State Journal* article, the one-time Badgers hosted a benefit performance of *Airplane!* at the Orpheum Theater and rode as grand marshals in the holiday parade.

Together the Shorewood friends as ZAZ Productions created the 1982 series *Police Squad!* and the 1984 film *Top Secret!* Though not as huge a commercial hit as *Airplane!*, the ZAZ players had established themselves as the barometers by which future spoof comedy will be measured.

They measured their success by screening movies at colleges, including their Madison alma mater, recalls Jim Abrahams. "After we showed the movie, we had a question and answer period. While it was always apparent that the Wisconsin kids were as smart and funny as kids at Harvard, the Wisconsin kids were always nicer, more respectful and more polite even when they had something critical to say."

In 1986, the trio broke its own mold a bit by directing a different kind of comedy, *Ruthless People*, a successful film starring Danny DeVito that proved to be the Shorewood friends' last directing collaboration for a long time.

"We were so encouraged (by our success) that we decided to split up," David Zucker told Jess Bravin November 19, 1991, in *The Los Angeles Times*.

"As we grew older, our interests and tastes changed. It became harder to find one movie that would interest all three of us. Additionally, once we directed on our own, we realized we each liked being the captain of the ship," says Jerry Zucker, who adds that the three friends wouldn't change one moment of their collaborations.

"Working together, starting in this business as we did together was great fun," he says. "I don't think any one of us could have done it alone. We all had a great time together and are still friends, and brothers.

David and Jerry Zucker continue to share offices and occasionally collaborate on producing projects, like *Walk in the Clouds* (1995), through their company called Zucker Brothers Productions.

The three stayed together to cowrite the first *Naked Gun* movie starring Leslie Nielsen, and Jerry Zucker and Jim Abrahams continued to serve as executive producers on the three-film series, but the success of the *Naked Gun* trilogy — *The Naked Gun: From the Files of Police Squad!* (1988), *The Naked Gun 2 ½: The Smell of Fear* (1991), and *Naked Gun 33 1/3: The Final Insult* (1994) — lies mostly on the shoulders of David Zucker, who filled his famous spoof-based stories with background sight gags and punch lines.

The elder Zucker remained loyal to the satirical comedies that earned ZAZ its Hollywood fame, producing *High School High* (1986) and directing *BASEketball* (1988), the latter of which was a offbeat comedy based on one of those creative games the Zuckers had been inventing since grade school, this one using a basketball and a baseball diamond and featuring a defensive style that allows players to psyche-out shooters both physically and verbally. Zucker tapped into his Milwaukee roots for much of the film's backdrop with stars who played for the Milwaukee Beers and fans who wore "Foamheads" as they battled the Dallas Felons and San Francisco Ferries.

David Zucker worked with Wisconsinite Chris Farley on the movie *Toddlers,* which was cancelled after Farley died in 1997. In 2002, Zucker was working on a screenplay for a movie called *Santa Claus Conquers the Martians.* He also was developing *The Onion Movie,* based on the satirical newspaper that started in Madison, and headed for New Zealand to film *Harv the Barbarian* starrring Rob Schneider.

Meanwhile, Jim Abrahams also preferred to stick with comedies and wrote, directed, and produced such movies as *Big Business* (1988), *Hot Shots!* (1991), *Hot Shots! Part Deux* (1993), and *Mafia!* (1998).

In 1993, after the Los Angeles riots, David Zucker teamed up with television producer Rich Markey, a college roommate, to create a comedy video with a very serious twist — producing *For Goodness Sake, For Goodness Sake II* (1996), and *For Goodness Sake III* (1998), with the aim of teaching (not preaching) moral values, using comedy to get the message across in vignettes that feature people confronting issues like racial jokes. David Zucker said the series is his proudest production.

"With all the craziness going on, seeing people looting stores, … we just felt like we had to do something," he told the *The Capital Times* in 1992, adding that, "everyone — the writers, actors, crew — is either taking a deferred salary or working for nothing on the project," including its producer who put up the seed money to make the films.

Abrahams style took on a more serious tone in some of his other films as well including in *Welcome Home, Roxy Carmichael* (1990) and especially in a TV movie about epilepsy that he produced for ABC in 1997, called *First Do No Harm,* starring Meryl Streep. Abrahams made the movie after he and his wife, Nancy, were told their third child Charlie had epilepsy and discovered that an unusual high-fat, low-protein, low-carbohydrate diet called the ketogenic diet seemed to keep his seizures at bay. The couple also founded the Charlie Foundation to spread the word about pediatric epilepsy and the diet.

Today, Abrahams still considers producing movies, but focuses most of his creative energies on running the foundation and promoting the diet. "You can't make a movie painting by numbers, you have to feel passion for the project. Right now, I feel the most passion for this diet and for letting others know that there are alternative, successful treatments for epilepsy."

Meanwhile, Jerry Zucker, who recently produced such films as *First Knight* (1995), *Rat Race* (2001) and *Unconditional Love* (2002), branched off from the spoof genre in 1990 and decided to direct a love drama movie starring Patrick Swayze and Demi Moore, called *Ghost* — a concept the director's older brother was concerned about at first, David Zucker admitted in an interview with *The Onion* in 1998.

"Jerry and I have totally different interests in what kind of things we think would make good movies (so) with almost every movie the two of us have done separately, one has tried to talk the other out of doing it," he said. For instance, when David wanted to do a movie series based on the TV show *Police Squad*, Jerry thought the concept wouldn't work and tried to talk him out of it.

Likewise, David Zucker recalled asking his younger brother, "'You're not gonna do this *Ghost* thing, are you? ... No matter how you slice it, you end up with a dead guy at the end. He's killed in the first fifteen minutes.' And then I thought, 'well, maybe he can be revived and brought back to Earth or something.' And (Jerry was) like, 'No, he's dead.' ... When I saw the movie, I thought it was great."

Family members continue to appear in Zucker and Abrahams's films, though Charlotte Zucker still gets the most recognition for her performances. In return, the former theater actress says that motherhood aside, she's been impressed with the boys' directing talents.

"There are directors who have a reputation for yelling, but my boys don't. They go over to the actor and explain; nobody hears tantrums or bad language," Charlotte Zucker stresses. "As an actress, I'm very admiring of their polite, calm personalities on the set."

Still, it took a minute or two to adjust to the idea of having the kids in charge, Jerry Zucker jokes, saying his mom once said that we were "finally getting back at her for telling us what to do" all those years.

"Mom is a really good actress and she loves it," he adds. "She's very much a trooper, too, and refuses special treatment on the set. While filming *Rat Race*, for example, I asked her to come eat in my trailer because it was so hot out. But she said, 'no, no, I'm going to eat with the actresses,' and off she went to the tent."

Charlotte Zucker adds that she is equally impressed by how much the Shorewood friends have learned about filmmaking over the years. "I'm constantly amazed at how spread out into the field they are knowledge wise. They know about editing and costuming and music and I keep thinking 'How do they know all that? I never taught them any of that,' she says. "From what I do know both professionally, and as their mom, they amaze me."

The Zuckers insist that if they are well mannered on the set, they have their parents and Wisconsin upbringing to thank.

"I always felt I had a huge advantage coming from Wisconsin," says Jerry Zucker. "Though you can grow up funny anywhere, there's just a different kind of funny in the Midwest.

"Wisconsinites have a great sense of humor that's a little self-deprecating, but they love to poke fun at the big guys. And, that's what we do in our satires, poke fun at movies and television," he adds. "In New York and L.A. they take show business a little too seriously to do that, but we grew up in a place that media usually comes to, not from, so it's easier to ridicule."

The brothers and Abrahams have remained loyal to their home state, even though they've both lived in Los Angeles for decades — Jerry with his producer wife Janet and 14-year-old daughter Katie and 10-year-old son Bob, and David with his doctor wife Danielle and 3-year-old son Charles and new baby girl Sarah.

In 1986, the Zuckers and Abrahams were inducted into the Wisconsin Performing Artists Hall of Fame and were introduced by their family friend and fellow inductee Charlotte Rae. In turn, they got to introduce Fred MacMurray, a man they watched on TV as teen-agers.

The Zuckers are longtime Packer and Badger fans who used to camp out overnight in downtown Milwaukee to get Packer tickets and still don Cheeseheads at game time. When the Badgers went to the Rose Bowl in 1994, David Zucker pulled out all the Wisconsin stops, filling a motor home with brats and Pabst beer for a huge tailgate party in the Rose Bowl parking lot.

As proud as they are of their football teams, the Zuckers and Abrahams remain proudest of their home state and return as often as they can, with Abrahams traveling each summer to a home he has near Eagle River.

"I thought summers in Eagle River were the best parts of my youth, and I always counted the days until we got to go up north. Today, I take my children there. We fish where I fished as a kid

Famous Wisconsin Film Stars

and enjoy the beauty of Wisconsin," Abrahams says.

In short, the Zuckers may still joke around a lot but the truth is they're serious about the strong roots and values Wisconsin instilled in them years ago.

"The fondness I have for Wisconsin isn't in the buildings or farmland or festivals," Jerry Zucker said. "My fondest memories and my pride is the people. Wisconsin people are great because they're more sane and down to earth and they've got good values — the kind of values that stay with you."

ON SCREEN

David Zucker wrote and then directed and/or produced the following motion pictures:

Phone Booth (2002) (producer)
Harv the Barbarian (2002) (director, producer)
The Guest (2001) (director)
H.U.D. (2000) (TV) (director)
For Goodness Sake III (1998) (producer)
BASEketball (1998) (producer, director)
For Goodness Sake II (1996) (director)
High School High (1996) (producer, director)
A Walk in the Clouds (1995) (producer)
Naked Gun 33 1/3: The Final Insult (1994) (producer)
For Goodness Sake (1993) (producer, director)
The Naked Gun 2 1/2: The Smell of Fear (1991) (director only)
The Naked Gun: From the Files of Police Squad! (1988) (executive producer, director)
Our Planet Tonight (1987) (TV) (executive producer)
Ruthless People (1986) (director only)
Top Secret! (1984) (executive producer, director)
Police Squad! (1982) TV Series (executive producer, director)
Airplane! (1980) (executive producer, director)
The Kentucky Fried Movie (1977)

Jerry Zucker wrote and then directed and/or produced the following films:

Unconditional Love (2002) (producer)
Rat Race (2001) (producer, director)
My Best Friend's Wedding (1997) (producer)
First Knight (1995) (producer, director)
A Walk in the Clouds (1995) (producer)
Naked Gun 33 1/3: The Final Insult (1994) (executive producer)
My Life (1993) (producer)
The Naked Gun 2 1/2: The Smell of Fear (1991) (executive producer)
Ghost (1990) (director)
The Naked Gun: From the Files of Police Squad! (1988) (executive producer)
Our Planet Tonight (1987) (TV) (executive producer)
Ruthless People (1986)
Top Secret! (1984) (executive producer, director)

Police Squad! (1982) TV Series (executive producer, director)
Airplane! (1980) (executive producer, director)
The Kentucky Fried Movie (1977)

Jim Abrahams wrote and then directed and/or produced the following movies (Louise Yaffe has appeared in all the films her son directed):
Mafia! (1998) (producer, director)
... First Do No Harm (1997) (TV) (producer, director)
The Naked Gun 3 1/3: The Final Insult (1994) (executive producer)
Hot Shots! Part Deux (1993) (director)
The Naked Gun 2 ½: The Smell of Fear (1991) (executive producer)
Hot Shots! (1991) (director)
Cry-Baby (1990) (executive producer)
Welcome Home, Roxy Carmichael (1990) (director)
The Naked Gun: From the Files of Police Squad! (1988) (executive producer)
Big Business (1988) (director)
Ruthless People (1986) (executive producer, director)
Top Secret! (1984) (executive producer, director)
Police Squad! (1982) TV Series (executive producer, director)
Airplane! (1980) (executive producer, director)
The Kentucky Fried Movie (1977)

Parents Burton and Charlotte Zucker and sister Susan Breslau have appeared in most all of the Zucker brother's movies, including in the following roles:
Rat Race (2001) with mom as Lucy and Susan as a rental car manager
BASEketball (1998) with mom as a surgery nurse
My Best Friend's Wedding (1997) with mom, dad and 'sis' as customers
High School High (1996) with mom as a pipe smoker, Susan as a secretary and dad as an extra
First Knight (1995) with mom and dad bread vendors and Susan as a wedding guest
Naked Gun 33 1/3: The Final Insult (1994) with mom as a nurse, dad as a clinic patient, and Susan as a train passenger
My Life (1993) with mom and Susan as wedding guests
Brain Donors (1992) with mom as a woman with program
The Naked Gun 2 1/2: The Smell of Fear (1991) with mom and Susan as banquet ladies and dad as a lab technician
Ghost (1990) with mom as a bank officer and Susan as an extra.
The Naked Gun: From the Files of Police Squad! (1988) with mom as Dominique, dad as an airport photographer, and Susan as a woman at the police station
Ruthless People (1986) with mom as the judge and Susan as an extra
Top Secret! (1984) with mom and Susan as a cafe diners and dad as a chef
Airplane! (1980) with mom as the lipstick lady and Susan as a ticket agent
The Kentucky Fried Movie (1977) with mom and Susan as jurists

JERRY ZIESMER

If behind every good man is good woman (or vice versa), then behind every good director is Jerry Ziesmer. As a first assistant director, the Milwaukee native was the right hand man whom movie directors turned to when they needed more extras, their star on the set, a fast solution to an impossible problem, or just somebody to yell at.

"All I ever wanted to do was bring the paints to Van Gogh," Ziesmer says. And for thirty years that's what he did as well, if not better, than anybody else.

Ziesmer brought creative solutions through the tropical storms and stifling heat of a Philippine jungle to director Francis Ford Coppola while filming *Apocalypse Now.*

He herded hundreds of star-struck extras into position and away from Barbra Streisand, for Sydney Pollack during the creation of *The Way We Were.*

He coordinated the filming of 86,000 extras for John Frankenheimer in *Black Sunday.*

He finagled Amy Irving through a maze of parking lot red tape to visit her boyfriend Steven Spielberg as he filmed *1941.*

He played the parts for Cameron Crowe while they created *Say Anything, Singles, Jerry Maguire,* and *Almost Famous.*

He assembled a marching band of extras for Peter Bogdanovich to never use in *Illegally Yours.*

He jogged a street filled with running extras alongside Sylvester Stallone in *Rocky II.*

He waited for Al Pacino to get it perfect while Brian De Palma directed *Scarface.*

And, he brought a large-screen TV to John Huston so the famous director could watch the Kentucky Derby while everyone else filmed *Annie.*

Most of all, Ziesmer brought together the best talent palettes of Hollywood long enough that its most famous directors could paint their unique magic upon the Silver Screen.

Ziesmer was born May 31, 1939, in Milwaukee, to postal employee Herbert Ziesmer and his wife, Billie. He grew up on 34th

Street and often visited relatives in Oconto, Green Bay, Pensaukee, and especially Waupun, Wisconsin, where his mother's Dutch immigrant parents lived.

The future moviemaker first found a passion for performing at Rufus King High School where English teacher Evelyn Crowley taught students how to paint pictures with words, and drama teacher Catherine Miller encouraged Ziesmer's involvement in school and community theater.

In addition to school plays, Ziesmer acted in such Milwaukee Players productions as *Romeo and Juliet* and *Ondine* and performed as well in Mount Mary College's *Anastasia*. In the summers he performed at the Norman Players stages in Milwaukee's Lake Park and helped stage Port Players (by then in Oconomowoc) productions at the high school.

When his local theater thoughts turned to Hollywood dreams, Ziesmer looked to other Wisconsin stars who'd made it on the big screen for inspiration, he notes. "Just to be a 'screen struck' kid in Wisconsin in the 1950s and 1960s, you had to grab on to anything that would allow you to dream and to believe you could catch your dreams and be a 'somebody' in Hollywood."

Specifically Ziesmer took careful notes on how fellow Milwaukee and Northwestern University alum Jeffrey Hunter (of Whitefish Bay) made it into pictures. And, "I looked at the careers of my Wisconsin and acting idols Fred MacMurray and Fredric March," the one-time aspiring actor reports.

Ziesmer's most notable high school performance — and one of the defining moments of his young life — was when he landed the part of a Greek god football player in *The Member of the Wedding* being performed at the Fred Miller Theatre in Milwaukee.

The teenage actor's costar was Ethel Waters. His opportunity to act with, and speak with, Waters "strongly influenced my ideals and goals for my eventual film career," the now retired assistant director stresses.

In his 2000 autobiographical book, *Ready When You Are, Mr. Coppola, Mr. Spielberg, Mr. Crowe*, Ziesmer relays a most important discussion he'd had with the actress while waiting for his girlfriend Suzanne to pick him up in her dad's pink and white Buick for a cheeseburger at Shorty's.

"Ethel Waters was staring at me like we were friends … I knew it was my turn to speak. I smiled and tried to get the right words together," Ziesmer wrote. He said, "'You're so real on stage. The play's so perfect.'

Actor-comedian Richard Pryor with Jerry Zeismer.
Photo courtesy of Jerry Zeismer.

"'It doesn't happen often,' (Waters) said and laughed gently ... 'When a play like this one comes along, when it's your play, you got to grab on,' she said, and laughed again. 'Remember that.'"

Suzanne soon arrived and, with cheeseburgers on his mind, the young thespian left the accomplished actress waiting in the wings for her ride.

While Ziesmer was on stage, his girlfriend was behind the curtain working as the first girl on the Rufus King High School stage crew thanks to her encouraging teacher Mr. Seibrecht. Together with friends, the two would visit other Milwaukee hangouts like Doege's Frozen Custard, the George Devine Ballroom and such theaters as the Ritz, Egyptian, and, when money allowed, Riverside.

"I remember too ice skating, canoeing, and the lagoon and swans at Brown Deer Park, the "submarine races" at Bradford Beach, listening to WOKY and Mad Man Michaels, and going to a Wisconsin Avenue restaurant near Milwaukee County Stadium that served the *best* hot fudge sundaes in the world," Suzanne recalls of her days with Ziesmer.

Born in Texas, the future movie crew production assistant also remembers her high school attempts to be cool during Wisconsin winters. "I put my winter boots in the mailbox just before I got on the school bus and retrieved them when I got home. It was so 'uncool' to wear boots in high school," she says, noting that, "four years later, our mailman reminded me of how my boots shared the mailbox with the mail."

Ziesmer and his Rufus King girlfriend went to senior prom in 1957 and then parted ways after graduation, at least for a while.

Suzanne first went to Marquette University and then Oshkosh State University, now the University of Wisconsin-Oshkosh, and worked in between at Browns' Lake Resort in Burlington where the New York Yankees stayed while in town for the World Series. "I took the bus to Milwaukee with the team to attend my classes at Marquette while they practiced and played," she recalled, stressing that she remained loyal to her Milwaukee Braves. "I loved going to Milwaukee County Stadium and watching a game. I still haven't gotten over (the Braves) leaving Milwaukee," she notes.

Suzanne became a grade school teacher after college and married Ted Hartkopf in 1963. He died in 1979.

Her prom date left for Northwestern University in Illinois, a destination Ziesmer says he reached thanks to his high school teachers.

It was homeroom teacher Elaine Steiger, "who guided this immature, clumsy boy through those difficult years and helped provide that 'divining board of education' that enabled me to compete ... in the world of Hollywood," Ziesmer says.

And, it was speech and drama teacher Miller who steered Ziesmer down the road to a college education. Miller urged Ziesmer to apply to Northwestern University's Cherub Program (its high school institute). After he was accepted "totally because of Ms. Miller," Ziesmer received a full scholarship to the university gaining him entrance to a college education that "this son of a U.S. mailman from Milwaukee would never have been able to do financially."

On summer breaks from Northwestern, Ziesmer returned to Wisconsin, though not always to Milwaukee. He performed two summers at the Tower Ranch Summer Theatre outside Rhinelander, near his parents' new cottage on Lake Buckatoben. There he performed with Tom and Theoni Aldredge, who he would run into on a movie set seventeen years later.

After graduating in 1961, Ziesmer headed west in a packed VW Beetle, took a post office job in Beverly Hills and tried to work his way into movies as an actor.

He did have some success, landing tough kid or soldier roles, mostly in television shows filmed on the Metro-Goldwyn-Mayer lot in Hollywood. The Milwaukee native was especially thrilled when he got a part in an episode of *My Three Sons* starring Fred MacMurray, one of the Wisconsin stars he idolized as a teen.

In the meantime, Ziesmer pursued a graduate degree in theater at UCLA. For his master's thesis, Ziesmer interviewed comedian Stan Laurel of Laurel and Hardy fame at length about his theories of comedy.

While looking for steady work as an actor, Ziesmer found the love of a UCLA actress instead, and married Mary Kate Denny in 1964. They eventually had three children: Chris, Tim, and Jillian.

To make ends meet, Ziesmer took a job teaching English, American literature and journalism to junior high kids at the John Adams School in Santa Monica.

The actor loved his new occupation and, even after working with some of the most famous people in the world for thirty years, Ziesmer said he still loved teaching most.

"I'd do it all again, but I do miss the classroom and the joy of seeing a student 'learn,' that moment of 'CLICK'…he's got it!" Ziesmer said.

It was a student who finally convinced the teacher to chase his dreams, Ziesmer writes in his book, *Ready When You Are…*. After being accepted into an assistant director training program, Ziesmer asked his pupils if their teacher should leave them for Hollywood.

At the "very end of fourth period, (a) quiet boy in the back of the second row raised his hand. … 'Mr. Ziesmer, I think you should leave because I believe that's what you want most, but you must try to only do the very best movies.'"

With that challenge before him, Ziesmer set out for a destiny behind the camera on some of the best movies of the past thirty years.

He did not leave his teaching behind completely when he went into Hollywood movies, however, he told Tim Ryan of the *Honolulu Star Bulletin* in 1997. "Egos among these people are gigantic. My background as a junior high teacher … prepared me well to be an assistant director," Ziesmer said.

As part of the AD training program, Ziesmer was eventually assigned to work as an assistant director trainee on *Hello, Dolly* (1969) starring Gene Kelly and worked with his Wisconsin idol Fredric March on the actor's last picture, *...tick...tick...tick* (1970).

March was just one of dozens of top stars Ziesmer would come to know well over the next thirty years. Names on the long list include Tom Cruise, Barbra Streisand, Richard Pryor, Rita Hayworth, John Belushi, Mel Gibson, Martin Sheen, and Robert Redford.

Ziesmer got his first official second assistant director job, awarded after four hundred on-set days of training, on the movie, *Tell Me That You Love Me, Junie Moon* (1970), directed by Otto Preminger. He followed with a second assistant job in the boxing movie, *The Great White Hope* (1970), which gave Ziesmer his first taste of the travel involved in moviemaking when he flew to London and Spain to help film location scenes.

By 1972, Ziesmer had the 600 additional on-set training days needed to work as a first assistant director. And he landed a pristine opportunity to work on *The Way We Were* (1973), starring Robert Redford and Barbra Streisand.

The Milwaukee native followed with work on such movies as *Harry and Walter Go to New York* (1976) and *Black Sunday* (1977). Then, in 1976, he got a call to be assistant director for Francis Ford Coppola on a six-week war movie shoot that the Oscar-winning director of *The Godfather* (1972) was filming in the Philippines.

The six-week job lasted nearly a year thanks to a typhoon, a strange tropical illness that hospitalized half the crew, a moody Marlon Brando, and a temperamental Hollywood tiger. All complicated and delayed the completion of the now legendary film, which then took Coppola two years to edit and finally release in 1979.

After months of frustration, Coppola asked his assistant director to play a one-line part as a civilian who meets in a bar with Martin Sheen, G.D. Spradlin (the general) and a nearly unknown actor, Harrison Ford, as the colonel. Ziesmer told Sheen to "terminate with extreme prejudice" — a line that became the most memorable of the movie. While he was concerned with his performance, Ziesmer was more worried about the former Ripon College acting student they'd hired to play the colonel in the movie, he recalled in *Ready When You Are...* .

Of all the "thousands of actors in Hollywood, Fred Roos hired one who coughed and cleared his throat all the time as if he had consumption. I hoped this guy had a trade he could fall back on," Ziesmer thought of the actor who soon played Han Solo in *Star Wars* (1977) and is now a major Hollywood star.

One of a passel of snags that the assistant director and crew encountered was knee-deep mud on the set after a typhoon swept through the Philippines.

"You were lucky if you could keep stepping across the mud field," Ziesmer recalled in *Ready When You Are...*. "What happened to a lot of us was that our shoe or boot would stay down in the mud and our foot would come out. Soon, at least half of us were trudging through the mud field in our stocking feet. The Playboy Bunnies were carried across the field ... (and) an outbreak of skin rashes on any surface that had touched the mud spread throughout the company."

Coaxing Marlon Brando onto the set also proved challenging. However, Ziesmer had more problems with one of the film's "larger stars," the trained tiger "Gambi" who leaps at Martin Sheen in one scene. To get the tiger to spring from the jungle underbrush, trainers waived chickens in the air off camera. When the tiger remained uninterested for the better part of the day, trainers eventually got a pig. A squeal, they promised, would arouse the mild-mannered tiger to action.

A frustrated crew member volunteered to lie on the ground out of camera angles, hold the pig between his legs and make it squeal, Ziesmer recalled in *Ready When You Are...*. "Terry (Leonard) said, 'when Gambi leaps out, I'll turn and cover the pig. Gambi'll see (the trainer) with the chickens and we'll get the shot."

"I wished there was a chapel nearby," Ziesmer recalled of his nervousness about the idea everyone else seemed so sure of. "'Action,' Francis (Ford Coppola) said. ... 'Squeal!' ... In a tenth of a second, before any of us could move, even Terry, Gambi leaped out, took the squealing pig from between Terry's legs and bounded back into the jungle! We were all in total shock. Nothing moved that fast," Ziesmer recalled. He added that the tiger eventually charged through the set, sending crewmen scurrying to the river. The crew hid behind cameras and climbed a grip stand before Gambi settled back to being the quiet, lazy Hollywood tiger they'd all come to trust.

Ziesmer moved from tigers to prisoners and the challenges of working with first-time director Dustin Hoffman on *Straight Time* (1978). After a frustrating first day of indecision, Hoffman, who also was producer of the film, fired himself as director. Remembering his quality promise to that junior high student years earlier, and knowing he'd no longer be a part of Hoffman's first directing role, Ziesmer bowed out of the movie.

In 1978, he got a call from another actor who'd already directed his first low-budget movie to astounding success, *Rocky,* and accepted Sylvester Stallone's offer to be assistant director on the 1979 box-office smash sequel *Rocky II.* He followed as assistant director on *Annie* (1982) and the hit Al Pacino film *Scarface* (1983). In between, Ziesmer had a last-minute AD job with a new Hollywood director on the last scenes of his movie, *Close Encounters of the Third Kind* (1977).

Ziesmer recalls Steven Spielberg as completely focused on the film as they drove endlessly in search of the right desert location for the famous spaceship shot. "We all had done years more filmmaking than him. He'd done maybe one-fiftieth of what the rest of us had done, but we chased him across the desert and he told us where things would go," Ziesmer told Tom Alesia in a June 15, 2001, article for the *Wisconsin State Journal.* "He was a leader. We knew at an instant he was going to be a major force in filmmaking."

The Wisconsin native worked with Spielberg again on his not so spectacularly received comedy, *1941.* The movie starred onetime University of Wisconsin-Whitewater student John Belushi, who arrived by driving up the studio's Hollywood Boulevard in a New York taxi with Dan Aykroyd and danced onto the set. "It was quite an entrance for the two leading comics, ... and I already felt I was in for some rough times with those two," Ziesmer wrote.

Toward the end of his career, Ziesmer began working with new Hollywood director and writer Cameron Crowe. Their first film together was *Say Anything* in 1989 in which Crowe cast Ziesmer in a small role as a U.S. attorney. The director repeated the tradition, casting Ziesmer as a councilman in *Singles* (1992) and as the trainer that treats Cuba Gooding Jr. on the field in *Jerry Maguire* (1996).

But mostly the director relied on his experienced AD for, well, everything, he wrote in a foreword to Ziesmer's book.

"No movie has ever been made, or made well, without the character who toils just outside the spotlight. Hell, he arranged for that spotlight, hired the spotlight operator, and even made sure it was trained correctly on the stars," Crowe noted.

"As a director of three movies, I can now peel back the veil and speak the truth," he added. "There would be nothing on movie screens, no teary-eyed Oscar winners, no finished films, good or bad, without the assistant director. And, in that world, I have been fortunate enough to work with the best — Jerry Ziesmer."

In a July 2001 issue of the Directors Guild of America's *DGA Magazine*, writer David Hakim noted that the secrets to Ziesmer's talents were his "calm and quietude that many admire but few can emulate" ... and his "uncanny ability to be liked. He does not 'make people like him,' nor does he especially go out of his way for acceptance. But people trust Jerry Ziesmer and that has been a large part of his success."

The Wisconsin native humbly has his own assessment of his contributions to Crowe's and other directors' films, explaining that, "I like to think I helped create the environment that allowed both the student and the acting artist to 'bloom," he notes. "I did a small part, but I contributed."

It's a contribution that Ziesmer would repeat if he could. "Though my life has experienced great personal tragedy, I would stand on the beaches in Southeast Asia filming *Apocalypse Now* with Francis Coppola and Marlon Brando ... on the deserts with Steven Spielberg and Francois Truffaut filming *Close Encounters of the Third Kind* ... and even the cold, dusty Hollywood studio stages filming *Scarface* with Al Pacino or *The Way We Were* with Robert Redford and Barbra Streisand. I'd do it all again."

And, Suzanne would do it all again too, adds the former Ziesmer prom date who became his wife and production assistant.

Suzanne was a widow teaching fifth and sixth graders at Huntley School in Appleton when Ziesmer called her from Los Angeles in 1981. A newly divorced father of three, her old friend said he needed help trying to put his life back together. By the end of the call, the high school sweethearts had fallen in love all over again. They were married December 18, 1982.

When she wasn't at home with Chris (who soon lived with them) and Tim and Jillian (who visited often in a joint custody agreement), Suzanne worked on movies sets, too. She started as a tutor for student actors filming *The River* (1984). One "student" proved especially problematic, Ziesmer relayed in *Ready When You Are*....

"Mel Gibson would ... quietly take a seat in her classroom ... until one day (he) raised his hand and said, "'You know, I only went to school until I was 16. And I think that was the biggest mistake as an actor.' ... 'That's right,' Mel continued. 'I never should've gone to school. Not one day. No actor should. It's best if you know nothing.'"

Ziesmer wrote that he wasn't sure if it was the first time Gibson "had been asked to leave a schoolroom, but it was the first time Suzanne had told a movie star to 'go to the principal's office.'"

Suzanne Ziesmer had an even more memorable and enviable experience on the set of *Jerry Maguire*. The film's star, Tom Cruise, gave her a friendly kiss. Though she was by then an experienced production assistant (having worked on movies like *Say Anything* and *Singles*), Ziesmer admitted she became a blushing fan who "didn't want to wash her face" for a while.

Suzanne Ziesmer and Mel Gibson. Photo courtesy of Jerry Ziesmer.

The two also had an encounter with the nemesis of any Packer fan, Dallas Cowboy quarterback Troy Aikman, who was on the set for his cameo appearance. The Ziesmers recall that the many Wisconsinites on the crew were ready for Aikman when he arrived. "Wisconsin folk working on our set gave him an Old Wisconsin welcome with every kind of Packer sign, symbol, and apparel we could find" — a jab that Aikman took in good stride with a sense of humor, the assistant director noted.

For all the good that happened filming *Jerry Maguire*, the Ziesmers suffered a painful loss when their son Chris died. Their friend and fellow Wisconsin stage star and movie actress Salome Jens, who had been Chris's drama instructor, read a Dylan Thomas poem *Fern Hill* at his funeral.

The Ziesmers have worked their way past the grief and again retired, as they had until Crowe called Ziesmer into *Jerry Maguire* and called again for his 2000 movie *Almost Famous*.

During his so-called retirement, Ziesmer wrote his book and continues to teach film classes through a UCLA extension, to mentor promising students and to lecture about the film industry including at Edgewood College in Madison, where he spoke at a 2001 Technology, Media, and Design Conference.

Despite their decades in California, the Ziesmers remain diehard Packer fans and Wisconsinites.

"Suzanne and I watch the Packers, Badgers, and the Northwestern Wildcats on TV now, though there's a certain bar out in Chatsworth, California, that totally specializes in the Green Bay Packers; maybe we'll get there this season," he says, adding that the two are also regulars at Wisconsin Film Commission tailgate parties in Hollywood.

"We love brats and cheese curds," adds Suzanne, noting that they can get Wisconsin brats in California but had to write home to Johnsonville Brats for the address of California stores that carry them. "Cheese curds are *not* the same here, even if we can get them," laments the one-time teacher who still asks Wisconsin friends to send cheese and curds from home in care packages.

The Ziesmers return to the Badger State at least every five years for class reunions and other activities.

Sometimes, Wisconsin finds the Ziesmers in California. And, they say, it's always a pleasant, occasionally funny, experience.

The latter was especially true at the premiere for their last movie *Almost Famous*, somehow an appropriate title for the last film of a behind the scenes assistant director and (on that movie) a producer.

Looking back on the incident now, the Ziesmers laugh about how their Wisconsin roots shined through the Hollywood glitz and spotlights.

"We were retired and relaxing in our home when we received a charming set of tickets to a showing of *Almost Famous* at the Directors Guild, and we gave it little thought," Ziesmer recalls.

"The night of the showing, Suzanne and I noticed a lot of lights and news trucks around the Directors Guild but thought nothing about it as the Directors Guild has two main theaters and anything could be showing in the other theater.

"As is our custom, Suzanne and I were dressed all in denim — our denim shirts emblazoned with Green Bay Packer insignias," he recalls. "When we reached the lobby, we were stunned and totally embarrassed when we realized that this event was the premiere for *Almost Famous*!

"Our embarrassment didn't end until we began to pass along the food and drink line," Ziesmer recalls. "The wonderful catering folk cheered us as fellow Green Bay Packer fans because they were all young kids from Wisconsin working their way toward a foothold in Hollywood!"

Just as the movie's respected and retired filmmaker had been all those years ago.

ON SCREEN

Jerry Ziesmer worked on the following Hollywood movies, as a first assistant director, unless otherwise noted in parenthesis.

Almost Famous (2000)
Jerry Maguire (1996)
Singles (1992)
Deep Cover (1992)
Secrets (1992/II) (TV)
Out for Justice (1991)
Marked for Death (1990)
Solar Crisis (1990)
Love at Large (1990)
Say Anything... (1989)
Illegally Yours (1988) (assistant director)
Midnight Run (1988)
Some Kind of Wonderful (1987) (assistant director)
Jumpin' Jack Flash (1986)
Short Circuit (1986)
Jo Jo Dancer, Your Life Is Calling (1986)
American Flyers (1985) (assistant director)
The River (1984) (assistant director)
Scarface (1983)
Blue Thunder (1983) (assistant director)
Annie (1982)
History of the World: Part I (1981) (assistant director)
Life on the Mississippi (1980) (TV) (assistant director)
1941 (1979)
Apocalypse Now (1979) (assistant director)
Rocky II (1979) (assistant director)
Close Encounters of The Third Kind (assistant director)
The Bad News Bears Go to Japan (1978) (assistant director)
King (1978) TV Mini Series (assistant director)
Black Sunday (1977) (assistant director)
Harry and Walter Go to New York (1976) (assistant director)
Mitchell (1975) (assistant director)
The Way We Were (1973) (second assistant director)
Lost Horizon (1973) (assistant director)
The Wrath of God (1972) (assistant director)
J.W. Coop (1972) (second assistant director)
Honky (1971) (assistant director)
Fools' Parade (1971) (assistant director)
Something Big (1971) (assistant director)
Tell Me That You Love Me, Junie Moon (1970) (assistant director)
The Great White Hope (1970) (assistant director) (uncredited)
tick...tick...tick (1970) (uncredited)
Hello Dolly! (1969) (uncredited)

COLLEGIATE CLOUT

Dozens of screenwriters, production crews, producers, directors, actors and actresses hang their Hollywood hats on Wisconsin college memories. In fact, two of the most recognizable action heroes ever in movies, Harrison Ford and Arnold Schwarzenegger, cut their acting teeth on Wisconsin's collegiate stages.

HARRISON FORD found scripts far more interesting than textbooks at Ripon College in Wisconsin, and dropped out of college his senior year to pursue an acting career.

"When I first considered being an actor for money, I knew I had to go either to L.A. or to New York, and damned quick, 'cause it was starting to snow in Wisconsin. So I flipped a coin. It came up New York, so I flipped it again so I could go to L.A. (because) I wasn't gonna starve *and* freeze," he explained to *Rolling Stone* magazine July 24, 1980.

Ford first found the thrill of performing his senior year of high school when the C student was the first to broadcast over the Maine Township High School's new radio station, WMTH-FM, in Park Ridge, Illinois, in 1960.

Born July 13, 1942, in Park Ridge, Ford followed his parents' wishes that their son pursue a degree and enrolled at Ripon College in 1960 as a philosophy major. Like famous Ripon alum Spencer Tracy, Ford fell ever more in love with acting at college and started working on backstage crews for such Ripon College Red Barn Theatre productions as *Come Back Little Sheba* in 1963 and *Antigone* in 1964.

Ripon College's most lasting contribution to Ford's future was not in what the less-than-stellar student learned academically. Instead, it was introducing Ford to acting, his life's passion. In time, Ford directed at least two college productions: *The American Dream* and *The Zoo Story*, and starred as Mac the Knife in the college's 1963 production of *The Three Penny Opera*. Ford apparently also played George Antrobus in *The Skin of Our Teeth* in 1963 and El Gallo in *The Fantasticks* in 1964.

In between semesters, Ford performed with the summer stock theater in Williams Bay, Wisconsin, and lent his voice to shows on Ripon's WRPN-FM radio. The college's yearbooks also note that Ford was a member of the Zeta Tau chapter of the Sigma Nu fraternity, served on the Union Board, and was an illustrator for the *MUG.*

Ford reportedly took his first drama class to improve a struggling grade point and perhaps meet some beautiful girls. Though he found the passion for drama that he lacked in his other studies, Ford's grade point scarcely improved. The actor's love of the stage and lack of academics caught up to him his senior year and he was either asked to leave or volunteered to leave college, heading out to fulfill his dream in California.

The same year he left Ripon, Ford married fellow Ripon actress Mary Marquardt. They had two children, Willard and Ben, before they divorced in 1979. Ford married screenwriter Melissa Mathison in 1983, shortly after she wrote the screenplay for the 1982 hit *E.T. the Extra-Terrestrial,* and had two children, Malcolm and Georgia. Since their 2001 separation, Ford reportedly has been dating actress Calista Flockhart.

Though Ford landed a few memorable roles in such 1960s TV shows as *Ironsides* in 1967, the Midwest actor was relying more on his skills as a carpenter to make a living in Hollywood. Still, he didn't give up acting and enjoyed his first break when he was cast as Bob Falfa in *American Graffiti* in 1973, a role for which he was reportedly paid about $500 a week.

Though he earned praise for his work in the movie, other film opportunities weren't plentiful enough to support a family. He returned to carpentry and was reportedly doing remodeling in George Lucas's offices when the director cast Ford as Han Solo in *Star Wars* in 1977. The smash sci-fi blockbuster, and its two sequels (*The Empire Strikes Back* in 1980 and *Return of the Jedi* in 1983), along with appearances in other top films such as his small role as Col. Lucas in *Apocalypse Now* (1979) and his portrayal of the futuristic cop in 1982's *Blade Runner,* made Ford a certifiable movie star.

The star's portrayal of action-packed artifact seeker Indiana Jones in *Raiders of the Lost Ark* (1981), *Indiana Jones and The Temple of Doom* (1984) and *Indiana Jones and The Last Crusade* (1989) propelled him to superstar status, a position he's never relinquished.

Since his *Star Wars* debut, Ford has appeared in seven of Hollywood's top grossing films of all time, and the one-time $500 a week actor now gets $25 million per movie.

While Ford continues to star most often as the action hero, such as in his string of movies as Jack Ryan in *Patriot Games* (1992), as Ryan again in *Clear and Present Danger* (1994), as Dr. Richard Kimble *The Fugitive (1993)* and as the president in *Air Force One* (1997), he's earned critical acclaim for playing the softer leading man, such as for his portrayal of an idealistic inventor in *The Mosquito Coast* (1986), his Oscar-nominated performance as the big city cop tracking a murderer in Amish country in 1985's *Witness* and his Golden Globe winning performance as Linus Larrabee in *Sabrina* (1995). Ford played Capt. Alexei Vostrikov in the 2002 release *K-19: The Widowmaker* and agreed to portray his now legendary character, Indiana Jones, for a fourth and, he says, final time.

The megastar has never given up the bread and butter master carpenter skills that sustained him in his early Hollywood days. Today, however, carpenter Harrison Ford builds strictly for pleasure at his Jackson Hole, Wyoming, home, where he also owns and flies a single-engine airplane and helicopter, which he piloted in July 2000 to rescue a hiker from Table Mountain in Wyoming.

Though he rarely if ever speaks publicly about his years in Wisconsin, preferring not to talk about his "not so pleasant" college experience, another university unknowingly brought Ford's Wisconsin ties back into the limelight in 1994.

That year, as Ford's Hollywood star rose ever higher, UCLA presented him with the Spencer Tracy Award, an acting honor named for another Ripon College student turned movie superstar.

As Ford accepted his accolades, the Badger State's other top action star **ARNOLD ALOIS SCHWARZENEGGER** was enjoying the public and critical acclaim of his then latest hit *True Lies*, co-starring Jamie Lee Curtis.

Schwarzenegger was already performing as a world-famous bodybuilder and muscle man movie actor when he graduated from the University of Wisconsin-Superior in 1979 with a major in international marketing and business administration.

The athlete actor came to UW-Superior in the mid-1970s from Graz, Austria. He was born in the village of Thal Styria, Austria, July 30, 1947, where he grew up as the son of a police officer and got into bodybuilding.

"I was always interested in proportion and perfection,"

Schwarzenegger is quoted as saying in an Internet Movie Database biography. "When I was 15, I took off my clothes and looked in the mirror. When I stared at myself naked, I realized that to be perfectly proportioned I would need 20-inch arms to match the rest of me."

Eventually, the Austrian Oak, as he was soon called, developed the perfect proportions he dedicated himself to as a child — with a chest at 57 inches, waist at 34 inches, biceps at 22 inches, thighs at 28½ inches, and calves at 20 inches — and enjoyed unparalleled success in international bodybuilding competitions.

Schwarzenegger reportedly competed in his first bodybuilding competition in Graz in 1963. He won the Austrian Junior Championship in 1964. By 1969, Schwarzenegger had moved to the United States and won his first professional world championship in bodybuilding in 1970.

In all, he won three Mr. Universe and seven Mr. Olympia titles and eventually earned the *Guinness Book of World Records* praise as "the most perfectly developed man in the history of the world."

Schwarzenegger used his bulk to break into movies, gaining muscle-bound roles in such low-budget movies as *Hercules in New York* (1970) under the stage name Arnold Strong.

After he was featured in the bodybuilding book and film *Pumping Iron* in 1977, he was cast as a bodybuilder in *Stay Hungry* in 1976.

At the same time, Schwarzenegger was working toward his college degree. After studying acting and other subjects at California schools like Santa Monica College and UCLA, the bodybuilder enrolled at UW-Superior, studying mostly via exchange and correspondence courses.

In 1977, Schwarzenegger contributed to the first of his books on bodybuilding, *Arnold: The Education of a Bodybuilder* by Douglas Kent Hall for Simon & Schuster Pocket Books. Simon & Schuster published *Arnold's Bodybuilding for Men*, coauthored with Bill Dobbins, in 1981.

In between writing and studying, Schwarzenegger was pumping up his acting talents, working to soften his thick accent and improve his skills.

His hard work in all arenas paid off in 1979. He earned his college degree and earned regular roles in movies, beginning with *Scavenger Hunt* in 1979.

In 1982, the Austrian Oak graduated into movie stardom, as

the lead in *Conan the Barbarian* and *Conan the Destroyer* in 1982 and 1984. In between, he became an American citizen.

It was his role as a different kind of destroyer, a killer robot from the future in *The Terminator*, that pumped up Schwarzenegger's movie career for good and created the line for which he'll forever be known, "I'll be back."

The actor did come back in a long line of action thrillers, which included *Commando* (1985), *Predator* (1986), *Total Recall* (1990) and *Terminator 2: Judgment Day* (1991). He's played Jericho Cane in *End of Days* (1999) and Adam Gibson in *The 6th Day*. He also starred in the Sept. 11-delayed *Collateral Damage* (2002) and planned to appear in sequels to some of his biggest action hits in *Terminator 3* and *True Lies 2*.

Schwarzenegger has also proven he could bring more than a few laughs as a comedic leading man, mostly poking fun at his macho image, in movies like *Twins* with Danny DeVito as Schwarzenegger's pint-size brother in 1988 and as a tough cop pulling the tougher assignment of kindergarten teacher in *Kindergarten Cop* in 1990. The muscle-bound star even played a pregnant man in 1994's *Junior*. Most recently, Schwarzenegger has been trying out his talents behind the camera, directing an episode of *Tales from the Crypt* and a TV movie *Christmas in Connecticut*.

But movies aren't Schwarzenegger's only headline-making roles.

In 1986, he married TV journalist and Kennedy clan member Maria Shriver and now is the father of four children: Katherine, Christina, Patrick, and Christopher.

The actor also put his UW-Superior business administration degree to good use by wisely investing his bodybuilding winnings and $25 million per picture salary in such businesses as the Planet Hollywood string of restaurants.

Schwarzenegger has long been a political activist for the Republican Party and a spokesman for physical fitness. He was appointed chairman of the U.S. President's Council on Physical Fitness in 1990 and has served as sports director of the Special Olympics, one of a small group charged with the international organization's summer and winter Olympics. His Special Olympics work and his Hollywood success led his hometown's city council to present Schwarzenegger with the Graz Ring of Honor April 24, 1997.

The actor hasn't forgotten the small Wisconsin university that helped him reach the stars. In May of 1996, Schwarzenegger returned to his alma mater to give a short commencement speech and accept an Honorary Doctorate of Humane Letters, presented to the star for all of his charitable efforts as well as his career successes.

Many other Wisconsin-educated artists have left their marks on the screen. A short synopsis of some of the dozens of famous Wisconsin-educated film stars follows.

MASON ADAMS. Born in New York City on February 26, 1919, Adams graduated from the University of Wisconsin in Madison before heading to Hollywood. Though Adams appears in more than forty feature and TV movies, many know his voice best as the Smuckers jam spokesman who for twenty years said, "With a name like Smuckers, it has to be good."

Much of Adams's most memorable work has been in television series and movies. He was nominated for a Best Actor Emmy for his role as Managing Editor Charlie Hume on CBS's *Lou Grant*. Most recently, in November 1999, he made a guest appearance as Justice Joseph Crouch on *West Wing*, starring for an episode with Wisconsin actor Bradley Whitford.

One of the UW graduate's first feature film roles was a small one in *The Happy Hooker* (1975). Other feature credits include narrating several films as well as playing: the father in *The Lesser Evil* (1998), the boss in *Houseguest* (1995), Walter Sr. in *Son in Law* (1993), Colonel Mason in *F/X* (1986), and the president in *The Final Conflict: Omen III* (1981).

RALPH BELLAMY. Born June 17, 1904, in Chicago, the one-time student at the University of Wisconsin in Madison was one of the best-known actors in Hollywood in his heyday, not only for the 100 feature films he acted in but for helping other actors by founding the Screen Actors Guild and serving on its board. He served four terms as president of Actors' Equity.

Bellamy's heart wasn't in his UW studies, and the future star spent as much time as he could acting, apprenticing at stock companies, and eventually founding his own after leaving college behind for Broadway. By 1929, Bellamy was acting to New York City accolades and eventually won both Tony and New York Drama Critics awards. He broke into the Hollywood limelight in 1931 with a role in *The Secret Six*. For fifteen years thereafter, Bellamy filled the screen, usually as the second leading man in pursuit of a leading lady. He played the suitor so well that Hollywood rewarded him with an Oscar nomination for his 1937 portrayal of Cary

Grant's rival.

Bellamy was married and divorced three times — to Alice Delbridge (1927-30), Catherine Willard (1931-45), and Ethel Smith (1945-47) — before finding a lasting relationship with his fourth wife, Alice Murphy, whom he married in 1949.

In between, Bellamy starred in several mysteries, mostly B movies, including as detective Ellery Queen in *Master Detective* (1940). Among his best-played roles are a hilarious parody of himself in *His Girl Friday* (1940) and his performance of Franklin Delano Roosevelt in *Sunrise at Campobello* (1960).

By the late 1940s, Bellamy was concentrating more on stage work and only worked occasionally in movies and television. In an Internet Movie Database biography by Leonard Maltin, Bellamy explained that his return to the stage came when he overheard how typecast he'd become in Hollywood.

"One day in Hollywood I read a script in which the character was described as 'charming but dull — a typical Ralph Bellamy type.' I promptly headed for New York to find a part with guts," he said.

For all his roles, Bellamy is probably most remembered by audiences as one of the rich-turned-poor, stock-hungry brothers with Wisconsinite Don Ameche in the 1983 hit *Trading Places*.

Hollywood remembered him, though, for all he'd done on screen and off for the industry by presenting Bellamy with an honorary Oscar in 1986. Bellamy died in Santa Monica November 29, 1991.

JOHN BELUSHI. For a short time in the mid-1960s, the *Saturday Night Live* funny man attended the University of Wisconsin-Whitewater. Born January 24, 1949, in Chicago, Belushi starred in the university's spring 1968 production of *A Night Must Fall* among other productions before transferring to the College of DuPage, a junior college near his hometown of Wheaton, Illinois.

Though he'd been co-captain of the football team, variety show performer and homecoming king in high school, some of those who knew Belushi at Whitewater remember a much different image.

In perhaps a foreshadowing of the fraternity-bashing, college party movie *Animal House*, in which he would one day star, Belushi bucked the discipline, structure, and pretense of the college fraternity and study scene.

"We thought he was kind of an outsider," recalled then

Whitewater sorority girl Barbara Riemer. "He was much more an anti-establishment type than I was at that time, though today I respect someone who can stand up against such peer pressure. He had long hair and was just sort of gross, so I was pretty surprised when he became such a star."

Belushi started down the road to stardom at DuPage where he founded an improv comedy group known as the West Compass Players. By 1971, Belushi was performing his trademark physical comedy with Second City in Chicago. Within a year, he and his high school girlfriend Judy Jacklin moved to New York so Belushi could perform in National Lampoon's off-Broadway revue *Lemmings*. After writing for two years for the *National Lampoon's Radio Hour*, Belushi took his famously expressive eyebrows and live comedy talents to a new TV variety show, *Saturday Night Live*, in 1975. He married Jacklin the next year.

Though most famous for his four years on *Saturday Night Live*, Belushi also starred in several movies, two of which, *Animal House* and *The Blues Brothers*, have reached cult status.

His first movie performance as Hector in *Goin' South* (1978) earned him one of his most recognizable roles, that of the antiestablishment, beer guzzling, "g-r-o-s-s" Bluto in *National Lampoon's Animal House* (1978). After he and fellow *Saturday Night Live* performer Dan Aykroyd quit the show in 1979, they teamed up as Jake and Elwood Blues in John Landis's *The Blues Brothers* movie. The two comedians had often performed as the Blues Brothers to warm up the *Saturday Night Live* set, and even produced an album, "A Briefcase Full of Blues" featuring the brothers' songs. The John Landis movie transformed the duo's black-suited, briefcase-toting, blues-swinging, characters into comedy legends.

Belushi and Aykroyd teamed up again for *Neighbors* in 1981. Then, the one-time Whitewater freshman went solo and portrayed a Chicago newspaperman in love with a Colorado eagle expert in *Continental Divide* (1981). It was his last movie performance.

While Belushi's film career had been taking off, so was he. Cocaine and heroine became his drugs of choice, and he chose them once too often.

The 33-year-old Belushi was found dead of a drug overdose in the Chateau Marmont hotel in Los Angeles on March 5, 1982, after a night of partying with Robin Williams and Robert DeNiro. The drug dealer companion who gave him his final dose, Cathy

Smith, was sentenced to three years jail time for supplying the drugs.

ANDREW BERGMAN. Before he became the writer and director of such well-known comedy films as *Honeymoon in Vegas*, Bergman was just another University of Wisconsin student trudging down State Street in Madison. He eventually earned both a masters and doctoral degree in history and later published his college dissertation, *We're in the Money,* as a book.

Born February 20, 1945, in Queens, New York, the Wisconsin alum got his Hollywood start helping to write *Blazing Saddles* for one of Hollywood's zaniest funny men, Mel Brooks, in 1974, which starred Wisconsin actor Gene Wilder.

Bergman, who is also sometimes credited as Warren Bogle, wrote his first full screenplay for *The In-Laws* in 1979. He then tried his hand at writing and producing for the lesser-known, and less-well-received movies *So Fine* (1981) and *Big Trouble* (1985).

He reclaimed his comedic screenplay success by writing or cowriting *Oh God! You Devil* (1984), *Fletch* (1985) and *Soapdish* (1991) and writing and directing *The Freshman* (1990). He received perhaps his biggest accolades for writing and directing the hit comedy *Honeymoon in Vegas* (1992) starring Nicholas Cage. Bergman's next directorial effort, *Striptease* (1996), did not receive such high praise. Since then, Bergman directed *It Could Happen to You* (1994) and was executive producer for *Undercover Blues* (1993) and *Little Big League* (1994).

MARSHALL BRICKMAN. Born August 25, 1941, in Rio de Janeiro, Brazil, this Oscar winning comedy writer and Emmy-winning TV producer is another graduate of the University of Wisconsin-Madison.

Brickman's first entertainment gig was in music, not movies. While he was playing with The Tarriers, the band — which also featured actor Alan Arkin — had a brief spot in the movie *Calypso Heat Wave* (1957). Though he didn't have a part in any more movies for more than fifteen years, the UW graduate became friends with actor/director Woody Allen.

During the 1960s and early '70s, Brickman put his talents to work for television, writing for such shows as *The Tonight Show.* He teamed with Allen on the screenplay for *Sleeper* in 1973 and then cowrote Oscar's Best Picture of 1977, *Annie Hall,* for which he and Allen shared an Academy Award for the screenplay. The comedic writing duo was nominated again for an Oscar for their

1979 movie *Manhattan* before Brickman branched off to direct some of his own material. In 1980 he cast "Tarriers" alum Arkin in *Simon*. He directed *Lovesick* (1983) and *The Manhattan Project* (1986) and made an appearance with Dick Cavett in *Funny* in 1989. Eventually Brickman rejoined Allen to create the *Manhattan Murder Mystery* in 1993 and has since written the screenplay for *Intersection* (1994) and directed a made-for-TV movie *Sister Marie Explains It All* (2001).

JOAN CUSACK. An alumna of the University of Wisconsin-Madison, Cusack got her acting feet wet in a Madison improvisational comedy group called the ARK Repertory Theatre.

The comedienne was born into the acting family of Dick Cusack on October 11, 1962, in New York City. After her college days in Wisconsin, the star of the *What About Joan* (2001) TV series, was a *Saturday Night Live* regular from 1985 to 1986 before she got her first Hollywood job in *My Bodyguard* (1980). She earned an Academy Award nomination for Best Supporting Actress in her role as Cynthia in *Working Girl* (1988). She also starred as Blair Litton in the 1987 film *Broadcast News* and lent her voice to the yodeling cowgirl character in the 1999 hit children's movie *Toy Story 2*. Some of her big screen films include: *Where the Heart Is* (2000), *High Fidelity* (2000), Run*away Bride* (1999), *Arlington Road* (1999), *Grosse Pointe Blank* (1997), *Addams Family Values* (1993), *Hero* (1992), *My Blue Heaven* (1990), *Married to the Mob* (1988), *Sixteen Candles* (1984), and *Cutting Loose* (1980).

TOM EWELL. Though he attended law school at the University of Wisconsin in Madison with Don Ameche, Yewell Tompkins dropped out after four years, just a few credits shy of graduating, to sell magazines, he told the *Wisconsin State Journal* August 12, 1951.

"I waited tables at the Sigma Phi Epsilon house. One year when they had too many waiters, they gave me a job as second floor maid. I had 17 beds to make," he recalled of his college days in an Earl Wilson interview for the 1951 article.

Born April 29, 1909, in Owensboro, Kentucky, Ewell (then Tompkins) played a bit role to Ameche's lead in the campus production of *Lilliom* and worked with Ameche in summer stock productions with the Al Jackson players.

When World War II started, Ewell enlisted in the Navy. Though he eventually made lieutenant second grade, he was for a time, he told the *State Journal*, surely the "the oldest living ensign," in the Navy. After the war, the actor married Marjorie Sanborn April 29, 1948, and had one child.

Though most remembered as the man who stood watching Marilyn Monroe's skirt blowing skyward in the 1955 movie *The Seven Year Itch*, Ewell was a popular comedic actor who starred in such films as *Adam's Rib* (1949), *The Girl Can't Help It* (1956), *State Fair* (1962) and his last film appearance in *Easy Money* (1983). Ewell died September 12, 1994, in California.

MICHAEL MANN. The Emmy-winning director attended the University of Wisconsin-Madison before transferring to the International Film School in London, where he launched his movie and television writing and directing career.

Born February 5, 1943, in Chicago, Mann was most recently lauded for his direction of Will Smith as Muhammed Ali in the 2001 hit *Ali*. He is probably best known as the creator of the hit 1980s TV series *Miami Vice*, starring Don Johnson.

After graduate school in London, Mann directed the short film *Juanpuri* in 1970 and won the Cannes Film Festival Jury Prize for his efforts. His first television job was as a writer on the *Starsky & Hutch* TV show in the early 1970s. In 1974, he married Summer Mann and eventually had four children before they divorced, and he married Diane Venora in 1995.

Mann won two Emmys, for outstanding miniseries for *Drug Wars: The Camarena Story* in 1987 and for outstanding writing for *The Jericho Mile* documentary in 1979 for which he was also named Best Director by the Directors Guild of America.

Mann's first release as a Hollywood movie writer and director was *Thief* (1981) starring James Caan, followed by *The Keep* (1983) and the thriller *Manhunter* (1986). He then returned to TV for a few years before cowriting and directing the hit movie *The Last of the Mohicans* (1992) as well as *Heat* (1995), *The Zen Confidential* (1997) and *The Insider* (1999).

As a director, Mann reportedly prefers to operate the camera himself on occasion, a technique he used while shooting the critically acclaimed *Ali* in which he directed actor Will Smith to an Academy Award nomination for Best Actor in 2001. In 2002, Mann was producing a TV series he created called *R.H.D./LA*.

FRANCES LEE MC CAIN. She was born in York, Pennsylvania and graduated in 1966 from Ripon College, the same college attended by Spencer Tracy and Harrison Ford.

McCain made her first film appearance as a prostitute in the

1973 movie *The Laughing Policeman*. Since then she has been featured as a supporting character in such movies as *Footloose* and *Gremlins* (both in 1984), *Stand By Me* (1986), *Scream* (1996), *Patch Adams* (1998), and *True Crime* (1999).

WALTER MIRISCH. This movie producer and former president of the Motion Picture Academy was born November 8, 1921, in New York and graduated from the University of Wisconsin in Madison with a degree in history in 1942. Mirisch produced his first movie, *Fall Guy*, in 1947. He followed with a string of westerns and other films, including a series of "Bomba" movies, which included *Bomba on Panther Island* (1949), *Bomba and The Hidden City* (1950), and *Bomba and the Jungle Girl* (1952).

During a fifty-plus year career in Hollywood, the UW graduate produced some 100 films, including such Academy Award winning movies as *West Side Story* (1961) and *In the Heat of the Night* (1967) as well as hit movies like *The Magnificent Seven* (1960) and *Midway* (1976).

The producer told a UW alumni publication in 2000 that regardless of how many movies he's made, he still loves creating. "There is great excitement in simply starting with an idea ... molding it into a screenplay, casting it and seeing it come to life," he said, adding that "seeing it realized ... has immortality."

Though the producer has made it as big as anyone can in Hollywood, he's never forgotten his Wisconsin ties and he returned to Madison to accept an honorary degree in 1989. In 1995 he served as the first chairman of the UW-Madison Alumni Committee in Los Angeles and served as a board member of the University of Wisconsin Alumni Association from 1967 to 1973. Mirisch also returned in 2000 for a film retrospective of his movies during the Madison Film Festival.

JAMESON PARKER. Francis Jameson Parker Jr. was born November 18, 1947, in Baltimore, Maryland, to foreign service parents. Parker traveled most of Europe before he was out of high school and he graduated from Beloit College with a degree in theater arts in 1972. Though he is best known for his television work on *Simon & Simon* (beginning in 1981), as well as such TV shows as the soap opera *One Life to Live* (from 1976 to 1978), Parker has appeared in several big screen and TV screen movies.

The father of four, who was shot though not seriously injured in 1992 by a neighbor upset over dog waste, starred in TV movies like *Simon & Simon: In Trouble Again* (1995) and *The Immigrants*

(1978). He also appeared in such films as *The Bell Jar* (1979), *A Small Circle of Friends* (1980), *White Dog* (1982), *Jackals* (1986), *Prince of Darkness* (1987), and *Curse of The Crystal Eye* (1991).

DAVID SUSSKIND. Though best known for his television production and talk show hosting roles, the one-time University of Wisconsin student did produce in several movies, including the 1981 hit *Fort Apache-The Bronx*. Other films he produced include *Edge of the City* in 1957, *A Raisin in the Sun* in 1963, *All the Way Home* in 1963, and *Alice Doesn't Live Here Anymore* and *All Creatures Great and Small* both in 1974.

Susskind's list of TV movies includes: *The Glass Menagerie* (1973), *A Moon for the Misbegotten* (1975), *Eleanor and Franklin* (1976), *Johnny, We Hardly Knew Ye* (1977), *The Plutonium Incident* (1980), and dozens more, including specials on John F. Kennedy, Harry Truman, and Winston Churchill.

Born December 19, 1920, in New York City, Susskind began his screen production career on the 1951 TV show *The Goodyear Television Playhouse*. He stepped in front of the camera most notably as producer and host of the *Open End* interview program (1958-1966), which featured such guests as Rod Serling. Susskind died February 22, 1987.

JENNIFER WARREN. Born August 12, 1941, in New York City, this actress, director and producer made her big screen break a few years after graduating from the University of Wisconsin in Madison in 1969 when she played Erica in the movie *Sam's Song*. She played Mary Sikes in the 2000 movie *Partners in Crime*. She's also appeared in such films as *SlapShot* (1977), *Ice Castles* (1978), *Night Shadows* (1984), *Fatal Beauty* (1987), *Life Stinks* (1991), and *The Beans of Egypt, Maine* (1994). Warren also appeared regularly on *The Smothers Brothers Comedy Hour* and in the TV series *Paper Dolls* (1984) as well as in several made-for-TV movies, including: *First, You Cry* (1978), *Champions: A Love Story* (1979), *The Intruder Within* (1981), *Confessions of a Married Man* (1983), *Full Exposure: The Sex Tapes Scandal* (1989), and *Dying to Belong* (1997).

DAVE WILLOCK. Dave Willock was the other half of several acts with Milwaukee actor Jack Carson, both in vaudeville and on radio before each actor made a name for himself in movies. Willock, who was born in Chicago in 1909, teamed with Carson in the *Willock & Carson* vaudeville show after attending the University of Wisconsin in Madison and starring in several campus productions.

When their national vaudeville tours tapped out, the lifelong friends teamed up on the air with Willock acting as neighbor Tugwell, among other characters, on Carson's radio program. The friends soon made their way onto Hollywood movie sets, and Willock debuted in 1939 in such uncredited movie roles as a student in *Good Girls Go to Paris* and a guard in *Mr. Smith Goes to Washington* (in which Carson also appeared). That same year, he played radioman Blinky in *Legion of Lost Flyers*.

For the next forty years, the one-time UW student played small and sidekick roles to other movie stars' leads.

After playing bellhops, desk clerks and elevator operators through the early 1940s, Willock began getting bigger supporting roles in 1944, such as his portrayal of Ensign Hans Jacobson in *A Wing and a Prayer* and Dud Miller in *Pin-Up Girl*. That same year, Willock played a soldier in Wisconsin-born actress Carole Landis's movie *Four Jills in a Jeep*. In the 1940s and 50s, Willock alternated between uncredited and larger roles such as Dr. Daily in *This Love of Ours* (1945), a taxi driver with former Wisconsin teacher Agnes Moorehead in *Hush... Hush, Sweet Charlotte* (1964) Foggy in *The Fabulous Dorseys* (1947), Franklin in *Ma and Pa Kettle on Vacation* (1953), Joe Keaton in *The Buster Keaton Story* (1957), and Peter Tillig in *Ten Seconds to Hell* (1959).

Willock found bigger stardom on a smaller screen, beginning in the 1950s when he starred as himself in the 1952 TV series *Dave & Charley* and cohosted the 1955 series *Do It Yourself*. Audiences still remember him as Harvey Clayton on the TV series *Margie* (1961-62), Tom Blackwell from the hit series *Green Acres* (1966-67), and as Ozzie from the 1969 series *The Queen and I*. In 1963, Willock also played Speedy Jackson on several episodes of the *Temple Houston* series, which starred Wisconsinite Jeffrey Hunter.

The aging actor found fewer roles in the 1960s and '70s but still kept his name on screen in supporting roles such as Ray Hudson in *What Ever Happened to Baby Jane?* (1962), Alfred in *4 for Texas* (1963), Rocky in *The Grissom Gang*, and Groundhog in *Emperor of the North Pole* before ending his screen career much as it had begun, with a small role, that of a liquor store clerk in 1975's *Hustle*. Willock died November 12, 1990, in California. He was 81.

AMY WRIGHT. The Beloit College graduate, who was born in 1950, first made a name for herself on stage, where she continues to star, but has also appeared in many Hollywood movies, mostly in the 1970s and 1990s. Her movie debut came in 1975's *Not a Pretty Picture,* and she also appeared in 1978's *The Deer Hunter,* 1979's *Breaking Away, Wise Blood,* and *The Amityville Horror,* and the 1980 film *Stardust Memories.*

In 1988, Wright returned to movies as a member of William Hurt's family in *The Accidental Tourist* and as Ricki in *Crossing Delancey.* She played Karen Weaver in *Love Hurts* (1991) and Shelley in *Hard Promises* (1991). In addition to several made-for-TV movies, such as *In the Line of Duty* (1991), *To Dance With the White Dog* (1993), and *Oprah Winfrey Presents: Amy and Isabelle* (2001). Wright appeared in *Where The Rivers Flow North* and played Aunt Polly in *Tom and Huck* (1995), May in *Joe the King* (1999), and Mona in *Besotted* (2000).

THEY ALSO STARRED

Many other Wisconsinites have starred in or contributed to Hollywood movies, though they may be better known for their writing, production or TV roles. The following is a short description of just some of the dozens of other stars who once called Wisconsin home.

BONNIE BARTLETT was born June 20, 1929, in Wisconsin Rapids, to actor-turned-insurance salesman E.E. Bartlett. The future actress grew up in Moline, Illinois, and attended Northwestern University where she met and married fellow actor William Daniels, former Screen Actors Guild president.

Bartlett first starred on the small screen as Vanessa Raven on the CBS soap opera *Love of Life* in the 1950s. She also played Aunt Myrtl in the movie *The Meanest Men in the West* in 1967 and had a recurring role as Grace Snider-Edwards from 1974 to 1977 on the hit TV series *Little House on the Prairie*. But mostly, though, Bartlett raised two adopted sons.

The Wisconsin Rapids native did not return to acting full time until the 1980s and hasn't stopped since. Most memorably, Bartlett and her husband each won Emmys for their portrayals of Dr. and Mrs. Mark Craig on the TV show *St. Elsewhere* in 1986.

Through the years, Bartlett has made one-time appearances on such TV shows as *Hart to Hart*, *The Rockford Files*, and *The Waltons*, and also has performed in TV roles, including Barbara on *Once and Again* (1999), Ruth Greene on *ER* (1994), the dean of admissions in *Boy Meets World* (1993), Lucille on *Home Improvement* (1991), and Hillary Townsend-King on *Midnight Caller* (1988).

The actress has kept busy in the movies, too, including playing Mary Ann Benedict in *Twins* (1988), a senator in *Dave* (1993), Martha Harris in *Primary Colors* (1998) and, most recently, Charlotte in the 1999 TV movie *Tuesdays with Morrie*.

JEFF CESARIO was born in Kenosha and is now an Emmy-winning writer for *The Larry Sanders Show* and *The Dennis Miller Show*. He also cowrote the script for the 1998 movie *Jack Frost* and, as an actor appeared as Todd Lackey in the Charlie Sheen movie *Five Aces* and as Brian in *Kiss of a Stranger*, both in 1999. He is also the voice of Marv Albert on the *Futurama* TV cartoon series.

Famous Wisconsin Film Stars

EDWARD "EDDIE" F. CLINE was born November 7, 1892, in Kenosha. The actor, writer and director started his movie career in 1913, acting in such silent films as *The Knockout* (1914) and *A Dog Catcher's Love* (1917). After playing a hobo in the film *Cops* in 1922, Cline stopped acting to direct full time. In all, Cline directed nearly 150 films from 1916 through 1948, including *Bubbles of Trouble* (1916), *Circus Days* (1923), *Kitty from Killarney* (1926), *Don't Bite Your Dentist* (1930), *High Flyers* (1937), *Cracked Nuts* (1931 & 1941), *He's My Guy* (1943), and *Bringing Up Father* (1946). His last film was *Jiggs and Maggie in Court* (1948). Cline died in Hollywood May 22, 1961.

ROBERT EASTON was born Robert Easton Burke November 23, 1930, in Milwaukee and is respected as one of the greatest dialogue coaches in motion pictures. He was even pictured on the cover of *Life Magazine*.

DAVE ERICKSON of Spring Green is an award-winning documentary filmmaker whose historic and cultural movies mostly air on Wisconsin Public Television. Through his company, OOTEK Productions, Erickson has produced such documentaries as the internationally award-winning *Raising Crane* about the International Crane Foundation's crane-rearing project, *Powder On The Prairie* about the Badger Ammunition Plant, *The Rush for Grey Gold* about Wisconsin's lead mining history and *The World's Greatest Showmen* about the history of Barnum and Ringling Brothers circuses, which features Wisconsin sportscaster Bob Uecker as the voice of P.T. Barnum.

BERT I. GORDON was born September 24, 1922, in Kenosha and attended the University of Wisconsin in Madison. Nicknamed "Mr. Big" for his initials, the director, writer and producer created many of the low-budget creature features of the 1950s and 60s, including *The Cyclops*, *Earth vs. The Spider* and *Attack of the Puppet People*. Other films include, *The Magic Sword* (1962), *Necromancy* (1972) which featured legendary Wisconsin actor Orson Welles and *Picture Mommy Dead*. His last picture was *Satan's Princess* in 1990.

ERIK GUNNESON of Madison directed his first feature film, *Milk Punch*, in 2000.

UTA HAGEN was born in Gottingen, Germany, June 12, 1919. She is perhaps the world's best-known drama instructor, and nearly every drama student has read the book she wrote on the subject, *Respect for Acting*.

Hagen was raised in Madison, and after studying at the Royal

Academy of Dramatic Arts, she made her Broadway debut in 1938 with two other legendary Wisconsin resident actors Alfred Lunt and Lynn Fontanne in *The Seagull*. Hagen later stared on stage in *The Country Girl* and *Who's Afraid of Virginia Woolf?* winning Tonys for each performance.

In 1938 she married actor Jose Ferrer, whom TV audiences may remember as Arthur Vanderkellen on the *Newhart* TV show of the early 1980s. They had one daughter and divorced in 1948.

Hagen then married actor Herbert Berghof in 1957 and still runs the legendary HB Studio acting school he founded in 1947 in New York.

Hagen made just a few movie appearances over the years, including roles in *Boys From Brazil* (1987), *Seasonal Differences* (1987), and *Reversal of Fortune* (1990). She also had a part in the 1945 TV show *Victory*, played Gloria in the 1985 Library episode of *The Twilight Zone* TV series and recently lent her voice to Tilly's Friend on the *King of the Hill* animated series.

Hagen remained friends with her debut partners Lunt and Fontanne and often visited the couple's Ten Chimneys estate in Waukesha County on her trips back to Wisconsin.

The theater has always been her first love, however, and the 83-year-old Hagen continues to teach and act. In 2001, the 1981 Theater Hall of Fame inductee danced the tango and fox trot in the Los Angeles Geffen Playhouse production of *Six Dance Lessons in Six Weeks*.

DEIDRE ANN HALL and her twin sister Andrea were born in Milwaukee October 21, 1947, but grew up in Florida where Deidre was elected Junior Orange Bowl Queen when she was 12. Hall is best known as *Days of Our Lives* soap opera's Dr. Marlena Evans, a character she's portrayed for more than twenty years. Andrea portrayed her evil twin on the soap opera. Prior to *Days of Our Lives*, Hall starred as Electra on the 1976 series *Electra Woman and Dyna Girl*.

In addition to television work, which included starring in her own series *Our House* (1986), Hall has appeared in such TV movies as *A Reason to Live* (1985), *And The Sea Will Tell* (1991), *Woman on the Ledge* (1993), and *Op Center* (1995). Hall also produced a 1995 film about her struggles with infertility, called *Never Say Never: The Deidre Hall Story*. She is married to novelist Steve Sohmer, her third husband, and they have two children.

SALOME JENS was born in Milwaukee May 8, 1935. Though she has appeared in more than thirty Hollywood and TV movies,

Jens is best known for her exemplary stage performances on and off Broadway and is often called the "contemporary grand lady of theater." When not acting, Jens teaches future actors as a drama instructor at UCLA.

Some fans may recognize her name, though probably not her face through all the dramatic makeup, as The Founder on *Star Trek: Deep Space Nine* (1993) or from her other regular roles on TV series like *Melrose Place*, *Falcon Crest* and *Mary Hartman, Mary Hartman*.

After appearing on stage as a teenager in Swan Theater (now the Milwaukee Repertory Theater) productions and in college productions at Northwestern University, Jens made a name for herself on Broadway. In 1956, she made her first screen appearance in *Showdown at Ulcer Gulch*. She has since appeared in such movies as *Angel Baby* (1961), *Savages* (1972), *The Jolly Corner* (1975), *Diary of the Dead* (1980), and *Uncommon Valor* (1983). Jens also narrated the 1986 movie *The Clan of the Cave Bear*, the acclaimed PBS mini series *The Great War and the Shaping of the Twentieth Century*, and played Diantha Krohn in the independent film *I'm Losing You* (1998).

"She is loved by her students and brings out the best in them," notes movie production assistant Suzanne Ziesmer, who worked with Jens on a film the Wisconsin actress recently produced and directed, *A Ceremony for a Midget*. " Salome has a way of bringing zest and life to all that she does. She is a talented actress and a truly caring person."

KRISTEN JOHNSON was born September 20, 1967, in Washington, D.C., where her father was a U.S. senator. The 6-foot-tall blonde is probably best known for her role as Sally on the hit TV series *Third Rock from the Sun* (1996-2001).

Johnson graduated from Whitefish Bay High School in 1985, though she spent much of her teenage years as an exchange student in South America and Sweden.

The Wisconsinite made her film debut in *The Orkly Kid* in 1985. She next appeared as Alice Kosnick in *The Debt* (1993). More recently, she played Ivana Humpalot in *Austin Powers: The Spy Who Shagged Me* (1999), Wilma Slaghoople in *The Flintstones in Viva Rock Vegas* (2000) and a judge in *Queen of the Whole Wide World* (2001).

JANE KACZMAREK was born December 21, 1955, in Milwaukee and raised in Greendale as the oldest of four children. Though she is most recognized today for her portrayal of the mother on the hit Fox TV show *Malcolm in the Middle*, the 2001 Emmy-nominated actress boasts a long list of TV and movie credits.

Kaczmarek studied at the University of Wisconsin-Madison, where she met Green Bay born actor Tony Shalhoub, who encouraged her to pursue acting, according to Internet Movie Database biographer John Sacksteder.

During her senior year of college, Kaczmarek taught high school seniors and once said "that being a student teacher is the hardest job there is."

After attending Yale Drama School, the UW-Madison graduate made good on Shalhoub's advice and was soon appearing on New York stages.

By 1991, she was appearing on Broadway in Neil Simon's *Lost in Yonkers* and dating her future husband, Wisconsinite Bradley Whitford (star of *The West Wing* TV show), whom she met on a blind date in 1990. The two were married in 1992 and have two children, Frances and George, and were expecting a third child in the fall of 2002.

In the movies, the Wisconsin native played Katharine Holloway in *Door to Door* (1984), Ann Raftis in *Falling in Love* (1984), Dr. Anne Biddows in *The Chamber* (1996) and, most recently, Valerie in *Jenifer* (2001).

But, Kaczmarek remains best known for her television roles. In addition to her starring role on *Malcolm in the Middle*, she played Sandy Burns on *St. Elsewhere* (1982), Officer Clara Tilsky on *Hill Street Blues* (1981) with Wisconsin native Daniel J. Travanti, Holly on *Cybill* (1995) with Wisconsinite Tom Wopat, and Carol Anderson on *Felicity* (1998).

KATHY KINNEY was born in Stevens Point, Wisconsin, November 3, 1954. Best known as the make-up rich Mimi Bobeck on *The Drew Carey Show*, Kinney unknowingly studied for her role when she was a real-life secretary at WCBS-TV in New York in the 1980s. The actress began as a comedian with improvisational theater groups and tours now with The Improv All Stars.

In addition to *The Drew Carey Show*, Kinney has appeared on numerous TV shows and in several films. She got her first movie break when she was cast as Joan in *Parting Glances* (1986) and as a nurse in *Scrooged* (1988). Kinney has also played Blaire Kendall in *Arachnophobia* (1990), a homeless lady in *Mr. Jones* (1993), and Mrs. Tattler in *Picking Up the Pieces* (2000).

DAN KLEIN is a Madison West High School graduate whose mentor is movie director and Shorewood native Jim Abrahams of

Airplane! and *Naked Gun* fame. Klein wrote and directed his first feature, *Pig Music*, filmed in Colgate, Madison, Mount Horeb, and Milwaukee.

TERRY LEONARD is a West Allis native who has made some of Hollywood's top stars look brave and daring as a stuntman and coordinator on movies since 1963. He performed stunts in such movies as *The Planet of the Apes* (1968), *Blazing Saddles* (1974), *The Wind and the Lion* (1975), and *Apocalypse Now* (1979), where he came closer than anyone should to a pouncing tiger. He also performed stunts in later movies like *Conan the Barbarian* (1982), *Backdraft* (1991), *Far and Away* (1992), *Patriot Games* (1992), and *My Fellow Americans* (1996).

Wisconsin native and Hollywood first assistant director Jerry Ziesmer is impressed not only by Leonard's bravery in facing that jungle tiger with him on *Apocalypse Now* but by the stunt man's professionalism and hard work on other movies.

"Terry has become one of the truly legendary stuntmen and stunt coordinators and second unit directors of our era," Ziesmer says.

Leonard coordinated stunts for such movies as *Raiders of the Lost Ark,* where he was one of the stunt doubles for one-time Ripon College student Harrison Ford, *Romancing the Stone* (1984), *Dragnet* (1987), *The Fugitive* (1993), *Rush Hour* (1998), *Joy Ride* (2001) and *Impostor* (2002).

Since 1978, the West Allis native has also helped make movies behind the camera as a second unit assistant director on such films as *Used Cars* (1980), *Buffy the Vampire Slayer* (1992), *The Fugitive* (1993) in which he designed the famous "leap from the dam" shot, *The Quick and the Dead* (1995), *Die Hard: With a Vengeance* (1995), *Mighty Joe Young* (1998), *Sum of All Fears* (2002), and *Agent Cody Banks* (2003).

In between, he's been cast in bit parts and supporting roles in some twenty movies. In addition to his appearance in the 2002 TV show *Behind the Action: Stuntmen in Movies*, Leonard played the chief of the Shoshones in *A Man Called Horse* (1970), 'Handsome Jack' Klutas in *Dillinger* (1973), a Crow brave in *The Mountain Men* (1980), and a bartender in *Joy Ride* (2001).

Asked why he jumps off of high buildings, climbs under a team of running horses, and crashes trucks to make another star look invincible, Leonard once explained, "Stunt work to me is memories, friends and eight-by-tens."

JIM MALLON produced and wrote *Mystery Science Theater 3000* and also directed a 1986 movie, *Blood Hook,* filmed in Wisconsin, about a deadly giant fishhook terrorizing a muskie fishing contest.

MARK METCALF was born in Ohio in 1946 and is most famous for portraying Douglas Niedermeyer in the movie *Animal House* (1978). An actor featured in twenty-five other movies, Metcalf now lives in Mequon, where he owns a restaurant and bar. The actor most recently played Bill Harris in *Lone Hero* (2002) and John Closs in *Sorority Boys* (2002). He is also known for his recurring TV roles as the Maestro on the hit series *Seinfeld* and the Master on *Buffy the Vampire Slayer.*

JACQUELYN MITCHARD is a *Milwaukee Journal Sentinel* columnist and author whose best-selling book, *Deep End of the Ocean,* was turned into a movie of the same name in 1999.

AL MOLINARO was born June, 24, 1919, in Kenosha and is most famous for his portrayal of Al on *Happy Days* and its spinoff *Joanie Loves Chachi.* He also played a drapery man in the 1976 movie *Freaky Friday,* played Joe Alberghetti in the 1990-91 TV series *The Family Man,* and has since opened a chain of diners called Big Al's.

CHRISTOPHER DAVID NOTH was born in Madison November 13, 1954, and is most famous for his role as Detective Mike Logan on *Law & Order* from 1989-1995. The son of a CBS reporter, Noth lived in England, Yugoslavia, and Spain before studying drama at Yale University. In addition to *Law & Order,* Noth has appeared on TV shows like *Touched By An Angel* and *Hill Street Blues,* and plays Mr. Big on the hit cable show *Sex in the City.*

The actor and writer started his screen career as a prostitute in *Smithereens* in 1982 and as Jimmy/Dean Whitney on *Another World* from 1985 to 1988. Since then, he has costarred in Hollywood movies like *Baby Boom* (1987), *The Deli* (1997), *Getting to Know You* (1999), *Cast Away* (2000), and *Double Whammy* (2001), as well as in such recent TV movies as *Exiled* (1998), *Someone's Watching* (2000), *The Nightclub Years* (2001), and *Sudden Fear* (2002).

NANCY OLSON was born in Milwaukee July 14, 1928, and attended the University of Wisconsin in Madison before finding fame mostly as a stage actress. Olson appeared in several Hollywood movies including *The Absent Minded Professor* (1961) and *Son of Flubber* (1963) with fellow Wisconsinite Fred MacMurray and made an uncredited cameo as a secretary in the Robin Williams remake of MacMurray's role in *Flubber* (1997). The Milwaukee actress was nominted for an Oscar for her role in *Sunset Boulevard* (1950) and also starred in such films as *Pollyanna* (1956) and *Airport 1975* (1974). According to the Internet Movie Database, her husband Alan Livingston created Bozo the Clown in 1946 and is also the man responsible for signing Frank Sinatra and the Beatles to Capitol Records.

JOHN RIDLEY is a Mequon native writer who recently produced the film *Undercover Brother* about rescuing a black candidate's derailed presidential campaign. Ridley also wrote and produced the *Three Kings* (1999), and *U Turn* (1997), and wrote and directed *Cold Around the Heart* (1997). In addition, Ridley has been a writer for such TV series as *Third Watch*, *The John Larroquette Show*, *Martin*, and *The Fresh Prince of Bel-Air*. He is also a commentator for National Public Radio.

JOHN ROACH is a Madison writer and columnist who turned the true story of lawn mower riding 73-year-old Alvin Straight into a movie screenplay with writer Mary Sweeney. *The Straight Story* premiered in 1999.

LARRY SHUE was born in New Orleans July 23, 1946, and educated in Milwaukee. He became a successful playwright and stage actor and played Sayeville druggist Bill Edson in the 1986 movie *Sweet Liberty*. His career was cut short when he was killed in a Sept. 23, 1985, plane crash on the way to the opening of his play *Foreigner* in Washington, D.C. He was inducted posthumously into the Wisconsin Performing Artists Hall of Fame.

KURTWOOD LARSON SMITH was born in New Lisbon on July 3, 1943. Though he's appeared in more than fifty movies, today's fans best recognize Smith as dad Red Forman on the hit Fox TV show, *That 70s Show*.

His character reminds Smith of his own Wisconsin parents, he told the *Pittsburgh Post-Gazette* January 1, 2002. "(Red) grew up in the same era as my parents. He shares a lot of those values. People took responsibility for themselves and then found out that maybe the American Dream wasn't all it was cracked up to be," the actor noted.

Smith had his film debut as a security guard in the 1980 movie *Roadie* and he played a choreographer in 1983's *Staying Alive,* but he probably first caught moviegoers eyes as a CIA agent in 1984's *Flashpoint*.

The New Lisbon native's next big roles came as drug czar Clarence Boddicker in *Robocop* (1987), which also starred Wisconsinite Peter Weller, and as the *Dead Poets Society* (1989) father who drove his son to suicide.

Since then Smith has starred as Cliff Forrester in *The Crush* (1993), General Cooper in *Under Siege 2* (1995), Stump Sisson in *A Time to Kill* (1996), the secretary of defense in *Broken Arrow* (1996) and Otis Hefter in *Deep Impact* (1998). Most recently, Smith's movie roles have included Dr. Crumble in *Girl, Interrupted* (1999), and Secretary of Transportation William Easter in *Teddy Bears' Picnic* (2002).

He played the federation president in the movie *Star Trek VI: The Undiscovered Country* in 1991 and has portrayed three different characters on the *Star Trek* TV series, including Annorax in *Star Trek: Voyager* (1995) and Thrax in *Star Trek: Deep Space Nine* (1993) with Wisconsinite Salome Jens (a space shifter) in addition to appearing in many TV movies, such as a *Bright Shining Lie* (1998) and *Murder in Texas* (1981), and on other television shows like *Picket Fences* (1992) and *A-Team* (1983).

Smith is married to actress Joan Pirkle and has two children from a previous marriage.

CONCETTA TOMEI was born December 30, 1945, in Kenosha and has appeared in several TV movies and shows, including the new hit *Providence*, where she portrays the lead character's deceased mother. Tomei graduated from the University of Wisconsin-Madison with a degree in education and taught school in Milwaukee for four years before earning a bachelor of fine arts degree in theater from the Goodman School in Chicago.

Tomei began her screen career as lawyer Susan Hauber on *LA Law* (1986) and Dr. Estelle Kramer on *Falcon Crest* (1986). She's played Major Lila Garreau on *China Beach* (1988) and was a regular on the *Hollywood Squares* game show in 1998.

In between, the one-time Milwaukee teacher has performed in such movies as *Don't Tell Mom the Babysitter's Dead* (1991), *The Goodbye Bird* (1993), *Deep Impact* (1998) with Wisconsinite Kirkwood Smith, *The Muse* (1999) with Wisconsinite Bradley Whitford, and most recently as Lily Elias in *Purpose* (2002).

DANIEL J. TRAVANTI was born Danielo Giovanni Travanti March 7, 1940, in Kenosha, and is most famous for his portrayal of Captain Furillo in the hit TV series *Hill Street Blues*. He has appeared in some thirty movies and TV shows and debuted on the screen in *Who Killed Teddy Bear* (1965), *The Love War* (1970), *It's My Turn* (1980), *Millennium* (1989), *Skin* (1990), and *Just Cause* (1995).

In addition to starring as Spence Andrews on *General Hospital* in 1979, the Kenosha native also portrayed Edwin R. Murrow in the 1986 TV movie *Murrow* and played Peter Mallow in the 2002 movie *Design* and Harrison in 1999's *Something Sweet*. He was inducted into the Wisconsin Performing Artists Hall of Fame in 1994.

PETER WELLER was born in Stevens Point on June 24, 1947. His father was an Army helicopter pilot and the family traveled the world. Weller eventually graduated from high school in Texas and built a successful acting career on Broadway where he studied under Wisconsin acting coach Uta Hagen.

The actor, writer, and director debuted in the 1973 TV movie *The Man Without a Country*. His Hollywood debut came in *Butch and Sundance: The Early Years* in 1979. Weller then appeared in such films as *Shoot the Moon* in 1982 before landing a role as a half-man, half-robot officer Alax Murphy in the 1987 hit *Robocop* and its 1990 sequel *Robocop 2*. He has since starred in movies like *Of Unknown Origin* (1983), *Sunset Grill* (1993) and, most recently, *The Contaminated* (2000), *Styx* (2001) and *The Sin Eater (2002)*.

In 1993 Weller was nominated for an Oscar for the short film he directed and co-produced, *Partners*. He has since directed television episodes for such shows as *Homicide: Life on the Street* (1993), *Gold Coast* (1997) and the new series *Odyssey 5* (2002).

BRADLEY WHITFORD was born October 10, 1959, in Madison and graduated from Madison East High School in 1977. Today, Whitford is best known as Joshua Lyman on the hit TV series *The West Wing*, a role he won a supporting actor Emmy for last year.

Whitford studied theater and English literature at Wesleyan University, in Middletown, Connecticut, and earned a master's degree in theater from the Juilliard Theater Center. After starring roles on and off Broadway, he appeared in such TV films as *C.A.T Squad* (1986) and also played Jack Ford in the 1987 TV movie *The Betty Ford Story*, which starred Wisconsinites Gena Rowlands as Betty Ford and Concetta Tomei as Jan.

He made his Hollywood movie debut as Terry Reilly in *Dead as a Doorman*. After appearing as Roger in *Revenge of the Nerds II*, Whitford played Jamie Kemp in the 1990 Harrison Ford movie *Presumed Innocent* and Charles Phalen in *Young Guns II*. He has also appeared in such films as *Scent of a Woman* (1992), *Philadelphia* (1993), *Billy Madison* (1995) and *Red Corner* (1997).

Whitford married fellow Wisconsin actress Jane Kaczmarek of Greendale. They have two children.

In 1999, Whitford played Lloyd Charney in the Robin Williams film *Bicentennial Man* and Hal in *The Muse*. That same year,

Whitford was cast as Joshua Lyman on the hit TV series *The West Wing*, where according to the Internet Movie Database the Madison native is earning at least $70,000 per episode.

Whitford and his wife return to Wisconsin often, such as when Whitford visited Madison in May 2002 to lend a hand to the "Hammer With a Heart" project that repairs low-income homes.

"Madison has always been a place that I have been proud to call home," Whitford told *The Capital Times* May 4, 2002. "One of the things that I love about Madison is its sense of community. I'm glad to give back to the town that gave me so much as I was growing up."

TOM WOPAT was born into a dairy farming family of eight on September 9, 1951, in Lodi. He is still best remembered as Luke Duke on the high-flying *The Dukes of Hazzard* TV series from 1979 to 1985. The 1969 Lodi High School football star and graduate, is better remembered on the University Wisconsin-Madison campus for his musical talents, though some also remember him as the self-employed roofer who laid their shingles.

While in Madison, Wopat sang with a band called Skyway and played guitar and trombone. Wopat's baritone voice became part of the university's *Opera Chunks*' concerts and he returns to Madison occasionally to sing at the Wisconsin Varsity Band's annual spring concert, as he did in 1981, 1997, and 2001. Wopat debuted on Madison stages as Tony in *West Side Story* and Judas in *Jesus Christ Superstar*, and also performed at the Wilson Street East dinner theater, playing a "policeman who went down to his underwear" in *What the Butler Saw*.

After six years of college, Wopat left Madison without a degree in 1976, explaining to the *Wisconsin State Journal*'s Nadine Goff April 19, 2001, that "I never finished the piano requirement because I just couldn't stand piano class."

Wopat debuted on Broadway in 1978 and landed his *Dukes of Hazzard* role the following year. He has since starred in two *Dukes of Hazzard* reunion movies and the short-lived TV shows *Blue Skies* (1988) and *Peaceable Kingdom* (1989). Since then, Wopat played Jeff Robbins on *Cybill*, where he often appeared wearing Wisconsin Badger sweatshirts, guest starred on *Home Improvement* and played Hank Pelham on the soap opera *All My Children*.

Always the musician, Wopat continues to sing with his own band and has produced four country albums from his home in Tennessee.

Wopat has also appeared in such TV movies as *Burning Rage*

(1984), *Christmas Comes to Willow Creek* (1987), *Contagious* (1997), and *Meteorites* (1998), and he narrated the 2001 TV movie *Bear: The Legend of Coach Paul Bryant.*

In 1999, Wopat received a Tony nomination for his Broadway portrayal of Frank Butler in *Annie Get Your Gun* and returned to Madison in 2002 to play Emile de Becque in the CTM Madison Family Theater Company's production of *South Pacific,* a musical he first appeared in during a UW-Madison production in 1974.

Wopat says he likes coming back to Wisconsin to perform and to help out on the dairy farm that he and his brother still own.

"Wisconsin is a great place to be from," Wopat told Kelly Radloff of the *Wisconsin State Journal* February 15, 1996. "…in Wisconsin, people stick together."

LIGHTS, CAMERA, ACTION!
... IN THE BADGER STATE

In 1916, silent film director Harry Beaumont came to Wisconsin to film *The Truant Soul*, a 120-minute movie about a surgeon with a split personality starring Henry B. Walthall. Since then many movies, large, small and independent, have been filmed, at least in part, in Wisconsin, according to the Wisconsin Film Office and Internet Movie Database.

Madison and Milwaukee claim the greatest number of movie sites, some of which are noted below.

MADISON
• **The Boy Who Drank Too Much** (1980), a TV movie starring Scott Baio.
• **Back to School** (1986), starring Rodney Dangerfield, as a self-made millionaire who returns to college was filmed at the University of Wisconsin in Madison.
• **I Love Trouble** (1994), starring Julia Roberts and Nick Nolte, has scenes filmed in Dane County, including at the Majestic Theater in Madison
• **Chain Reaction** (1996), starring Keanu Reeves and Morgan Freeman, included an iceboat chase on Lake Geneva and a scene at the Yerkes Observatory there. Scenes were also filmed in Williams Bay and Madison, used to depict Washington, D.C.
• **For Keeps** (1988), starring Molly Ringwold as a Kenosha teen who gets pregnant, has scenes filmed in Madison and Kenosha.

MILWAUKEE
• **Gaily, Gaily** (1969), starring Beau Bridges and George Kennedy in a movie about a newspaperman's life.
• **Dillinger** (1973) was partly filmed in Milwaukee and southeastern Wisconsin.
• **The Blues Brothers** (1980), starring Dan Aykroyd and one-time University of Wisconsin-Whitewater attendee John Belushi, ended with a car chase down an uncompleted Milwaukee freeway.
• **Major League** (1989), starring Charlie Sheen and Corbin Bernsen as Cleveland Indians ballplayers, was filmed in the old Milwaukee County Stadium, using local fans for crowd scenes.
• **Dillinger** (1990), TV movie starring Mark Harmon, filmed in the Milwaukee area as did other TV movies, like **Lies and Lullabies** (1992) and **Family of Cops** (1995), starring Charles Bronson.

Famous Wisconsin Film Stars

- **Aswang** (1994) a horror movie directed by Barry Poltermann of Lake Geneva and Wrye Martin of Racine for Purple Onion Productions, Milwaukee, also contains scenes shot in Lake Geneva.
- **Rudy** (1993), a hit movie about a Joliet, Illinois boy who fulfills his dream of playing football for Notre Dame has scenes filmed in the Milwaukee area.
- **Hoop Dreams** (1994), an award-winning documentary about two inner city kids' dreams to be basketball stars, contains scenes filmed at Marquette University.

The small, northern Wisconsin community of Gleason has its movie fame to claim as well since low-budget horror movie director, and then Gleason resident, Bill Rebane shot many of his B-movie scenes in and around Gleason and the Wausau area. His films included:

- **Rana: Legend of Shadow Lake** (1975) about a strange half-man/half frog monster living in a lake.
- **The Giant Spider Invasion** (1975) about enormous, flesh-eating spiders that sneak through a black hole into Northern Wisconsin.
- **Stroszek** (1976) a film about a German ex-con who wants to quit drinking and moves to Wisconsin to work as a mechanic.
- **The Alpha Incident** (1977), about a Mars microorganism, which kills victims when they sleep.
- **The Capture of Bigfoot** (1979).
- **Blood Harvest** (1987), starring Tiny Tim as a psychotic killer.

In addition, England's Windsor Lake Studios produced several films in the Eagle River area after it set up a studio there during the 1980s. Their films included:

- **Hellraiser** (1987), a horror movie.
- **Children of the Night** (1985), a TV movie.

Eagle River and Lake Geneva were also the sites of several scenes in **Damien-Omen II** (1978), starring William Holden in a sequel to "The Omen."

Many Wisconsin towns reportedly had several movie scenes shot in their vicinity. Those locations include:

DELAFIELD
- **The Major and the Minor** (1942), starring Ginger Rogers and Ray Milland, includes scenes filmed in Delafield.

MELLEN
- **Hemingway's of a Young Man** (1961), has scenes depicting parts of Hemingway's youth filmed in Mellen.

ELKHART LAKE
- **Winning** (1969), starring Paul Newman as a race car driver, Joanne Woodward and Robert Wagner was shot at Elkhart Lake.

DODGEVILLE
- **F.I.S.T.** (1978), starring Sylvester Stallone, has a few scenes filmed in Dodgeville.

NORTH FREEDOM
- **The Immigrants** (1978), a TV movie starring Sharon Gless and Roddy

McDowell, and **Mrs. Soffel** (1984), starring Diane Keaton and Mel Gibson, includes scenes shot at the Mid-Continent Railway Museum.

KENOSHA
- **The Betsy** (1978), starring Laurence Olivier and Tommy Lee Jones
- **Fever Lake** (1995), a horror movie, also used scenes from Twin Lakes as the setting of the fictitious Fever Lake.

DICKEYVILLE
- **Take This Job and Shove It** (1981), starring Robert Hays, Art Carney, Barbara Hershey, and Martin Mull.

APPLETON/FOX CITIES
- **Meet the Applegates** (1989), starring Stockard Channing and Ed Begley, Jr. as a family of insects posing as people, has scenes in the Fox Cities area.

BURKHARDT
- **Rachel River** (1987), starring Craig T. Nelson, has scenes filmed in Burkhardt.

ST. CROIX
- **The Mighty Ducks 2** (1993), starring Emilio Estevez, contains scenes at Interstate Park.
- **Angus** (1995), a movie about an overweight boy, and **The Cure** (1995), a movie about a boy with AIDS, include some scenes in Hudson and the St. Croix River area.

SUPERIOR
- **Iron Will** (1993), starring MacKenzie Astin, Kevin Spacey and Brian Cox, includes dog sled race scenes filmed in Superior, Oliver and the Brule River State Forest.

MORE MOVIES

The Wisconsin Film Office in Madison, and the Internet Movie Database (*www.imdb.com*), report that the following are among dozens of films, including many horror and B movies, that were filmed at least in part in Wisconsin.

1970s
- **Things in Their Season** (1974), a TV movie about a Wisconsin dairy farmer's son who moves out just as his mother discovers she has incurable leukemia.
- **The War at Home** (1979), a documentary about resistance to the Vietnam War in Madison.

1980s
- **Not a Love Story: A Film About Pornography** (1981)
- **The Pit** (1981), a horror film about an autistic boy seeking revenge.
- **Clash of the Titans** (1981), a depiction of the ancient Greek myth of Perseus and Andromeda.
- **Cremation of Sam McGee: A Poem ...** (1982), a short independent film.
- **Dreams Come True** (1982), about a boy who travels in his dreams.
- **The Devonsville Terror** (1983), a horror movie about a witch's curse.
- **28 Up** (1985), a British documentary.

Famous Wisconsin Film Stars

- **Blood Hook** (1986), a horror comedy about a giant fish hook that kills participant's in a Wisconsin town's annual Muskie Madness festival.
- **Patti Rocks** (1987), a relationship comedy.

1990-1995
- **Mindwarp** (1990), a science fiction-style horror movie
- **Pierced Tongue** (1991), a documentary
- **The Paint Job** (1992), a romantic thriller/comedy
- **Trauma** (1992), a horror movie about an anorexic girl who investigates her parents' gruesome murder.
- **Severed Ties** (1992), a horror film about a regenerated arm.
- **America's Deadliest Home Video** (1993), a TV movie.
- **Blessing** (1994), about living on a failing farm in Wisconsin.
- **Hysteria** (1993), a Finnish film.
- **Hank Aaron: Chasing the Dream** (1995)
- **All You Can Eat** (1995), a horror movie.
- **The Hunted** (1995), a Ninja action movie.

1996-1999
- **The Marksmen** (1997), about a native Wausau baseball player who leaves the team in disgrace and comes home to make amends.
- **Sleepers** (1996), about abused friends who grow up to seek revenge.
- **Reggie's Prayer** (1996), starring Green Bay football legend Reggie White.
- **Coven** (1997), about a demonic self-help group
- **The Big One** (1997), Michael Moore's expose' on greedy big businesses.
- **One Night Stand** (1997), about a director who discovers the woman he had a fling with is his brother's new wife.
- **The Wrestling Game** (1997), a TV movie.
- **A Simple Plan** (1998), about two brothers trying to keep millions of dollars that they found.
- **Houdini** (1998), a TV movie.
- **Dario Dare: Go to Hell** (1999), a horror comedy about a young journalist trying to steal back his soul.
- **Deep End of the Ocean** (1999), a movie based on a book by Wisconsin author Jacquelyn Mitchard.
- **American Movie: The Making of Northwestern** (1999), a documentary about the difficulties in producing *Coven*.
- **The Straight Story** (1999), about a 79-year-old Iowa man's travels via riding lawn mower to see his brother.
- **Expecting Mercy** (1999), a B-movie thriller.
- **The Last Great Ride** (1999), a family adventure starring Ernest Borgnine.

2000s
- **Lady in the Box** (2000), a murder mystery filmed in Milwaukee about a man accused of a crime he didn't commit.
- **First Nations Removed** (2000), a documentary about Native American assimilation.
- **Chump Change** (2000), a comedy that looks at what happens when "cheese

and beer" meet L.A. lifestyles.
- **Dexter Dickie** (2000), about small town political race.
- **Novocaine** (2001), starring Steve Martin as a dentist led toward crime by a patient.
- **Hollywood, Wisconsin** (2001), about a kids who try to turn a small town play into a big-time movie.
- **All for Ashley** (2001), an independent movie by student filmmaker Brent Sandrock from Middleton High School that premiered at the Wisconsin Film Festival in 2001.
- **Britney Baby, One More Time** (2001), about an independent filmmaker seeking an interview with Britney Spears.
- **No Sleep Til Madison** (2001-02), a comedy about a man confronting his obsession with attending the Wisconsin State High School Hockey Tournament each year.
- **The Red Betsy** (2001)
- **The Return of Shamus Poole** (2001)
- **The Wildwood Project** (2001)
- **Milwaukee, Minnesota** (2001)

Editor's Note: *The above list is meant to provide only an overview of the many movies filmed in Wisconsin and is not to be taken a complete list or description of all the movies made in Wisconsin.*

ACKNOWLEDGMENTS

These profiles of Wisconsin's famous movie stars would not have been possible without the research and assistance of other less famous but no less hard working Wisconsinites.

I'd like to thank Scott Thom at the Wisconsin Film Office in Madison, Jim Van Ess at Carroll College in Waukesha, Robert Noll of the Dodge County Historical Society in Beaver Dam, yearbook advisors Corin DeHartog and Paul Felhaber of Shorewood and Whitefish Bay High Schools respectively, John Sime of the Agnes Moorehead Film Festival Committee in Viroqua, Rick Peterson from the Lawrence University public relations office in Appleton, the Beloit Historical Society in Beloit, the South Wood County Historical Society and the research staffs at the Universities of Wisconsin in Whitewater, Superior, and Madison as well as Ripon College and Carroll College in addition to the countless reference librarians at public libraries in Madison, Milwaukee, Beloit, La Crosse, Racine, Kenosha, Appleton, and Beaver Dam, among many others.

Most especially, I'd like to thank Jerry and Suzanne Ziesmer, the Wisconsin State Historical Society Film Office, Madison researcher Steve Dhuey, Marion Rose of Whitefish Bay and the family and friends of Jeffrey Hunter, James and Tyne Daly, Chris Farley, Gregg Sherwood Dodge and Fred MacMurray, some of whom preferred not to be quoted in this book but who nonetheless helped immensely in providing the personal details for these profiles.

My appreciation, as always, goes to my parents, Renee Halverson, Dee Halverson, my little sisters Breona and Kristy and my publisher Marv Balousek for their support and encouragement — especially for their enthusiasm about this book and the famous Wisconsinites in it.

Finally, *Famous Wisconsin Film Stars* would still be just an idea had it not been for my silent partner in my every endeavor, my husband, Steve Halverson, who is always there to encourage me to put pen to paper, to critique and compliment my work, to endure my frustrations and to actually and sincerely miss me when

I'm locked to my keyboard for hours, and days, on end.

In addition to the people behind the book, and personal interviews with such moviemakers as Jerry Zucker, David Zucker, Jim Abrahams, Bill Rebane, and Jerry Ziesmer, I acknowledge the following sources of my research.

Thanks to the Internet Movie Database and the All Movie Guide for helping to provide the film listings at the end of each chapter.

Besides the numerous newspaper and magazine articles credited within the profiles themselves, I credit Associated Press Biographical Service biography articles and, most especially, Amazon.com's *Internet Movie Database Ltd.*, at *http://us.imdb.com*, including mini 1994 biographies by Leonard Maltin (used by arrangement with Signet, a division of Penguin Putnam, Inc.) as well as mini biographies written for the database by: Ed Stephan, Jane Byron Dean, Volker Boehm, Ray Hamel, Jan Wilm, Kay Peracca, Denny Jackson, Dave Curbow, Bill Takacs, VidMan, Tony Fontana, Steven Dhuey , Bill Takacs, Denny Jackson, David Montgomery, Matt Patay, Peter Vietze, Stephen Currence, Stacey Sanders , John Sacksteder, David L. Gorsline, Herman Seifer , Natasha Hall, Grace Z, and Ian Doyle.

Other sources include:

Academy of Motion Picture Arts and Sciences Web site at www.oscars.org. 2002.

All Movie Guide Web site, at www.allmovies.com, including biographies by Hal Erickson. 2002.

*The American Theater Wings Tony Award*s Web Site, at www.tonyawards.com. 2002.

An Affair to Remember. Christopher Anderson. William Morrow & Company, New York. May 1997.

Bunny, Bunny: Gilda Radner: A Sort of Love Story. Alan Zweibel. Random House, Inc., New York. August 1994.

Carroll College: The First Century 1846-1946. Ellen Langill. Carroll College, Waukesha, Wisconsin. 1980.

Citizen Welles: A Biography of Orson Welles. Frank Brady. Scribner, New York. March 1989.

Colleen Dewhurst: Her Autobiography. Colleen Dewhurst and Tom Viola. Simon & Schuster, New York. 1997.

Cult Movie Stars. Danny Peary. Simon & Schuster Fireside Books, New York. 1991.

Dennis and Lillian Morgan's Interview with Marilyn Williams Linley, History of Education Theater. Marilyn Williams Linley. Marquette University, Milwaukee/Waukesha. 1969.

The Complete Films of Spencer Tracy. Donald Deschner. The Citadel Press, New York. 1968.
E! True Hollywood Story: Chris Farley Biography. E! TV. July 23, 2002.
The Films of Fredric March. Lawrence Quirk. Carol Publishing Group, New York. March 1974.
The Films of Joseph Losey. James Palmer and Michael Riley. Cambridge University Press, Cambridge, England. August 1993.
The Film Encyclopedia: Third Edition. Ephraim Katz, Harper Perennial. New York. 1997.
Fred MacMurray Web site, www2.powercom.net/~fredmac. Ron Noll. Beaver Dam. 2002.
Fredric March: Craftsman First, Star Second. Deborah C. Peterson. Greenwood Publishing Group. April 30, 1996.
Gene Wilder Tribute Web site, at www.wilder.narod.ru. Sandra Brennan & John A. Simone, Jr. 2002.
Hollywood Babylon. Kenneth Anger. Dell Publishing Company, New York. May 1983.
Hollywood.com Web Site at www.hollywood.com. 2002.
I Was Interrupted. Nicholas Ray and Susan Ray. University of California Press, Berkeley, Calif. April 1995.
In Hollywood Album: Lives & Deaths of Hollywood Stars From the Pages of the New York Times. Edited Arleen Keylin & Suri Fleischer. Arno Press, New York. 1979
Internet Broadway Database Web Site at www.ibdb.com. 2002.
Joseph Losey-A Revenge on Life. David Caute. Oxford University Press, Oxford, England. October 1994.
Me: Stories of My Life. Katherine Hepburn. Ballantine Books Inc., New York. July 1996.
Metro-Goldwyn-Mayer Presents Samuel Bronston's Production of King of Kings. Metro-Goldwyn-Mayer, Los Angeles. 1961.
The Movie Stars. Richard Griffith. Doubleday & Company Inc., New York. 1970.
Movie Stars of the 1930s: A Complete Reference Guide for the Film Historian or Trivia Buff. Donald Ragan. Prentice-Hall Inc., Englewood, Cliffs, N.J. 1985
Movie Stars of the 1940s: A Complete Reference Guide for the Film Historian or Trivia Buff. David Ragan. Prentice-Hall Inc. Englewood, California. 1985.
Nicholas Ray: An American Journey. Bernard Eisenschitz, Tom Milne. Faber & Faber, London. May 1993.
*Old Familiar Faces: The Great Character Actors and Actresses of

Hollywood's Golden Era. Robert A. Juran. Movie Memories Publishing, Sarasota, Florida. 1995

Orson Welles: The Rise and Fall of An American Genius. Charles Higham. St. Martin's Press, New York. 1985.

Ready When You Are Mr. Coppola, Mr. Spielberg, Mr. Crowe. Jerry Ziesmer. The Scarecrow Press Inc., Lanham, Maryland. 2000.

Spencer Tracy: Tragic Idol. Bill Davidson. E.P. Dutton Publishing, New York. 1988.

Spencer Tracy: A Biography. Larry Swindell. Coronet Books, Philadelphia, Penn. 1973.

Stars in Blue: Movie Actors in America's Sea Services James E. Wise and Anne Collier Rehill. Naval Institute Press, Annapolis, Maryland. 1997.

The Three Stooges Scrapbook. Jeff Lenburg, Joan Howard Maurer, Greg Lenburg, and John Howard Maurer. Citadel Press, Sacramento, California. September 1997.

Three Stooges Web site, at www.threestooges.com. 2002.

This is Orson Welles. Orson Welles & Peter Bogdanovich. De Capo Press Inc., Cambridge, Massachusetts. 1998.

Together Again: Stories of the Great Hollywood Teams. Garison Kanin. Doubleday & Company Inc., New York. October 1981.

TV TOME television reference guide Web site, at www.tvtome.com. 2002.

The Wind at My Back: The Live and Times of Pat O'Brien. Himself (Pat O'Brien). Doubleday & Company, New York. 1964.

The World's Most Famous Movie Ranch: The Story of Ray 'Crash' Corrigan & Corriganville. William J. Ehrheart. Ventura County Museum of History and Art. Ventura, California. 1999.

Wisconsin Performing Artists Hall of Fame Web Site at www.marcuscenter.org. Marcus Center for Performing Arts, Milwaukee, Wisconsin. 2002.

Wisconsin State Historical Society Film Office archives. Madison, Wisconsin. 2002.

ABOUT THE AUTHOR

Kristin Gilpatrick Halverson was born Aug. 26, 1968, in Edgerton, Wisconsin, and is a graduate of Cedarburg High School, where she appeared in her senior class play, Woody Allen's *Don't Drink The Water.*

The author still clearly remembers watching her first big screen movie, *Cinderella,* at the Al Ringling Theater in Baraboo when she was 4 and admits she's been a popcorn-munching, die-hard movie fan ever since. (She even saw *Tootsie* 13½ times at Cedarburg's Rivoli Theater in 1982.)

Gilpatrick had her screen debut, and simultaneous grand finale, in the 1997 Wisconsin lead mining documentary *The Rush for Grey Gold,* where she played an 1820s "working girl" who scantily reveals … her ankles!

A graduate of the University of Wisconsin-Eau Claire — where she double majored in journalism and Spanish and studied a semester abroad in Valladolid, Spain — Gilpatrick worked as an award-winning newspaper and magazine editor for ten years before becoming a full-time author and freelance writer.

For the past five years, Gilpatrick has dedicated herself to recording and telling the stories of Wisconsin war veterans in her popular book series, *The Hero Next Door*®, which includes *The Hero Next Door*® *The Hero Next Door® Returns,* and *The Hero Next Door® of the Korean War,* coming in 2003. In addition to Korean War profiles, Gilpatrick is completing a book about a Bataan Death March survivor, *Footprints in Courage,* due out in late 2002.

Gilpatrick's most recent work is *Destined to Live,* which tells the story of incredible World War II airman "Wild Bill" Scanlon who survived seventy-seven combat missions with air forces of three countries before being shot out of a B-17 bomber and escaping back to freedom through the French Underground.

When she is not writing and rewriting, the author volunteers with the Big Brothers/Big Sisters program where, for fourteen years, she's been a big sister to two girls.

Gilpatrick lives in Monona with her best friend and husband of five years, Steven Halverson, an Edward Jones investment representative.

(Discover more about Gilpatrick, her *Hero Next Door*™ series and other upcoming books at *www.heronextdoor.org* or at the Badger Books Inc. web site, *www.badgerbooks.com*.)

INDEX

Symbols

20th Century Fox Studios 17-19, 56, 57, 65, 101, 121, 149-150, 197

A

Abbott and Costello 76, 80
ABC 72, 93
Abraham, F. Murray 221
Abrahams, Jim 273, 277, 314
Abrahams, Nancy 278
Academy Award 12, 29, 31, 45, 104, 121, 125, 126, 169, 179, 221, 243, 250, 303, 305
Adams, Brooke 268
Adams, Joe 177
Adams, Josie 268
Adams, Lynn 269
Adams, Marion 243
Adams, Mason 300
Ade, George 35
Africa 41, 197
Agnes Moorehead Film Festival 33
Ahwahnee, California 180
Aikman, Troy 292
Al Jackson Players 304
Alaska 224
Albert, Marv 311
Albright, Lola 190
Aldredge, Tom and Theoni 286
Alesia, Tom 273, 279, 290
All Movie Guide 149
Allen, Woody 231, 303
Alpha Delta Phi 118
Alpha Epsilon Pi 229
Altman, Robert 269
Ameche, Don 98-105, 301, 304
Ameche, Jim 98
American Academy of Dramatic Arts 15, 28, 132, 133, 145, 158
American Cancer Society 183
American Film Institute 45, 49
American International Pictures 248
American Legion 88, 91
American Playhouse 221
American Repertory Theater 268
Amici, Dominic Felix *(see Ameche, Don)* 98
Amici, Felix and Barbara *(see Ameche, Don)* 98
Anderson, Broncho Billy 13
Anger, Kenneth 58
Aniston, Jennifer 122
Ann Arbor, Michigan. 220
Annapolis, Maryland 196
Appleton, Wisconsin 131, 132, 138, 173, 217, 238, 239, 241, 242, 243, 244, 245, 252
Appleton East High School 239, 240
Appleton Post Crescent 137, 138, 238, 239, 242, 244
Arbuckle, Fatty 265
Arizona 67, 104
ARK Repertory Theatre 304
Arkansas 60
Arkin, Alan 303
Armendarez, Pedro 32
Armus, Si 81
Arnold, Maxine 178, 181
Arnold, Tom 262, 266
Arnold: The Education of a Bodybuilder 298
Arnold's Bodybuilding for Men 298
Arpe, Janet 85
Arrow Collar 197
Art Institute of Chicago 247
Asner, Ed 124
Associated Press 20, 21, 69, 85, 168, 183, 254
Astaire, Fred 179
Astin, MacKenzie 324

Athens, Wisconsin 207
Atlantic City, N.J. 223
Attic Theater 238, 239, 245
Aurer, James 239
Austrian Junior Championship 298
Aykroyd, Dan 265, 266, 290, 302, 322

B

Bacall, Lauren 17
Badger Annual 118
Badger Brass and Bain 36
Baio, Scott 322
Baker, Ellis 120
Balfour, Malcolm 85
Balloonatics 149
Baltimore, Maryland 120, 306
Bancroft, Ann 230
Baraboo, Wisconsin 176
Barbary Coast 197
Bard, Ben 187
Barnum & Ringling Brothers Circus 311
Barnum, P.T. 311
Baron Group International Ltd. 249
Bartlett, Bonnie 310
Bartlett, E.E. 310
Bartlett, Joan 69
Beach, Guy 166
Beach Nuts 149
Beatles 317
Beaver Dam, Wisconsin 87, 90, 91, 93, 96
Beaver Dam School Board 95
Begley, Ed 65
Begley, Ed, Jr. 324
Belinda, Johnny 29, 33
Bellafante, Ginia 264
Bellamy, Ralph 99, 104, 106, 113, 299
Beloit 76, 77, 79, 80, 81, 82, 86
Beloit College 76, 306, 308
Beloit Daily News 79, 80, 82
Beloit High School 80, 84

Belushi, John 255, 258, 289, 301, 322
Benard, Bernard A. 201
Benard, Ray 201
Bendestorf Film Studios 247
Bennett, Richard Dyer 215
Benny, Jack 190
Benson, Rex 251
Bergen County (N.J.) Record 241
Bergen, Polly 67
Berghof, Herbert 312
Bergman, Andrew 302
Bergman, Ingrid 135
Bernsen, Corbin 322
Bernstein, Dr. 37, 38, 40, 48, 50
Beta Pi Epsilon 177, 182
Beverly Hills, California 32, 122, 287
Bible 243
Bickel, Ernest Frederick McIntyre 117-120
Bickel, John 117
Biggs, Lucia R. 132
Bill Halley's Comets 251
Billen, Andrew 158
Black-Foxe Military Institute 229
Blystone, Jasper 149-157
Blystone, John 149-157
Blystone, Stanley 149-157
Blyth, Ann 66
Bogart, Humphrey 17, 168
Bogdanovich, Peter 35, 45, 46, 48, 50, 283
Bohemian Club 178
Bohn, John 189
Bondi, Jerry 159
Boody, H.P. 14
Borgnine, Ernest 325
Boston Globe 272
Bowers, Ronald 30
Boyd, William "Bill" 16, 106
Boy Scouts 12
Boyer, Charles 31
Boyer, Karen 235
Boys Town 18

Bradford Beach 285
Bradley University 28
Brando, Marlon 127, 288, 289, 291
Bravi, Jess 276
Brazil 39
Brecht, Bertolt 210
Breslau, Susan 281
Brickman, Marshall 302
Bridges, Beau 202, 322
Bridges, James 221
Bridges, Lloyd 275
Briggs, Lucia 132
Bristol Old Vic Theatre School 229
British Isles 56
Bronson, Charles 322
Brookings Hollow, Oregon 205
Brooks, Mel
   229, 230, 231, 232, 303
Brown Deer, Wisconsin 138
Brown Deer Park 285
Brown, Kathryne Dora 145
Brown's Lake Resort 285
Brule River State Forest 324
Brussels, Belgium 48
Bullock, Sandra 164
Burkhardt, Sandra 324
Burlington, Wisconsin 285
Burlington Railroad 210
Burma 113
Burns, Walter 112
Burrows, Nick 256
Burton, Richard 213
Byron, J. Dean 197

C

Caan, James 305
Caeser, Julius 29, 43, 64
Caesar, Sid 228, 235
Café Arabica 268
Cage, Nicholas 303
Cagney, James 16, 106, 113, 115
California 32, 61, 64, 73,
  84, 89, 90, 93,
  101, 115, 120, 122,
  123, 142, 170, 182,
  193, 211, 223, 231, 252,
  262, 298, 305, 308
Callaway, Tom 239
Callow, Simon 221
Cambria, Wisconsin 158, 159, 162
Cambridge (Massachusetts) Drama
   Festival 230
Cambridge, Masssachusetts 268
Camp Indianola 39
Canada 60, 135, 212
Canadian Football League 129
Canfield, Alice 102
Cannes Film Festival 305
Canton, Ohio 113
Capitol Hill 212
Capitol Records 317
Carleton College 186
Carman, Manitoba 186
Carney, Art 324
Carpenter, Chuck 118
Carroll College
   88, 173, 174, 176, 177, 182, 183
Carroll College Bulletin 174
Carroll Echo 173, 174
Carson, Elmer L. 186
Carson, Jack 43,
  115, 178, 179, 183, 186-
  192, 207, 307
Carson, Johnny 50
Carson, Robert 186
Cason, Colleen 204
Cassavetes, John 159, 164
Cassavetes, Nick 161
Cassel, Seymour 160
Catholic Actors Guild 114
Caute, David 211, 212
CBS 30, 43, 190, 316
Center Stage 238
Central High School, La Crosse 166,
  168, 210
Cesario, Jeff 310
Champion, Marge and Gower 66
Channing, Stockard 324
Chaplin, Charlie 58, 151, 233

Chapman, Dorothy 38
Charles, Arthur 60
Charles, Daisy 27, 33
Charlie Foundation 278
Chateau Marmont Hotel 169, 302
Chatsworth, California 202, 292
Cheyenne, Wyoming 179
Chicago 14, 35, 37, 38, 39, 42, 44, 80, 89, 91, 93, 101, 108, 111, 117, 132, 171, 176, 178, 179, 183, 193, 215, 247, 259, 264, 301, 302, 305, 307
Chicago Daily News 42
Chicago Drama League 39
Chicago Music College 178
Chicago Opera Company 40
Chicago Sun Times 264
Chicago Symphony Orchestra 178
Chicago Tribune 243
Children's Theater of the Air 63
Chris Farley Foundation 266
Christ Episcopal Church 60
Christophe, Henri 43
Chudnow, Dick 274
Churchill, Winston 307
Cincinnati, Ohio 16
Circus World 169, 171
Civil War 144, 208
Clark, Dane 67
Clark, J. Graham 14
Cleveland, Ohio 196
Cleveland Indians 322
Cline, Edward "Eddie" F. 311
Clinton, Massachusetts 26
Cochran, Steve 66
Coffer-Miller Players 193
Cohan, George M. 16
Coker, Flora 240
Colbert, Claudette 90, 101
Colgate, Wisconsin 315
Colgate Comedy Hour 272
Colleen Dewhurst: Her Autobiography 129
College of DuPage 301
Colorado 301
Columbia 18
Columbia Academy 99
Columbia Pictures 47, 247
Columbus, Christopher 125
Columbus, New Mexico 196
Communist Party 168
Confidential 81, 82, 83
Connecticut 145, 236
Connery, Sean 164
Connor, Edward 71
Cooper, Gary 127
Coppola, Francis Ford 2913
Corby, Ellen 223-227
Corby, Francis 223
Cornell College 140
Cornell, Katherine 41
Corrigan, Ray "Crash" 201-206
Corrigan, Rita 204
Corrigan, Tom 204
Corriganville 202, 204
Cotton, Joseph 44
Counter-Attack Magazine 124
Cox, Brian 323
Crawford, Joan 12, 169, 201
Crime in Connecticut: The Story of Alex Kelly 216
Crosby, Bing 93, 106, 115, 180, 188
Crowe, Cameron 138, 283, 290
Crowley, Evelyn 284
Cruise, Tom 293
CTM Madison Family Theater Company 321
Cuba 40
Cukor, George 21
Culver City, California 95
Curtis, Jamie Lee 219, 297
Curtis, Tony 66
Cusack, Dick 304
Cusack, Joan 304

D

D.W. Griffith Award 49
Dafoe, William and Muriel 238, 242
Dafoe, Willem 238-246
Dailey, Dan 80
Daily Tribune 141
Daily Variety 12, 39, 45
Daily Yomiuri 212
Dairy Queen 272
Dallas Morning News 264
Daly Ice & Coal Co 140
Daly, Jim 140-148
Daly, Mel 142, 143, 145
Daly, Timothy 145, 148, 269
Daly, Tyne 143, 145-148
Dane County, Wisconsin 322
Dangerfield, Rodney 322
Daniel Freedman Hospital 262
Daniels, William 310
Darrow, Clarence 125
Dartmouth College 210
Davidson Theater 111
Davies, Don 162
Davis, Bette 45
Davis, Lisa 274
Day, Doris 189
Dayton Memorial Park 32
Dayton, Ohio 32
De Palma, Brian 283
Dean, James 169
Del Rio, Delores 46, 201
Del Mar Race Track 115
Delafield, Wisconsin 186, 196 322
Delbridge, Alice 301
Demarest, William 94
DeMichele, Gary 137
Democratic Party 122, 124
DeNiro, Robert 301
Denny, Mary Kate 286
Denver, Colorado 120, 201
Department of Commerce, Wisconsin 251
Department of Tourism, Wisconsin 251

Derek, John and Pati 67
Des Moines, Iowa 112
Deschner, Donald 13-18, 21, 23
Detroit, Michigan 220
Detroit Free Press 99, 102
DeVito, Danny 276, 299
Dewhurst, Colleen 129-139
Dewhurst, Fred 129
Dexter, Anthony 66
Dies, Martin 124
Diller, Phyllis 73
DiMaggio, Joe 76, 79
Directors Guild of America 49, 290, 293
Disney, Walt 69, 87, 219
Disraeli 174
Dobbins, Bill 297
Dodge, Gregg Sherwood 76-86
Dodge, Horace 80, 84
Dodge, John Francis 85
Dodge, Johnny 82, 84, 85
Dodgeville, Wisconsin 323
Doege's Frozen Custard 285
Donlevy, Brian 196-200, 207
Doolittle, Jimmy 21, 58
Door County 186
Dorsogna, Gene 250
Douglas, Kirk 159, 190, 230
Douglas, William O. 24
Downer College 131, 132
Dreyfus, Lee 229
Dru, Joanne 66
Dublin, Ireland 40
Dubuque, Iowa 99, 104
Dunn, James 80
Dunne, Irene 92
Dunne, Red 110
DuPont, Elaine 204

E

E! 73, 255, 258
Eagle River, Wisconsin 249, 251, 280
Eagle's Nest Productions 252

Earhart, Amelia 129
Easton, Robert 311
Eau Claire, Wisconsin 150
Eder, Shirley 99, 102
Edgewood College 256, 292
Edgewood High School 254
Edison, Thomas 19
Edwards, Hilton 41
Edwin Booth Society 119
Ehrheart, William 202
Einstein Junior High School 239
Eisenhower, Dwight D. 58
Eisenstein, Sergei 210
Eldridge, Florence 120
Eliot, T.S. 244
Elkhart Lake, Wisconsin 323
Ellis, Aline 119, 120
Emerson, Ralph Waldo 24
Encino, California 191
Encyclopedia Britannica 161
Engel, Dave 141
England 57, 58, 114, 212, 213, 229, 235, 315
Erickson, Dave 311
Erickson, Hal 149
Ermini, Cecilia 222
Escadrille, Lafayette 196
Estevez, Emilio 324
Estonia 247, 252
Europe 41, 47, 73, 108
Ewell, Tom 99, 304

F

Fairchild, Wisconsin 55
Falco, John S. 80
Falk, Peter 160
Farley, Chris 254-267
Farley, John 267
Farley, Kevin 263, 267
Farley, Paul 63
Farley, Tom 266
Faye, Alice 101, 102
FBI 72, 194, 212
Fedderson, Don 93

Fehlhaber, Paul 74
Feldman, Marty 232
Fenster, Bob 261, 262
Ferrer, Jose 312
Filmograph 61
Films and Filming 170
Films in Review 71
Finn, Patrick 257
First Drama Quartette 31
Firth, Peter 220
Fjelstad, Dora *(see Gregg Sherwood Dodge)* 76
Fjelstad, Mons 76
Fletcher, Lucille 30
Flockhart, Calista 296
Florida 85, 220, 245, 312
Flynn, Errol 189
Foersche, William 252
Foley, Matt 260
Fonda, Bidget 138
Fonda, Jane 213
Fontanne, Lynn 311
Ford, Betty 164
Ford, Harrison 233, 288, 295, 297, 305, 315
Ford, John 17, 23, 114, 170, 208, 210
Forest Lawn Cemetery 225
Forman, Milos 221
Foster, David 181
Foster, Jodie 137
Fox News Service 147
Fox River Baptist Church 243
Fox River Mall 244
Foyle, Kitty 179
France 196, 213
Francis, Kay 58
Franco, Generalissimo Francisco 113
Frank Elementary School 98
Franken, Al 261
Frankenheimer, John 283
Franz, Eduard 193-195
Franz, Eduard Schmidt 193
Frautschi, Lowell 38
Frawley, William 93

Fred Miller Theatre 283
Frederick, Oklahoma 57
Fredric March Theater 126
Fredric March: Craftsman First, Star Second 117
Freedom Communication 261
Freeman, Morgan 322
Freise, Bill 171
French Foreign Legion 197
French Riviera 81
Fresno, California 184
Frost, Robert 24
Fuller Opera House 119

G

Gable, Clark 18, 19, 202
Gabor, Zsa, Zsa 84
Galesville, Wisconsin 166
Galileo, Galilei 211
Garbo, Greta 122
Garden, Mary 178
Gardner, Ava 171
Garland, Judy 207
Garrick Theater 99
Gary, Indiana 133
Gates, Nancy 67
Gaylord, Janet 122
Gaynor, Mitzi 67
Gazarra, Ben 135, 160
Gensler, Barbara 272
George Devine Ballroom 284
George Olsen Band 89
Georgetown University 99
Gere, Richard 268
Germany 40, 247, 248
Gesu Catholic Church 106, 107
Gibbons, Cedric 201
Gibson, Mel 291, 323, 324
Gilda's House 235
Gill, Doris E. 204
Gilligan's Island 249, 255
Gimbel's Department Store 106
Gingrich, Newt 260
Girls Town Inc. 85

Gish, Lillian 135
Gist, Robert 30
Gleason Days, festival 249
Gleason, Jimmy 111
Gleason, Wisconsin 247, 248, 249, 323
Glendale, California 225
Gless, Sharon 323
Gobel, George 92
Goddard, Paulette 151
Godunov, Boris 213
Goff, Nadine 320
Goff's Restaurant 177
Golden Mike Award 30
Good Samaritan Hospital 74
Gooding, Cuba, Jr. 290
Goodman, John 266
Gordon, Bert I. 311
Gordon, Herschel Lewis 248
Gottingen, Germany 310
Gottlieb, Herman 230
Grable, Betty 56
Graham, Alexander Bell 98
Graham, Professor 24
Graham, Renee 136
Grahame, Gloria 168
Grand Detour, Illinois 37
Grand Theater 250
Granger, Farley 168
Grant, Cary 179, 300
Graz, Austria 296
Great Britain 212, 235
Great Depression 60, 193, 223
Great Lakes Naval Training Station 14, 108
Greco, Jose 83
Green Bay, Wisconsin 164, 176, 268, 269, 283, 314, 325
Green Bay Packers 292, 293
Green, Blake 240
Greendale, Wisconsin 313, 319
Greer, Jane 29
Grcy, Yvonne 197
Griffith, Richard 121
Grosson Brian Boru Donlevy 196

Guardian 162, 163
Guinan, Texas 101
Guinness Book of World Records 298
Gunneson, Erik 311
Gurda, John 189
Gus Arnheim Orchestra 89

H

Hagen, Lois 84
Hagen, Uta 311, 319
Hakim, David 290
Hale, Alan Jr. 249
Hall, Deidre Ann 312
Hall, Douglas Kent 297
Hamburg, Germany 247
Hamner, Earl 225
Hampshire House 81, 82
Hanks, Tom 18, 126
Hansen, Ellen 223
Hansen, Peter 67
Hardwicke, Sir Cedric 31
Harlem, New York 43
Harmon, Mark 322
Harrison, Rex 58
Harsch, Rick 166, 167
Hart, Edie 190
Hartkopf, Ted 285
Hartford Avenue Grade School 186
Harvard University 210
Harver, June 80, 92, 96
Haunted Honeymoon 234
Having a Wonderful Crime 58, 113
Hawaii 92
Hawn, Goldie 324
Hayes, Bill 67
Hayes, Helen 230
Hayes, J.J. 41
Hays, Robert 324
Hayward, Susan 32
Hayworth, Rita 46, 47, 56
Hazelton Clinic 262
Head, Norma 110
Head, Robert 61, 110
Healey, Don 255

Hearst, William Randoph 45
Heart Ball 85
Heinen, Tom 96
Helgeson, Orland 27
Heller, John 80
Hemingway, Ernest 323
Hendrix, Wanda 66
Henie, Sonja 101
High Mount Grade School, 186
Hibbard, Edna 16
Hiegel, Mrs. Ernest 171
Higgins, Jack 89
Higgins, Robert 103
High Noon 211
Higham, Charles 35, 37, 38, 39, 40, 41, 42, 44, 46, 48
Highland Park, Illinois 38
Hill, Roger 39, 41
Hinakaga yearbook 88, 177
Hobson, Louis B. 254
Hoffman, Dustin 127, 288
Holiday Hotel 103
Hollywood Album: Lives & Deaths of Hollywood Stars 123, 124
Hollywood Canteen 21
Hollywood Cavalcade 101
Hollywood Magazine 102
Holy Cross Cemetery 95
Honolulu Star Bulletin 286
Hope, Bob 73, 92, 93, 180, 188, 205
Hopkins, Anthony 220
Hopper, Dennis 170
Horne, Lena 46
Horror-Wood Webzine 250
Houdini, Harry 245
Houseman, John 29, 42, 167
Howard, Cy 168
Huber, Russell 171
Hudson, Wisconsin 324
Hudson, Rock 66, 76, 80
Hughes, Howard 112, 211
Hulce, Thomas Edward 219-222
Hunt, Willis Jr. 56

Hunter Enterprises 71
Hunter, Christopher 73
Hunter, Jeffrey 23, 30, 60-75, 110, 114, 170, 214, 243, 308
Hunter, Scott 70
Hunter, Todd 71
Huntley Grade School 239
Huntley School in Appleton 291
Hurley, Wisconsin 252
Hurt, William 308
Huston, John 17, 49, 282

I

Illinois 28, 39, 41
Improv Olympic Theater Company 259
Indiana 119
Indianola Trail 39
Interlochen Arts Camp 220
Interlochen, Michigan 219
International Crane Foundation 311
International Film School, London 305
International Showtime 103
Internet Movie Database 46, 51, 112, 298, 301, 314, 317, 320, 324
Interstate Park 324
Iowa City, Iowa 140
Ireland 40
Ireland, John 66
Irving, John 222
Irvy, Bob 241, 243
Italy 212
Iverson Movie Ranch 202
Ives, Lucy 36
Ives, Richard Welles 36

J

Jabas, Debbie 261
Jacklin, Judy 302
Jackson, Al 99
Jackson Hole, Wyoming 297
Jahiel, Edwin 171
Jameson, Francis Parker 306
Jamestown, S.D. 197
Jardine, Cassandra 228
Jarvis Repertory Theatre 158
Jean Evans 167
Jennings, William Bryan 125
Jens, Salome 291, 312
Jensen, Don 98
Jesup, Olin 176
John Adams School 287
John Tracy Clinic for the Deaf 16
Johnson, Hildy 112
Johnson, Kristen 312
Johnsonville Brats 293
Joliet, Illinois 323
Jones, Allan 178
Jones, Jane 222
Jones, Tommy Lee 323
Joseph Losey: A Revenge on Life 211
Joseph Losey: The Man With Four Names 212
Joy, Tom 88
Juarez, Mexico 73
Juilliard Theater Center 319
Junior Achievement Inc. 66

K

Kaczmarek, Jane 312, 319
Kahn, Madeline 232
Kanin, Garson 17, 19
Kankakee, Illinois 87
Kankakee State Institution 39
Kansas City, Missouri 13, 186
Katzenberg, Jeffrey 264
Kayalli, Randa 268
Kaye, Danny 228
Kazan, Elia 167
Keaton, Buster 51, 149
Keaton, Diane 135, 322
Keene, Chris 274
Kellogg, Blake 182
Kennedy, Arthur 66

Kennedy, John F. 307
Kennedy, George 322
Kenosha, Wisconsin 35, 37, 38, 39, 40, 98, 99, 309, 311, 316, 318, 322, 324
Kenosha News 98
Kenosha School Board 35
Kentucky Derby 283
Kentucky Fried Theater 273, 274
Kerrigan, Nancy 260
Key Club 84
Kickapoo Scout 26
Kienzle, Raymond *(see Nicholas Ray)* 166
Kimbrough, Mary 98
King, Larry 230, 232, 236
King, Randall 137
Kinney, Kathy 313
Kirk, Phyllis 66
Klein, Dan 314
Klug, Scott 260
Knute Rockne, All American 108, 113
Kodar, Oja 48
Kohl, Herbert 229
Kramer, Stanley 18, 23, 159
Kroger, Larry 219
Kupcinet, Irv 84

L

La Crosse, Wisconsin 166, 167, 171, 210, 212, 243
La Crosse Tribune 166, 167, 169, 171
Lac du Flambeau, Wisconsin 41, 181
Lake Geneva, Wisconsin 321, 322
Lamont, Lillian 90
Landis, Carole 55-59, 113
Landis, Dorothy 55
Landis, Lawrence, 55
Landis, John 220, 301
Lane, Marjorie 197
Langford, Frances 102

Larson, Kurtwood Smith 317
Larson, Lee 177
Las Vegas, Nevada 90, 190
Latvia 249
Laughton, Charles 31
Laurel and Hardy 149, 150, 151, 286
Laurel, Stan 287
Lawford, Peter 67
Lawrence College 137, 138
Lawrence, Larry 62
Lawrence University 131, 132, 135, 173, 176, 239, 240
Leachman, Cloris 217
Lear, Norman 216
LeCompte, Elizabeth 241
Lee, Canada 45
Lee, Jack G. 28
Lee, Peggy 66
Leigh, Janet 67
Lennon, John 247
Leno, Jay 264
Leonard, Terry 315
Leslie, Joan 180
Letterman, David 255, 260
Lewis, Jim 211
Lewis, Monica 67
Life Magazine 310
Lincoln, Abraham 126
Lindy, Elizabeth 187
Liotta, Ray 219
Livingston, Alan 317
Llamas, Fernando 80
Lodi, Wisconsin 320
Lodi High School 320
Logan, Michael 146
Lombard, Carol 122
London 160, 161, 170, 219, 220, 239, 288, 305
Loohauis, Jackie 29, 180
Los Angeles 74, 84, 91, 126, 145, 193, 216, 220, 229, 234, 274, 277, 279, 291, 302
Los Angeles Citizen News 70, 72

Los Angeles Civic Light Opera Company 178
Los Angeles Geffen Playhouse 312
Los Angeles Times 142, 161, 202, 203
Los Angeles Times Press 122
Losey, Joseph 114, 166, 168, 210-218
Losey, Louise 211
Losey Memorial Arch 171
Loyola University 89
Lucas, George 252, 296
Luchetta, Stella 224
Lugosi, Bela 199
Lugosi, Lillian 199
Lundstrom, Jim 137
Lunt, Alfred 22, 174, 142, 311
Lux Radio Theatre 123

M

MacDonald, Katherine 256
MacLiammoir, Micheal 41
MacMurray, Fred 69, 87-97, 283, 286, 316
MacMurray, Maleta Martin 87
Mac's Melody Boys 88
Mad Magazine 272
Mad Man Michaels 285
Madison, Wisconsin 28, 38, 39, 44, 71, 82, 99, 100, 114, 118, 143, 145, 158, 176, 182, 193, 235, 254, 258, 261, 266, 292, 300, 303, 306, 311, 312, 315, 317, 319-324
Madison Capital Times 82, 84, 86, 256, 261, 273, 277, 279
Madison East High School 318
Madison Film Festival 306
Madison Repertory Theater 263
Madison West High School 314
Madrid, Spain 72
Maine 220
Maine Township High School 295

Majestic Theater 80, 322
Malaga, Spain 51
Mallon, Jim 316
Maltin, Leonard 32, 46, 74, 112, 117, 187, 198, 207, 301
Mankiewicz, Herman 45
Mann, Michael 305
Mann, Summer 305
Manufacturers Bank 117
Maple Bluff, Wisconsin 254
Marathon County 249
March, Florence 125
March, Fredric 23, 117-128, 207, 284
Marcus Theater Corporation 243
Markey, Gene 58
Marquardt, Mary 296
Marquette Academy 13, 15, 108, 109
Marquette High School 108
Marquette University 99, 108, 109, 110, 174, 257, 258, 266, 285, 322
Marshall Field & Co 183
Marshfield, Wisconsin 173, 176, 184
Martin, Dean 79, 224
Martin, Dewey 80
Martin, Steve 22
Martin, Wrye 323
Mary of Scotland 122
Mason, Edith 40
Mason, James 169
Massachusetts 129
Mathison, Melissa 296
Matthau, Walter 169
Mature, Victor 58
Maxwell, Marilyn 66
Mayfair, Mitzi 58
Mayo Clinic 32
McBride, Joseph 35, 38, 39
McCain, Francis Lee 305
McCambridge, Mercedes 169
McCormick, Robert 44

McCrea, Joel 66
McDowell, Roddy 323
McFadden, Bernarr 201
McGuire, John M. 31
McHugh, Frank 16, 106, 114
McInerney, Jay 170
McIntyre, Ian 211, 213
McKinley, Dennis 256
McKinnies, Edith 62, 66
McKinnies, Henry 62
McKinstry, Randall 88
McLaughlin, Bobby 73
McLaughlin, Emily 73
McNeeny's 83
Me 20, 24
Mehigan, "Cyclone" 106
Mehigan, Irving "Stuts" 106
Mehigan, Frank 108
Mellen, Wisconsin 323
Mequon, Wisconsin 316
Mercier, Mary 230
Mercury Productions 46
Mercury Theater 29, 46
Mercury Wonder Show 47
Merrill, Wisconsin 249
Mertz, Fred 208
Metcalf, Mark 316
Methou, Jason 176
Metro-Goldwyn-Mayer (MGM) Studios 18, 21, 70, 122, 178, 201, 211, 287
Mexico 120, 196, 198
Michaels, Lorne 259, 266
Michigan 220
Mid-Continent Railway Museum 323
Middleton High School 326
Middletown, Connecticut 318
Mike Zoler's Sweet Shop 177
Milland, Ray 197, 322
Miller, Arthur 125
Miller, Catherine 284
Milwaukee, Wisconsin 12, 13, 14, 16, 17, 18, 19, 23, 29, 60, 61, 62, 65, 66, 70, 72, 94, 99, 106, 107, 108, 109, 110, 111, 114, 115, 129, 130, 132, 133, 138, 176, 177, 179, 180, 182, 183, 186, 188, 190, 191, 195, 201, 214, 216, 217, 228, 229, 233, 240, 257, 271, 276, 283, 284, 286, 288, 312, 313, 315, 316, 322, 323, 325
Milwaukee County Stadium 285, 322
Milwaukee Journal 62, 65, 66, 67, 84, 94, 175, 177, 179, 181, 183, 184, 238, 258
Milwaukee Journal Sentinel 29, 94, 96, 136, 137, 138, 161, 180, 189, 228, 257
Milwaukee Magazine 176, 178, 181
Milwaukee Players 284
Milwaukee Playhouse 229
Milwaukee Repertory Theater 221, 312
Minneapolis Star Tribune 244
Minnesota 142, 262
Mirisch, Walter 304
Miss America Pageant 77
Miss USA Pageant 77
Mississippi River 171
Mitchard, Jacquelyn 316, 324
Mitchella, Greg 122
Mitchum, Robert 168
Mix, Tom 62, 149, 150
Mockley, Mary 63
Modern Screen 60, 62, 69, 70
Moe, Doug 84, 86
Molinaro, Al 316
Moline, Illinois 310
Monroe, Marilyn 55, 99, 304
Montana 39
Montgomery, Elizabeth 31
Montreal, Quebec 129

Moore, Demi 278
Moore, Garry 190
Moorehead, Agnes 26-34, 43, 44, 46, 70, 170, 308
Moorehead, Reverend John H. 26
Moorehead, Mary 26, 32
Moran, Dennis 84, 86
Morgan, Jaye P. 251
Morgan, Dennis 88, 106, 113-115, 173-185, 186, 188-191
Mori, Paoli 48
Morner, Stanley *(see Dennis Morgan)* 173, 178
Moscow, Russia 210
Motion Picture 102
Motion Picture & Television Magazine 60, 65, 67
Motion Picture County Hospital 199
Mount Horeb, Wisconsin 315
Mount Sinai Hospital 126
Mount Vernon, Iowa 140, 142
Movie Encyclopedia 187, 198
Movieland & Times 73
Mozart, Amadeus 221
Mount. St. Mary College 284
Mull, Martin 324
Muller, Frederick 38
Murphy, Alice 301
Murphy, Audie 66
Murray, Bill 269
Murrow, Edwin R. 318
Muskingum College 26

N

Napoleon 47
NASA 249
National Music Camp 219
National Pro Football Hall of Fame 113
National Public Radio 317
National Society of Film Critics 269
Naval Institute Press 109
Navidad, Joe 73
NBC 28, 42, 72, 92, 190, 211
Neenah, Wisconsin 176
Nelson, Craig T. 323
New Concord, Ohio 26
New Jersey 110, 111, 191
New Lisbon, Wisconsin 317
New Milford, Connecticut 123
New Orleans, Louisiana 60, 317
New York 15, 17, 28, 39, 41, 42, 44, 45, 62, 65, 76, 77, 78, 79, 81, 82, 84, 85, 90, 98, 101, 110, 112, 120, 123, 132, 133, 145, 180, 193, 197, 210, 211, 215, 220, 222, 230, 235, 241, 247, 261, 268, 295, 302, 312, 314
New York City 28, 41, 76, 79, 84, 99, 120, 158, 220, 269, 271, 300, 304, 307
New York Courier 85
New York Herald-Tribune 210
New York Shakespeare Festival 134, 220
New York Times 85, 210, 220
New York University 171
New York Yankees 79, 284
Newell, Hope 143
Newman, Paul 190, 322
Newsday 240
Nicholson, Jack 127
Nicholson, Virginia 42
Nielson, Leslie 277
Ninth Naval District Headquarters 64
Nobel Prize 126
Noll, Robert 87, 91, 93, 96
Nolte, Nick 322
Noonan, Elmer 63
Norfolk Navy Yard 14
Norman, Jack 257
Norman Players 284
North Africa 56, 113
North Carolina 77, 78

North Carolina School of the Arts 220
North Hills County Club 183
North Star Communications Corp. 249
Northern Westchester Center for the Arts 136
Northfield, Minnesota 186
Northwestern University 63, 64, 176, 214, 284, 309, 313
Noth, Christopher David 316
Notre Dame University 108, 113, 323
Nyack, New York 145

O

O'Brien, Eloise 182
O'Brien, William Joseph 106
O'Brien, Margaret 106
O'Brien, Pat 13, 15-17, 21, 23, 45, 106-116, 182, 211
O'Brien, William "Tip" 106
Observer 245
Oconomowoc Lake Club 183
Oconto, Wisconsin 282
O'Donnell, Cathy 168
O'Donnell's Saloon 106
O'Hara, Fisk 101
Ohio 32, 196, 316
Okinawa, Japan 114
Old Chicago 197
O'Leary, Dorothy 60, 64, 68
Olivier, Laurence 324
Olson, Nancy 65, 316
O'Neill, Eugene 125, 134
OOTEK Productions 311
Orange Bowl 312
Orchestra Wives 56
Ordonez, Antonio & Ronda 51
Orpheum Theater 117, 276
Orson Welles and People 49
Osborne, Robert 20
Oshkosh, Wisconsin 72

Osmond, Donny 254
Our Lady Queen of Peace Roman Catholic Church 266
Owensboro, Kentucky 304

P

Paar, Jack 29
Pabst Theater 110
Pabst, William 183
Pacelli, Christine 133
Pacific Palisades 67
Pacino, Al 290, 291
Page, Mary 38
Paget, Debra 65, 66
Palm Beach, Florida 81, 82, 84, 85, 86
Palm Springs, California 208
Palmer House 178, 179
Palmer, Lilli 58
Paramount Studios 30, 65, 90, 91, 121, 178, 180, 275
Paris, France 39, 72, 80
Park Ridge, Illinois 295
Parker, Dorothy 35
Parnell, Peter 221
Paul, Les 88
Paul Masson wine 50
PBS 221
Peace Corps 217
Pearl Harbor 142
Pearlman, Cindy 238
Penn, Sean 164
Pennsylvania 64, 223, 229
Pensaukee, Wisconsin 283
People Magazine 241
Pepin, Cora Sue 182
Performing Garage 241
Perkins, Dean 177
Perkins, Tony 220
Perry, Matthew 264
Peterson, Deborah C. 117, 118, 120
Petrified Forest 191
Phi Kappa Delta 14

Famous Wisconsin Film Stars

Philippines 242, 283, 288, 289
Philips, Don 176
Photoplay Magazine 30
Pickwick 215
Picturegoer Magazine 68
Pierce, Mildred 187
Pinter, Harold 210, 212, 213
Pirkle, Joan 318
Pitt, Brad 122
Pittsburgh Post-Gazette 317
Plainfield, New Jersey 111
Planet Hollywood 261, 299
Playboy Magazine 163
Plymouth, Michigan 219
Plymouth Theatre 78
Poitier, Sidney 20
Polacco, Giorgio 40
Pollack, Sydney 283
Poltermann, Barry 321
Pope John XXIII 170
Port Players 62, 214, 284
Port Washington, Wisconsin 62
Portadown, Ireland 196
Potomac River 81
Powell, Dick 32
Power, Tyrone 58
Powers Modeling School 77
Preminger, Otto 288
Prendergast, Honore 99
Prentice, Wisconsin 173
Prince Edward Island 135
Provincetown Players 193
Pryor, Richard 232, 233
Pulitzer Publishing Company 124
Purple Onion Productions 323

Q

Queen Elizabeth 114, 122
Queens, New York 303
Quindlen, Anna 220

R

Racine, Wisconsin 117, 118, 120, 121, 125, 223, 323, 324
Racine Hardware Manufacturing Company 117
Racine High School 117
Radio City Music Hall 210
Radloff, Kelly 321
Radner, Gilda 233, 234, 236
Rae, Charlotte 62, 214-218
Ralston cereal 62
Ramsey, Jack 118
Randolph, Susan 66
Randolph, William Hearst 44
Random House 57
Ray, Ida 201
Ray, Nicholas 49, 70, 71, 166-172, 210, 243
Ray, Susan 169
Raye, Martha 57
RCA Victor 89
Ready When You Are... 234, 284, 288
Reagan, Ronald 94, 108, 113
Rebane, Barbara 249, 252
Rebane, William 247-252
Red Barn Theatre 295
Redford, Robert 291
Reedsburg, Wisconsin 26, 32
Reedsburg High School 26
Reeves, Keanu 322
Reilly, Charles Nelson 216
Republican Party 299
Resurrection Cemetery 104, 266
Reynolds, Debbie 67
Reynolds, Joseph C. 57
Rhinelander, Wisconsin 286
Rhodes, Joseph 76
Rice Lake, Wisconsin 149, 150
Richards Grade School 61
Richland Center, Wisconsin 32
Ridley, John 317
Ridste, Lillian Frances Mary *(see Carol Landis)* 55
Riemer, Barbara 300
Riga, Latvia 247
Ring, Blanchc 208
Ringwold, Molly 322
Rinka, Chester 273

Ripon, Wisconsin 14, 15
Ripon College 14, 24, 288, 295, 306, 315
Ripon's College Days 15
River City Memoirs 141
River Hills, Wisconsin 72
River's End 179
Riverside High School 130, 131
Riverside Theater 29, 179, 186
Rizzo, Frank 143
RKO 44, 45, 46, 90, 113, 114, 179, 187, 233
RKO Radio Pictures 44
Roach, Hal 55
Roach, John 317
Roberts, John 141
Roberts, Julia 136, 137, 164, 322
Rochester, Minnesota 32
Rock, Chris 266
Rockefeller, Barbara 84
Rockefeller Foundation 211
Rockhurst Academy 13
Rockne, Knute 113
Rogers, Ginger 179, 322
Rogers, Roy 190
Rogers, Will 16, 150, 208
Rolling Stone Magazine 294
Rome, Italy 72
Romney, Jonathan 239, 244, 245
Roosevelt, Eleanor 28, 85
Roosevelt, Franklin 47, 300
Roosevelt, Teddy 118
Rose Bowl 263, 279
Ross, Ann 63
Rotary Club 176
Rowlands, E.M. 158
Rowlands, Gena 158-165, 318
Royal Purples 89
Rubirosa, Porfino 81
Rufus King High School 283, 284
Rush, Barbara 69, 169
Russell, Lillian 101
Russia 210
Ryan, Meg 269
Ryan, Robert 168

Ryan, Tim 286

S

S & H Pool Hall 167
Sacksteder, John 313
Salzburg, Austria 219
San Bernardino, California 55
San Diego Zoo 202
San Fernando Valley, California 17, 189
San Francisco, California 18, 55
Sanborn, Marjorie 303
Sandell, David 82
Sanderson, Mrs. Arvon 162
Sandler, Adam 266
Sandrock, Brent 325
Santa Monica, California 95, 115, 286, 300
Santa Monica Bay 199
Santa Monica College 297
Santa Ynez Inn 67
Sargent School of Theater 110
Saturday Evening Post 94
Schaefer, Ed 171
Schlitz Brewery 201, 228
Schlitz Brown Bottle Pub 30
Schlitz Hotel 13
Schmidlapp, Horace W. 58
Schmitt, Joan 70
Schneider, Rob 266
Schutz, Mary Joan 230
Schwarzenegger, Arnold 201, 294, 296
Scotch Oil Supply 254
Scott, Alex 137
Scott, Campbell 133, 136, 137
Scott, George C. 133, 135, 136
Screen Actors Guild 124
Screen Snapshots 190
Scripps Howard New Service 204
Seattle, Washington 138, 219, 222
Second City 259, 301
Secret Service 78
Selig, Bud 229

Seltzer, Frank 55
Serenity Prayer 266
Serling, Rod 306
Shakespeare, William 37, 43, 131
Shalhoub, Tony 143, 164, 268-270, 313
Shawano, Wisconsin 177
Sheboygan, Wisconsin 175
Sheen, Charlie 310, 322
Sheen, Martin 287, 288
Sheffield House Hotel 37, 38, 40
Shepard, Sam 268
Sherwin, Walter 79
Shewey, Don 221
Shields, Brooke 164
Shooting Ranch Ltd. 250, 251, 252
Shorewood, Wisconsin 94, 130, 235, 271, 276, 279, 314
Shorewood High School 214, 271
Shriver, Maria 298
Shue, Larry 316
Sigma Nu fraternity 295
Sigma Phi Epsilon 303
Silberman, Jerome "Jerry" 228
Silva, Mario 181
Silver Street Festival 252
Sime, John 26
Simi Valley 202
Simon & Schuster Pocket Books 297
Simonson, Eric 137
Sinatra, Frank 84, 316
Sinclair, Upton 122
Singapore 221
Sivage, Gerald 183
Skywalker Ranch 252
Smith, Cathy 301
Smith, Ethel 300
Smith, Les 177
Smith, Lori J. 238
Smith, Will 304
Sohmer, Steve 311
Soldier's Grove, Wisconsin 26, 28, 32
Solvang, California 198

Sophomore Society of the Skull and Crescent 118
South America 46, 312
South by Southwest Film Festival 270
South Salem, New York 135
Spacey, Kevin 324
Spade, Dennis 262
Spain 41, 73, 287, 315
Spanish Civil War 113
Spears, Britney 325
Special Olympics 298
Speilberg, Steven 282
Spencer Tracy Award 296
Spielberg, Steven 210, 289, 290
Spiro, J.D. 72
Spokesman Review 147
Spring Green, Wisconsin 167, 311
St. Croix River 324
St. Germaine, Kay 187
St. John's Cathedral School 13
St. John's Hospital 115
St. John's Military Academy 186, 196
St. Louis, Missouri 26, 31
St. Louis Municipal Opera Company 28, 193
St. Louis Post Dispatch 31
St. Mary's High School 13
St. Patrick's Cathedral 84
St. Patrick's Parish Grade School 254
St. Rosa Parochial School 12
St. Rosa's Catholic Church 12
Stack, Robert 275
Stage Door Canteen 124
Stalin, Joseph 212
Stallone, Sylvester 282, 288, 322
Stanford, George 145
Stanley and Livingstone 19
Stanwyck, Barbara 30, 91
State Farm Insurance 249
Steele, Jimmy 266
Steiger, Elaine 285
Sterling Motor Truck Company 12
Stevens, George 187

Stevens Point, Wisconsin 313, 318
Stewart, Jimmy 179, 224
Stiltz, Moses S. "Bud" 204
Stone, Oliver 242
Stowell, Jean 77, 79
Strauss, John 215
Streisand, Barbra 282, 290
Stuker, Steve 275
Sundance Film Festival 164
Superior, Wisconsin 323
Susann, Jacqueline 58
Susskind, David 305
Svejda, John 239
Swan Theater 114, 191, 313
Swayze, Patrick 278
Sweden 312
Switzer, Carl 204

T

Table Mountain, Wyoming 296
Taliesin 167
Tanaka, Hideo 212
Tarcai, Mary 215
Tarkington, Booth 46
Taylor, Elizabeth 22, 213
Taylor, Eloise 112
Ted Weems Orchestra 178
Temple Houston 71
Temple Theater 26
Tennessee 319
Termini Station 136
Texas 193, 284
Thalberg, Irving R. 122
Thal Styria, Austria 293
The Arizona Republic 261
The Calgary Sun 254
The Capital Times 319
The Clown's Prayer 266
The Daily Telegraph 228, 235, 236
The Films of Spencer Tracy 13, 24
The London Observer 158, 159
The Los Angeles Times 143, 276, 277
The Milwaukee Journal 72
The Music Box Theatre 222
The New York Times 41
The Observer 170, 239, 244
The Onion 278
The Record 243
The Tarriers 303
The Theater History Studies 30
The Times, London 164, 180, 211, 213
The Undertones 120
The World's Most Famous Movie Ranch: The Story of 202
Theater X 240
Theta Alpha Phi 14, 177
Theta Pi Delta 175
Thomas, Bob 69
Thomas, Danny 190, 194
Thomas, Dylan 291
Thompson, Bob 164
Thompson, Kevin D. 147
Thoreau, Henry David 24
Three Stooges 149, 150, 201, 207, 224
Time Magazine 43, 71, 171, 242; 264
Tiny Tim 251, 323
Todd School 39
Tokyo, Japan 212
Tomahawk, Wisconsin 249
Tomei, Concetta 317, 318
Tony Award 125, 134, 146
Topeka, Kansas 13
Topkins, Yewell *(see Tom Ewell)* 99, 303
Toronto, Canada 262
Toronto Sun 164
Tower Ranch Summer Theatre 285
Tower Theater 186
Townsend, Leo 211
Tracy, California 183
Tracy, John Edward 12
Tracy, Spencer 12-25, 61, 70, 106, 108, 110, 114, 121, 125, 126, 294, 304
Treadwell, Louise 16
Treasure Island 29, 50

Truffaut, Francois 169, 290
Truman, Harry 307
Tucker, Forrest 251
Tucker, Sandy 190
Turner Classic Movies 20
Turner, Lana 80
TV Guide 78, 144, 214, 215
TV Picture Life 27, 33
Twin Lakes, Wisconsin 89, 324

U

U.S. Army 119, 196, 229
U.S. House Un-American Activities Committee 124, 168, 211
U.S. Marines 13
U.S. Naval Academy 196
U.S. Navy 15, 143
U.S. Office of Price Administration 158
U.S. Office of War Information 21
U.S. President's Council on Physical Fitness 299
U.S. Supreme Court 24
U.S. Work Progress Administration 42
UCLA 64, 287, 292, 297, 298, 313
Uecker, Bob 311
Union Club 110
Union Vodvil 119
United Artists 197, 275
United Press International 45, 47, 79
Universal Studios 48, 199
University of Chicago 167, 178
University of Iowa 140, 229
University of Michigan 220
University of Southern Maine 268
University of Wisconsin 28, 46, 99, 100, 106, 118, 143, 145, 149, 158, 173, 178, 182, 184, 193, 240, 271, 273, 300, 303, 306
University of Wisconsin Alumni Association 306
University of Wisconsin-Madison 104, 119, 126, 144, 263, 303-307, 311, 314, 316, 320-322
University of Wisconsin-Whitewater 255
University of Wisconsin-Oshkosh 285
University of Wisconsin-Superior 297, 299
University of Wisconsin-Whitewater 301, 322
USO 124
Utah 32
Utey, Betty 167

V

Valley Forge Hospital 229
Van Cleve, Henry 101
Van Cleef, Lee 32
Van Devere, Trish 133
Variety 121, 235
Vatican 71
Vedder, Lillian 173
Venora, Diane 305
Vickery, Joseph 133
Vietnam War 242
Villa, Pancho 196
Village Vanguard 215
Vince Lombardi Memorial Golf Classic 183
Virgin Islands 67
Virginia 14
Viroqua, Wisconsin 26, 27, 33
Vognar, Chris 264
Von Braun, Wernher 143
Voice of America 167
Voight, Jon 163, 247

W

Wagner, Robert 66, 67, 69, 323
Wake Island 198
Walker, Alexander 59
Walker, Gertrude 208

Wallace, Thomas C. 57
Wallis, Hal 30
Walt Disney Studios 92
Warner Bros. 18, 55, 56, 71, 89, 113, 175, 177, 179, 180, 187-189
Warren, Jennifer 307
Washington, D.C. 81, 99, 158, 313, 317, 322
Washington High School 229
Washington Park 181
Washington Post 240, 245
Waters, Ethel 284
Watersmeet Chamber of Commerce 252
Watersmeet, Michigan 252
Waukesha, Wisconsin 89, 173, 177, 182
Waukesha County 311
Waukesha Freeman 89, 182
Waupaca, Wisconsin 173
Waupun, Wisconsin 261, 284
Wausau, Wisconsin 248, 250
Wauwatosa High School 13
Wauwatosa, Wisconsin 158
Waxman, Sharon 240
Wayne, John 32, 69, 92, 135, 168
WCBS-TV 313
Weight Watchers 255
Weissmuller, Johnny 201
Weller, Peter 319
Welles, Beatrice 35, 37
Welles, Mary 37, 38
Welles, Orson 29, 35-54, 167, 210, 224
Welles, Rebecca 47
Welles, Richard 35, 37
Wells, H.G. 29
Wenders, Wim 172
Wendt, George 266
Wesleyan University 319
West Allis, Wisconsin 60, 315
West, Bill 274
West Compass Players 301
West, Mae 207

Westwood Village 67
Wheaton, Illinois 301
Wheeler, Irving 55
White Plains, N.Y. 16
White, Reggie 325
Whitefish Bay, Wisconsin 60, 62, 63, 66, 74, 110, 129, 130, 214, 243
Whitefish Bay High School 63, 74, 130, 313
Whitewater, Wisconsin 219, 302
Whitford, Bradley 299, 314, 318, 319
Whitney, Dwight 214
WIBA 44
Wilde, Oscar 35
Wilder, Billy 91
Wilder, Gene 228-237, 303
Wilder, Thornton 41, 167, 230
Willard, Catherine 301
William, Marilyn Linley 174
Williams Bay, Wisconsin 294, 322
Williams, Jay 162
Williams, Richard 161
Williams, Robin 302, 316, 319
Willock, Dave 178, 186, 190, 191, 307
Wilson, Earl 99, 304
Wilson Street East Dinner Theater 320
Windsor Lake Studios 323
Wink Magazine 78, 79
Winninger, Charles 207-209
Winninger, Karl 207
Winnipeg Sun 137
Winslow Grammar School 117
Wisconsin Journal Magazine 240
Wisconsin Children's Theater 62
Wisconsin Film Festival 326
Wisconsin Film Office 251, 291, 324
Wisconsin Film Society 49
Wisconsin Movie Scrapbook 252
Wisconsin Performing Artists Hall of Fame 33, 94, 115, 126, 136, 183, 189, 194, 317

Wisconsin Players Theater 99, 193
Wisconsin Public Television 311
Wisconsin Rapids, Wisconsin 140, 145, 310
Wisconsin State Historical Society 32
Wisconsin State Journal 35, 38, 39, 44, 99, 159, 162, 240, 241, 255, 263, 266, 276, 290, 304, 320, 321
WKBT-WKBH 166
WKOW 182
WMTH-FM 294
WOKY 285
Wolfe, Thomas 230
Wolheim, Louis 197
Women's Division of War Finance 113
Wood County Players 184
Wood, Natalie 169
Woodland Hills, California 199
Woodstock, Illinois 39, 41
Woodward, Joanne 323
Woolcott, Alexander 41
Wooster Group 241, 244
Wopat, Tom 314, 320
Works Progress Administration 167
World Powderpuff Championship 249
World War I 13, 108, 110, 119, 196
World War II 21, 64, 113, 124, 133, 142, 168, 181, 189, 190, 211, 224, 244, 247, 304
Wright, Amy 308
Wright, Frank Lloyd 167
WRPN-FM 296
WTMJ 62, 63, 176, 177, 178, 186
Wyman, Jane 183, 189
Wynn, Ed 190
WZEE 266

X

Xerxes 178

Collect the whole series!

The first four titles in our FAMOUS WISCONSIN SERIES will be published in 2002-03:

• FAMOUS WISCONSIN AUTHORS by James P. Roberts, ISBN 1-878569-85-6, $14.95

• FAMOUS WISCONSIN FILM STARS by Kristin Gilpatrick, ISBN 1-878569-86-4, $16.95

• FAMOUS WISCONSIN INVENTORS & ENTREPRENEURS by Marv Balousek, ISBN 1-878569-87-2, $14.95

• FAMOUS WISCONSIN MUSICIANS by Susan Masino, ISBN 1-878569-88-0, $16.95

MUCH MORE TO COME!

Badger Books Inc.
P.O. Box 192
Oregon, WI 53575
(800) 928-2372
www.badgerbooks.com